Historic Places in Greene County
NEW YORK

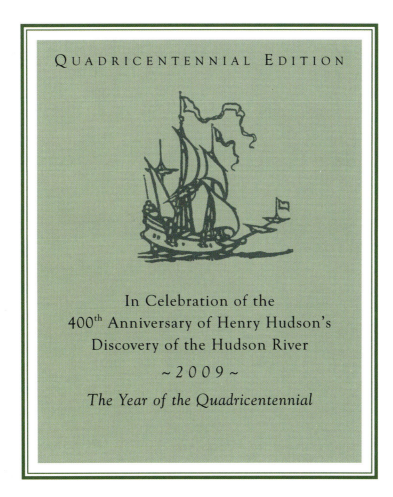

Quadricentennial Edition

In Celebration of the
400th Anniversary of Henry Hudson's
Discovery of the Hudson River

~ 2009 ~

The Year of the Quadricentennial

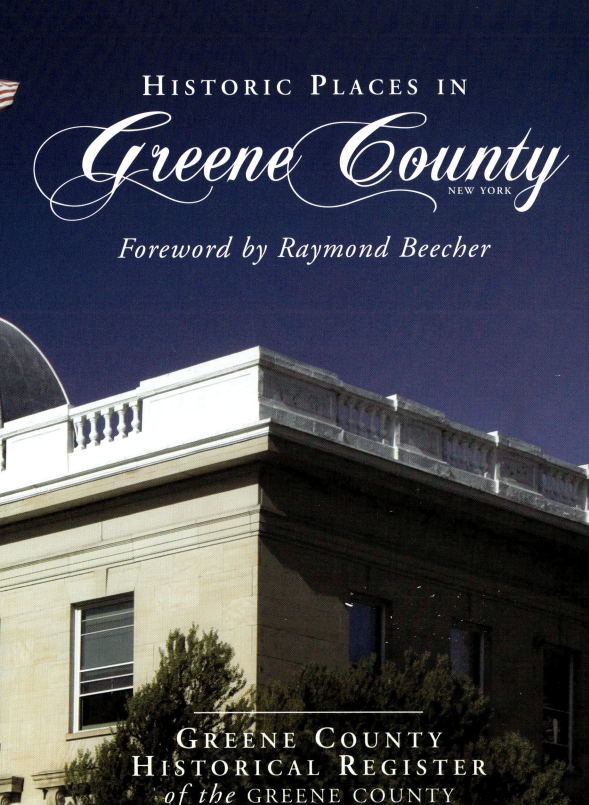

Historic Places in Greene County
NEW YORK

Foreword by Raymond Beecher

GREENE COUNTY HISTORICAL REGISTER
of the GREENE COUNTY HISTORICAL SOCIETY

by Jean M. Bush, Natalie E. Daley, Kenneth E. Mabey
& the Historical Register Committee

Photography Assistance: Thomas J. Satterlee
Editing Assistance: Robert D'Agostino
Introduction by Ted Hilscher

FLINT MINE PRESS
Coxsackie, New York

Copyright © 2009. The Greene County Historical Society and Flint Mine Press, LLC

All rights reserved.
No part of this book may be reproduced or transmitted in any form
or by any means, electronic or mechanical, including photocopying, recording,
or by any information storage and retrieval system,
without the written permission of the authors and publisher.

Printed and bound in the United States of America.

ISBN: 978-0-9825208-1-9

Library of Congress Control Number: 2009933446

Published by
Flint Mine Press, LLC
PO Box 353, Coxsackie, NY 12051

www.flintminepress.com

Dedicated to

Raymond Beecher (1917–2008),

whose presence is still felt

in all aspects of

The Greene County Historical Society

*The Greene County Historical Register is deeply grateful to the following individuals and organizations.
Their generosity allowed this book to be published in color.*

DIAMOND

Furthermore: A Program of the Kaplan Fund

GOLD

Athens Community Foundation
Bank of Greene County Charitable Foundation
Raymond Beecher
Clesson and Jean Bush
County of Greene Quadricentennial Funding
Greene County Tourism
Robert C. and Ann B. Hallock
Palmer Foundation

SILVER

Jane Van Loan Erickson

BRONZE

Academic Exchange Quarterly
Frank and Natalie E. Daley
L. Ruth and William A. Day

ASSOCIATE

Albright/Conine/Palmateer,
　gift in honor of Natalie Daley
Timothy A. and Elizabeth Albright
Joel I. Berson
Robert D. & Joan G. Carl
Franklin B. & Winifred J. Clark
Barbara T. Corning
Natalie E. Daley,
　in memory of Beatrice Bergamini
Carol S. Doney
Harvey J. and Kathleen M. Durham

Muriel H. Falkey
Priscilla Fieldhouse
Greene County Historical Register
Committee Members,
　gift in honor of Josephine Blakeslee
Steve Hartman
Donald M. and Joan S. Howard
Suraj and Emily Kunchala
Lloyd M. Loop
Kenneth Mabey and Natalie E. Daley,
　gift in honor of Dr. Olga Santora

Elizabeth A. and Richard G. Mason
Shirley R. Mc Grath
National Bank of Coxsackie
New York Community Trust,
　Gloria and Barry H. Garfinkel Fund
Oak Hill Preservation Assoc.
Dennis R. and Julia L. O'Grady
Hugh J. and Margaret Quigley
Richard and Sybil Tannenbaum
Barbara T. Tolley

SUPPORTER

Charles L. Baker, C. Glenn Baker,
and Leslie Baker,
　in memory of Kathryn Baker
Leonard and Janet Bazzini
John Cannon and Alta Turner
Arnold H. Chadderdon
David C. and Wanda J. Dorpfeld
Helen Mary Eckler
Shirley L. Ermine
Arthur A. & Marion K. Fazzone
Norman & Charlotte Fuller

Thomas and Linda Gentalen
Jean Gwynn
Betty Roefer Haude
Paige A. Ingalls
Stephanie Ingalls
Tracy L. Karlin
John F. Jr. and Lisbeth L. Lamb
Audrey B. Madison
Richard B. and Virginia Mather
Marjorie S. McCoy

Clarice E. Millspaugh &
　Mary F. M. Hoyt
Charlotte P. & Mary C. Randall
Judith G. Rundell
Lillian Salvino
Phyllis E. Silva-Keith,
　in memory of Raymond Beecher
Irving & Doris Smith and
　Mr. & Mrs. Todd Smith
Martin C. Smith
D. Wubben

*This book is supported in part by Furthermore, a program of the J. M. Kaplan Fund.
Joan K. Davidson, President, Ann Birckmayer, Administrator*

CONTENTS

Foreword . . . . *ix*

Acknowledgments . . . . *x*

Introduction *1*

TOWNS

Ashland *5*

Athens *17*

Cairo *47*

Catskill *55*

Coxsackie *113*

Durham *133*

Greenville *155*

Halcott *173*

Hunter *177*

Jewett *189*

Lexington *195*

New Baltimore *201*

Prattsville *225*

Windham *243*

APPENDIX

Photography & Illustrations *264*

Sources *265*

Index *271*

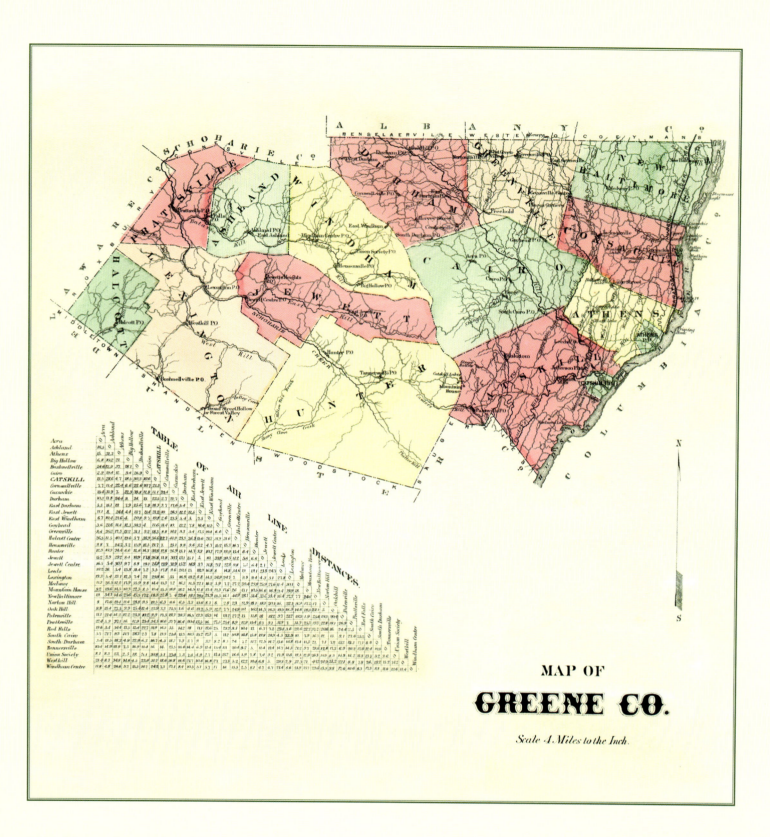

Map of Greene County adapted from the Beers' 1867 Atlas of Greene County, New York.

FOREWORD

The County of Greene, State of New York, whose settlement commenced under the Dutch, continued under the English Crown, and expanded significantly during the post-Revolutionary centuries, has an architectural heritage of telling proportions. The Greene County Historical Register strongly reflects the intrinsic building components of the North European architectural tradition of using both dressed and rubble stone, brick and timber. The post-Revolutionary centuries have added Federal, Greek Revival, Victorian in all its multiple phases, and modernism to this earlier wealth of architectural styles. Many structures, such as the several-building Bronck Homestead, are located on historic plots of land grants.

The Greene County Historical Register was established in 1990 by The Greene County Historical Society for the express purpose of identifying sites of cultural value in the history of the county. By doing so, it has sought to encourage property owners to adhere to acceptable standards of historical restoration efforts. Its success is reflected in the continued flow of applications submitted to the diligent supervisory committee.

The publication of Historic Places in Greene County brings together in one useful volume a wealth of such information not readily found elsewhere. With supplements in the years ahead, it will continue to serve researchers and readers as a significant resource volume. The all-volunteer countywide committee merits the gratitude of all those individuals who have come to appreciate the architectural, historical, and scenic strongpoints of the County of Greene in the State of New York.

Raymond Beecher (1917–2008)
Greene County Historian

ACKNOWLEDGMENTS

In addition to our many donors we are grateful to the nearly 400 owners of the historic sites whose applications to the Greene County Historical Register made this volume possible. Their application files were invaluable for writing these individual texts. Extensive research by committee members and other interested volunteers, working tirelessly, fleshed out the historic stories.

In May 1990 Raymond Beecher convened the first Register meeting at the Windham Mountain home of Dr. Robert and Josephine Blakeslee. Sadly, Josephine passed away on December 31, 2008, just as her dream for a book was nearing completion. Along with charter members Justine Hommel and Winifred Clark, Josephine provided the original spark. She chaired the committee for years, relinquishing the post—but twice—due to family illness. Josephine remained a working member after her retirement as chair in 2006. Our profound gratitude is melancholy.

The next chair, Jo Anne Makely, gave the committee expert architectural lessons. Philip Kesinger, as chair, lobbied for a book version. The longtime secretary, educator Kathryn Baker, was the heart of the committee, passing away before her time in the midst of writing a children's book. These early visionaries were joined by volunteers, Elizabeth Vaughn, Jeff Flack, and Mary Heisinger, among many others.

Throughout the years, publication committee members Ken Mabey, Jean Bush, and Natalie Daley have been the chief motivators. They continued to push for a publication, always reminding the Register Committee of the importance of a volume in book form. Through the tasks of research, writing, and fund-raising they gave support to their fellow volunteers, and through perseverance and resolve for a professional, color publication, they have made this book possible. We also appreciate the extra workload handled by Jean Bush in recent months, from researching and scanning archival photographs to responding to last-minute edits.

A hearty thanks to all who advised, led, and agreed and disagreed with us neophytes as we began an unknown journey. It must be a "good read," admonished Nicki and Barry Henks, who joined the original book meetings, serving for a time as collectors of texts. Robert D'Agostino, whose editorial expertise shines throughout the volume, has earned our sincere appreciation. His efforts at writing, collecting, and tweaking hundreds of narratives deserve a large thank-you.

Our gratitude also extends to many for their interest, help, and professional guidance. Debbie Allen met with us for years as an adviser. Sincere appreciation also to Timothy Albright, Jr., Timothy Albright, John Bonafide, Clesson Bush, David Dorpfeld, Christy French, Robert Hallock, Ann Hallock, Steven Hoare, Shelby Mattice, Charles Schaeffer, Ron Toelke, and the Greene County Historical Society's trustees. We gratefully acknowledge Thomas J. Satterlee's photographic skills and calm demeanor, and for the hours spent in teaching us about communicating with Society members and community organizations. We especially appreciate Tom's willingness to photograph and reshoot many of the images that appear in the book.

A special debt of gratitude is extended to Sylvia Hasenkopf, whose website "Greene County New York Genealogy and History" was an invaluable reference tool in leading us to original sources and materials.

Thanks to Justine Hommel and Robert Gildersleeve of the Mountain Top Historical Society, and Carol Bennett of the Zadock Pratt Museum for their assistance. Also, thanks are due to the various Town Historians and individuals whose knowledge and interest contributed to this project.

Special gratitude goes to Laura Pierce for her efficiency and welcomed secretarial skills. The staff of the Vedder Research Library was always there for us—Shirley McGrath, Judy Rundell, Stephen Schwebler, and Steve Pec, among others, are heartily appreciated. We are heavily indebted to Ted Hilscher, who used his legal expertise to guide us over rough spots and through necessary documents. Publishing a book requires elbow grease, patience, and perseverance. To those volunteers who stuffed envelopes, xeroxed, typed, ran errands, and mailed while doing liaison and public relations work—Janet Daly, Patty Daley, Allaire Moront, Elizabeth Craigmyle, Penny Ashby, Suzanne Daley, Charlene Mabey, and others—we thank you.

We are grateful to our publishers, Linda Pierro and Robert Bedford of Flint Mine Press in Coxsackie. Their optimism, support, and willingness to persevere brought *Historic Places in Greene County* to fruition in 2009.

Finally, great appreciation is proffered to our authors: the late Josephine Blakeslee, the late Jane P. Bostrom, Jean M. Bush, Christine Cepale, Winifred Clark, Robert A. D'Agostino, Natalie E. Daley, Carol S. Doney, Ralph Grinnell, Theodore Hilscher, Kenneth Mabey, Nick Nahas, Betty O'Hara, Robert Bedford, and Linda Pierro. Their expertise, research, writings, and knowledge of various locales were indispensable to this publication.

A final note: Featured in *Historic Places in Greene County* are homes and sites that are on the Historical Register of Greene County, with the exception of recent additions to the Register. Since the research and writing of this publication began, more than forty-five sites have been added that will not be part of this work, but will be considered for future projects by the Register Committee and the Greene County Historical Society. Those owners who were approved after this volume began may look forward to an addendum or a future volume. Additionally, there are certainly many fine, worthy historic sites that are not on the Register, and we are always looking to add these if individuals or groups wish to make an application to the Register Committee.

The research, writing, and editing of the text have been accomplished by the several members of the Register Committee over several years, and we have attempted to be as accurate as possible. The information taken from the original submissions covers nearly two decades of application files. We note that history is provisional, and is correct only until the next new discovery of information is forthcoming. Much of the text comes from additional research conducted by the members and editors, and we have tried to be diligent and assiduous in this task. As to be expected, we have found inconsistencies and contradictions in some of the sources, and have tried to resolve the issues as best we could. In some instances corrections could be made. In others, we have noted the contradictory data when documentation could not be found. Any ommissions, errors, or inaccurate representations due to conflicting historical data and sources, are purely unintentional.

Every effort has been made, as well, to the correct usage of names, surnames and place names. Over several generations, not only have the names of towns, hamlets and villages changed, but as properties and houses changed hands, so did the names of many sites. Furthermore, it is not unusual to find different lines of the same family using a slightly different spelling of their names, especially when given the casual nature of spelling during the 18th and 19th centuries. We have endeavored to use the spellings that appear most consistently in our sources, and which seem to be the most valid and historically accurate.

The Greene County Historical Register Committee

Jean M. Bush, Winifred Clark,
Natalie E. Daley, Roy Davis, Carol S. Doney,
Ralph Grinnell, Emily Kunchala,
Kenneth E. Mabey, Nick Nahas, Betty O'Hara

On behalf of the Historical Register Committee, I would like to express our gratitude and appreciation to Natalie Daley for all of her many contributions to this book. Natalie led our committee in fulfilling the concept of a book, and stood fast in her goal for a hardcover, full-color version. She hosted publication committee meetings at her home, wrote grants and conducted fund raising, researched, wrote, and edited the numerous Catskill texts, and found Flint Mine Press for us when we needed a dedicated publisher. Those who know Natalie, will know without doubt that she would not wish to be singled out for any accolades, but we would be remiss if we did not acknowledge and credit her for the inspiration and role model she has been for us all.

Kenneth E. Mabey, Chairperson
The Greene County Historical Register Committee

INTRODUCTION

The buildings and sites on the following pages are recorded on the Greene County Historical Register, representing the fourteen towns in Greene County. This publication has been an ambitious undertaking. A few hardy Historical Society volunteers, putting in very long hours, have attempted to document and record these historic homes and structures using written and oral histories to evoke the lives and personalities of their former owners.

Historic buildings are preserved and studied and photographed, and enjoyed, because they help us to understand how we got to where we are today. They are, after all, the tangible past. On a deeper level they heighten our sense of place, reinforcing warm associations, providing roots and familiarity and balance as we head out into the world each morning. Hopefully, this book will both teach us about Greene County history and be something of a record of our connections to Greene County.

Some of these buildings are noteworthy because they are representative; the others because they are extraordinary. There will be plenty of discussion about types and efforts to pigeonhole each building into this category or that. There is a value to this. First of all, it gives us a vocabulary to use and directs our attention to specific features so that we better appreciate what we are looking at: the low-pitched roof accented by brackets says Italianate, the mansard roof Second Empire. Second, as we learn to read the landscape, the tangible past, we can teach ourselves how to associate different styles with approximate dates of construction and thus begin to organize along a timeline what we see as we travel around.

However, identifying architectural styles holds the danger that each building is expected to fit neatly into a particular mold. A house or building may feature some of the elements of one style alongside the elements of another style. This often occurs as a result of a later addition or renovation. Many examples follow. The focus of this volume is to record the individual homes and sites of the Register, and it is not intended to be a discourse on architectural design or style. Rather, it should be viewed as a resource to the diverse styles, personal tastes, and individual histories that have shaped our region.

When the first European settlers arrived here in the late 1600s and early 1700s, they often settled in clearings that were once the sites of Algonquin dwellings and gardens. They built vernacular (or folk) buildings, in the centuries-old traditions that had evolved slowly back in Europe, then were adapted to accommodate New World conditions. The Dutch pioneers built stone, brick, and wood houses with ethnic features such as gable-end parapet walls (walls extending above the roof line), double doors, garret ventilating holes, and dormers. Dutch architecture is well represented on the Register by the Bronck House (Coxsackie), the Albertus Van Loon House (Athens), and the northern end of Klinkenberg (Coxsackie). Other influences in the region during colonial times came from English and German settlers.

While vernacular buildings can sometimes be identified by distinctive exterior features, folklorist Henry Glassie believes the best way to classify vernacular buildings is by their floor plans, which tell us a lot about how the owners intended to use their buildings. Landscape historian John Stilgoe speaks of vernacular buildings being of the people, born of common sense.

In contrast to vernacular architecture is an approach in which typology or categorization is based largely on ornamental rather than functional features, or "style." The *idea* of the house built in an architectural style originates with a distant designer, not the owner or the builder, as it does in a vernacular building. Architectural styles traveled from urban areas out to small towns and the countryside. The owner of a new Federal or Georgian house, or, later, one of the types associated with the Victorian era, wants his neighbors to know he has attained some level of success, and he is able to afford a modern, sophisticated home. In some neighborhoods there was a great competitive drive to build or renovate in the latest vogue. You will find many of the homes on the Register next to, or nearly next to, others on the

Above: Gable-end parapet wall, Bronck House, Coxsackie.

Register, on Prospect and Broad Streets in Catskill, Franklin Street in Athens, and Main Street in Windham.

The earliest architectural styles found in Greene County are the Georgian (after the English kings) and its descendant the Federal, utilized in homes during the nation's infancy. Both styles followed classical and formal rules of symmetry and balanced proportions, with a central entry and chimneys on the end walls. The entry usually features columns of fixed glass panes called sidelights flanking the door, and a fan light over the door. Second-floor Palladian windows above the entry are a High-style elaboration.

The Greek Revival movement (1825–1860) reflected an increasing interest in democratic values such as universal education and an enlarged electorate. A road-facing gable is the most indicative element, perhaps combined with round, or squared, columns supporting a triangular pediment, a central door, and wide cornice mimicking the temples of the people credited with democracy. The Register abounds with churches in this style, built by the second generation of settlers who wanted to display their egalitarian spirit. Likewise, many backcountry farmhouses were embellished with flat imitation columns, known as pilasters, as corner boards. Greek Revival symbolism retained its power long after the early National era, as illustrated by the entranceway in the 1901 Catskill Library and the portico on the 1909 Courthouse.

By the middle of the 19th century, architecture began to reflect an increase in wealth, and demonstrate the use of mass-produced ornamental elements and balloon frame construction. Homes were built on a significantly larger and more decorative scale, often referred to today as "Victorian." "Victorian" is not a style of architecture, but an era during which buildings more specifically identified as Gothic Revival (1840–1880), Italianate (1850–1890), Second Empire (1860–1890), and Queen Anne (1880–1910) were built.

Gothic Revivalism was advocated by Andrew Jackson Downing, the landscape designer and arbiter of taste from downriver at Newburgh, who bemoaned Greek Revivalism as being too pretentious for country houses. "The Greek temple disease has passed its crisis," he said in 1846. "The people have survived it." Applying to both homes and small churches, typical Gothic Revival features were prominent front gables, steeply pitched roofs decorated with arched or pointed windows, and board and batten siding. On the Episcopal churches in Ashland and Greenville and the Episcopal parsonage in Prattsville, the verticality is intended to direct your attention upward to the heavens. Downing, through his bestselling books, did as much as anyone in American history to tell us what a desirable house should look like. For instance, he was our foremost proponent of porches—he called them verandas—which were additions on perhaps two dozen Register buildings.

In the Italianate style, homes normally featured a low-pitched roof, accompanied by wide, overhanging eaves and decorative brackets. After the Civil War, Main Streets across America adopted the Italianate style for most commercial structures. The rectangularity of the upper floors provided the most square footage on a building footprint and therefore the highest possible return for investment in a commercial lot. That's why the Day and Holt Building in Catskill had a false Italianate façade added to its early-19th-century roofline, to make it compatible with its surroundings.

The dominant identifying element of the Second Empire style, which incorporated the French elements so in vogue during the era of the Second French Empire, was a patterned "mansard roof." This "roof" is actually a slightly pitched, full upper story, distinct from the lower stories by its siding. At times this architectural style showcased a central tower, perhaps dismantled in ensuing years.

The most flamboyant of the Victorian-era styles is the Queen Anne. Steeply pitched roofs, towers, turrets (which look like giant upside-down ice cream cones), wrap-around front porches, various patterned sidings, and "Painted Lady" colors are representative. These homes are at the opposite end of the spectrum from the vernacular.

Existing alongside such popular architectural styles is the eccentric Van Gelder Octagon House in Catskill. The variety to be found in the county is further demonstrated by the newest structure on the Register, the Art Deco jewel that today is headquarters of the Bank of Greene County (Catskill).

The largest buildings on the Register, and the largest buildings ever built in Greene County, remind us of our role in the leisure industry. Due to the proximity to New York City and innovations like the steamboat and steam railroad engine, hotels like the Kaaterskill Hotel, Laurel House, and Prospect Park Hotel became great attractions. The world-renowned Catskill Mountain House, which for 140 years was perched literally on the ledge of South Mountain in Hunter with its Corinthian columns and breathtaking view, deserves a special place in the history of Greene County buildings. Once the most heavily patronized of all the grand hotels in the region, and noted as one of the greatest hotels of the country, its slow decline spanned several decades of the 20th century. After it fell into neglect and decay, it was ultimately demolished by intentional fire in January 1963, but the site of the former Mountain House has been fortunately preserved as a state park. Examples of resorts on a smaller scale, though, like Winter Clove (Cairo), the Thompson House (Windham), and the Windham House are represented on the Register, along with numerous places that served at one time or another as boardinghouses.

Ultimately, this is a book not about architecture, but about people. You will meet artists, industrialists, and a Socialist, a pioneering black minister and then a pioneering woman minister, and John "Legs" Diamond, the mythic bootlegger who couldn't be killed by bullets (until he was). And of course you will meet farmers. Greene County agriculture has never meant industrial agriculture, so prevalent today, but rather the small family farms of people like Russell Sutton in Coxsackie, who kept cows, chickens, and fruit trees; raised nine children with his wife, Irene; and made time to serve for many years on the school board and as town assessor.

Here is Greene County, one anecdote at a time. Wherever we call home, the stories of our communities, and our place in them, begin with the stories of our historic buildings and the lives lived around them. Among and between communities are common themes and common traits. Once you compare and contrast information collected from one place to that from others, the bits and pieces coalesce into patterns. Macrohistory emerges from microhistory. James Joyce was thinking of his own roots in Dublin when he captured the significance of local history done well, the close study of certain people at a certain place and time. "In the particular," Joyce observed, "is contained the universal."

Ted Hilscher
Assistant Professor
Columbia-Greene Community College
August 2009

Opposite left: Palladian window on the 1813 Courthouse, Catskill.
Opposite right: Mansard roof on the Bedell House, Athens.
Above: The Catskill Mountain House at the turn of the century.

Panoramic bird's-eye view of Ashland, along the banks of the Batavia Kill, circa 1900.

TOWN OF ASHLAND

In 1787 the area known as Scienceville had yet to become Ashland, the place where "one could find peace and strength." After Prattsville had been set off in 1833, this attractive mountain town was carved from the western part of Old Windham in 1848. The natural surroundings of Ashland are often compared to the mountainous landscape of Switzerland. Oral history has it that the town was named for Henry Clay's home, as Clay supposedly had close friends in this mountain town.

It has also been said that those who settled in Ashland were of more than ordinary education, and made special effort to establish schools of the highest quality. And in fact, Ashland Village could boast the first public school for boys. It was constructed of logs with a fireplace at one end and a box stove at the other. Ashland was also home to the Ashland Collegiate Institute & Musical Academy. While short-lived—built in 1854 and destroyed by fire in 1861—it can claim John Burroughs, the famed naturalist, as one of its students. The Institute's original bell still exists, housed in the Trinity Episcopal Church on Route 23.

Elisha Strong and his family were probably the first settlers in the present-day hamlet of Ashland, coming here from Connecticut with his family in 1785.

George Stimson was the first settler at Windham, living near the current village of Windham. It is likely that he or members of his family were among the first in what would become the Town of Ashland, as well. In 1785 his family of four sons and five daughters arrived from Massachusetts. Not troubled by Indians, they nevertheless were harassed by wolves and other wild beasts that killed their cattle and sheep.

ASHLAND

HUBBARD/BENHAM/TOMPKINS HOUSE
THE 1867 EPISCOPAL HOUSE PARSONAGE

This house was built on the property of Deacon Jedediah Hubbard, who originally built a cabin here in approximately 1793, not long after he had arrived from Connecticut. Father and sons did not arrive alone: they were among the very earliest settlers, and had traveled along with others from the same area who also decided to settle here. This cabin was one in a line of contemporary dwellings that were built along the Batavia Kill. Below Hubbard's was the house of John Prout; above, the home of Foster Morss. Morss' son Lyman built a tannery near his father's house, also above Hubbard's cabin.

In his *Old Times in Windham*, the Reverend Henry Hedges Prout recounts a tale regarding a plot by Hardenburgh and Livingston Patent land agents to steal Jed Hubbard's land away. Realizing what was going on, Hubbard's friends and neighbors dressed up as Calico Indians and hid in the nearby woods. Spying so many "Indians" around them, the land agents decided that they were in the wrong place, and left.

Jedediah Hubbard is an important figure in the history of the area, as he was one of 28 persons who signed the covenants incorporating the First Presbyterian Church on October 24, 1808, and was elected its first deacon. Timothy, one of his sons, also served as deacon. The act of incorporation was recorded in the Greene County Clerk's Office on pages 21 and 22 in Liber [Book] A of the Records of Religious Societies.

Dr. Thomas Benham and his son Thomas likely lived in the house after Hubbard himself. At some point Jedediah's house was used as a store, the proprietor being Sidney Tuttle. Then, in 1867, the Trinity Church purchased this property from a William Marner. In that same year, 1867, the church purchased a small house from Austin Smith and moved it from Ashland village, attaching it to the original house. From that point on, it became known as the Episcopal Parsonage. The Reverend Henry H. Prout lived there from 1867 until 1871 while rector of the Trinity Church.

In 1957, the property was sold to A. Gould, and then transferred again in 1986 to Audrey Tompkins. Many alterations have been made to the building and grounds throughout the years. The garage was built in 1984; a year later the main house was renovated and a new addition was added to the east end. Audrey Tompkins lived in the house from 1986 until recent years.

Physical proof that Jedediah's original cabin had existed in this location had been lost to history until proof of that structure was uncovered in 1990—the base of a fireplace. Other items found at the site include various knives, a one-cent coin dated 1847, and a clay pipe. These artifacts were uncovered by Frank Tompkins while digging up the flower garden, not far from the present house, according to the Tompkins' neighbor Pauline Lawrence.

ASHLAND

WEST SETTLEMENT METHODIST CHURCH

West Settlement Methodist Church is a noteworthy building, and currently holds a place on the National Register of Historic Places, as well as on the Greene County Historical Register. The building is quite similar to the North Settlement Church, and from the exterior appears nearly identical. It has the same single-story, four-by-three bay plan with hand-hewn post and beam construction on a high foundation of uncoursed, mortared limestone blocks.

At the top sits a moderately pitched gable roof clad in asphalt shingles. Narrow clapboard siding with wide corner pilasters supporting the architrave frieze and molded box cornice presents an attractive representation of the period in which it was built. The decorative elements encircle three sides of the building, ending in a simple return on the rear façade. A molded, raked cornice, which creates a tympanum of narrow wooden clapboards, abuts the frieze on the gable. An octagonal vent is centered on the tympanum. The windows throughout the church are elongated twelve-over-twelve sashes, and add to the charm and balance of the building.

Dorothy Talmadge, Windham's town historian in 1976, wrote, "In 1823 the West Settlement organization was part of the Durham circuit as an out-appointment with meetings held in the Richmond Corner's schoolhouse. On April 6, 1832, a meeting was held in the schoolhouse, with Phillip Conine and Samuel Tompkins presiding. Trustees were elected and this organization was named the Second Methodist Episcopal Church of Windham." She continued, "On May 2, 1832, a deed of land was given by Isaac Hull, for where the church now stands. In April of the same year the church was made a part of the Windham Charge and the church building was begun and completed in the same year."

Built in 1832, West Settlement is the second church to be constructed in Old Windham. Both the North and West Settlement churches today are in the present Town of Ashland, which was formed in 1848 from the western part of old Windham.

Talmadge also noted that "the period of 1880–1890 appeared to have been the most prosperous times in the church's history." After that time, however, the church stood vacant and deserted for many years. In recent years the church has been rescued, and renovations by the Ashland Historical Society are progressing.

NORTH SETTLEMENT METHODIST CHURCH

In the early years people were interested in perpetuating their denominations, and it was the Methodist Episcopal Church that seemed most successful in bringing together these disparate groups. At first, traveling preachers would meet the people in homes, schools, and inns or taverns that were the public houses of the day, and were large enough to accommodate growing congregations.

Members formed this Methodist Society in 1805, when Windham became part of the Albany Circuit, with the Methodist Episcopal Church at Coeymans as the Mother Church. In 1826, under the guidance of Reverend Seth Crowell, a minister assigned to the Albany Circuit, the congregation built this church—the oldest church in Windham, according to a 1934 article by Donald F. Munson. Munson further stated that the early settlers there were of Puritan stock and arrived around 1786, mostly from Connecticut.

This little country church is almost hidden in the woods of Windham on County Route 10. The interior has wide plank floors and hand-made pews. In 1856, 30 years after its construction, the parishioners decided that the old edifice needed to be re-erected because of its old and decayed condition. The horse stalls the parishioners had to use might have had something to do with it as well. They called a meeting to decide whether to build fresh, or repair the original structure. The vote was to re-erect the old church, and subscriptions of more than $900 were raised for that purpose.

This little country church also holds an important place in Methodist history. In the early 1800s, a young black boy from Albany, who had been hired to do chores for a farmer in North Settlement, became a Christian. His name was Francis Burns, and he went on to become the first black missionary bishop in the Methodist Church in America.

SHRINE CHURCH OF ST. JOSEPH
St. Joseph's Chapel

St. Joseph's, located below the Village of Ashland itself, is claimed to be the oldest Roman Catholic church in the Catskill Mountains. The exterior of the building is wood, as is the interior of the chapel, the altar, and other structures. A very old cemetery lies peacefully beside the chapel.

According to a history written in 1957 by an unidentified author, St. Joseph's Chapel is believed to have been built in 1833 by immigrant weavers who built a mill nearby, and imported cottons and wools from Ireland. This would date St. Joseph's to long before the establishment of the Albany Roman Catholic Diocese in 1847. During those early years before 1847, the congregation was served by the Reverend Michael Gilbride, who was pastor of the Roman Catholic church at Saugerties.

In 1877, while the Reverend McCarthy was attempting to establish a Presbyterian church in Prattsville, the Reverend Father S. J. Cannime of Stamford was serving Mass at the Roman Catholic Chapel—now called Fatima Chapel—beyond Red Falls.

Once the mill closed down, however, the church stood deserted until 1948. Then, in 1950, under the direction of Father Rennie, the Shrine Church of St. Joseph was refurbished and rededicated on August 14, during a Triduum to our Lady of Fatima. A shrine to Our Lady of Fatima was also established in the area at that time.

Above: South façade, overlooking the small St. Joseph cemetery.
Below: Interior view of the nave.

Crescent Lawn/Jeralds House

This historic home's exterior is done in a Victorian/Italianate style with stained glass windows in a solarium, topped by a bracketed, sunlit cupola. The two front doors contain etched glass. The interior contains a "parson's cupboard," and the rooms have wainscoting. The house also boasts original woodwork, doorknobs, and latches, as well as its original fireplace and fire screen.

Crescent Lawn is a composition of three separate structures. One section, probably the oldest, was the parsonage of the Presbyterian Church of Ashland, which was built on a one-acre lot purchased by the Society in 1854. On June 11, 1856, Rev. Edward Stratton was ordained at Ashland and took up residence with his family in the parsonage. His successor and brother-in-law, Rev. Charles H. Holloway, was the last pastor to occupy the parsonage.

After Rev. Holloway and his family left, the parsonage was rented to various individuals, until it was purchased by Albert Tuttle, a prominent member of the church. Albert also purchased a piece of land between the parsonage and the old Strong family (brick) homestead next door from his wife's siblings. Many objected to the sale of the parsonage, but it was ratified at the annual meeting in 1869.

At some time the parsonage was moved a little farther from the church and nearer the Strong homestead. There is conflicting information about whether Albert or, later, his son-in-law, Thomas W. Jeralds, moved the parsonage. The Jeralds family did combine a Strong Homestead with the parsonage but this may have been at a latter date. It seems likely Albert would have had a substantial house due to his prominence as a farmer, merchant, and politician. When he was a member of the New York State Assembly he introduced the act to incorporate the Town of Ashland in 1848.

Albert's daughter, Frances, married Thomas W. Jeralds in 1860. Thomas was in the mercantile business for one year in Ashland, and then they moved to Connecticut, where they raised their children. By 1880 Thomas and Frances had returned to Ashland and were sharing the Tuttle home. Albert Tuttle died in 1883, followed by his wife, Aurelia, in 1890. Their home was inherited by daughters Ellen Tuttle and Frances Tuttle-Jeralds.

After retiring from active business, Thomas served as Ashland supervisor for the years 1891–92. He spent his retirement watching over his various business interests and management of the estate, known as Crescent Lawn. With major additions and remodeling of two substantial residences adjoining each other, the Jeralds created a residence noted for its beauty and splendid gardens. The valuable property consisted of 150 acres used chiefly for dairy and the cultivation of small fruits.

After Frances' passing in 1898, she left a large personal estate, which included her one-half interest in the family home to be inherited by her children and husband. Later that year Thomas purchased the shares of his children and sister-in-law, Ellen. Two years later, Thomas married Caroline Prout of Ashland. Thomas and Caroline spent the summer and fall months with his family at Crescent Lawn and wintered in New Haven, Connecticut. After Thomas W. Jeralds' death on January 19, 1917, the estate was inherited by his children. It remained in the Jeralds family until the 1960s.

Strong Farmhouse

Strong Farmhouse was begun in 1797 and completed in 1803. The house is Federal in style and has three fireplaces, including a beehive oven. Even today the interior of the house has the original wide-board floors. The trim and early integrity are maintained.

Elisha Strong, an early settler, founded the first permanent settlement in 1785 by the West Hollow Brook, still called Windham at the time, and owned the land upon which the Village of Ashland now stands. He came from Sharon, Connecticut, and he engaged in woodcutting. Two years later he brought his wife and seven children to the village, which was later named "Scienceville" because of its Academy and its Literary Institute. At this point he purchased all of the land now occupied by the Village of Ashland, and with the help of his four sons, he built himself a house, which was near a tavern built by his son Elijah. One of his other sons, Jairus, had a wood-framed store building, later building a brick store near the other one. In 1805, he lived in a brick house located across the street from this Federal-style store.

Elisha, unfortunately, did not live long to enjoy his new home, because in 1805 a horse kicked him and he died, at age 62, as a result of his injuries. His widow, however, continued to live in the house for many years, and is said to have lived until age 92. Two of the Strong sons, Jairus and Elijah, continued to live nearby, as did some of their sisters and their husbands. The two other brothers and two sisters moved to Friendship, in Allegheny County.

The Strong family—Elisha, his children, and their families—were prominent both in the community and as founding members of the Presbyterian church. Three of the early and most impressive homes in the village were built and owned by members of this family, and are an indication of their industry, business enterprises, and standing in the community.

One of the stories about the family concerns son Jairus, who was said to have a very fine racehorse that he hooked to a two-wheeled cart. It has been claimed that this horse would get Jairus to Catskill in four hours and return him the same day, dubbing him, no doubt deservedly, "a legend in his own time."

Trinity Episcopal Church

The church as we see it today was completed in 1879. The first service was held on June 27th of that year, when the Right Reverend William Croswell Doane, first Bishop of the Diocese of Albany, consecrated it. The trees that now tower over the building are likely the same trees planted in the spring of 1879 by the vestrymen whose names belong to old families in the area, and whose descendants are still to be found living here or nearby.

The church bell is original from the old Ashland Collegiate Institute & Musical Academy, which was built in 1854 and destroyed by fire in 1861. The bell bears the inscription "Hedding Literary Institute, Ashland, New York, 1854," and was cast by Jones & Hitchcock, Founders at Troy, New York.

As a body of worshippers, if not as a building, the history of this church goes back to 1793. However, the "official" organization of this church began May 20, 1799, under Philander Chase, a missionary. At that time it was known as the "Protestant Episcopal Church in the towns of Freehold and Windham vicinity and counties of Ulster and Albany," as neither the town of Ashland nor Greene County itself had been formed at the time.

The first building where this congregation worshipped was the First Congregational Church of Windham. It seems, in fact, that when this old meetinghouse was built, it was in some sense a union house to whose construction at least two denominations contributed, and it was used as such for a number of years. Troubles began to arise when both pastors scheduled activities at the same time and disagreements ensued. By 1808 the members began "to study the standards of Presbyterianism, and on October the 26th, 1826, were received under the care of Columbia Presbytery at a meeting in Greenville."

The old meetinghouse continued to be the place of worship for the members until the new building was completed at Windham Centre in 1834, then called Osbornville. The meetinghouse, which stood on part of the land of the Pleasant Valley Cemetery, was eventually torn down in 1896, and a New York State Historic marker now notes its location. A watercolor sketch of the "Old Meetinghouse" was painted from memory, possibly by Harry Addison Steele (a Bump descendant) or his wife, Frances Vosburgh Steele, who was the organist at the Centre Presbyterian Church in Windham for many years. The painting is in the possession of Pauline Munger Lawrence, to whom we are indebted for preserving the history of Trinity Church. She herself is a longtime member, as are past and later generations of her family, and as are the members of other families who have kept the church going for so many years.

In 1817 the wardens and vestry met at the home of John Tuttle to consider the "Building of a House of Public Worship," and resolved that a church be built after the model of the Trinity Church of Rensselaerville, designed by Ephraim Russ, a famous builder of churches and houses, many of which still stand within the region. The Trinity Church building here was 45 by 34 feet, and the growing congregation probably outgrew the building quickly. In 1879 the present Ashland Trinity Church building replaced the earlier one.

Sadly, the congregation has decreased in numbers and faced with mounting expenses, it turned the property over to the Diocese when other options were unavailable. This is, unfortunately, a common story among small rural churches.

It should be noted that this church congregation contributed greatly to the clergy as younger members grew to adulthood and entered the ministry, becoming rectors and bishops. The Right Reverend Daniel S. Tuttle, D.D., was the first Bishop Missionary of Montana, Idaho, and Utah, and also served as Bishop of Missouri. The Reverend Henry H. Prout was rector of the Trinity Episcopal Church from 1867 to 1871. He then was called to assist his old mentor, Bishop Tuttle, in Utah.

Inset: The Right Reverend Daniel Sylvester Tuttle, D.D., Bishop of Trinity Episcopal Church, circa 1860.

Above: "A simple sketch from memory" of the Old Meetinghouse—the First Congregational Church of Windham.

Second Street, looking east toward the Hudson River, circa early 1900s.

TOWN OF ATHENS

Bounded on the north by the Town of Coxsackie, on the east by the Hudson River, on the south by the Town of Catskill, and on the west by the Town of Cairo, the Town of Athens measures about seven miles at its longest point, and five and a half miles at its widest. Beers' 1884 *History of Greene County* describes the geography contained there as "exceedingly diversified," citing stretches of hills, areas of "flats" (valleys), and multiple streams.

The Town of Athens was formed from lands taken from Catskill and Coxsackie. The New York State legislature passed the bill creating the town on February 25, 1815. The town sits on portions of patents and land grants: the Loonenburg Patent, the Catskill Patent, the Corlaers Kill Patent, and the Roseboom Patent.

The three original settlements in the area were Loonenburg in 1685, Esperanza in 1794, and Athens in 1800. Before the American Revolution, the number of settlers in the area was small, limited mostly to those families living close to the Hudson River.

Esperanza, a speculative venture to create a city to rival the City of Hudson across its namesake river, was created with an eye toward becoming the western terminus of a great canal into the western parts of New York state and beyond. But the great speculation was never realized, the Erie Canal was built farther north, and the grand plans for a courthouse, a marketplace, and a "city tavern" only exist on maps.

Despite its hopeful name, the area planned as Esperanza has been assimilated into Athens itself. The incorporation of the Village of Athens took place on April 2, 1805. It was the first incorporated village in Greene County, and the third oldest in New York state. The area was once the home of the Mohican Indians, as evidenced by artifacts unearthed at Black Rock, a site in the southern part of the village. It was in 1609 that the English navigator Henry Hudson, sailing for the Dutch East India Company, made contact with the Indians living just west of Athens.

As Dutch settlers came to the Hudson River Valley, land was purchased from the Indians and confirmed by patent. By 1765 most of what has become the Village of Athens was owned by Jan Van Loon, and the subsequent hamlet was called Loonenburgh. A full 75 percent of the shares of this new town were owned by the Livingston family; names of the founders were given to the east-west streets. Then Isaac Northrup acquired the "Lower Purchase," the future site of downtown Athens, in 1800. In fact, Northrup was so successful in attracting the right businessmen that Loonenburgh soon outstripped Esperanza, and both were incorporated as the Village of Athens.

Over the years, many industries have existed in the town. The brickyards began operating in 1800, as did Athens Pottery, the latter lasting a hundred years. The brick industry carried on until the 1940s, when the last plant shut down. 1813 saw the start of the boat-building industry in Athens. Hundreds of boats were built here: steam-powered tugboats, diesel-powered freight and tow boats, sloops, barges, and lifeboats. The largest—and arguably the most famous—boat ever constructed here was the side-wheeler *The Kaaterskill*. Boat-building ended in Athens during the mid-1940s.

In the summer and fall during the 1800s, farmers like Cornell Vosburgh, who had the most important truck farm in the country, shipped produce by boat to the New York City market. During the winter, ice-cutting was an important industry here. Nine icehouses lined the Athens shores, providing off-season work for farmers and brick makers alike. Herman F. Dernell's Ice Tool Company became the largest manufacturer of ice tools in the United States.

Ferry service across the river to Hudson began in 1778, the boats and service improving until 1947, when the ferries finally fell victim to competition from the nearby Rip Van Winkle Bridge, which opened in 1935.

Today the Town of Athens is the site of the Cohotate Preserve and the Greene County Environmental Education Center, as well as restaurants, antique shops, and the like.

Athens has been in the movies as well. Some of the interior footage in *Ironweed* was shot at the Stewart House; Meryl Streep's death scene was filmed there as well. More recently, Steven Spielberg's production company did a week of location shooting for *The War of the Worlds* along the Athens waterfront, turning North Water Street into a ferry slip and railroad station, employing close to a hundred local people as extras, and bringing business to the area.

Jan Van Loon House

Jan Van Loon's modest two-room stone house, with a cellar kitchen, was built near the Indian site "Black Rock," where Indians of the Algonquin nation, mostly Mohicans and Delaware, congregated. The present house likely dates from the late 18th or early 19th century, with one wall remaining from the original structure. One of two stones salvaged from the original structure bears the inscription "1706, JVL."

Jan Van Loon was the earliest European settler in Loonenburgh (now Athens) and was the chief holder of the Loonenburgh Patent, securing title to the land in 1685. Jan's land holdings included a large bowery, part of which in 1800 was sold by his descendants to Isaac Northrup, who was the founder of the Village of Athens.

Born about 1650 in Liege, the capital of an independent bishopric, Jan Van Loon was formerly a Netherlander, although no citizen of the Dutch Republic: he was one of the few Netherlanders who, immediately after the final surrender of New Netherlands by the Dutch to the English in 1674, settled in this country. He arrived in New York in 1675. The minutes of the Common Council of the City of New York, dated November 24, 1675, stated that on that day he took an oath of allegiance to the king of Great Britain. In 1676, two months after his naturalization, he married Maria Jansen Van Ilpendam in New York, in the Dutch Reformed Church; the couple moved to Loonenburgh that same year. Maria had been born in New Amsterdam in 1656. Jan was well educated and spoke French as well as Dutch.

Jan and Maria had four sons, Jan, Albert, Nicholas, and Matthias. Their two daughters, Elsje and Maria, added the names of La Grange and Van Schaack to the family tree. The sons married into the Hallenbeck, Clouw, and La Grange families.

During 1937, this cherished landmark came close to demolition when the highway passing the stone house was realigned. Albert Van Loan (no longer spelled *Van Loon*) started a petition to save this historic structure, and thanks to Colonel Frederick Stuart Greene, the head of the Department of Public Works, a revised map with an alternate highway route was drawn to save the site.

The descendants of Jan Van Loon held title to his residence into the 21st century. In 2001, Eugene Van Loan, Jr., of Bedford, New York, transferred the house, which now stands on a small triangular-shaped parcel of land, to the Greene County Historical

Society. The Society signed a long-term lease with the Village of Athens for its use as a visitor center.

A grant from Athens Generating Corporation, funds from members of the Van Loon family, as well as monies from other contributors allowed the Village to obtain the necessary professional services for the project. The work was administered by the New York State Office of Parks and Recreation.

Archaeological requirements were completed in 2005, and the structural repairs began in the fall of 2006. Randy Evans and his crew rebuilt or restored the east, west, and south walls, south chimney, fireplace, and long-disappeared bake oven. Due to deterioration, similar stone was required to complete the restoration and was obtained from a building foundation on Howard Hall Road.

Since the archaeological study turned up items such as clay smoking pipes and Indian flint tools, and as the building was so near *Black Rock*, one would wonder if the original structure may have been used as a trading post.

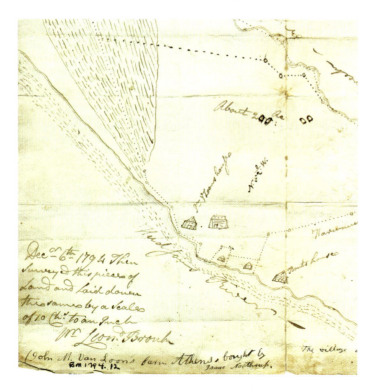

Left: Portion from December 6, 1794, survey map featuring Jan Van Loon's farm in Athens.

Above: North view of the Van Loon House, on the shore of the Hudson River, circa 1890.

Sketch of one of the cornerstones from the original 1706 home, bearing Jan Van Loon's initials.

HAIGHT/GANTLEY/VAN LOAN HOUSE

The Haight/Gantley/Van Loan House is the best-known house in Athens, as it is referenced in several publications as a particularly fine example of Federal architecture, designed by the architect Barnabas Waterman.

General Samuel Haight, soldier and merchant, chose the site for its panoramic view of the Hudson River. Before the house was completed, General Haight was called into active service in 1812. His wife, the former Jane Van Loon, a descendant of the first Van Loon patentee, was a woman of great social ambition and desired an oval ballroom like those in fashionable New York City mansions. When General Haight returned from the War of 1812, he found that the rectangular house now included an oval ballroom at the rear! On November 1, 1817, a Grand Open House was held. Etched into a pane of glass looking out on the verandah are the names of Samuel Haight, William Haight (his son), and Lydia Haight, William's wife.

Daniel W. Gantley, the "owner" from 1848 to 1905, was a wealthy merchant who, with his wife, Maria Hosmer, and family in tow, made the move from New York City to Athens in 1848. In his youth he had been the youngest passenger in Robert Fulton's steamboat *The Clermont,* and according to Van Loan family lore, he had spied this house from the river and decided he would like to live in it someday. Daniel Gantley was loved and revered by several generations in his lifetime. He lived to the ripe old age of 94, and died at his home on March 8, 1881.

In 1905 Thomas Van Loan of Brooklyn, a coffee and spice import and wholesale merchant—and a descendant of Jan Van Loon—bought the property from the Gantley heirs. In 1912, Thomas persuaded his son, Eugene Van Loan, and Helene, Eugene's wife, to take up residency on the Athens property. Thomas' extensive collection of paintings and objets d'art was moved to Athens. Paintings by European and American artists such as Church, Kensett, and Cropsey, among others, hung in tiers on every wall space of the ballroom, the halls, and the bedrooms. Thomas also built an addition for a new kitchen wing to replace the outmoded 19th-century area beneath the ballroom.

Eugene Van Loan's children, Mary Helene, Eugene, Jr., and Jane, grew up in this house. Being community-minded, Mrs. Eugene Van Loan opened her home to various civic groups for meetings and for special occasions. The young people of Athens in the 1930s and 1940s remember that the highlights of their Christmas holidays were the dances held in the oval ballroom.

In 1968 a Coxsackie merchant, Francis Hallenbeck, and his wife, Catherine, purchased the part of the property belonging to Eugene Van Loan, Jr., exclusive of the small Jan Van Loan house. In 2006 the property, including the mansion, the carriage house, and "the necessary"—the privy—were purchased by Ashton Hawkins and Johnnie Moore. These new owners are now restoring this home with care and sensitivity.

Inset: Daniel W. Gantley.

Below: The original privy, built circa 1813.

BLACK ROCK FARM

Originally a tenant farmhouse, built circa 1820 with unusual barns, this house was part of the properties owned by General Samuel Haight. In 1812 Haight built a Federal-style mansion (see Haight/Gantley/Van Loan House, page 21). At a later date, a carriage house, Black Rock Farm, and barns were constructed.

After the ownership had passed to Daniel W. Gantley, in 1913 Thomas Van Loan, the grandfather of the present owner, bought the property for his retirement from a thriving coffee, tea, and spice import business in New York City.

Upon Van Loan's death in 1930, the property was divided between his sons: Eugene, who inherited the mansion and carriage house; and Schuyler, who inherited Black Rock, Black Rock Farm, and the barns. When Schuyler died in 1981 his niece, Jane Van Loan Erickson, the present owner, inherited his property.

BLACK ROCK SITE

Black Rock was a part of the Loonenburg Patent of May 25, 1667, and deeded in part to Jan Van Loon in 1688. The landmark mentioned in the Indian deed as Machawamick was called by the Dutch settlers "Vlught Hock," or "Flying Corner." It is now known as Black Rock; it projects into the river at the southern end of the Village of Athens. When Route 385 was straightened, the "new"—prior to 1948—road separated Black Rock from the rest of the properties owned by Schuyler Van Loan, the uncle of the present owner.

This was the site of a large Indian encampment in prehistoric times. The soil around this camp is black for 10 to 12 acres, caused by campfires burned there for a number of years. The site is believed to have been occupied first by Delaware Indians, and in later years by the Mohicans. Nearly all the relics, broken pottery, arrow heads, and other stone implements that have been found are of Mohican manufacture.

An original Indian deed shows five Indian names: Keesie Wey, Sachemoes, Papeuna, Masseha, and Mawinata—alias Schermerhorn—granting area lands.

Above: Looking south from South Washington Street with Black Rock to the left, circa 1962.

Livingston/Coffin/Apfel House

Built for Anthony Livingston in 1825, this high-style Federal brick building was designed by the "master builder" Barnabas Waterman, who also designed the House of History across the Hudson River, in Kinderhook, New York. Anthony Livingston was the kin of Philip Livingston, one of the signers of the Declaration of Independence. The house, with its double-storied portico, four 22-foot Corinthian columns, and its Hudson River location, was a tribute to the Livingstons' wealth and prestige. The doors and windows are trimmed with Vermont marble. The interior has 12-foot ceilings, seven working fireplaces, a Dutch oven, 12-inch crown moldings, and three Bohemian crystal chandeliers.

In 1845 the house was sold to Judge Sylvester Nichols, a respected justice as well as the Athens town supervisor and Village clerk. By 1871 the property had new owners: Lydia and Reuben Coffin. Lydia was the daughter of William Coffin, the founder of Athens' largest shipyard. The current door, which shows Lydia's taste for the Italianate style, with its ornate detailing, was meant to impress visitors and announce the family's prominence in the community. Lydia held a large wedding reception at her home in 1897 after her granddaughter married a nephew of President William McKinley.

Unfortunately, between 1906 and 1935 the house was not kept up to standards set by the previous owners. In 1935 James Hyer, a prominent lawyer, purchased the house. To provide ample living space for his growing family of a dozen children—eleven of whom survived childhood—and the need for office space, the original ell-shaped building was extended. Hyer's law office, library, and insurance company were located in the basement (i.e., the ground floor). The kitchen was moved from the basement to the first floor, and central heating and modern bathrooms were installed.

In 1972 the balusters around the portico and the four Corinthian columns were removed due to decay. Since acquiring the property in 2003, however, the current owners, Richard and Janet Apfel have been busy re-creating the portico to its former glory of Corinthian column supports encased by 19th-century-styled balusters.

The property includes the bay area of the Hudson River adjacent to the Athens Riverfront Park.

ATHENS

ALBERTUS VAN LOON HOUSE

This early-18th-century Dutch stone house was built by Albertus Van Loon, the fourth son of Jan Van Loon, the original patent holder of Loonenburg, the original name for the Athens area. An erection date of 1724 was established by two date stones, one in the lower southwestern corner of the house and the other, newly uncovered, on the upper southeast corner.

The southern half of the stone house was first erected with a very steep gable roof of 60 degrees, in the common urban Dutch style of the time; one entered the premises from the north wall side. About the middle of the 18th century, the northern half of the stone house was added, and the orientation of the entire house was shifted west, to the road side. The English-style gambrel roof is original over the northern half, but the southern half of the roof is framed differently. The dormers were added in the 1830s.

The original one-room stone house had a jambless fireplace and one or two garrets, but was renovated in the 1760s to the Georgian style, and retains its paneling and elaborate fireplace mantel. At about this time the clapboard addition on the south end was added. The Georgian room is known as "the Dueling Room." A liquor license was obtained in 1774, and it is possible a tavern was operated in the southern addition at that time. The many pieces of pottery shards, musket balls, and coins attest to a great deal of activity in this area.

The wooden addition to the north end may have been on-site earlier than the stone building, as a reference to its existence in 1717 is mentioned in *The Albany Protocols*. That building used an even earlier Dutch construction type than the stone house, but shows evidence that it may have been moved from elsewhere. Connecting two wooden additions at the rear of the stone house, facing the Hudson River, is a Victorian addition from approximately the 1880s that enclosed what was originally a long Dutch porch.

The property descended down to the fourth-generation Albertus/Albert Van Loon, who died in 1838. According to his will the house was bequeathed to an adopted daughter, Cornelia. The will was contested by relatives and a lengthy trial ensued. The challenge led to an argument between Anthony A. Livingston, one of the executors, and the attorney James Byrnes. It is said that Byrnes stabbed Livingston in this house, so perhaps this is where the legend of the Dueling Room materialized. The lengthy 140-day trial ended on November 7, 1839, with the will being sustained.

The house then passed through several private owners, followed by the New York Ice Company in 1858, and the Knickerbocker Ice Company in 1867. After numerous year of deterioration, in the late 1990s the current owners, Randy Evans and Carrie Feder, purchased the house. The couple has performed a great amount of preservation work to stabilize and restore the structure.

Inset: Sketch of the 1724 cornerstone, from the lower southwestern corner.

DERNELL-CLARK HOUSE

In 1854 Herman F. Dernehl, age 18, arrived in the United States from Germany. Four years later he settled in Athens, where he began general blacksmithing. The rapid rise of the ice harvesting industry on the Hudson River caused him to concentrate on ice tools. Due to the quality of his work and certain inventions, he soon became a leading manufacturer of ice tools in the United States, with additional customers in Germany and Sweden.

HERMAN F. DERNELL & CO.

MANUFACTURERS OF

All Kinds of Ice Tools,

ATHENS, N. Y.

Dernehl anglicized the spelling of his last name to Dernell and was locally known in Athens as Harmon Dernell, Harmon being the Dutch version of Herman. As Harmon Dernell, he served as the Athens Village president three different times: 1870–71, 1884–85, and 1902.

The present property was acquired by Dernell in three stages. The original oblong structure, built circa 1840, consisting of two rooms downstairs and two rooms upstairs, was purchased in 1861. In 1868, after buying the lot to the north, he added a wing to the house. In 1893 the lot and house to the south were acquired, and by moving the second house back he could add another "wing," making the house T-shaped and allowing more room for a garden. The structure moved to the back housed his full-time gardener, and provided temporary quarters for the immigrants working for his ice tool foundry.

This Victorian house, with Stick, Queen Anne, and Second Empire architectural touches, was purchased in 1921 by William J. Clark from the estate of Emilie Dernell Lang, the deceased sister of Herman Dernell. William Clark was the owner of Clark's Variety Store, and was the father of subsequent owners Harriet Clark Peloubet (deceased), and Franklin B. Clark and his wife, Winifred. For a number of years Harriet was the Town of Athens tax collector, with her office in this house, and Franklin, as a New York State Superintendent of Schools, had his office here for most of his tenure.

Herman Dernell also had his office in this house. It was located in the southeast room with a secondary front access. The room now serves as the Clarks' living room, which still contains Dernell's standup desk and his numerous built-in bookcases.

There are still a few Dernell plantings in the Clarks' garden: deutzia bushes, cabbage roses, ribbon grass, tree peonies, and sweet woodruff. The huge Norway spruce planted by Dernell, which survived being struck by lightning in 1978, was pronounced unsafe in 1990 and had to be removed. Since the tower was now the tallest structure in the area, lightning rods were installed on the house.

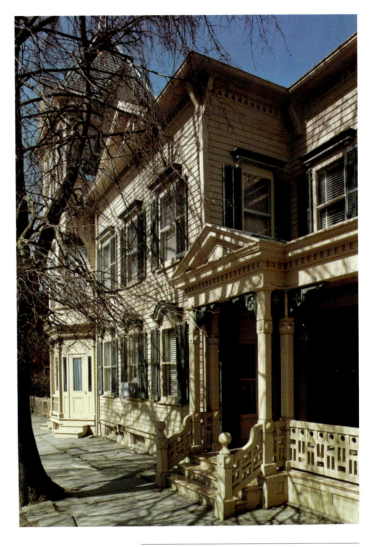

Left: Advertisement for the H. F. Dernell Ice Tool Company, circa 1900.

Above: Façade as viewed from the northeast.

Below: Close-up of the downstairs windows.

Eichorn / Zar / Kurdziel House

This house was originally built in 1880 as a rectangular Italianate house, and a large Queen Anne turret was added at the turn of the 20th century. The front porch was deepened at the same time. This house could be described as an "in-law" house, one of those structures built by the upper-middle class that, in scope and comfort, is one step below houses built by the most prominent members of a community. Such "in-law" houses are often associated with sisters or daughters who are given a boost by their affluent families to ensure that, once married, they can live in appropriate style and comfort.

In this instance, Charles Eichorn had married Leonora Dernell, the sister of Herman Dernell, the man who had established a major ice-tool manufactory in Athens. Dernell's house is shown on the previous page. Mr. Eichorn worked in the Dernell plant. After the death of Mr. Eichorn's wife his daughter, Laura, and son-in-law, Ben Hoff, moved into the house to care for Mr. Eichorn.

After a succession of owners, the house deteriorated. The back porch was removed, aluminum siding was used, and, at one point, the house was divided into a two-family structure. The present owners have carefully restored both the exterior and interior. The Queen Anne turret and front porch have been painted using a turn-of-the-century original decorative scheme.

Cornelius Van Loan House

Built in the Georgian style during the Federal period, this house was constructed in 1795 for Cornelius Van Loan. The fine entrance door is within an arched and recessed vestibule. The archway over the entrance is of painted marble, as are the lintels under the front windows. The Palladian window above repeats the delicate design in the fan and sidelights of the door. The American eagle symbol of the Federal period can be seen in the center of the fanlight over the door and the Palladian window.

From 1795 to 1923 Cornelius Van Loan, and his descendants, retained ownership of the property. But through the years after that the house was altered, abused, and allowed to deteriorate to the point that, by 1993, it was no longer habitable. It was from 1993 to 1996 that Robert Keeper and Arthur Marquis began the essential task of restoration, retaining as many of the original features as possible and removing the extra kitchen and two side porches not appropriate to the original house. The present owners, Robert and Andrea Smallwood, now maintain this home in pristine condition.

In 2007, Andrea was elected mayor of Athens, the first woman to hold that position.

Close-up of the front entrance, with Palladian window and archway of painted marble.

BEDELL/NICHOLS HOUSE

In 1872, 57-year-old George S. Nichols, custom house officer in New York City, sold to Abram Bedell four and a half lots in the village of Athens described as "up to 4th street running 274 feet westerly from Franklin Street." The following year, Abram Bedell built this Second Empire Victorian house. The mansard roof with its dormer windows is typical of the period.

When the house was built, 54-year-old Abram Bedell was already retired from the Athens firm Van Schaack & Bedell Glue Manufacturers. When he passed away during 1890, Adam bequeathed to his wife, Sarah W. Sanderson-Bedell, "my present place of residence, consisting of house and lands situated on the westerly side of Franklin Street in the Village of Athens, also household furniture, wearing apparel, silverware and plated ware, watch and jewelry, books, works of art, fuel and provisions and all other consumable stores, chattels and effects belonging to me." While Sarah also received a bequest of $25,000, the remainder of Abram's personal estate was divided among his children, Bradbury, Minnie (Mary), and Margaret. Sarah, her two unmarried daughters, and their servant remained in the house into the early 20th century.

The three Bedell women purchased a house on William Street during 1902 and named it Bradbury after their recently deceased son and brother. Sarah died in 1910, followed by her daughter Mary in 1917. Margaret lived in the house on William Street until her death in 1932 at age 71. She was buried in the family plot with her parents and sister in Athens Rural Cemetery.

In 1904 this house and adjoining land were sold to John Nichols, a relative of George S. Nichols, who had sold the land to Adam Bedell. It appears that the Bedell and Nichols families may have had a shared family connection, or a long friendship. Their relationship certainly started as young men prior to the transfers of this house. Documentation comes from the 1855 census, which lists Abram and George, along with their families, living in a duplex brick dwelling in the Village of Athens.

The Nichols family came to this country from England and some of the individuals settled in Athens as early as 1800. Being honorable members of the community, they were active in the civic affairs of both the town and village. They were a wealthy family who owned tugboats and engaged in shipping on the Hudson River. At the time John purchased this house, he was earning wages as the superintendent of a steamboat company, perhaps in the family business.

At the death of John Nichols, his daughter, Edna Nichols Van Deusen, inherited the property. Edna, in turn, passed it on to her daughter, Barbara Van Deusen Euiler. Seventy-seven years of ownership by the Nichols/Van Deusen/Euiler families ended when the house was sold in 1981.

The property was purchased by Earle S. Olsen, who takes pride in maintaining this house with its slate roof and original clapboards. Many rooms still have the original Victorian moldings and marble fireplaces.

Inset: George Sylvester Nichols.
Above: Original Victorian balustrade that frames the front porch.

Titus / Conine / Palmateer House

When historical research is undertaken it becomes obvious that many houses constructed in the 19th century manifest a blend of differing architectural styles. This fact is well illustrated in the stately red-brick residence of the Palmateer family. Located on the corner of Second and Warren Streets, the original section of the house was erected circa 1803, before the Village of Athens had even been incorporated. The symmetrical five-bay front was built in the Federal style. Yet the original section's classic Federal front, with its symmetry and Georgian-style entrance, harmonizes perfectly with the late-1870s Greek Revival design used in the rear section. The blending of these two popular styles is seen in many structures throughout Greene County, and generally suggests the work of master craftsmen, as apparent in this attractive house.

The building was constructed on a raised basement with the front steps erected sideways, leading to the handsome center portico. There, a heavy wooden doorway with egg-and-dart molding is flanked by fluted Ionic columns and a pediment. A center Georgian-type hall, replicated on the second floor, once led from the doorway to the rear of the house, but the building of a first-floor powder room in the 1950s interrupted this space. The windows, made beautiful by dark shutters contrasting with the brick, contribute to the total historic picture. "Eyebrow" windows were built into the heavy cornice surrounding the attic area. A striking cupola with eight windows tops the handsome historic structure.

Fireplaces, many still working, enhance every room, including the attic and the basement. During cold winter days those working fireplaces provide a welcome aura of warmth. Three mantels on the first floor are of black marble, and glow with the flames reflection.

Original inner shutters, most likely used in earlier times to shut out the winter weather, grace the three tall French-style windows. Two sections of six-over-six windows brighten the splendid southwest interior. Four rooms on each side of the first- and second-floor halls illustrate the mix of Federal and Georgian design. Surrounded by heavy original crown moldings, the high ceilings and early plaster work have been carefully preserved. A carved medallion centers the northwest formal parlor. The pineapple, the colonial symbol of hospitality, along with an acanthus leaf, is carved into the corners of door moldings.

An original tin ceiling tops the attractive dining room just north of the kitchen. In the kitchen itself two large hearthstones, uncovered when flooring was installed in recent years, correspond with the antiquity of the building. One probably served as the base for a wood stove, while the other protected against fireplace ashes.

Late in the 1980s, a fire destroyed sections of the roof while workmen were repairing the area. Luckily, the cupola suffered only slight damage. The roof was subsequently restored and an elliptical leaded-glass window, centered in the west peak, damaged when firemen were forced to enter the attic, was skillfully repaired by Michael Black, a well-known local artisan. This historically significant window illustrates outstanding artistry. Black used antique glass, creating two new casts of rosette moldings to produce the elegant restoration.

The area on which the house is sited reflects the Dutch concept of building in a rural village along the Hudson River. That is, a house should be set on or very near the street, with an expansive ground

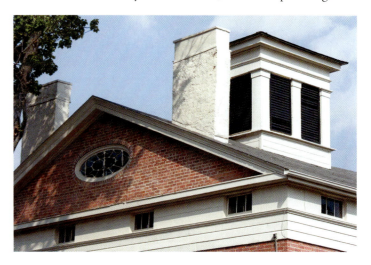

area in the rear where family activities take place and gardens produce family provisions. In general this land was fenced to give privacy and safety from animals. In this instance the tall wooden fence, stretching for about 191½ feet along Warren Street, encloses the large backyard and has illustrated this concept for over a century. The fence was completely restored in 2006. Within its boundary lie the flower/vegetable gardens and a rather unique building, the original two-sided privy, with three holes on each side. The sides sit back-to-back: one side for family, the other for servants.

The Palmateers have refurbished both the interior and exterior with careful attention to historical and architectural detail. As they have phrased it, "It is part of your job and your responsibility to take care of historic sites when you purchase them." Nancy and Lee Palmateer have embodied that principle since purchasing the property on August 25, 2000, and have enjoyed the professional advice of popular designer Timothy Albright, Jr., Nancy's brother. Together with their three young sons (Benjamin and twins Elliot and Samuel), Lee, an attorney, and Nancy, an educator, represent the fourth and fifth generations of a family who has owned this residence since 1930. To maintain a safe environment for their family of three young boys, extensive lead abatement was done on the interior in 2002 and on the exterior in 2004.

Rumor suggests that at one time this property was known as Goose Meadow, although the reason for this nomenclature has not yet been uncovered. While it is known that the house was constructed circa 1803, the history of owners at that time is vague. The first known owner was James Koster, who sold the house to a William Tolley in 1838. While it is possible that Koster could have erected the house 35 years earlier, it is probable that both Koster and Tolley were farmers. In 1866 a Fred Tolley sold the property to

Epenetus Titus for the sum of $5,000, a hefty sum indeed for that day and age! Epenetus had the greatest impact on the early significance of the house, and it was most likely he who constructed the Greek Revival rear section of the house in 1870.

Born in New Baltimore in 1822, Epenetus married Catherine Miller, a Greene County woman. Together they birthed five children. George Titus, Epentus' bachelor brother, also lived with them in this beautiful house, and probably worked with Epenetus on their extensive farm. Various censuses describe Epenetus as follows: farmer (1850), boatsman (1855), and retired farmer (1870). In 1870 he recorded $5,000 worth of real estate and $45,000 in personal property.

George's statistics are less varied until 1870. Listed as a farmer in the 1850 federal census, 1855 New York state census, and 1860 federal census, he reported $20,000 worth of real estate and $4,000 of real property. But by the 1870 federal census he regarded himself as a retired manufacturer, with $6,000 worth of real estate and $125,000 of real property. The Titus brothers were arguably the wealthiest farmers in Greene County at that time.

When Epenetus died in January 1903 his executors, daughter Emily Day Seymour and grandnephew Fred Titus, recorded the house—by then "very much out of repair"—at a value of $4,000; cash on hand was listed at $29.53, and total worth was $138,613.63.

By 1914 the structure was involved in the brick industry, which had arisen in parts of Greene County, notably Catskill and Athens. The Stanley Gladfelters, shipbuilders and major owners of the Athens brickyard, purchased and began to refurbish the house when, unfortunately, the brickyards folded. On September 22, 1930, Jennie Gladfelter, in payment for a large loan on the brick industry and house, transferred the property's title to Eleanor D. Lassen, Annie Shufelt, and Dr. Alton B. Daley, the latter an Athens physician. Dr. Daley bought out his two co-owners.

Thus, in 1930 the modern family ownership began. With the approach of World War II, and during the war as well, the house was leased to several families as new industries supporting the war became an important economic feature in the Hudson River Village of Athens. In 1955 title was transferred through purchase to Frances Daley Conine, whose family had been dwelling in the residence for several years. Their daughter, Elizabeth Conine Albright, was raised in this home since she was a toddler. In 1987 Elizabeth and her husband, Timothy Albright— current owners of another historic house—received title to this house, which they sold to their daughter and son-in-law, current owners Nancy and Lee Palmateer.

Opposite: Southwest corner view of cupola, eyebrow windows, and the restored leaded window.

First Reformed Church

As early as 1811, prayer meetings and Sunday school were held at the corner of Market and Franklin streets, at the home of Ebenezer King, a schoolmaster. The early church fathers' initial direction was not Reformed but Presbyterian, and articles of incorporation for a Presbyterian church were filed at the Greene County Courthouse in 1814. However, since the Reformed Dutch vastly outnumbered the Presbyterian Scottish in the area, it was felt that a Reformed church would be more in line with the needs of the community.

On November 22, 1824, a meeting was held at Ebenezer King's schoolroom to discuss the building of a church. Reverend Isaac N. Wycoff of the Leeds Reformed Church was requested to officiate as chairman, and the Reverend Gilbert R. Livingston of the Coxsackie Reformed Church to act as secretary of the meeting. The total of the subscriptions promised amounted to $1,635.

This house of worship was built between 1825 and 1827, at a cost of $2,213.52. Later additions to the building included the "old" Sunday School Room, built in 1886. The latter is now labeled "old" because in 1975 a new Sunday School Room, office and study were added. It is a classic example of an early-19th-century colonial brick structure with a splendid slate-clad steeple topped with an original weather vane.

The twelve stained-glass windows in the sanctuary are of exceptional quality. The one to the left of the altar was placed in memory of Emilie Dernell-Lang, sister of Herman Dernell. Altered brick on the outer walls signify that the windows were at one time squared at the top, not arched as they are now. These early windows probably had plain glass panes. In the past, the church interior was open with a vaulted ceiling and a plainer balcony.

A parcel of land divided by a 20-foot alley was given by Isaac Northrup, founder of the Village of Athens, to be equally divided among the Presbyterians/Dutch Reformed, and the Episcopalians. The Reformed church chose the northern half. Since Northrup had influence in naming the streets in Athens, it seems likely he chose the name Church Street.

The first minister, the Reverend David Abeel, was installed immediately after his graduation from the New Brunswick Seminary, class of 1826. His salary was $15 a month. After three months his salary was increased to $33 a month with a later salary increase. He served the church from 1826 through 1828. In that year, at age 24, he left this pastorate to become the first foreign missionary to Asia; he also became the founder of the Amoy Mission. This Reformed church in Athens was the only church in this country in which Abeel served as pastor.

It was during the pastorate of the Reverend Cornelius Van Cleef (1828–1833) that one of Athens greatest religious revivals took place, with 60 being received into the church at one time. In the mid-19th century, General George S. Nichols, a much esteemed Athenian, was a member of this congregation. At the close of the Civil War he was made a brigadier general.

The congregation became very large and people were traveling long distances to attend services. In 1833 there was an appeal to build a chapel west of the village near High Hill. The chapel was built in 1837 and sat on the hill with a few old cemetery stones in the Coleburg Cemetery to the west.

Some years later, the First Reformed Church conveyed the chapel to the consistory of the Second Reformed Church of Athens, with the condition that it would remain a Dutch Church. Services continued at High Hill until 1903, and then in 1904 the congregation disbanded. On June 26, 1908, an auction was held at the Sager Hotel located on Lime Street, High Hill, to sell the building. Several years later the chapel was destroyed by fire.

During 1901 the Sunday school of the First Reformed Dutch Church purchased a large building north of the village (12 Brick Row) that for a short time was used as a "mission." Also during 1901, in celebration of the church's 75th anniversary, the interior was redecorated and the roof received new slate.

The Carnegie Corporation of New York pledged half of the cost of a new organ in 1913. The cost was not to exceed $2,500. This instrument was installed in the front, rather than in the back balcony where the previous organ was located. A new organ was dedicated in 1998.

Above: Reverend David Abeel.

ZION EVANGELICAL LUTHERAN CHURCH

The Zion Evangelical Lutheran Church is the oldest continuously active congregation of the Lutheran Church in America! The current red church building of classic design was erected in 1853. It was to cost "no more than $7,000." The building was enlarged and remodeled first in 1897, and then again in 1924, 1953, and most recently in 1996. Straley Hall was built in 1963, named out of respect for Reverend Luther Straley, who served as pastor for 44 years.

Being much larger than the original church, the new building was erected farther back from Washington Street. The 1924 renovation included creation of a partial basement and the installation of electricity and central heating. Also, the arch behind the altar was created and the current altar, pulpit, and lectern installed.

The Hook and Hastings tracker organ, donated to the church in 1913 under the terms of the will of Nicholas Van Hoesen, was replaced in 1971. The new organ was built by the L. A. Carlson Company of East Greenbush, at a cost of approximately $12,000.

The actual date of the founding of the congregation is lost in obscurity. However, the fact that records begin in 1704 appears to indicate that there was an organization before that time. The Reverend Justice Falckner, whose 1703 ordination in Philadelphia is believed to be the first in America, was to be the minister of a congregation in Albany. However, when he reached Albany during June 1704, he found the congregation practically disbanded. Most of the members had moved south along the Hudson River to Loonenburgh [Athens]. While Pastor Falckner held services in both Albany and Loonenburgh, the new Loonenburgh congregation overshadowed the one in Albany. He made this his upstate headquarters and was still pastor at the time of his death in 1723.

It is not known where the congregation first met, but it is generally agreed that the first building was constructed in 1724. That first building was known in the community as the "beehive" due to its unique shape: four roofs forming a peak topped by a small steeple. It served the congregation until the current one was erected. Reverend Wilhelm Chistoph Berkenmeyer was probably the first to preside over services in the beehive, since he was the second established minister of Albany and Loonenburgh.

Reverend Berkenmeyer died in 1751 at age 69. At his request his remains were buried in the beehive. A sandstone tablet was placed over his crypt, situated either in front or beneath the altar. The tablet is now located on the outside east wall between the entrance doors of the present church. It is possible that it still identifies the location of Reverend Berkenmeyer's tomb.

Apparently the beehive was erected on Van Loan family land holdings, since in 1727 a farm of undetermined acreage, which came to be known as the "glebe farm," was deeded by Jacob Van Loan, Albertus Van Loan, and Mathyes Van Loan for use by and on the behalf of the Lutheran minister and the Lutheran congregation. While a lot of approximately 150 feet by 100 feet on Washington Street was reserved as the church ground, the remaining land was to be the glebe, land used for the benefit of the church. The land was divided into lots, which yielded revenue to the church. Even today, while the present owners can own the buildings on this glebe land, the land itself is still subject to the glebe rent. This is the oldest and longest continuous glebe in New York state.

Inset: The 1792 seal of the "Evangelical Lutheran Zion's Church in Loonenburg," featuring a sketch of the original church structure.

D. R. Evarts Library

The Beaux-Arts style of architecture was quite popular in public buildings in the early years of the 20th century. Built in 1907, the D. R. Evarts Library is fine example of this style.

Daniel Redfield Evarts came from a large family with limited income, and had no free access to books or a quiet place to study. He spent his formative years in Athens longing for books to read. Due to the kindness of the Dutch Reformed pastor and congregation, he was allowed to use a small room attached to the rear of the church as a place to study with access to books. Working after school in his uncle's grocery and bakery, he then landed a position with the New York and Philadelphia Transportation Company. He left Athens to fill this position, but as he prospered he never forgot his hometown and the kindness shown to him. On his death he bequeathed Athens the money to build a library, with additional funds to be invested for further income.

The laying of the cornerstone in July of 1907 was a great occasion, touching off a three-day celebration called "Old Home Week" with speeches, parades, concerts, ball games, a motorboat race, and carnival. A church service closed the festivities. The cornerstone, laid with Masonic rites by the Civil War general George S. Nichols, assisted by S. H. Nichols, H. F. Dernell, Harmon Van Wort, and C. Porter, contains a box with copies of the wills of Daniel R. Evarts and his wife, Elizabeth, American flags, old coins and currency, an ice-tool catalog of H. F. Dernell and Company, business cards, and assessment rolls. The silver trowel used to lay the cornerstone hangs proudly, displayed on one wall of the library with portraits of D. R. Evarts and his children.

When the library was opened to the public on June 18, 1908, the eloquent Reverend M. Seymour Purdy, pastor of the Reformed Church, said in his address, "Each age is the heir of all the ages that have come before us. The past is ours mainly through the medium of books. It is no slight gift that the donor has bestowed upon us in giving to Athens this library. Just how much benefit you or I derive from his gift depends altogether upon ourselves."

Matthias Van Loon/Palmer House

Matthias Van Loon, who was a descendant of one of Athens' earliest settlers, Jan Van Loon, owned the Athens Shipyard. Among other vessels, this shipyard produced the day boat Kaaterskill, the largest boat constructed in Athens.

In 1872, Matthias had a house constructed for his personal use. This transitional house in the Italianate style, it incorporated the elements of large Doric columns of the Greek Revival period. The interior has ten-foot-high ceilings and wide, distinctive moldings.

Matthias Van Loon, born in 1822, was a direct descendant of Matthias Van Loon, the youngest son of Jan Van Loon. In 1871, with Peter Magee as a partner, Van Loon bought the shipyard that had been established in 1843. This shipyard of Van Loon and Magee became the most important shipyard on the Hudson River, building a variety of boats including a three-masted schooner, a steam yacht, barges, ice barges, tugboats, and the ferry boat the *A. F. Beach*.

The house was purchased in 1900 by William C. Brady, the founder of W. C. Brady's Sons, Inc., funeral home. First based in Athens, it is now located in Coxsackie.

When the funeral home maintained its office in Athens, it became the gathering place for retired old men and unemployed seasonal workers. In fine weather, they would sit on chairs outside; in inclement weather they met in the front room. They referred to these visits as "going to the morgue." The rear room would contain the cadavers.

In 1910 the marriage of the Bradys' daughter Edith to Benjamin Whiting was held on the front lawn. At William Brady's death in 1938, the Whitings moved into the house to care for their widowed mother. When Edith Whiting was widowed, her daughter Jeannette and her husband, Harry Palmer, came to be with their mother and to raise their family here. Since 1900 three generations have lived here.

Above: Matthias Van Loon House, circa 1884.

Nichols/Daley/Albright Home

The main structure of this two-story Federal-style brick house was built in 1846. Additions were constructed later in the 19th century, and a wood-framed addition was built during the 1920s. The floor plan and most of the moldings and basic structure are original.

John Bennet, a merchant in Athens, purchased the property in 1846 and is believed to be the first occupant. John and his wife, Phebe, were natives of Connecticut. Hobart Bennet, probably their son, and Elsie Scot were residents in the Village of Athens when they were married on February 18, 1849, by clergy of the Athens Trinity Episcopal Church.

Hobart and Elsie took up residence with John and Phebe and started to raise a family. Sadly, the early years of their marriage were filled with tragedy. John Bennet passed away during 1852, and two years later funeral services were held at the Trinity Episcopal Church for four-year-old Abby and her younger sister Mary Elisa. Another daughter, Amanda, died in 1856 at the age of one year.

This house was also owned by various members of the Coffin family, who were prominent citizens in Athens. From 1843 until its closing in 1941, the Coffin shipyards were the center of industry in Athens. At first, canal boats and barges were constructed, and later towboats, schooners, and steamboats.

Sarah Nichols purchased the house from the Coffin family. After the death of Sarah in 1913, her children sold the house to Frank R. Shufelt and his wife, Annie Nichols Shufelt. The Shufelts presented the house as a wedding gift to their daughter Frances and Dr. Alton B. Daley.

Numerous Athens residents passed through the doors of the wood-framed addition where Dr. Daley had his medical practice. After retiring, the doctor remained in this house until his death in 1971. His granddaughter Elizabeth and her husband, Timothy Albright, purchased the property from his estate.

Witherill/Stalker House

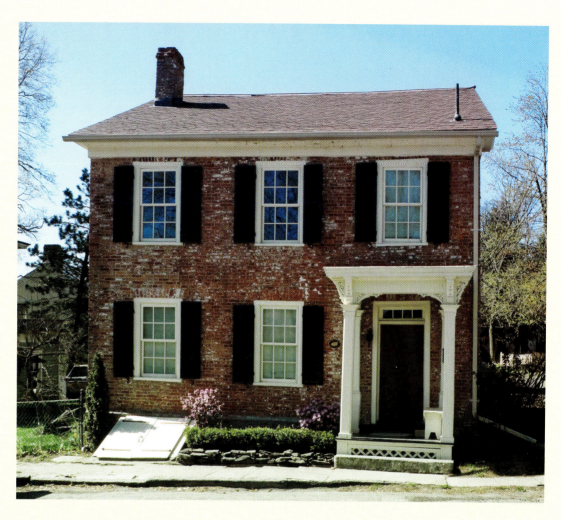

Constructed of brick laid out in a Flemish pattern, this two-and-a-half-story house is late Georgian in design. The original construction dates to circa 1824. The front portico was a Victorian addition similar to other porches and porticos in Athens.

The front door and the four panes of glass above it are replacements but it is believed they are quite similar to the originals. The original six-over-six windows have also been replaced. The interior has the original plaster walls, wide-board floors, and the original woodwork and moldings. No original mantels or hearths still exist, but moldings and cut-outs in the floor suggest they were present.

The Hudson-Athens Ferry started operation in 1778, attracting individuals and industry to the west bank of the Hudson River. By 1805, when the village was incorporated, a number of elegant structures were built, each reflecting the wealth of the early settlers. Others would follow.

Elijah Spencer was one of the early settlers purchasing this property in 1824. It is unknown if the structure existed at that time, but based on the projected building date and his short ownership of nine months, it seems reasonable to think that perhaps he was the craftsman, or at least the entrepreneur.

The Spencer family resided in Athens at least as early as 1815; there is a record of their infant daughter's funeral held at the Athens First Episcopal Church. Elijah was one of the trustees of a Reformed Protestant Dutch church in Athens, who met on May 27, 1826, to incorporate under the name Dutch Reformed Church of the Village of Athens. Elijah's wife, Freelove Pratt, was baptized in the Reformed church as an adult during 1826, followed by their child, Edward, on October 7, 1827

It seems likely that the next owner of the property, Benjamin Haxton, was the first resident. Benjamin purchased the property from Elijah Spencer in January 1825 and owned it for the next ten years before selling to a William H. Spencer. The following year Benjamin sold his small farm at the south end of the village to the rector of Trinity Church.

There have been many owners of this house over the years, including Sylvester Nichols, Athens justice of the peace, whose ownership spanned the years 1860 to 1865; Herman F. Dernell, the important ice-tool manufacturer, who owned the property from 1869 to 1913; and Dernell's sister, Minnie Every, whose ownership ran from 1913 to 1939. For many years Orin Q. Flint, the first president of the Greene County Historical Society, had his law and insurance office here. Jeffrey and Ann Marie Stalker, who were the owners from 1994 to 1999, placed the house on the Greene County Historical Register.

Inset: Sylvester Nichols.

COUNTRY HOME

This Italianate-style house, with buttresses supporting the roof, was built circa 1868. The current wooden siding replicates the original wood siding. An original barn was torn down through necessity and replaced by the carriage house, constructed in a manner compatible with the main house. Restoration took place between 1984 and 1995 under the ownership of Thomas and Hope Lanahan, who placed it on the Greene County Historical Register.

Although the Decker family lived for many years in this house, the early occupancy is a bit uncertain. Three families, Sweeney, Waggoner, and Decker, were involved with ownership of the property during the years 1860 through 1872.

In 1860, four adjoining lots were sold by Israel Porter to John Sweeney of New York City. A court action was initiated against Sweeney, and the four lots were sold at public auction. Eunice Waggoner attended the December 23, 1872, auction held at the Wormer House located on Washington Street. As the highest bidder, she took immediate ownership of the four lots.

That same day, Eunice sold the two southernmost lots to Sephronia Decker, wife of Jacob Decker. Sephronia assumed one-half of the existing mortgage. Eunice kept ownership of the two northern lots until 1881. In 1884, the northern lots were purchased by Sephronia's son, Jacob H. Decker, Jr., bringing the four lots into single-family ownership once again.

The Decker family resided in this house just two blocks from the Hudson River for more than 80 years. Jacob Decker was a lifelong river boatman and pilot. Unlike his father, Jacob Jr. took a different career path; clerk and then buyer in a grocery, manager in a hardware store, bookkeeper and director of Athens National Bank.

After his parent's deaths, Jacob Jr. and other family members continued to live in the family homestead. Jacob died February 19, 1928, leaving no wife or children. He willed the five room, two-story frame residence, valued at $3,000, to his sister Mable Decker-Reynolds. Mable retained ownership until her death in 1958. Her executors put the homestead up for sale, ending the Decker heritage.

Northrup House

This Federal-style brick house built during 1803–1804 for Isaac Northrup, founder of the Village of Athens, is situated on a village lot only one block from the Hudson River. *The cornerstone on the northeast side of the house bears the date 1804, written in Dutch letters.*

The single-family residence contains eight rooms, with center hall and staircase. It has four original fireplaces, two upstairs and two down. A Franklin grate in the master bedroom bears the date 1877. In the cellar there is space for servant quarters, and this may be where Mr. Northrup quartered his slave.

Looking across the river from Hudson, where he had settled in 1787, Northrup was attracted by the advantages of the open land along the water. In 1800, at a cost of $3,000, Northrup purchased 200 acres of farmland from John M. Van Loon, the grandson of the early settler Jan Van Loon.

Intending to establish a large "city" on his new purchase, he had a survey and map drawn up by John D. Spoor in 1801. Northrup, his wife, Cynthia Morton, and their children moved into this house probably shortly after its completion in 1804. Soon, others of superior class were attracted to Northrup's "city."

The entrepreneur also took his civic duties seriously. When the Village of Athens was incorporated in 1805, Northrup served as its first president (mayor), and served again in 1810. During 1814 he was one of the trustees of Joint School District 13 (Catskill with Saugerties), and that same year he was appointed as the first justice of the peace of the Town of Catskill. When the Town of Athens was incorporated in 1815, he served as the first supervisor.

Sometime between the death of Cynthia in 1812 and 1820, Northrup left Greene County. Since that time there have been several different owners of this house, including J. P. and Frieda Mac Braswell. The Mac Braswells are credited with restoring this house during the 1940s. Restoration included refurbishment of all the windows, and replacement of all the floors in oak and mahogany using pegged construction. Unfortunately, the "widow's walk" that must have allowed a grand view down the river was removed in 1943.

Walter and Ilse Fox were the owners when an illustration of this house was drawn by Joel Naprstek. The illustration was used to represent the "Widow Douglas house" in June Edward's 1981 adaptation of *Tom Sawyer* by Mark Twain.

The house is also included on the New York State and National Register of Historic Places as one site within the "Village of Athens Multiple Resource Area," as well as in the "Athens Lower Village Historic District," where Northrup's basic "city" design is still retained in the streets and alleyways south of Market Street.

Morton/Reinsdorf House

Built circa 1860 using the Second Empire style, this house was first occupied by William H. Morton (1805–1888) and family. William married Maria Wait (1808–1892), a native of Massachusetts, and they had thirteen children. Their growing family, which included six by 1850, and William's success in the shipbuilding business most likely led them to their new home.

William's parents emigrated from Nantucket to Hudson, where William was born. The following year they moved to Athens, where William prospered as a businessman. William served as a land agent for his uncle Isaac Northrup, who is considered the founder of the Village of Athens.

In 1828, at age 23, William began his life's career as a successful businessman in the shipbuilding trade. Four years later, along with two other investors, he purchased property on the Athens riverfront, which included an active four-year-old dry dock and marine railway. During the next few years there were a number of changes in ownership and partners. By 1854 things stabilized, with William as one of the two principal owners. The firm of Morton & Edmonds prospered, and in 1872 was sold to Mathias Van Loon and Peter Magee.

On April 25, 1877, the New York–Catskill–Athens Steamboat Company Limited was organized by William and four other men. The company ran a number of boats, including the *City of Catskill*, which was launched May 29, 1880, and was recorded as one of the biggest and finest boats built on the upper Hudson.

During the Civil War, William served as postmaster at Athens. He also served twice as Athens Village clerk, and in 1846 served as town supervisor. His service to the community gained him the distinction of having the William H. Morton Steamer Company, a fire company in Athens, named after him. William and wife Maria were laid to rest in Athens Rural Cemetery, fittingly so, since during his lifetime the cemetery received much of its neatness and beauty from his care and skill.

As William was a prominent figure, it seems plausible that his important relative, Levi P. Morton, visited him in this house. Levi was a member of the U.S. House of Representatives (1879–1881), vice president of the United States (1889–1893), and the 31st governor of New York State (1895–96).

Ownership of the house passed from William and Maria to their son-in-law, Henry Van Loan. It remained in the hands of Morton descendants until 1961, when it was purchased by Walter and Lucille Reinsdorf. Beginning in 1969, restoration of the house by the Reinsdorf family was ongoing for a number of years.

DIMMICK HOUSE

This workingman's or artisan's house, circa 1810, is a good example of the type of vernacular, timber-framed Federal architecture that would have been popular in Athens, but is one of the few that remains largely intact today. The small portico with Doric columns that was added to this simple story-and-a-half house reflects the popularity of the Greek Revival style in Athens in the period between 1830 and 1845.

The structure started out as a center hall with a room on either side. The original beehive oven with cooking hearth remains, but was "Rumfordised"—made shallower and more efficient—sometime in the early 1800s. There are a total of five fireplaces in the house. A shed was added to the rear of the house soon after building, creating a saltbox configuration.

In the early to mid-1900s—perhaps even as early as the late 1800s—a fish market operated out of the lower back of the house, with an entrance on Warren Street. The basement entrance seems to have been added for this purpose. At some point the entire original first floor was restructured as an open room with horizontal wide-board wainscoting. This was how it was used when it was occupied by the Zion Evangelical Lutheran Church as a parish house in the mid-1960s. However, the floor plan has now reverted to the center hall layout.

In 1989 this property was purchased by Randall Evans and Carrie Feder of the Athens Architectural Workshop, building restorers and preservationists.

GABRIELE/MAHER HOUSE

Originally constructed in the late 1700s, the north wing was added in 1840 for use as a store, and in 1870 the south wing was added to the rear living area. In 1986 the entire brick surface was restored.

The earliest owner was Sylvester Nichols, who made large purchases of real estate in Athens for later resale. Subsequent owners maintained a general store in the upper village building, supplying the needs not only of the residents but also of the ship hands whose boats plied the Hudson River. In addition to food items, the store carried coal and livestock feed.

From 1926 until 1960, Rosario and Teresina Gabriele continued to operate the store. In 1973 the property passed to their son and his wife, Frank M. and Catherine Gabriele, and then in 1986 to Kathleen Gabriele Maher and her husband, William J. Maher. The bakery "Cakes by Kay" formerly occupied the first floor under the second-story porch.

A "Dinner Party" at the Cairo Fair, August 27, 1890.

TOWN OF CAIRO

The Town of Canton was established in 1803 from lands formerly held by Catskill, Coxsackie and Freehold (now Durham). In 1808 the name of this new town was changed to Cairo. The name change was made at the urging of Ashbel Stanley, a prominent local citizen who hailed from Cairo, Egypt. The pronunciation shifted to "KAY-ro" as the usage was anglicized. The Village of Cairo is the only incorporated area within the town. Other, more densely populated areas include Round Top and Purling.

The town is composed of several high rocky ridges that meet the foothills of the Catskill Mountains on its western border. As early as 1678, Sylvester Salisbury and Marte Geritse Van Bergen purchased land from the Indians. They were granted a patent by the royal governor two years later. The earliest area of settlement appears to have been in what is now Round Top, with the first log house there belonging to the ill-fated Strope family, who were massacred by the Indians.

Following several land grants and patents, the population of the area grew steadily. Settlers in surrounding areas, as well as others from Connecticut and Long Island, were drawn here by the great expanse of hemlock forests. Tanneries and sawmills were established, and those forests began disappearing from the ridges as the industry harvested the tree bark for use in the tanning process, the logs being used for lumber. General farming was also important, and many farmers used the excess wood in the area to manufacture shingles. As early as 1819, the Greene County Agricultural Society established a county fair where homegrown produce and baked goods were judged in addition to livestock. The most popular form of entertainment at the fair was horse racing.

By 1810, the town's population had boomed to more than 2,000. Schools and churches soon followed, after an initial period of holding meetings in private homes. A local post office was established quite early in the 19th century, as well.

Cairo's central location within Greene County—as well as easy land availability—saw the creation of the County Poor House within the township, in 1825. A bell foundry, a clock factory, and a nail factory provided employment. The hotel and boardinghouse industries have also been important to the town's prosperity.

The town retains much of its natural beauty today, its local roads offering views of beautiful cloves and overlooking magnificent vistas as they wind through the town's hamlets: Acra, Gayhead, Purling, Round Top, and South Cairo.

WINTER CLOVE INN

Snuggled at the base of North Mountain in the Catskill Mountains, the inn is surrounded by hundreds of acres of undeveloped land. The proprietors own more than 300 acres, and are in close proximity to the thousands of acres located within the Catskill Park and Forest Preserve. Originally a single-family residence, Winter Clove Guest House, as it was originally called, has been transformed into a modern inn with 49 guest rooms.

The name "Winter Clove" seems to have first appeared on a map of the Catskill Mountain area when surveyors configured survey lines through the clove, plotting out allotments for Revolutionary War veterans. During those early years, Elihu Slater, a pioneer from Connecticut, owned property in the area that he cleared for farming and built a log cabin. Elihu married a local Round Top girl named Sarah Beach, and, in 1838 or so, constructed a small saltbox-style house to accommodate their large family.

During 1850 Elihu and Sarah died seven days apart, and their sons succeeded Elihu in running the family farm. The oldest son, Hugh, had left the family farm at age 21 to live in East Jewett. There, he and his wife, Sally Woodworth, raised their family on their own farm. In 1862, their daughter, Mary E. Slater, married Henry Barber Whitcomb, also of Jewett; the young couple moved to her grandfather Elihu's property in Cairo, where they lived out the remainder of their lives.

It is unclear whether Elihu and his family took boarders into their farmhouse, but by 1863, under the proprietorship of H. B. Whitcomb, the farmhouse, by then known as Winter Clove House, was accommodating several guests. A photo, circa 1863, of the two-story saltbox pictures several guests on the lawn in front of a large porch with Victorian trim.

H. B. Whitcomb was an industrious man: in addition to running the hotel and possibly managing the family farm, he operated a saw mill and was involved in the tanning industry. By 1882 H.B. had completed a new addition on the original house to accommodate an increasing number of guests. Circa 1884 Winter Clove had the capacity to accommodate 60 guests. Whitcomb again enlarged the house during the 1890s, adding more guest rooms and installing its first indoor plumbing fixtures. Interestingly, the fixtures came from the 1893 Columbian Exposition in Chicago.

According to his descendants, at one time Henry owned the entire mountainside, obtained through his purchase of parcels allotted to the veterans, who had no interest in keeping them.

During the early 1900s H.B. sold off hundreds of acres to the State of New York; those became part of the newly created Catskill Park and Forest Preserve.

Mary Salter Whitcomb died in 1911, followed by H.B. in 1917. Two days before his death, H.B. wrote out his will—on Winter Clove House stationery. After the payment of debts, his property was equally divided among his four children. In the accounting of his property, his executors valued Winter Clove House and eight surrounding acres at $20,000. Approximately 700 acres of his mountain land in the town of Cairo were worth an estimated $5,000. Following his death, his children Edward Burdette Whitcomb and Lillie Plank took over the management of Winter Clove House.

The 20th century brought modernization to the inn and further changes in family ownership. Though the front porch was changed many times over the years, E. Burnett and Lillie were responsible for extending it across the front of the large mansard-roofed southern addition, and adding the additional arches to match the five that had ornamented the original saltbox portico. Circa 1920 the Whitcomb family built an outdoor swimming pool—believed to be the first in Greene County—in front of Winter Clove House. During the second half of the 20th century the Whitcomb family started adding private baths to the guest rooms. The north wing was altered to enclose an indoor pool, central heating was added, and the inn remained open year-round.

The modernizations at Winter Clove House led to the decision in 1980 to change the name to Winter Clove Inn. Although it has been reported that the original saltbox structure was torn down, no part of Winter Clove has ever been removed. Although it cannot be recognized as such, the original saltbox is indeed still there, located in today's lobby area.

Winter Clove Inn, circa 1912.

CAIRO

CASE STORE AND RESIDENCE

This Victorian-style residence and storefront sits on a small village lot that was once part of the Daniel Sayre farm situated along the Shinglekill Creek. The current building was constructed during the early 1890s, but there has been a store and dwelling at this location since at least 1867. The massive support beams under this building span the older foundation and extend out over a crawl space. The original retail area in the building, with its thirteen-foot ceiling, is now a large, attractive banquet hall that is rented for various social functions. The owners have their residence on the upper floor.

The designer was Henry S. Moul from Hudson, New York. In his portfolio Moul titles this structure as "Store and Residence, John Case, Cairo, NY." Mr. Moul is better remembered for the many large homes he designed in Hudson, as well as the design of the Columbia County Courthouse. This building appears to be one of only a few he designed in Greene County.

When John and Mary Case purchased the premises in 1890, they apparently had plans to tear down an existing building and rebuild, because the soda fountain, fixtures, and all the lamps in the store building had been kept by the previous owner. The current building was completed in 1894, substantiated by the date on the weathervane that was found in the basement and restored by John Gallagher. In 1895, Mrs. Case even spoke of their new store in her will.

Postcard view of the John Case Dry Goods store and residence, circa 1900.

John Case retained ownership of the property for 27 years; for part of that time he was the proprietor of John Case Dry Goods. Louis A. Miller purchased the premises in 1917 and, according to the 1920 U.S. census, he was living on Main Street and was an employer in the manufacture of souvenirs. Miller retained ownership until 1945, when he sold the building to Lester H. and Eva Story.

The Storys ran a dry goods and souvenir shop in the building. Lester had his carpentry shop in a building behind the store. They retained ownership until 1976, when they sold the premises to John A. and Claudette D. Schwerbel. Although the property was sold in 1991, Mr. Schwerbel continued to operate his auto-parts business in the storefront.

In 1999 the property was purchased by John M. Gallagher. Luckily, some of the original interior and exterior features had not been destroyed, but they were in need of attention. A leaky roof and burst pipes had taken their toll, and the storefront window had been covered with plywood following an auto accident in the early 1990s. Mr. Gallagher has been slowly restoring the building back to its original splendor. For his historic preservation of this building, Mr. Gallagher was honored in January 2007 by the Greene County Planning Board, who presented him with the Ellen Rettus Planning Achievement Award.

Calvary Episcopal Church

Calvary Episcopal Church is located on Jerome Avenue in the Village of Cairo. The Greek Revival wood-framed church, with its original white clapboards and square belfry, sits atop the hill where construction began in the early 19th century.

The process of its erection is summed up well by Robert Uzzilia, Cairo's town historian, when he describes it as "built by the gnarled hands of skilled craftsmen and trusty farmhands and graced by the irreplaceable touch of devoted church women." The pointed-arch stained-glass windows are complemented by the pointed-arch door that leads into the sanctuary with a vaulted ceiling. The pointed arch is again repeated by three arches that cover the entire front wall of the sanctuary. Access to an addition is through a door in the left arch. Encompassed in the central arch is the main altar.

The incorporation paper was signed on August 13, 1832, and witnessed September 5, 1832, establishing the fourth Episcopalian church in Greene County as a part of the New York City diocese. The money received toward the building fund amounted to $1,950, of which $500 came from New York City's Trinity Church. The consecration of Calvary Episcopal Church took place on August 4, 1833; the ceremonies were presided over by Bishop Onderdonk from New York City.

From 1835 to 1837 there were only eight communicants in the church, yet they were able to pay their first clergyman a salary of $125 yearly, and by 1840 the congregation was able to purchase a bell costing $153. Music must have been essential to these first communicants, because during their first year of incorporation a committee was formed to purchase an organ. That organ, now gone, remained in the church for many years, even after a new pipe organ was donated in March 1894.

The growing congregation, 58 by 1883, needed additional seating, thus several pews were added in 1876. The rental fees from the slips must have helped cover the $800 cost of church improvements during the early 1880s, including the cost to install the new stained-glass windows that were a gift from communicants.

The early 20th century saw many changes. The original bell that had called the parishioners to worship was replaced in 1903, and in 1906 electricity was installed. During 1907 the interior of the church was remodeled, including the removal of the galleries, the rebuilding of the chancel, and construction of a new pulpit. In 1928 the pipe organ was enlarged, and more interior redecorating took place. The chancel was again rebuilt, possibly due to the expansion project, and the old altar was placed in the rear to serve as a children's altar.

In later years the choir stall was moved from the front to the rear, and the children's altar moved to the front. After the pipe organ ceased to accompany the choir and the communicants in song, many of the pipes were removed from the right arch. Some of the pipes remain in storage in their original condition, while others serve a decorative function: painted gold and mounted in the rear over the church entrance.

Greene County Poorhouse/Almshouse/Home
The Greene County Office Building

This brick building was the third poorhouse to be administered by Greene County. The property along the Shinglekill was purchased in 1941 from Joseph and Lydia Carman. For a purchase price of $5,900 the county took ownership of approximately 130 acres of land that had been a portion of the former Carbine Farm. Included in the sale was the privilege of passing horses and cattle over land owned by Amos Cornwall. In later years the county purchased additional property, increasing the size of the farm property surrounding the Poorhouse to approximately 200 acres.

A wooden structure on the farm had earlier served as the county poorhouse—until a committee of the Board of Supervisors condemned it as unfit in late 1882. Over the next few months controversy over the building's fate arose, but the final resolution was to construct a new building, the cost not to exceed $15,000. Work began on August 1, 1883, by the construction firm Mull and Fromer, from a design by John B. Halcott.

The completed building has two-foot-thick masonry walls, an eight-foot-high basement under the entire building, and a stone foundation three feet thick at the base. The center pavilion, topped by a bell tower, measures 56 feet deep by 40 feet and the mansard roof allows for a third story.

When in use as the county poorhouse, the bottom two floors of the center pavilion were mostly occupied by the superintendent and his family. Staircases for their use connected with all the floors. In this section there was a general office, doctor's office, reception room, dining room, kitchen, three bedrooms, a large clothes press, and pantries. It appears that the third story was only used for storage.

Extending from each side of the pavilion are two brick wings measuring 42 feet by 50 feet. The interior corridors that stretch across the entire building are seven feet wide; platform staircases five feet wide lead to the second floor. When first built, the two wings accommodated approximately 90 residents, one for men and the other for women. Each wing had its own dining room, sitting room, bath, and washroom. On the second floor each wing contained large dormitories, some small rooms, a washroom, and an infirmary.

The interior woodwork was painted in colors but the main entrance and hall were faux-grained. This was a common practice in the 19th century, applying a superficial layer of wood-colored paint on soft, inexpensive woods or nonwood surfaces, to imitate expensive hardwoods. After the base coat was dry, the "graining" was achieved by brushing on a thin layer of darker brown color, then using a comblike tool to mimic the look of wood grain—including knotholes. Transoms still remain over the doorways today; they helped the air circulate.

The kitchen for the residents was located in the rear of the building, between the men's and women's dining rooms. Stairs went from the kitchen to a bakery in the basement. The basement also contained a laundry, two bathrooms, cisterns, the heating system, and compartments for storage and fuel. In fact, the only thing found lacking was adequate quarters for the sick and insane!

In May 1936 the old wooden structure, which had stood about 60 feet to the rear, still housing some of the residents, was torn down and the present two-story brick annex was constructed, including a connecting corridor to the main building. Assembly of the annex, measuring 45 feet by 91 feet with a full basement, was completed in early 1937. The construction work was performed under the New York Works Progress Administration at an approximate cost of $58,446, which included a $21,000 federal grant. It incorporated a new kitchen with modern equipment, dining rooms for both sexes, up-to-date bathrooms, showers, and sleeping quarters. There also were infirmary wards for both men and women,

attended by a staff nurse. A new coal boiler to heat the entire structure replaced the two old systems.

In June 1937 the Board of Supervisors allocated an additional $15,000 to make alterations to the main building, to bring it into compliance with requirements of the New York State Department of Social Welfare. The residents' area was thoroughly renovated. New steel stairways were erected, old partitions were demolished and new ones constructed. The two rooms formerly used as dining rooms became day rooms for the residents.

In 1939 the De Masi Sand Blasting Company of Schenectady, New York, was awarded a $3,650 contract to burn the paint off the brickwork and stone of the main building. When the brick on the main building was first painted is unknown, but postcard photos circa 1910 depict an attractive multicolored structure.

A resolution was passed by the Greene County Board of Supervisors to close the county poorhouse, by then known as the County Home, on June 1, 1962, or as soon as accommodations could be found for the remaining residents. They agreed that any personal property remaining at the home should be sold to the highest bidder. In the fall of that year, following a fire at the local school, several rooms and the kitchen facilities were leased to the Cairo Central School District No. 1 as temporary accommodations. Soon thereafter it was decided that the building should be used to house county offices.

ROUND TOP CEMETERY

Round Top Cemetery is located on South Road in the town of Cairo, situated in the foothills of the Catskill Mountains near some of the area's many resorts. It is partially surrounded by wooded areas and has many massive evergreen trees interspersed with the gravestones, which impart the feel of an earlier time. According to oral legend, this historic burial ground dates back to 1767, when Native Americans were first buried here.

During the late 18th and early 19th centuries, some early European settlers in the Round Top area were also interred here. Although not legally incorporated until April 23, 1909, it has been an active cemetery since those early times and today still remains a well-cared-for community cemetery.

The earliest burials in the cemetery for which the gravestones are still legible include James Cochran, who died July 10, 1797; Samuel Cochran, July 14, 1797, age 43; M. Vandervoort, December 23, 1798; and Howken Buckley, December 21, 1819, age 49.

The first church in the hamlet of Round Top was the Methodist Episcopal Church, established in 1838. It was situated close to the cemetery, and although it is not documented that the church sponsored the cemetery, some of the early church founders are buried here. Among others, they include Peter Fiero, who died in 1858, and his wife, Mercy Cochran, who followed him in 1871; Samuel Jones, who died in 1843, and his wife, Eve, who followed ten years later; Harvey Stoddard, who died in 1862, and his wife, Emily Hunt Stoddard, who died in 1886.

One of the earliest known settlers in Round Top was Elias Dutcher. The Revolutionary War veteran was born in Dutchess County, moved with his family to the Town of Cairo in 1790, and settled near Round Top. He and his wife, Elizabeth, are buried here together. They both died in 1887: Elizabeth passed in January, and Elias followed in December.

With more than six hundred graves, it is impossible to list everyone. It seems sufficient to say that they range from the common man to men of importance. But there is one who became a legend and whose story must be told; Frederick Schermerhorn, who is buried here with his wife, Sarah Van Hoesen.

In 1780 an Indian massacre took place in Round Top at the farmhouse of Johannes Strope. Frederick Schermerhorn, then a boy of 17, was visiting to help with the shepherding when the raid occurred. The Indians slaughtered the elder Stropes and captured young Frederick, who was taken to Fort Niagara and forced to enlist with the British army. Released after four years, he returned to Round Top. It is said that he intrigued his grandchildren with tales of the attack.

Schermerhorn's grave is marked by a plain uncut slab without an inscription, but a later tribute was erected by his descendants. It reads:

> FREDERICK
> SCHERMERHORN
> 1763–1847
> WHEN A BOY OF 17 WAS CAP-
> TURED BY INDIANS 40 RODS
> FROM THIS HIS LAST RESTING
> PLACE, TAKEN TO CANADA,
> SOLD TO THE BRITISH, FORCED
> IN ARMY, AND HELD CAPTIVE
> 4 YEARS.
> Peace to his ashes, erected by grand and
> great grand children.

View looking north, Main Street by the corner of William Street, circa 1900.

TOWN OF CATSKILL

The origin of Catskill began essentially in the spring of 1649 when land just west of the present village, at the intersection of the Kaaterskill and the Catskill Creek, was purchased from the Mohican Indians by Brant Arent Van Slichtenhorst, with others, as agents for the Patroon of Rensselaerswyck. The Mohicans received as payment a coat of beaver, a knife, and 17½ ells of duffels (duffel was a type of European cloth and an ell was a unit of measure equaling three quarters of a yard).

In 1684 Gysbert Cornelise uyt den Bogaert purchased a parcel from a band of Esopus Indians. The parcel extended north from the mouth of Catskill Creek to a small creek opposite Vastricks (Rogers) Island, then inland to a mill at the end of what is now Suburban Way, and then down the Catskill Creek to the point of beginning. From these auspicious beginnings grew the largest town in the County of Greene.

The first town meeting, held on April 8, 1789, laid a political foundation. The male citizens in attendance elected five assessors, two collectors, three constables, a commissioner of highways, two overseers of the poor, and four fence viewers and pound masters. Such data provide insight into the important aspects of living in the late 18th century—as the 24 taverns, 4 churches, 15 schools, and 8 attorneys extant in 1805 paint the picture of life in the early 19th.

The Act of March 24, 1772, erected the "Great Imboght District," larger than the present Town of Catskill, which was established by the act of March 7, 1788. The Village of Catskill was incorporated in 1806 at the mouth of the Catskill Creek in the Eckerson's Valley Swamp, near the Dutch-named Hop-O-Nose Indian Village. Catskill Landing was a safe and convenient harbor for sailing vessels at the dawn of the steamboat era. A drawbridge over the Catskill Creek, opened to great jubilation and ceremony in 1802, eased both land and water travel for the geographically-divided area. Stagecoaches left on Tuesdays and Fridays for Albany; mail was sent by water twice a week. From this bustling river town evolved the present-day Greene County seat of government.

During much of the 19th century, Catskill enjoyed world renown as the gateway to the beautiful Catskill Mountains. Passengers would debark from Hudson River steamers and board stages that took them up twisting and precarious mountain roads to the Catskill Mountain House. In the 1870s, however, local narrow-gauge railroads made the ride faster—and much more convenient! Boarding a Catskill Mountain Railway train after leaving a steamer at Catskill Point, passengers were whisked westward and came to the end of the line at the base of the Catskills' eastern escarpment. There they would transfer to a separate, steam-powered Otis Elevating Railway, which would take them straight up the side of the escarpment, either to the Catskill Mountain House or to the other luxurious resorts that had sprung up at the top of North and South Mountains. Once there, these vacationers hiked the paths where Thomas Cole, Asher Durand, and other famous Hudson River painters had earlier trod, and were awed by the vast valley views and unparalleled brilliance of the sunsets.

Catskill includes Leeds, Jefferson Heights, Kiskatom, Palenville, and Smith's Landing (formerly Cementon). Leeds, renamed from the earlier Madison in honor of Richard Hartwick, who hailed from Leeds, England, opened its post office in 1827, and prides itself on its ancient stone bridge, built between 1760 and 1792, and still functioning! Jefferson Heights, previously known as Jefferson Flats and originally referred to as "the Flats," was a sandy plain considered by the arriving Dutch to be of little value. The Imboght, which boasts no area center, was settled by commissioners of the Dutch and Portuguese before 1732.

Widespread flatlands and indefinite geographical limits describe Kiskatom as "the Place of the Hickory Nuts." This former Indian village was purchased by William Beckman in 1708. Beckman's 1718–1720 patent was confirmed and enlarged to 2,000 acres, joining the Catskill patent. Palenville, "the Village of Falling Waters," is the namesake of Jonathon Palen, owner of a large tanning business at or near the entrance of Kaaterskill Clove. Cauterskill should be noted, since like Kiskatom, it predates the Revolution and in 1690 was a collection of scattered houses. Branches of Catskill's Old King's Road transverse Cauterskill, Palenville, and Kiskatom.

At the southeast corner of Catskill lies the area known as Smith's Landing, purchased by Connecticut Yankees in 1779. Earlier in the 1600s this area had been the scene of a major battle between families of the Iroquois and the Algonquin nations, struggling for supremacy. Fishing, ice harvesting, and bluestone quarrying gave sustenance to the hundreds of immigrants who settled in this area from Ireland, Germany, Poland, Italy, Yugoslavia, and Russia. The limestone in the area led to the development of a thriving cement industry. It is most likely that Charles Cowles, the superintendent of Catskill Cement, was the person responsible for changing the post office name from Smith's Landing to Cementon in the early 1900s. In 1993, residents had the name changed back to Smith's Landing in honor of Rufus Smith, who arrived in the area in 1813 and developed it commercially.

Greene County Courthouse

One of the most impressive buildings in all of Greene County is the classical Ohio sandstone courthouse. Judge Emory Chase, a justice of the New York State Court of Appeals, was instrumental in the building of this magnificent structure. At ten in the morning on August 3, 1908, Judson A. Betts, then Greene County's treasurer, offered "for sale at public auction to the highest bidder" bonds to finance the new courthouse. According to the bond flyer, there were "One Hundred Coupon Bonds of the denomination of One Thousand Dollars each, with interest at four per cent, payable semi-annually . . . on February 1st and August 1st." Ten bonds were payable each year, from 1911 through 1920. The sale apparently went well, for the cornerstone for the much-anticipated building was laid on November 12, 1908.

Designed by William A. Beardsley of Poughkeepsie and constructed by Keeler and Company, the large building is topped with an ornamental balustrade. A frieze decorates the front gable. Four Ionic columns support the pediment, supplied by A. P. Lombard Company. The bas-relief on the pediment symbolizes the advancement of civilization under law. The Greeks are presented on the right, the Romans on the left, with the two striving toward the highest standard of civilization, represented by the solitary central figure: Justice.

As the center of county government from 1910 until the new Greene County Office Building was constructed at the start of the 21st century, the courthouse has served as the county's repository for deeds, mortgages, and other property records, as well as surrogate, criminal, civil, and family court records. As the automobile gained in popularity, the county clerk's office in the courthouse soon became home to a DMV office as well. Despite the need for such unplanned adaptations, most of the building's original interior, including its floor plan, courtrooms, and furniture remains basically unchanged, as does the wainscoting and trim that run throughout the building. The courthouse celebrated its Diamond Jubilee in 1985.

Formal ceremonies take place on the top platform of the long flight of stone stairs that lead up to the front entrance. Memorial Day parades end with speeches and music here. Luminaries such as Governor Nelson A. Rockefeller and Senator Robert Kennedy have addressed crowds of well-wishers from these heights.

Related outbuildings and properties include what was once the sheriff's residence (now offices), the county jail, and a garage.

By 2009 plans to rejuvenate the century-old courthouse were under way. All furnishings and materials were moved to the vacant St. Patrick's School on Woodland Avenue, which the county had rented, and heavy construction began in earnest.

Left: Notice of bond sale for the courthouse, which went on sale at a public auction on August 3, 1908.

Below: Assembly on courthouse steps with speaker Teddy Roosevelt at center, during his 1912 Bull Moose campaign.

CATWALK

This Hudson River estate, built circa 1866, sits atop a high cliff in the Town of Catskill, with sweeping views of both the Hudson River and the Hudson Valley, on approximately 60 acres of wooded land that slopes down to the west bank of the river. The original section of the house was built by, or for, landscape artist Charles Herbert Moore.

Moore was born and raised in New York City, where in 1858 he exhibited his extremely detailed paintings at the National Academy. He was a friend of Thomas Cole, Jr., and a regular guest of the Cole family in the 1850s and early 1860s, perhaps renting an existing structure either on the Cole property or on this acreage. Moore married Mary Jane Tomlinson on July 19, 1865. The following June it was she who, for $5,000, purchased 23 acres of land up the hill just north of the Cole estate. According to the biographer Frank Jewett Mather, Moore designed the "Lodge," a charming board-and-batten raftered cottage. The one-and-a-half-story home, built of fieldstone and wood with a gambrel roof, survives today as the southern section of the current house.

In 1871, Charles accepted a teaching position as watercolor instructor at the Lawrence Scientific School of Harvard University. Their Catskill home was sold to Benjamin Howland, a woolen manufacturer and partner in the Steam Woolen Company of Catskill. Tragically, on April 28, 1882, at the young age of fifty, Benjamin was struck by a plank at the Robert Fuller mill and died from his injuries. Benjamin's wealth was inherited by Louise and his five remaining children: Agnes, Clarence, Edith, Blanche, and Slocum.

Clarence, a prominent attorney in both Catskill and New York City, was their only child to marry; he and his family occupied a house close by. After Louise's death on September 9, 1900, the four unmarried children constructed a large addition, seemingly using their inheritance money. The *Catskill Examiner* newspaper reported that during November 1900 two wagonloads of odd-shaped stones were hauled to Catskill from various locations in the Catskill Mountains for use in the new Howland dwelling.

A stone-and-shingle addition with caretakers quarters and a studio with large windows to provide north light was constructed. Edith was a sculptress who had displayed her art in Paris during 1895; it can therefore be assumed the studio was for her use. In 1920 she shipped her household goods, personal effects, and studio property from France to New York.

The deaths of her siblings left Edith as the sole heir by 1943. When Edith died six years later, at the age of 86, her probated estate included the stone-and-frame dwelling, barn, stone shed, pump house, wood house, tool house, and boathouse situated on 35 acres of land.

With the death of Edith, the contents of "Hilltop" passed to the family of her late brother Clarence. In 1954, after 83 years of Howland family ownership, the property was sold by Clarence's son, William Slocum Howland; William's sister, Louise Howland Beddow Whelan; and their mother. The purchaser was Miss Katherine M. Finan of New Jersey, who, less than three years later, deeded the property to John J. Casazza.

Mr. Casazza was a prominent businessman in Albany, New York, and spent a great sum of money upgrading this house, including turning the living room into a bar. He and his wife, an actress featured in White Rain Shampoo commercials, lived here and owned the property until 1968, when it was purchased by Frederick L. Zimmerman and his wife, Grace.

In 1983 Eric N. Lasry, an investment banker, and his wife, Margaret, of New York City purchased the house and property, naming it Hudson Heights. At that time the 9,000-square-foot house contained seven bedrooms, six and a half baths, and ten fireplaces, plus guest and staff accommodations. The following year an extensive restoration began, which included replacement of the faulty wiring that almost killed Lasry's young son, Gabriel. The decoration of the house was influenced by Mr. Lasry's birthplace, Casablanca, Morocco. His library, called the Moorish room, was in the old section built by Moore.

In 2001 it was sold to the current owners, who own and administer the Palmer Foundation. The Palmers changed the name of this handsome eclectic Hudson River villa estate to Catwalk, a name derived from a ramp that spanned from the roof of the house to the top floor of the old water tower. Visiting artists still use the water tower with its panoramic views to create their works of art—views that feature the Rip Van Winkle Bridge, the castle-like Olana and the dramatic flow of the tidal Hudson River.

Inset: Charles Herbert Moore.
Above: View of eastern façade.

CATSKILL

The Chase/Lane/Shanks House

In July 1997 Richard and Sherry Shanks, having returned to Richard's hometown following his army career, purchased this elaborate high-style Victorian house. They immediately began restoration projects that have continued. Porch and balcony railings were discovered in a large outbuilding. The balustrades of the huge, wide wraparound Victorian verandah, as well as an ornate second-floor balcony, were restored. They scraped the earlier, 20th-century white paint down to the raw wood, replacing it with bright trim that enhanced the varied and more muted background tones of the original Victorian palette.

Patricia Lane, from whom the Shanks purchased the property, did extensive research on its history and ornate architecture during her 14-year residency. She stated, "I feel [the house] should be remembered as a tribute to the man who had it built. Judge Emory A. Chase was a well-known person who was loved and respected not only by those in this community, but also by the governor, the judges, and the attorneys with whom he worked. So much so that a memorial law library located in the Greene County Courthouse was named after him." In 1896, Chase was elected a justice of the Supreme Court of the State of New York, assigned by the governor to the Third Judicial District Appellate Branch in 1900. In 1905 he was designated an associate judge of the Court of Appeals, for which he was elected to a full term in 1920.

Next-door neighbor Charles Van Loan built the three-story edifice in about 1887, providing Judge Chase with his elegant residence for 34 years. The expansive verandah, the double-beveled glass entry doors, the second-floor bays, the attractive balustrade on the second floor balcony, and the large existing stepping-stone reflect small town Victorian life in the Gilded Age.

When the house was first constructed, an Italianate tower, dismantled in the 1900s, reached for the sky from the middle of the third floor. Between 1895 and 1903, a large two-floor outbuilding was erected, bay windows were added to the first-floor living room and second-floor bedroom. The dining room and front porch were extended out to the side. In 1912 a corner window was built into the master bedroom, and a widow's watch, removed by 1955, was constructed.

Entry is through two sets of double wood doors. The first set folds into the walls during summer; opened, they keep out frost during winter. Patricia Lane had carefully stripped them of paint, restoring them back to their original chestnut. Similarly, the newel post and dowels from the first to the second floor were returned to their original beauty. Four sets of working pocket doors in graceful arches greet visitors, as do four gas-fired fireplaces with tile faces and floors. Six fireplaces in all helped warm this 5,800-square-foot residence.

The Judge's 100 cubic feet of natural wood built-in bookcases with double drawers and glass doors still anchor the west wall of the library. The design on the living room fireplace mantel matches that on the ceiling. Delicately carved wreaths on the formal room ceilings surround gas/electric chandeliers of clear glass.

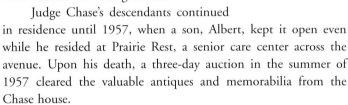

To ensure brightness when electricity failed—as it often did then, and even now—gas connections topped each electric globe.

A speaker tube from the kitchen to the third floor, where maids were housed, recalls the days of servants—as does the call-bell site in the dining room. The second-floor marble bath and the marble sinks in the bedrooms, among many other Victorian features, contribute to the total grandeur.

Judge Chase's descendants continued in residence until 1957, when a son, Albert, kept it open even while he resided at Prairie Rest, a senior care center across the avenue. Upon his death, a three-day auction in the summer of 1957 cleared the valuable antiques and memorabilia from the Chase house.

The next owners were Arthur and Lola Conklin, local entrepreneurs, who enclosed and adjoined the summer kitchen with the original indoor kitchen. With their daughter and son-in-law, Mary and James Leonard, they lived there briefly, leaving the dwelling after a short time. As though grieving for days past, the house sat dark for nearly seven years. Finally, on November 3, 1965, the Conklins conveyed the property to a local dentist, Dr. Paul Englert, and his wife, Marcia Englert. Their eight children increased the youth population to 30 within five historic houses along the avenue in the Catskill East Side National Historic Register District!

On January 16, 1978, Dr. Roger Van Winkle and his wife, Patricia, of Bel Air, Maryland, purchased the house from the Englerts. Roger Van Winkle had recently been appointed president of the Columbia-Greene Community College. He and his family spent the five years of his tenure at this elegant residence. During those years many celebrities were hospitably entertained. After lecturing at the college on April 8, 1982, former president Gerald Ford was honored at a school banquet. Earlier, in October 1981, astronaut James Lowell had received acclaim at this Van Winkle home by a reception attended by more than 400 community residents.

Today, Ricky and Sherry Shanks, who graciously opened their beautiful home for the Greene County Historical Society's 2006 tour, consider their ongoing restoration "a work in progress," while visitors view it as a portrait of charm.

Inset: Justice Emory A. Chase, justice of the New York State Court of Appeals.

CATSKILL

THE ADMINISTRATIVE CENTER OF THE BANK OF GREENE COUNTY

When this application was received, the Greene County Historical Register Committee made an exception to its strict rule that buildings on the Register be constructed during or before the 1920s, because the architectural and historical significance of the Bank of Greene County building deserved landmark status.

In 1931 the Commercial Mutual and Cooperative Mutual Insurance companies built this conservative Art Deco–style building for their home office. As designed by E. P. Valkenberg of Middletown, New York, the structure features a two-storied entry with bronze doorway, an arched window, and straight stone pilasters. The cream, white, and bronze façade has a skyward, tower-like effect that makes the building gracefully proportioned, and seem taller than it actually is.

Thought to be not only the first conservative Art Deco–style building in New York state but also the only example of Art Deco on Main Street in Catskill, this masterpiece embodies the belief that in planning its "home" a local business can, at the same time, create a spectacular community asset.

Purchasing the building in 1998, the Bank of Greene County precisely restored the structure to its original condition under the careful direction of Kevin Berry Builders and Timothy Albright, interior designer. Entering the building through the classic bronze doors, visitors today find themselves surrounded by the two-story foyer that is finished with travertine marble flooring and wainscoting. Decorative beads of marble run up and over the arched ceiling. Two cut-glass hanging fixtures highlight the area.

Most of the original furniture is still in use today. The original basement-level director's room of paneled pine recalls colonial days as much today as it did in 1931.

Central staircase, with marble steps and brass rails.

ROWENA MEMORIAL SCHOOL

The Rowena Memorial School was constructed between 1899 and 1901 in Palenville as a gift from Lysander Walter Lawrence to the children of the community in memory of his wife, Rowena Eloise Banning Lawrence.

This memorial school was constructed of rusticated gray granite blocks quarried from the Empire Quarry in Catskill by Master Mason James Holdridge of Catskill.

The August 16, 1899, edition of the local newspaper, *The Palenville Zepher,* carried a full-page image of the building accompanying the letter that had been received by the publisher: "How fitting it is that a village nestled at the foot of the grand old mountains should have a school building able to speak so eloquently of the skill of man—a building perfect as a work of art when viewed from an aesthetic point, or the more practiced one, the consideration of the child's health."

The school served the hamlet's children until 1970 when the Catskill school district centralized and the building was closed. For a time it served as a public library and community center. In 1989 it was closed and suffered much vandalism and neglect. Fortunately, it was rescued and revived as the shop/studio and home of world-renowned jewelry designer Steven Kretchmer, and his wife, Alma. Sadly, Steven lost his life to a careless driver in the summer of 2006; Alma passed away the following year.

This architecturally impressive school had been created according to the designs of the architect John A. Davidson, of 828 Flatbush Avenue, Brooklyn. It is now on the National Register of Historic Places.

Clarke House or Cowles House

This elegant stately redbrick house located at 166 Bridge Street in the Village of Catskill would be a fine subject for a volume on architecture. Unparalleled structure and historical significance abound in the harmonious blend of two distinct architectural styles. The popular mid-19th-century Italianate with Tuscan sub-style, known popularly as "Hudson River Bracketed," blends harmoniously with the early-20th-century Colonial Revival style.

The Clarke House reflects the prominence of the different residents who lived there for nearly 140 years. In 1868 Noble P. Cowles, a leading Greene County merchant, purchased a large lot from Joshua and Mary Fiero, building the house within a year. Cowles was a displaced New Englander from Connecticut who settled first on the mountaintop. Following the Civil War, he moved to the valley, where he made a fortune exporting farm products to the city. Cowles lived in the house until 1903 when his daughter, Hattie C. Carter, gained title. Ten years later William Donahue, the prominent postmaster, purchased the house, but in 1922 he deeded it over to the young and popular doctor Dean W. Jennings —cofounder of the Catskill Memorial Hospital—and his wife, Margaret. Sadly, only three years later the doctor passed away at age 41, a victim of hemophilia. The young widow sold the property to the couple who provided the spice that radiates throughout the walls even today.

Champlain Clarke, known as Champ or Chum to his close friends, was the son of a Catskill pharmacist. At the point when he enters the tale of the house, he had been married for about ten years to Rachel Fiero Clarke, an heiress to a large part of the Standard Oil fortune. When he and Rachel moved to this house, their love story became legend during the four decades they dwelt in their beloved home. Five years after Chum's death in 1964, Rachel passed away as well, leaving the property and all its furnishings—linens, family papers, and other items reminiscent of their 54 years of marriage—to their chauffeur/gardener, Valorous Sickles of Athens.

Retaining the Clarkes' large Cadillac, he, in turn, sold the majority of the estate to Catskill merchants Elizabeth (Betty) and Eugene Goldecklag. In 1995, they deeded the property to David Herman, an educational test consultant; Philip Kesinger, a retired FBI agent; and Richard Philp, the retired editor in chief of *Dance Magazine*. They have done extensive and continuous restoration, research, and analysis on the Clarke house.

The Greene County Historical Register's files at the Vedder Research Library contain an eloquent commentary by Richard Philp on the property at 166 Bridge Street. Describing the Clarkes and their philanthropy designed to assist future generations, he states, "Although the Clarkes were childless, their generosity has affected generations of children with a $13 million scholarship endowment for college-bound students attending Catskill High School." Today's students continue to reap the benefits of their philanthropy through this Clarke Scholarship, which is given every year to several recipients for use throughout each individual's four years of college.

Oral and written histories differ concerning the architectural changes made to the house over the years, and it is very difficult to pinpoint the times at which they were made. However, it is probable that after Mrs. Clarke received her fortune she made the significant and high-styled changes apparent today. Traces of former porches, added and subtracted, are evident. The 12 major rooms each originally had a fireplace; 10 were removed. Three hallways, each atop the other, have seen modification to make life easier and more comfortable.

Renovations, both interior and exterior, suggest the work of an unknown master architect, but Mrs. Clarke's name appears to be indelibly stamped on the beautiful building. The projecting cornice "supported" by paired brackets; the low-pitched hipped roof covering four stories; medallions and dentils; the tall, framed, hooded windows with heavy architraves and the Romanesque arches—all of these are characteristics of the Italianate style, while the front-view square shape and symmetry identify the Tuscan sub-style. As with the interior of many Italianate homes, the Clarke house illustrates the early Georgian center hall tradition and suggests the Colonial Revival period. In addition, Mrs. Clarke's love of everything English is evident in the charming English-style gardens surrounding the home.

View of the front Italianate with Tuscan sub-style façade.

Hull/Gamble-Roby House

This elegant Greek Revival house is one of the oldest in the Village of Catskill. That information comes down to us courtesy of a letter from John Bagley, the well-known local attorney, who was involved with the owner's legal work for decades.

Lydia Cooke Hull was the first known resident of a smaller house than exists today. When her son, Dr. A. Cooke Hull, inherited the property, he enlarged the house. Dr. Hull was a prominent homeopathic physician from Brooklyn who used this house as his summer home. Born in Utica, he was educated at the College of Physicians and Surgeons in New York City. The *Catskill Daily Mail* reported in the 1970s that Dr. Hull, who died in 1868, had treated "several of the worst cases" of the third cholera epidemic in Catskill in 1854, and that his "treatment was uniformly followed by recovery."

Dr. Hull was instrumental in establishing—and was a trustee of—some of Brooklyn's premium institutions, including the Art Association, the Athenaeum, the Academy of Music, the Philharmonic Society, the Historical Society, and the Brooklyn Club, among others. Along with a traditional physician, he was chosen to head the board of the new mental hospital in Poughkeepsie. He died suddenly at his Catskill home on July 3, 1868, and is buried in the Thompson Street Cemetery. His obituary was printed in *The New York Times*.

The four statuesque Ionic columns of the house, and the beautiful carved moldings around the interior doorways, attest to the historical significance of Dr. Hull's heritage.

Schuneman House

The oldest section of this Federal-style colonial home is the south end, where the kitchen is housed. The first known occupant of the house was William Schuneman, who lived here in 1829, although oral history suggests that residents did live in the earlier part of the building in the 1700s.

It is rumored to be the oldest "house" in the village and, as stated above, most probably served as a home even back in the 1700s when it was built. An 1847 sketch of the house done by Thomas Cole, considered to be the founder of the Hudson River School of Art, is part of the Thomas Cole Collection at the Albany Institute of History and Art. The western façade of the house is often mistaken as the front entrance. While most residents and guests do enter there, the architectural front façade faces north, sited on the corner of William Street and Prospect Avenue.

During the 1840s and the 1890s major alterations were made: the four-room brick addition, which included a library and parlor, was attached—as well as a second floor. Some evidence suggests that, at one time, a large porch, later removed, surrounded two sides of the house. Further alterations were made in the 1910s. Ten-foot ceilings and nine fireplaces throughout give an air of warmth, spaciousness, and beauty.

The house has been a home to many residents. During the early 20th century the house was well-known as the Kortz residence. In the 1930s and '40s Frank Cooke, secretary of the Catskill Board of Education, purchased and transferred his name to the dwelling. In the 1960s the daughter of historic preservationist Barbara Newcombe Weber, now Stephanie Walsh, lived there. Her mother at that time was refurbishing today's Greek Temple–like registered Tree House across the avenue. Soon thereafter, Cindy and Jack Van Loan purchased the house and undertook an elegant renovation during the many years they lived there—they recently sold to dwell in more rural environs. Holiday time was of special neighborhood significance. Paying tribute to the heritage of the house, they lit a single candle in every window.

VAN LOAN/DALEY HOUSE

In the early 1980s the owner of this modest Victorian house, an insurance agent, welcomed two elderly clients who arrived looking for advice. Upon leaving for a minute to retrieve his upstairs office files, he returned to find his senior visitors dancing, singing, and waltzing away in his 40-foot twin living rooms. Somewhat embarrassed, the guests explained that when they were teenagers, they had taken dancing lessons in that very same space: the daughter-in-law of the builder had given etiquette and dancing lessons there.

Built in 1879 by Charles Van Loan, Sr., this Victorian home has maintained most of its architectural integrity, including the Victorian front porch, the bay windows, the third-floor balcony with balustrade, the roof dormers, and the heavy decorative "gingerbread" in the north and south roof peaks. The exterior original wood clapboards cover double-thick brick inner walls.

In fact, Mr. Van Loan built many of the Victorian-era homes on Prospect Avenue. He constructed this particular house, less auspicious than its next-door neighbors, to live in himself. He also erected a large two-story barnlike out-structure (torn down in the 1980s) for storage of his building materials. They were brought in by horse and carriage through a still-existing back alley.

The house is entered through double doors leading to a long hall running the length of the residence. Wide Victorian arched doorways on either side of the front hall welcome guests to the double living room on the south and the parlor on the north. Six mantels, some marble, from the original seven fireplaces adorn six of the ten rooms, as does one of the builder's large handcrafted glassed-in cabinets. Carved medallions center the ten-foot ceilings of the first-floor formal rooms. Some original wide board floors remain. Two long Chinese pruned silks reflect the history of the builder's second daughter-in-law, whose first husband was an ambassador to Guatemala. There, the wife of the Chinese ambassador presented her with these two beautifully embroidered silks, which she gave to the next owners as a housewarming gift.

The five second-floor bedrooms have glass transoms over each doorway, suggesting that at one time, the Van Loans had paying guests, although no concrete evidence supports this theory.

Two generations of the Van Loan family dwelt in the house until 1957, when Frank Daley and his wife, Natalie, purchased the home from Louise Van Loan, the widow of Charles Van Loan, Jr., a well-known banker. Shortly thereafter other Victorian houses in the area were turned over to young couples and by 1960, forty-two children in one and a half blocks brought the Victorian houses of Catskill's east side National Historic District alive with activity. Frank, the insurance agent, and high school teacher Natalie still own this house where they raised their six children—a college administrator, two doctors, a teacher, and two nurses.

ELIZABETH HOUSE

This handsome brick and stone house is sited on the Catskill Creek with a picturesque view of the water and the old Leeds Bridge. Nearby cottages, once used for paying guests by former owners, are visible only by strolling the paths through surrounding trees and plants while enjoying the natural beauty of the grounds.

According to Beers' 1884 *History of Greene County,* this area of the plains in Leeds was once inhabited by Native Americans, probably of Mohican blood, mixed by the later 1700s with the Delawares, Penacooks, and Nanticokes. Jan Bronck, an astute Dutch colonial trader, purchased an estimated 300 acres from these Indians. This huge tract of land would be nearly the size of the modern village of Leeds. There, Bronck built himself a log cabin and spent the rest of his days working and enjoying his domain—although, rumor has it, he spent an inordinate amount of time in the gala atmosphere of Fort Orange (later known as Albany).

Other famous Greene County historical names enter the ownership of the Elizabeth House. Annatje Bronck conveyed the house and property to John Whitbeck and his wife, Catherine, a relative of the long-term reverend of the first Leeds Reformed Church. By the early 1800s the legendary Van Vechten family began their claims. In 1878 John and Anna Maria Van Vechten passed the property to Samuel and wife Sarah Van Vechten, who, in turn, conveyed it to Peter Van Vechten and his wife. Their house, which had burned around 1876, was replaced by Peter in 1891. The date, imprinted on a second-story lintel on the house's left side, verifies its construction. Additionally, the raised stone foundation provides evidence that this is actually the third house built on the site. A series of owners followed—the Peters, the Birds, and the Shannegers—until 1988 when the property was purchased by an interior designer and owner of an architectural restoration business, Stephen Shadley, who has been restoring and rejuvenating the house and landscape ever since.

Between 1910 and 1920 an enormous four-story wood extension was attached to the house. Alleged to accommodate 100 sleepers, it may have been a forerunner of the modern bed-and-breakfast or boardinghouse. One can only assume that business was not too brisk since the addition was torn down in 1930. The lumber and other materials from that demolition were used to build six cabins in the late 1930s or 1940s, most likely for paying guests. The present owner has converted one cabin to an open-air, gazebo-like structure for dining and relaxing. Work on the cabins has been done with deep respect for the history of the building. Similarly, the restoration of the house and property mirrors great understanding of the area's heritage. In the mid-1990s the National Historic Register added the Elizabeth House to its roster of important historic sites in the United States.

Shadley's interior restoration has respected the integrity of the original edifice even to the point of reproducing old-fashioned radiators for a heating system. Yet a rebuilt kitchen and new bathrooms have made the home comfortable and very livable for the modern lifestyle. Center halls and ten-foot ceilings contribute to the dwelling's spacious air. Pocket doors, stored in the basement, were retrieved and repositioned to supplement the original doors, casings, baseboards, and wide-plank floors. A mural of important Greene County sites graces the interior. Early cedar shakes are visible in the third story under the metal roof. Wide hemlock planks cover this "attic" area.

Unique positioning of this beautiful house enhances its charm. The front of the building facing the creek provides a breathtaking view of the water and the Old Leeds Bridge. The best photographs of this span are taken from the grounds of the Elizabeth House or from the center waters of the Catskill Creek. The recent purchase by Mr. Shadley of the surrounding acres where Native Americans once trod ensures the continued preservation of the area and its stunning views of the landscape and bridge.

Preservation was once an issue for the landmark bridge itself. On April 15, 1936, the *Cairo Herald* proclaimed that the famous old Leeds Bridge was doomed, undermined by a spring flood the previous month. This four-span masonry arch bridge was originally built in 1760 from native stone. The masons must have been extremely skilled, for it had survived 176 years of heavy use. Now threatened with becoming a "thing of the past," a mere memory, a huge public outcry begged for reconstruction and preservation, spearheaded by Greene County historian Jessie Van Vechten Vedder.

In June 1936 a temporary bridge constructed by Greene County engineers was opened to traffic, and in November 1937 the "new" Leeds Bridge replaced the temporary span and became available for public travel. Wider than the original old stone arch bridge, it is similar in many ways. In a successful attempt to have the old and new correspond as closely as possible, the construction engineers used stone from the old bridge to face the new version. The rebuilt arches provide an aura of antiquity, though the new version doesn't bow as much in the middle. For more than 70 years, travelers have crossed its 0.21-mile length, children have enjoyed swimming near its arches, and the occupants of the Elizabeth House have marveled at the scene.

Right: The "new" Leeds Bridge.

JUDD/OLNEY HOUSE

Local legend has it that Gideon Judd, the pastor of the Presbyterian church in Catskill, built this house in 1840. However, its style and ornamentation suggest a much later date. The present owners believe that Danforth Olney, who purchased the property in 1856, either built the house or completely remodeled a smaller, earlier house built by Judd.

In 1913, after a series of owners, the house and its lot became part of the large surrounding acreage, which included several houses, some owned by St. Elizabeth's Academy. In 1932 Our Lady of Lourdes Hospital of Camden purchased the entire property, including this house and lot, later building a large senior-care complex and turning the house into 16 small bedroom-bath apartments for seniors. Some records even indicate that there were 20 such rooms. The house was referred to as Holy Child by the Franciscan Order. The long, large senior-care center faces east to the Hudson River. Now "Home Sweet Home" on the Hudson River, under previous ownership the center was known as Saint Joseph's Villa for many years.

In 1989, Midstate Investors/Distefano purchased just the one house and the lot on which it was built. They, in turn, sold it to Barbara Weber one year later. Heavy restoration began in the 1990s. The interior of the home was gutted and original rooms restored. In 1996, Weber won the third-place award from the National Trust for Historic Preservation for the best restoration in the entire United States. They also cited her for stepping forward to save the structure, which, in all probability, would have been torn down.

Much credit for the superior revival of the ornate villa-style house goes to Barbara Weber, who has shown her passion for historic residences by restoring at least four significant houses in Greene County. Two others also are included on the Greene County Historical Register. In the February 4, 1996, edition of the *Albany Times Union* she was commended for her dedication to preserving the past and for saving the house from the "wrecking ball."

Mrs. Weber said that the beautiful staircase enticed her to purchase the house. In fact, it was the only original feature left. As her contractor, Glen Neal, described it, "The house was divided up into 20 bathrooms with bedrooms attached." The exterior was totally encased in asbestos shingles, and the interior had been stripped of all fireplaces and most of the wood ornamentation throughout.

Arched doorways, boarded up in plywood, with doors cut through, amazingly reappeared when the plywood was taken away. Many of the windows that had been altered during the rest-home conversion were returned to the two-over-two sash, matching the originals. When the dropped acoustical and tin ceilings were taken down, ten-foot-high plaster ones, some with carved medallions, were exposed and resurfaced. Four fireplace chimneys had been destroyed and most of the other fireplaces permanently removed. Two of the original white marble mantels were relocated and reattached. Beams and partitions that had marked the baths and bedrooms of the rest-home were torn out, leaving questionable support for the original house. New, stronger building materials were used to rebuild and replace those parts of the historic building. An architect, hired to create a floor plan, used as a model the structural remains from the early house unearthed after the senior residence was gutted.

In 1995 Anne Weber, a restoration architect, wrote, "The house is a very unusual example of the Hudson River Italianate villa. The main façade has four giant columns joined by wood filigree arches. The columns support an attic story with windows in a highly ornamented frieze. This interesting decorative treatment makes the house a very significant example of the architecture of the period . . . In other respects, the building is typical of Italianate architecture of the region, with bracketed overhangs and porches, bay windows, etc. Most exterior elements are original or reproductions of originals. [The house] originally had a cupola which has not yet been reconstructed. With this exception, the building retains its integrity to a high degree. It is significant in its design, and for the integrity of that design."

In 2007, Tom and Dianne Gibson purchased the house, after a two-year search. Tom retired as a VP in charge of financial affairs at Penn State. They used their talents to further enhance the house and designed an art gallery on the expansive first floor. "Gallery 42" is open to the public on selected weekends and by appointment.

Opposite left: The original staircase.
Opposite right: Italianate wood filigree cornice.

HALL/URSPRUNG HOUSE

This majestic historic residence illustrates the formal Federal rules of symmetry that evolved in the United States from the Georgian style between 1790 and 1830. Built in this modified English Georgian style, characteristic of post-Revolutionary architecture, the house was located on the site of the Catskill Packet, the first local periodical, published in 1792. Constructed of red brick in 1811, and supported by a stone foundation, it was first occupied by Lyman Hall and his wife, Electa Day Hall.

Following Lyman's death in 1816, Electa married General John C. Johnston, a Revolutionary War veteran. They resided in the house for more than forty years, moving from the area in 1857. The next owner, Joshua Atwater, left the house to son Henry, who conveyed it to Moses Staples in 1889. The family passed it on to John Cummings in 1916. Evidence exists that during these exchanges, Sybil Ludington Ogden operated a tavern there between 1904 and 1910. Other proprietors established a restaurant during World War I (1914–1918). If dates are accurate, that would mean that Cummings was the restaurateur. The next owners were Frank and Sarah Goldberg, who purchased the property on October 10, 1922. Finally, the home was purchased in 1931 by Dr. Mahlon Atkinson, renowned local physician, and his wife, Lillon. Dr. Atkinson's practice was housed in his offices, located in the attractive ground floor apartment. During World War II, their daughter-in-law dwelled with them awaiting their son's return from army service. On September 12, 1967, after 36 years, the Atkinsons sold their elegant home to Nancy Ursprung and her husband, Jack, who was an official in the family oil business. Their eight children grew to adulthood here.

At the rear of the main house is an older carriage house that reflects the post-Revolutionary development of Catskill as a creek-side village. The house itself, an excellent example of the five-bay -by-two-bay symmetrical Federal design, is enlivened by a simple cornice and frieze and exhibits identical north and south elevations dominated by the parapet gables surrounding four chimneys. A large oval window near the top of each parapet provides extra splendor. Ionic columns on both sides of the front arched recessed entrance doorway contribute to the Georgian picture, as does the Palladian window over the door with typical sidelights. A Greek revival porch attached to the south façade exemplifies the Greek, Roman, and other classic motifs that inspired details throughout the mansion. Fenestration represented by double-hung windows is but one example of the finely crafted architectural enhancements. An outstanding degree of integrity of design, materials, and craftsmanship, and a feeling for and association with the early 19th century are present.

Seven working fireplaces grace the interior of the home. Carved Adams period woodwork appears on a fireplace in the northeast dining room, as does delicate woodwork throughout the residence. High ceilings and the kitchen fireplace with its Dutch oven add to the historic picture. Ongoing restorations and the decor of the home reflect the owner's care and concern for maintaining local heritage (the owner is a Catskill native).

CATSKILL

RAMSEY SCHOOLHOUSE

Records describe an early schoolhouse in this area that was constructed in 1838 after "it was agreed by vote that there should be $120 paid to complete a schoolhouse and $12.50 to purchase the lot." The location was on the road leading past the home of John Ramsen—also spelled Remsen and now, through usage, corrupted to Ramsey. That early lot appears to be where the present building is sited. No account, however, of the end of that first school building remains, although financial records provide insight into the support of a school during the first half of the 19th century. In addition to a vote to complete the schoolhouse, on November 6, 1841, it was "resolved that 8 dollars be raised for stovepipe and finishing the schoolhouse"; in October 1863 it was "resolved that a tax of $17 [be] raised for the purpose of building a privy . . ."

Finally, at the beginning of the 20th century, a quarter acre was donated by Louis H. Schaefer and his wife "for the purpose of schoolhouse site and grounds." According to the Millers, the present building, known as the Ramsey (Remsen) Schoolhouse, was built in 1901 by Fred Fruisen of Catskill. During those days, it was a state-of-the-art rural educational center. For 50 years dozens of youngsters trudged through ice and snow to this hall of learning.

A former student, Carol Doney, whose mother, Virginia Story, taught there, recalls the large cast-iron stove that sat in the middle of the one room. On wintry days a neighbor started a fire to help warm the children who had all walked to school. She also remembers the hand pump in the entrance area, which supplied water for thirsty students. A privy attached to the back of the building allowed the children direct access so they wouldn't freeze their feet. Students from grade one through eight attended. This young scholar learned the grades ahead and was therefore able to "graduate" before her time.

The school closed in 1953. Following more than a decade of idleness, the property was purchased by Alex Grossman, an insurance agent, who sold it to Harry and Betty Miller in 1965. Two years later, the Millers had turned it into a gracious home where they resided for more than 30 years. Since the school had an outdoor privy for the children, the Millers installed indoor plumbing and later added a side bedroom. However, despite this partial modernization, the entry space and the one large classroom were maintained. Also left intact were the original slate boards covered with the signatures of many former students. Both Millers were deeply interested in education: Betty was a high school librarian for many years. When guests were entertained at this unique home, the blackboards and chalk awaited their signatures. As the boards filled up, guest books had to be used, much to the dismay of the owners. The Millers loved welcoming visitors to this historic, turn-of-the-century schoolhouse site, where they led many a tour.

CATSKILL

STILLWOOD

Seldom are houses honored with birthday parties, but in 1994 this elegant Victorian house was celebrated for its 100 years of existence. The owners at that time hosted a gala celebration under the stars as revelers from as far away as California dined on a catered gourmet buffet and danced to the strains of a swinging orchestra in a large, graceful white tent. A variety of mature trees surround the house: a weeping beech, Japanese maples, a European chestnut, and sycamores mix with holly plants and various evergreens. The interior of the home also reflects the beauty of wood. Extensive hand-carved woodwork abounds in oak, maple, and cherry. Additionally, five fireplaces, two with decorative glazed tile façades, provide visual warmth. The original stained-glass windows frame the front entrance door.

This house was designed by architect Warner F. B. Dayton. The builder erected it to the specifications of the first owner, Howard L. Boughton, for a 49-by-59-foot two-story building. On May 19, 1894, the *Examiner*, a Catskill newspaper, described the medleys of wood, including mahogany, oak, and ash, and added that "all modern improvements will be embraced in the structure." The original land spread from the Hudson River on the east to modern-day Spring Street on the west. Shortened through the decades by the sale of lots, the property still conceals the elegant clapboard house with high gambrel roofs as it blends into the surrounding deep woods.

Howard L. Boughton established the long-lived department store that bore his name. Born in Windham in 1849, he moved to Catskill at the age of 16 and worked for O. T. Humphrey, a dry goods merchant. Before he reached age 21 he formed a partnership with Lucius R. Doty: Boughton and Doty. Next there was Boughton and Warner, which became Catskill's popular business establishment, and finally Boughton's, which developed into the elite place for women's shopping needs.

During Boughton's short life he organized the Catskill Merchants Association, was a director of the Catskill National Bank, and the Building and Loan Association, and was a member of the Catskill Board of Education and the Wilson Fire Co. #5. When he died unexpectedly of "apoplexy" in 1905 at age 56, the *Catskill Examiner* of December 2, 1905, recorded that Boughton was stricken while preparing for bed. He was "his customer's personal friend. His integrity was unquestioned—he was essentially a man of gentleness and sincerity, honorable and charitable. In all things pertaining to the welfare of the village—its business, religious or educational interests—he was foremost and conspicuous. He believed in this community, and to him it was the center and the home of everything that was near and dear to his heart." He left Boughton's, the largest department store between New York City and Albany, to his heirs. His wife, who continued to manage the business, died in Atlantic City on January 5, 1928. A niece,

Antoinette Weed, became well-known and esteemed in Catskill for her business acumen, as she lived in the house until 1961 and managed the fashionable Boughton's located on Main Street just south of the theater, since replaced by other places of business.

In 1961 James and Jean Summers purchased the house, turning it over within eight months to Jack Lemelman, whose firm Greene County Property Inc. sold it to Bill and Mary White in May 1962. Bill was an entrepreneur and Mary an educator. In addition to rejuvenating the whole structure, they spent many months scraping white paint, applied by former owners, from the beautiful woods, and thus returned the handsome entrance room's tall-sided stairway and decorative beams and trims throughout the house to their original beauty. Raising their family of four children at this picturesque location, they finally conveyed the property to L. Scott Johnson, a landscape architect. Johnson, as might be expected, rearranged the entrance to the grounds, maintaining the statuesque historical trees. He renovated the kitchen into a *Better Homes and Gardens* modern picture of perfection and added a stunning large screened-in porch. Toward the end of 2005 he sold the house to two Hudson antique dealers, Frank Swim and Warner Shook. They, in turn, have been maintaining and revitalizing the historic, picturesque scene.

MYERS STONE HOUSE

Settlers who had come from Holland are credited with the of this sturdy but aging stone house on High Falls Road Extension. The stone home, with an original date stone above the front doorway dated 1807, has initials of possibly the original builders: I.M. and S.M. It is one of the earliest homes built in the Kiskatom area. There is a cellar space, just one main room with a large fireplace, and a steep stairway to a sleeping space overhead.

Several years ago, in conversation with Hattie Myers (at that time she was in her late 90s and totally blind but surviving alone in the home), it was learned that one of the Myers sons had worked in the quarry that supplied the slate to build the sidewalks around Macy's and Gimbels in New York City. She also told how the drivers of the horses and carriages that transported guests from the ferry in Catskill up to the Catskill Mountain House had also lived in this house.

The little stone home was last used by Ralph Schram who had a woodworking and chair-caning shop there.

It sits empty now—wishing and waiting for something to happen that will return it to its former charm and respect.

Below: Close-up view of the window, south side.

Thomas Cole's Cedar Grove National Historic Site

Due to its national significance, Thomas Cole's Cedar Grove was chosen as a national historic landmark in 1965. In 1979 Thomas Cole's great-granddaughter, Edith Cole Silberstein, sold the house and property to the Catskill Center for Conservation and Development. Nineteen years later, after a series of owners and caretakers, the Greene County Historical Society acquired the estate. In 1999 the U.S. Congress designated this house and its grounds as a National Historic Site. An affiliated unit with the National Park Service, Thomas Cole's Cedar Grove is now owned and managed by the Society through a board of governors. Although Thomas Cole never personally owned Cedar Grove, his impact is felt in every area of the house and landscape.

*O Cedar Grove!
When'er I think to part
From thine all peaceful
shades my aching heart
Is like to his who leaves
some blessed shore
A weeping exile ne'r
to see it more.*

—Thomas Cole, 1834

In the summer of 1827 Thomas Cole, who would become the internationally acclaimed founder of the Hudson River School of Art, first took up lodging at Cedar Grove and set up an artist's studio in an out-building. Cole spent hours hiking through the picturesque Catskill Mountains, which he came to love. He loved to walk into the deep woods of the mountains. The changing light and varying atmosphere inspired the strongly religious artist. Days passed as he traveled through the natural beauty of the Northeast, often accompanied by his close friend, painter Asher B. Durand. Cedar Grove, provided Cole with an uninterrupted panoramic view of the Catskills to the west, much as it does for visitors today. This home in Catskill provided him a haven from the city life in which he did occasionally dabble.

Cole fell in love and married Maria Bartow, the niece of his landlord, John Alexander Thomson. Affectionately known as "Uncle Sandy," Thomson was kin to Thomas T. Thomson, the first occupant of Cedar Grove, which was built in 1815. An 1812 bible of Alexander Thomson's notes that Maria Bartow, his niece, was raised at Cedar Grove after her parents were murdered in an Indian attack. Cole married Maria in the west parlor of the Federal-style brick home on November 22, 1836, and in that house the couple raised their children. It was Maria who would ultimately inherit the painted brick house and the surrounding property.

As time progressed, the household must have made for a lively existence: in addition to Thomson and the six members of the Cole family (Thomas and Maria had four children), Maria's three unmarried sisters—Emily, Harriet, and Frances—lived there along with assorted maids and manservants. For a time they were also joined by Cole's resident student, Frederick Church, later of Olana. The Hartford youth remained two years at Cedar Grove and was provided with studio space, access to the master, and trips into the mountains. Thus Cole started Church on his journey to celebrity and riches.

Cole himself never amassed great wealth. Life at Cedar Grove was simple and modest, but Cole was a major cultural figure in American art. He is credited with making the Hudson Valley and the Catskills into symbols of national greatness as well as a leading tourist destination.

It is easy to imagine Cole, the poetic artistic genius, dreamily staring westward toward the dramatic Catskill peaks. His voyage to Europe in 1842 and extended stay there are clearly depicted in his many letters home to his wife. To his love of nature he added his love for his church in later years. Cole's involvement with religion was noticeable after he unveiled his famous 1836 painting series known as "The Course of Empire" and the equally outstanding 1839–1840 "The Voyage of Life" series. When the original edifice of St. Luke's Church burned, he designed its replacement and was a loyal attendee. Unfortunately, the Cole-designed structure burned as well. The present-day St. Luke's records his son Thomas as an early rector. The current St. Luke's also contains a memorial stained-glass window given to the church by the Cole children in honor of their parents. The Cole family grave site can be found in Catskill's historic Thompson Street Cemetery.

Cole's original studio, remodeled into a caretaker's cottage, has been returned to the days when Cole worked at his easel. Though Cole built a "new studio"—which he designed in a modified Italianate style, facing west to the mountains that gave him his inspiration—and moved his work in during the Christmas season 1846, he sadly had but 14 months of pleasure in his new retreat before death took him. After his death, Maria and their children

maintained the studio as a shrine in his honor, with many of his works and artifacts on view for many years. Unfortunately, the "new studio" was demolished in 1973.

Cole's house became a focal point for colleagues, including writers, poets, and naturalists, who often met there. Credited as one of the nation's first environmentalists, Cole spoke out against the deforestation of the mountains and the encroachment of industry on nature's wonders. Even Cole's untimely death did not diminish Cedar Grove's appeal. During the 1850s and 1860s artists Benjamin Stone and Charles Moore rented rooms and studio space there. William Cullen Bryant eulogized Cole, claiming he was "the pre-eminent painter of his era." In honor of that eulogy Asher B. Durand painted the famous *Kindred Spirits,* showing Cole and poet Bryant standing on a rock ledge in the Catskills. The northern Catskills became a mecca for landscape artists, who followed in their friend and leader's footsteps.

Equally impressive to the family social history is the beauty of Cedar Grove and the architectural evolution of the house itself, built of brick in the Federal style. A three-story Victorian north wing added in the 1870s enhanced the house. Today the house features restored fireplaces, woodwork, and an awesome four-floor stairwell. Historic flower gardens, significant plants, and the 200-year-old towering honey locust tree surround the main house.

The ground floor may be entered through a door beneath the south porch. As would be expected, the house has an attic. Entering the symmetrical southern front façade through the center doorway, the

Opposite: Thomas Cole's studio, circa 1906.
Opposite inset: Thomas Cole.
Above: The fully restored, Federal-style privy, originally built to complement the house.

visitor steps into a central hall surrounded by a west parlor, east parlor, library, and pantry. High ceilings and tall windows provide an air of gracious spaciousness. The four bedrooms on the second floor, including a nursery, showcase the master west bedroom, facing the mountains, where Cole died. The ground floor includes a kitchen, pantry, wine cellar, and storage space.

A long verandah crosses the southern façade of the house, showcasing the dramatic mountains to the west for porch sitters. When the Greene County Historical Society took over this landmark property, Cedar Grove became an affiliated National Park Service site. Under their guidelines and those of the New York State Office of Parks, Recreation and Historic Preservation, the building was restored to the dignified presence tourists view today. The brilliant restoration was accomplished by Richard Rappleyea and his Dimension North, renowned for their historic restorations. This significant structure maintains the history of one of Catskill's most important personages for thousands of people annually. Cole's greatness complements the beauty of Cedar Grove. Although he never actually owned the house himself, it is undeniably his.

YE OLDE STONE HOUSE

This historic building is actually two houses: the native fieldstone main house, two and a half stories high, distinguished by fanlight windows in the east gable; and a second, smaller house known as the smokehouse, although the building is much too large to have been practical for that use.

The house was erected before 1783 and, although the original architect is unknown, the care and quality of the stonework suggest that a master mason was responsible. The first occupant was most likely Jan Persen, who built on land granted to him from Garret Van Bergen in 1749. John Person, Jan Person's son, and Jacob Newkirk, an in-law, owned two slaves in 1810, according to Beers' 1884 *History of Greene County*.

Local tradition has it that the stone structures were abandoned as homes by 1890 and were used as farm buildings for the next 60 years. Then, in the mid-1960s, the two stone buildings were joined by the addition of a kitchen and dining room. Such modifications and other alterations respected the architectural integrity of the original buildings.

The large size of the windows is characteristic of buildings extant in the Netherlands dating to the 18th century. An early form of solar heating, they provide the house with a great deal of sunlight and warmth in the winter. The stained glass is mid-19th century, having been retrieved during a renovation of the First Methodist Church on Catskill's Main Street.

The design of this intriguing structure manifests both a Dutch influence—the use of stone, with the gable end facing the road—and an English influence—the use of symmetry. The original mortar, needing repairs during the two centuries of its existence, still holds the "rubblework" walls securely. Richard Philp and David Martin, previous owners—now proprietors of the historic Clarke House in the Village of Catskill—placed this house on the Greene County Historical Register and did most of the research on this dwelling. As Mr. Philp noted and could rightly boast: "The house is a fine example of a stone dwelling dating from the early years of our Republic, adapted to contemporary use."

CATSKILL

TREE HOUSE

Today, local passersby would find it difficult to believe that this strikingly handsome, classic house was ravaged by flames on a chilly winter day in 1992. A tragic fire, starting in the basement, destroyed 80 percent of the interior as the sky brightened with red, yellow, and orange flames of destruction. Amazingly restored by historical restoration specialist Richard Rappleyea and his company, Dimensions North—also responsible for the rejuvenation of Thomas Cole's Cedar Grove—this true Greek Revival building is sited on its original 1838 base. Later additions, most likely in the 1860s, added 120 square feet to the already sizable structure.

The six elegant 24-foot-high Ionic columns with 26-inch diameters that grace the front entrance are original, unharmed by the devastating fire. The architrave and full-width pediment sit above them. The interior is enhanced by seven working fireplaces, three of which are marble. Five wood mantels remain. Five-foot-square mirrors, rumored to have hung originally in Hudson River dayliners, reflect the beauty of the home.

As with the histories of many old houses, differing versions and even various construction dates exist. The one most nearly accurate, as delineated in the Book of Deeds, is that the house was built for Mitchell Sanford of Schoharie on land purchased from James Powers, a prominent real estate investor, analogous to modern developers. A corner lot was specified; the one chosen lay at the corner of William and Orange (now Prospect) streets. The Hutchinsons later purchased the property from the Sanfords.

In 1845 the whole estate went at public auction to Daniel S. Gleason. He apparently purchased the property with his wife's money, but then transferred ownership to one of his own relatives. Needless to say, his wife, Helen, did not take kindly to this. Thus began a feud, primarily between husband and wife, over who had title and the right to transfer that title.

Following the Gleasons came the Cookes, whose descendants built the gracious home that stands across the avenue. The Cookes bought the property in 1850. Then in rapid succession came the Donnellys, Lydia Smith of New York, Amelia and Marie Badeau, Samuel Cornell, and Martino Niles Wilcoxson. The names of this last owner and that of his bride, Phoebe Badeau, became the title of choice for the property in that era. Wedded in the lovely drawing room, the couple honeymooned abroad for many months. Returning home, however, their increasingly negative feelings toward each other led to the dissolution of their seven-and-a-half-year marriage and to a major scandal related to their house.

A breath of fresh air finally arrived when Catskill businessman Michael Cimmorelli purchased the property in 1925, and for 51 years Catskillians knew the pillared home as the Cimorelli

House. In 1976 Pamela Newcombe Hobbs gained ownership, and in 1984 she sold the house to her mother, Barbara Newcombe (Weber), the later owner of the historic Judd/Olney house. She, in turn, after reviving its beauty, sold the property to three New Yorkers who used it as a weekend vacation home. Ironically, they had left to return to the city on the very morning of the devastating fire.

During one of the Greene County Historical Society's famous Homes Tours, the Rappleyeas, still in the midst of restoration, generously allowed the public to see their "work in progress." The Rappleyeas' three children named the house "the Tree House" and today it sits on the corner, anchoring the street of high-style Victorian homes.

CHERRITREE–RIVERVIEW COTTAGE

In 1999 Jay English, at that time the owner of this Victorian home, placed it on the Greene County Historical Register as "the Cherritree." Subsequent owners found through their research that the home had originally been named "Riverview Cottage" and decided to return to the original nomenclature. Before heavy brush and stands of trees on the opposite side of Prospect Avenue blocked the scene, Riverview Cottage most likely had a beautiful view of the Hudson River.

Olive Cherritree was an artist who had studied in Europe, preferring the milieu of France. Using oil on canvas, she painted landscapes in the style of the Barbizon School of Art. In 1888, Ms. Cherritree, then a resident of Oak Hill, had purchased this property from Joseph and Ellam Cornell. In the early 1890s she built this stately home with its expansive wraparound porch, following the plans of New York City architects Munn and Sons.

Between 1890 and 1894, the years when Ms. Cherritree was in residence, the *Catskill Examiner* always referred to the building as Riverview Cottage. Painted in Victorian shades on the exterior, the interior boasts two original stained-glass windows as well as all of the original floors and moldings.

After a series of five different owners, Alfred and Marjorie DiCaprio, educators at both the Catskill and Onteora school districts, purchased the home in 1954 and lived here for more than 40 years. Their estate sold Riverview Cottage to Jay English in 1998.

CATSKILL

First Reformed Church of Catskill

The First Reformed Church of Catskill might be considered an offshoot of the Leeds Reformed Church. In 1810 it was noted that Henry Ostrander of the Leeds Church was to preach at the Landing in Catskill. It was further stated that he should give his sermons in English—a large departure from the Dutch services in Leeds. Finally, for $600 yearly the Reverend Wyncoop answered the call and soon felt the need for a church in the village.

In 1828 the First Reformed Church was erected on the site formerly occupied by Charles Clark's harness shop on the east side of Main Street. Dimensions of the $8,000 structure were 40 by 70 feet. On one side of the church permanent seats were sold, while pews on the other side went to the highest bidder at public auction. When an 1851 disastrous fire started in the nearby livery stable, the original church was totally destroyed. The well-known architect Jackson and contractors Colgrave and Purdy were commissioned to design and construct a building that would provide facilities for a major cultural institution. Since 1852 the church, under constant maintenance, has done so for over 150 years.

Composed of large-scale red brick, the neoclassical-style building has a square bell tower. Interior simulated columns against the 80-by-50-foot sanctuary walls provide an aura of simple elegance. Details such as windows are designed in perfect proportion. A platform with a pulpit crosses the front. The organ is on the rear balcony. The stained-glass windows were changed in 1910.

Monies raised by the first church from the public auction of pews went toward the construction of the new church. Charging fees for the seating of the pews was the accepted practice of the day, and owners of paid-up pews continued to use the same numbers in the new church.

New York State abolished slavery as early as 1827 but the church continued to make arrangements "for people of color to occupy the tier of seats on the south gallery next to the pulpit." Pew 62 on the lower floor was also reserved, this one "for aged people of color."

The second minister of the church received $840 yearly and, since there was no parsonage, also received $160 for house rental. Today, friends and neighbors worship while seated in these historic pews, no longer for sale.

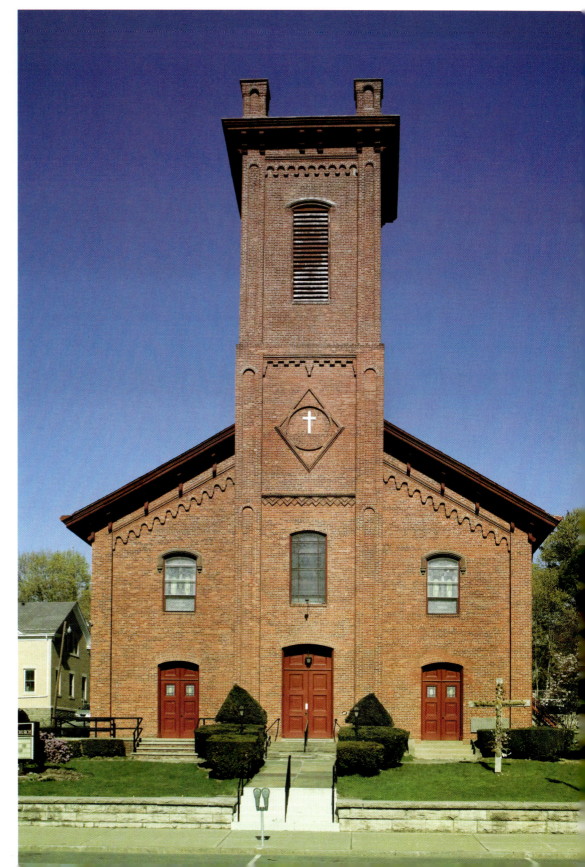

Harmon Pettingill House

This house is an excellent example of the Second Empire style, which has been influenced by both French architecture and the popular Italianate of the 1860s–1890s. Many notable Victorian exterior and interior features are illustrated by this elaborate building. The patterned multicolored slates of the mansard roof provide the visual design loved by the French, while the tower is Italianate.

It is probable that this central tower was changed at some point in time but evidence of such an alteration is nonexistent. A cupola, however, that originally topped the tower was removed in the 20th century. Both styles share certain features manifest in this building. The heavy bracketed cornice, the large decorative brackets, the bay windows, and the pedimented dormers are especially characteristic. The cornice, jutting out a distance from the brick wall, is both functional (covering the gutters) and aesthetic. A large front verandah facing east toward the Hudson River and the rising sun is interrupted by the left southeast front bay. Replicated on the southern side of the house, it provides the illusion of a sizable wrap-around porch. The third-floor mansard with its typical patterned dormers most likely housed the servants, as was the custom.

On April 8, 1795, a letter of patent for land in the Village of Catskill was granted to John Cantline, who issued a Deed of Trust on this property to four men, one of whom was George Clark (Clarke). These four proprietors agreed to the division of land in 1806. George Clark, among 11 parcels, drew Lot No. 15 stretching eastward, most probably from Main Street to the Hudson River. Sixty-four years later, in 1870, a 48-year-old son, also George Clark, living in Otsego County, New York, reported no occupation and real estate valued at $2,000,000. In October 1871 he transferred the eastern moiety (one of two parcels not necessarily equal) of Lot No. 15. This section included the 0.65 acre lot on which this house is situated. It is difficult to ascertain whether George Clark had this house built or just sold the property. The selling price of $6,500 is a large sum for that time period and owners in the 1950s and 1960s believed that this was evidence of a building. The wealthy George, or his representative, may have been living on the property, because when the sale to Oliver Bourke took place in October 1870, George reserved legal possession for an additional four months. In the 1880 census George listed his occupation as Proprietor of Real Estate. It seems likely that he is a direct descendant of George Clark, Esq., His Majesty's (King George II) Lieutenant Governor and Commander in Chief of the Province of New York, who obtained land along the Catskill Creek in 1741.

Oliver Bourke at a young age assisted his stepfather, James Kavelle, in a butcher business on Catskill's Main Street. Around 1839 Oliver established his own butcher business, becoming a prominent Catskill merchant. By 1853 he owned a meat market on Main Street and a slaughterhouse on Diamond Hill. In June of 1870 he lived with his wife's family on Bridge Street and was postmaster at 93 Main Street (probably his meat market). It must have been a proud day in 1871 when the Irish immigrant with his Catskill wife, Mary Bell, moved "up the hill" to this elegant house. In 1879 his residence was assessed at $2,200 and his store at $1,600. Oliver and Mary lived in this house for more than 30 years, some of which with their adopted daughter, Eleanor "Ella." Oliver died suddenly on November 13, 1902, from pneumonia and complications of diabetes. As was customary, his funeral was held at his residence. Sadly, six months following his death a public auction held at the Village Courthouse disposed of the property. The Catskill Savings Bank found it necessary to foreclose on both the house and market mortgages. By a deed dated May 21, 1903, the referee in the action transferred 17 Prospect Avenue to the highest bidder, Harmon P. Pettingill. Harmon paid $7,338.96, a fair offer considering it had been assessed at $6,000 in 1901. The residence became quickly known as the Pettingill house, a name lasting into the 21st century. Mary and Harmon Pettingill were leaders in the Catskill community who made a deep impression. He was a well-known and esteemed banker who owned a large share of Catskill Village's wool manufacturer, Malcolm and Company.

When the National Register of Historic Places accepted the Catskill East Side Historic District to the Register, this handsome house was referred to as the Pettingill House.

The Bunce House, however, is equally impressed on Catskill memories. Charles Bunce possessed the home from the late 1920s until the 1950s. He was a veteran of World War I, whose name is recorded on the memorial statue in front of the Greene County Courthouse. Bunce was, most likely, responsible for dividing the large residence into five (now four) lovely apartments, the top one providing a breathtaking 360-degree view of the mountains and the river. In a 1929 tax assessment the property was identified as an apartment house owned by Bunce while, his wife, Katherine, owned a "tenement in Leeds." Most likely, the Bunce's major holdings were in real estate. They did, however, let 17 Prospect remain idle for several years before refurbishing it in the early 1950s.

The high ceilings, large entrance hall, and handsome wide staircase help preserve the historic venue of this elegant house. A dumbwaiter extends from the solidly constructed basement to the third floor. In 1958 William Bull of Manhattan, an owner of private business schools, purchased the building, placed it on the

Greene County Historical Register, and made many cosmetic improvements. He named it "the Bull House." The residence was managed by the Bull's friends, Betty and Ray Light, who dwelled in the house for more than 30 years. Ray was with the New York State Education Department and Betty was a well-known community leader who cared for the architecture and historical details. Following the death of William Bull, the present owners purchased the property. Bob Barnes, now retired, was an editor and administrator for New York State. In 2006 he became involved in the antiques business. For more than 40 years George Jurgsatis has used his expertise as an antiques specialist in New York City, Hudson, and Catskill. He now owns and operates Townhouse Antiques in the Village of Catskill. They have continued to maintain their unique house beautifully in its distinctive historical style.

Opposite: The Victorian-style double front doors.

The Catskill Public Library

The Catskill Public Library sits solidly at the corner of Franklin Street and Bridge Street Hill, on land that once housed the Magilton Livery Stable. Directly facing its illustrious neighbor, the 1813 Courthouse, sited diagonally opposite the oldest church building in Catskill Village (the former Presbyterian church), and sited sideways to the newer, elegant Greene County Courthouse, the library forms a quadrant of historically significant buildings near the center of the Village of Catskill.

The mellow redbrick structure has served the community as a library for more than 105 years. In 1901 when the Catskill Public Library was constructed, tradition dictated, as it does today, that society's important institutions be housed in noble buildings. Victorian families, residing in their elaborate domiciles, required that libraries—as well as churches, schools, courthouses, and clubs —exemplify this concept. The library's neoclassical style and colossal portico entrance provide a perfect illustration.

The Gilded Age spawned a great desire for cultural institutions in the United States, and Catskill proved no exception. In the 1890s public agitation grew for a village library. In 1893 the State Board of Regents provided a charter incorporating the Catskill Public Library. The Catskill Library Association, formed that year, oversaw a small library, open Saturday afternoons in the then Catskill Village High School. In time, the 545 books constituting the nucleus of the library were moved to a store at 400 Main Street. The books had been contributed by the Catskill Free Academy and the beloved Emily F. Becker, who served as librarian for some 50 years.

Demand for a more suitable building, however, continued to grow exponentially. At a taxpayer meeting on April 28, 1899, it was voted to raise $3,000 in taxes toward the purchase of a site and the building of a library. In addition, contributions brought the amount to $8,000. Finally, Judge Emory A. Chase, a member of the advisory committee, and W. Irving Jennings, the library president, wrote to New York industrialist Andrew Carnegie requesting a grant to construct a library.

At that time, philanthropist Carnegie was awarding monies to cities throughout the United States for the purpose of establishing libraries to enhance nationwide cultural activities. After Chase and Jennings traveled by train to New York City to visit Carnegie and ask for the sum of $10,000, Catskill became the recipient of $20,000. It is believed to be the smallest town to receive such an honor. There was a catch, however: to accept the $20,000 award, taxpayers had to agree to spend a sum equal to 10 percent of the award—$2,000— each year for the maintenance of the building and its collections. The vote passed 22 to 1. As one trustee remarked, "This testifies to the intelligence and liberality of the taxpayer."

Many plans for the building were submitted, with the one by George C. Halcott, a Catskill native and member of the architectural firm Earle & Fisher of Worchester, Massachusetts, being chosen. Halcott was well-known as the architect of many Catskill buildings. George W. Holdridge of Catskill received the building contract.

The cornerstone was laid on October 24, 1901. In it were placed copies of the current local papers, *The New York World*, the *New York Times*, *New America,* and a copy of *Harper's Weekly* containing a report on President McKinley's assassination. In addition, 1901-dated United States coins of all denominations, a Pan-American souvenir, and a history of the library were included. The handsome new brick building, a three-story structure with a gray ashlar stone foundation, opened to the public on June 30, 1902. A painting of Andrew Carnegie greeted people in quiet dignity as they entered. The architects designed the main floor with book stacks at the north, the juvenile department in the northwest corner, a large reading room in the southeast, and a reference room at the southwest.

The basement originally contained a lecture room, a lavatory, a store room, and a kitchen serving as mending and packing room. Throughout the years the lecture room was used for various purposes. For a time kindergarten was held there. Civic organizations, including the Scouts, the Red Cross, and the Monday Club, were welcomed.

Customary for the time period, a museum was planned upstairs on the third floor. Geological specimens, stuffed birds, paintings, crafts, etc. were displayed along with books. Originally, this top-floor museum displayed Indian, Mexican, and geological relics, books in foreign languages, records in longhand of local genealogies for compiling family trees, and entrance papers for the Daughters of the American Revolution and other similar organizations. In time, these were removed to the Greene County Historical Society and are no longer available at the library. The practice of displaying exhibits of historical and contemporary interest, however, continues. In 2006, for example, the library presented the Saunders Hudson River Steamboat Collection with pictures and notes.

Prometheus Bound, the famous painting by Thomas Cole, donated by Cole's granddaughter Florence Vincent, hung for years in the library. A print now hangs there, as the original is on permanent loan to the Thomas Cole National Historic Site, and is sent to the Frances Lehman Loeb Art Center at Vassar College for the winter months.

Relatively, little has changed. Despite the passing of the century, much of the original furniture and the classical charm remain. Of course, the original coal furnace has been replaced by oil, gas lamps have given way to electricity, and fluorescent lights illuminated the stacks for the first time in the 1950s. The early dumbwaiter, which carried books to and from the kitchen and the upper stacks, and even the kitchen itself, are no longer. The several computers available for public use reveal that the library has kept abreast of the times.

OVERBAGH/EVERITT CEMETERY

The dates on the headstones marking the graves in this family cemetery range from 1732 to 1998. Some older stones are becoming illegible, probably due to acid rain and air pollution. The cemetery is part of an old farm and is located near a barn built in 1743 and a house constructed in 1801. A Revolutionary fire site is nearby, completing the aura of antiquity. All are part of the original farm. Eight generations of one family found their resting place here, along with four local Revolutionary soldiers. The 1732 inscribed stone marks the oldest known grave here, just east of the Kykuit; it is one of the oldest in the Town of Catskill.

The first identified occupant of this area was Johann Peter Ober Back (Overbagh), founding father of the Overbagh line, who was buried here in 1734. In 1992 it was still owned by the same family, reflecting six generations of Overbaghs and three of Everitts. In 1879, Mary Overbagh married Charles Everitt, thus changing the name but not the family. An 1899 bluestone post fence with iron chains encircles a 50-by-50-foot raised landscape marking the cemetery.

1813 Courthouse

Nancy and Ted Hilscher, attorneys at law, are just the fourth owners of the austere brick structure, built in 1813 to serve as the Greene County Courthouse. It is the sixth-oldest building in New York state to have been used as a county courthouse, and is one of the oldest surviving courthouses in the United States. Befitting of its stature as a beacon of self-government, the county fathers built the courthouse on the hill, next to the Presbyterian church, and above the mere commercial pursuits of Main Street.

Until 1910, this building housed the county and supreme court for several terms, and was also the seat of county government. The board of supervisors convened here, on the main floor. The building also housed the county clerk's office and the sheriff's office. Speakers such as General Tom Thumb and Orson Fowler, the man who promoted octagon-shaped buildings and determined personality traits by reading the bumps on people's heads, were heard by the people of Catskill when the courthouse also served as a community auditorium. Martin Van Buren and Theodore Roosevelt spoke here in their prepresidential days. Theodore A. Cole, son of the great landscape painter, was the building superintendent in the 1880s.

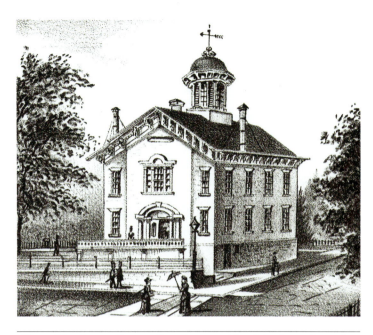

Above: The Greene County Courthouse, with original cupola, and before the addition of the Greek Revival portico, circa 1884.

Post–Civil War, a large addition was made to the east end of the building. Near the turn of the last century, the current Greek Revival portico with four Ionic columns was installed and the brick foundation was dressed up with a stone facing to match the 1901 Carnegie Library across the street. Georgian elements such as second-floor Palladian windows and a double-door entrance bordered by sidelights and a transom have been retained from the original construction. The projection of the central bay on the west elevation, breaking the structure's rectangularity, serves to further emphasize the entrance.

Between 1910 and 1990, this served as Catskill's Lodge #468, F. and A. Masons. The cupola was removed, and substantial changes were made to the main floor. Interior walls and doors opening onto the central hallway, which runs the full 90 feet of the structure, were relocated. The Masons maintained recreational space and rented offices to attorney Francis Ruf in the 1930s and 1940s, and in the 1970s to the county treasurer. The former courtroom on the upper floor, 41 by 49 feet in size, contains a tin ceiling installed during the post–Civil War renovations, and elaborate Greek Revival molding. In this room, men were

found guilty of murder and sentenced to death four times in the 19th century. Hangings took place outside the jail on Clarke Street. An inventory from 1886 notes the placement of 30 cuspidors in the courtroom, including one for each of the jurors.

The Masons sold the building to Community Action in 1990. It was purchased by the Hilschers for use as law offices in June of 2005. The main floor offices and conference room now provide a handsome historical milieu for clients and visitors.

Freightmaster's Building at Historic Catskill Point

Catskill Point, where the Freightmaster's Building is located, played a dominant role in the development of the Village of Catskill and the County of Greene. In the 19th century the Point was a major gateway to the great Northern Catskills.

Until the 1880s, visitors departing from New York City aboard Hudson River steamers landed at the Point to board horse and carriage to carry them to the base of the eastern escarpment of the mountains. Then the carriages would slowly wind their way along the narrow road across the mountainside until they reached the top of North Mountain, where the famous Catskill Mountain House was located. Both the carriages and the great hotel were properties of the Beach family.

Keeping up with the times—as well as trying to cut down the onerous amount of time spent cramped in the carriages—in the latter part of the 19th century the Beach family replaced the horse-drawn carriages with the Iron Horse. After that, visitors debarking from the steamers at Catskill Point boarded the carriages of the Catskill Mountain Railway, which took them to the base of the escarpment. There, they transferred to the famous Otis Elevating Railway, which afforded the passengers spectacular views of the Hudson Valley as their railcars were pulled up the steep incline by a steam-driven power plant located at the summit. Once there they could go to the Mountain House itself, or—by that part of the century—to any of the other grand hotels that now dotted the picturesque landscape.

Meanwhile, back at Catskill Point, by the year 1880 the large brick Freightmaster's Building had been turned into a hotel. The small guest rooms still exist today on the second floor. Around 1885 the Knickerbocker Ice Company purchased the building for their business. Then, in 1890, the Hudson River Day Line bought the building to use as its freightmaster's office. All boats carrying produce stopped here. Barges and night boats carried hay, fruit, and all types of items as well as passengers.

In the 1940s Greene County took over the building, using it as a highway garage until 1998, when the Greene County Legislature received a grant of approximately $3 million from the Canal Corridor Fund for restoration of the Point. Today exhibits and entertainment educate residents and tourists alike, enhancing historic Catskill Point. A medley of impressive displays of and lectures on 18th- and 19th-century life along the Hudson River and the Catskill Creek delight the visitors.

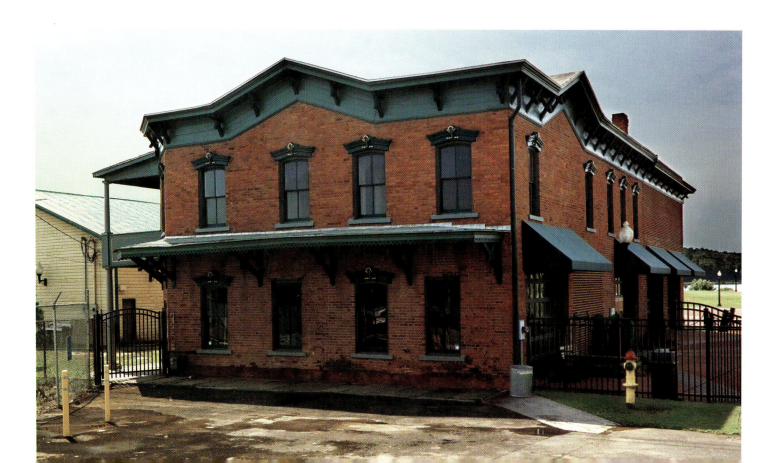

GRANT/FOOTE HOUSE

An old Dutch principle for building a house was to make each section square, and this home is a perfect illustration of the squaring concept. Unlike many surviving Dutch stone structures of the early 19th century, this house, constructed in two sections, was built of wood. The northern part, built in 1820, is 32 feet square. The southern part, probably built by 1840, is 22 feet square. The cupola also was constructed to old Dutch standards, as was the farmhouse fireplace. Brackets under the roof, Italianate in style, suggest that the roof may have been changed at some point in time.

The southern, newer section of the house contains the kitchen, dining room, and powder room; while the northern section, the older and larger area, contains a hall, living room, and parlor space. Here the early brick fireplace, painted white by former occupants, forms a natural mantel as it juts from the wall. Many old glass windows can still be found in this part of the house.

The house stands on land of the old Van Vechten patent. By 1866, Alexander Grant, owner of a large part of that patent, sold land to John B. Foote and thus they became co-owners—as oral history affirms. The first occupant of the house was John B. Foote, who, it is believed, had also received a land grant for 29 acres.

John B. Foote was born in Franklin, Delaware County, October 11, 1826. Moving with his parents to Catskill at the age of 15, he showed ambition by first clerking at his brother's grocery but soon went into business for himself. As an extensive fruit grower, he was lauded in his September 15, 1905, obituary in the *Recorder* for "his fine orchards on the Heights ranking with the best in the state" and as "a pioneer shipper of apples and pears to the European markets principally to Liverpool, England and Glascow [sic], Scotland." He was also praised for his 60-year membership to the Methodist church, where he served as Sunday school superintendent for 36 years.

His property remained in his family for years until his distant namesake, John C. Foote, was declared incompetent. The controller, Roy C. Moon, sold the estate to McTague in 1949. In 1952 Ed Brandow purchased the property, which he in turn sold to Edwin Grossman in 1960. Grace and Victor Smith finally purchased the home and worked to return some of its original beauty.

Other research done by the Smiths revealed that John B. Foote ran a lumberyard as well as a farm. The house was used as an inn, and the barn used as a cooperage. Most interesting is the belief, founded on some evidence, that the farm was the first to ship apples overseas. Freight boats would carry the freshly picked produce down the Hudson River to the port of New York, where ocean-going ships would take them to foreign lands. Grace, a teacher in the Catskill school system, undertook intensive research on the entire Jefferson area.

For many years during the Smith family's nearly-40-year tenure, the house was known as Fiddler's Green. The Smiths placed the house on the Greene County Historical Register using that nomenclature. Victor, a banker and veteran of World War II, enjoyed the British legend of Fiddler's Green, a place between heaven and hell where old soldiers rest in peace after their demise. Their children remember that a family outing would end when

"Dad said, 'Time to go to Fiddler's Green!'" Victor died in the 1990s and Grace in 2001.

Mr. Mack Schlefer, a pianist for the New York City Ballet, purchased the property in January 2001. He returned to the historic name of the Grant/Foote House in order to maintain centuries-old accuracy, and is restoring the house with great attention to architectural and historical detail. During ongoing major reconstruction, several antique items of interest have been uncovered. Beneath a porch in need of rebuilding, a zinc stencil was discovered. Used to brand fruit boxes with "J. B. Foote," the stencil provided historic evidence of Mr. Foote's commercial activities. A piece of hand-painted wallpaper—probably dating to the 1920s and uncovered when kitchen renovations were undertaken—is now framed and hangs in that area. Continuing research also has led him to an increasingly accurate understanding of life in this house and in the Jefferson area from the early 19th century to the 21st.

LITTLE RED SCHOOLHOUSE

Built in 1832–1833 by Peter and Jan Van Vechten on land they owned, this schoolhouse was erected to replace an earlier building—which had been sold to the highest bidder for the princely sum of $13. Oral tradition has it that the first school in the Jefferson area was built on a grassy knoll by the south side of Snake Road with a ravine near that wooded spot.

There the sons of Teunis Van Vecten were taught to read and write. From June 1771 to December 1772, John McRobert was teacher for "six gallons of rum for two years." Rum was, of course, the drink of choice in colonial times. In 1812 an act was passed to establish common schools. Jefferson's first district #11 came into existence on February 23, 1814. According to school records, there were 50 children in the area, with 25 attending school.

On the January 28, 1833, according to school records, Abner Austin, a landholder of large acreage throughout the Jefferson area moderated a school meeting called for the purpose of auctioning off the old school. He succeeded in getting a bid of $13. Daniel Crane, a resident of district #11 in the town of Catskill, with a building committee of three decided that a new school, 32 feet by 22 feet, should be erected with a "good, substantial hemlock frame or timber of as good quality." It was to be "covered with good shingles, enclosed with good merchantable siding not exceeding six inches to the weather." Some other requirements called for a one-and-a-quarter-inch spruce plank floor, and eight windows, each containing 24 panes, with shutters. The building was to be in-filled with brick and erected on a foundation of good stone wall, one foot under and two feet above the ground, at least 18 inches thick and painted 18 inches from the sill down.

By 1882, attendance had risen in this "newer" building to 38 (the child population was 77). The teacher was paid $8 a week. Between 1833 and 1948, hundreds of children learned their ABCs in this rare surviving example of early-19th-century revival schoolhouse architecture. A high level of integrity remains in terms of scale, form, exterior construction, and interior design, with the stage—that is, the teacher's platform—still intact.

This red-painted wood structure is an excellent example of the type of one-room educational school that serviced small rural agricultural communities. Simple mid-19th-century alterations had been recommended by lmater educational reform movements to improve rural school districts and were carried out here. For more than 105 years of its 170-year existence, children were in attendance. Modern pupils, transported to larger, newer schools in yellow buses, are reminded of their ancestors' days of learning.

Today the building serves as a meeting place for the community, for outings and local programs, and as the official voting location for the residents of Jefferson Heights.

HILL/TANNENBAUM HOUSE

Gaslights on the front lawn of this beautiful home reflect the antiquity of the building, as do the slate hip roof, the four chimneys, and the attached wood shed. A full brick-lined basement supports the wood-framed two-story house. The large interior Georgian center hallway, the wide floorboards throughout, the eight working fireplaces, and the dining room's original French crystal chandelier provide an aura of historic splendor.

A handsome 16-by-31-foot formal living room dominates the southern section of the house. The exterior symmetrical five-bay federal front is complemented by a large porch. According to the present owners, that porch was constructed when the house was built.

Another fascinating feature of the property is the extra-large greenhouse located in the rear of the main house. Graced by two exceptionally large glass windows, it was built at the same time as the main house and is attached to next-door neighbor, A. Cooke Hull's barn. It is probable that these friends or cousins—Hill, builder of this house, and Hull, owner of next door—made some agreement at the time Hill gave or sold Hull some land. No demolition of these structures can ever be carried out. Historically, the greenhouse was most likely used for farm equipment, years later sharing the space with the new Tin Lizzie contraptions when the automobile appeared. Today it can easily house two cars, leaving plenty of space for other equipment. Whatever its use, it has stood for over 150 years. As one current owner recently said: "Everything is historic here."

Some evidence suggests that this was the first house in Catskill to boast an indoor bathroom. And while the home is furnished with period antiques in keeping with its heritage and that of the surrounding area, modernization of the large country kitchen and the two baths has made the residence ideally livable. Built circa 1842, the house was originally occupied by Frederick Hill, the first cashier of the Tanners Bank. He passed the property to his grandson, also Frederick Hill, through his attorney and trustee, Emory A. Chase. Although it is rumored that Mabel Elliot ran a boardinghouse with gaslit chandeliers here in 1906, other descendants after Frederick's death gained title through trustee and well-known attorney Howard C. Wilbur. Accordingly, it remained in the Hill family, occupied by another Frederick Hill and his wife, Katherine, beginning in 1925. When Katherine died, circa 1930, Frederick remained there until his death on March 4, 1952. The Hill family, therefore, had dwelled in their stately house for more than 110 years. Then it was conveyed to Minetta Close. Within a year she sold to Carlos Dunn, Jr., and his wife, Nancy. They raised two young sons, who, as adults, have also purchased historically

significant houses. Carlos owned and operated Dunn Builder Supplies—which until 2008 was actively owned and managed by his son, Steven.

In 1969 the Dunns conveyed the house to Richard and Sybil Tannenbaum. Richard is a well-known pharmacist who for years has owned and operated a pharmacy in the Jefferson Heights area. Sybil is active in the community as a leader, and for several years has been head of volunteers at the Thomas Cole Cedar Grove National Historic Site. The Tannenbaums brought up their three sons, now adults, in this house. Mark, a West Hartford, Connecticut, businessman-musician; Keith, a chef in Steamboat Springs, Colorado; and Matt, a pathologist with a specialty in hematology in Idaho Falls, Idaho, provide their parents with varied and enjoyable vacation locales. Between visits they continue to enhance and maintain the elegant historical legacy of their family home.

KING HOUSE

This old landmark is an interesting mixture of Federal and Victorian Italianate Hudson River Bracketed styles. This combination belies the fact that it was first constructed circa 1790. At that time the north end provided the entrance to a farmhouse. In 1850 the Honorable Rufus King changed the location of the entrance and erected the three-story bay windows and cupola at the south end, turning the building into an elegant home. Three marble fireplaces, plaster moldings, sconces, medallions, and the original wide-board flooring grace the interior, which is foreshadowed by the beautiful walnut exterior entrance doors.

Rufus King is a former U.S. congressman after whom King Street is named. He was also a presidential elector for Ulysses S. Grant, and one of the first directors of the reincorporated Tanners National Bank. After his death on September 13, 1890, he was interred in Catskill's Thompson Street Cemetery, where his headstone can still be seen today.

The house was left to his wife, Lucia, who died in 1894. Nieces inherited the property, living there for many years before moving to Albany and leaving it unoccupied for 35 years. Older native Catskill residents remember it as the Haunted House on Chestnut Hill.

Dubois/Fray/Pouyat House

This beautifully maintained late-19th-century Victorian house was constructed of wood clapboards in 1882 by William Larremore Dubois in a landscape abounding with trees and variegated foliage. Built with a classic Georgian interior, it originally had an exterior Italianate mansard roof. Little of the Italianate remains, however, because that roof burned in 1922. It was skillfully replaced with a hip roof and two wide dormers, one each on the east and west side. Alterations made in 1929 and 1930 were designed by Keefe Architects, renowned for their Catskill Savings Bank and Catskill Middle School buildings. The interior was modified by a handsome enclosed porch on the southeastern side with a balustrade topping this one-story piazza. Currently, two giant blue spruce guard each side of the front entrance, providing a landmark for the stunning home.

According to tradition, Dubois, owner and operator of the first and oldest drugstore in New York state, purchased the property for his house from Minerva Congdon on May 1, 1882. By that time he'd been partnered with Benjamin Wey for almost 20 years, their business association stretching back to 1863. Wey's grandfather, Dr. Thomas O'Hara Croswell, had established his Catskill drug business in 1793. Some competitive evidence, however, purports that a Samuel Gale had opened an apothecary shop in Vanderheyden, now Troy, in 1787, which later developed into a large wholesale drug establishment, John L. Thomson Son & Co. That the Catskill drugstore was the second-oldest business established in the Village of Catskill is not disputed. The *Catskill Recorder*, the first publication, took precedence by only a few months.

In 1822 the Catskill store was moved from the east to the west side of Main Street and so remained throughout the 65 years of Dubois' management into the 90th year of his active life. In this house his family celebrated that birthday with a small dinner party. Known as the "Grand Old Man from Catskill" to the New York State Pharmaceutical Association, he was congratulated by many out-of-town colleagues at their convention in August 1928—his birthday was August 25—which he had attended, and was feted in his own house by many hometown admirers. Less than a year later, on May 3, 1929, he passed on.

The funeral was held in this house with the rector, Reverend William E. Howe of St. Luke's Episcopal Church, officiating. Dubois had been a lifelong member of St. Luke's, a vestryman, a warden, and a Sunday School superintendent. Although he had never been active politically, he had served on the board of education and as a village trustee. At the time of his death he was president of the Jefferson Rural Cemetery Association.

His dedication to his business was legendary. One eulogy from the Pharmaceutical Association decried the changes in drugstores: "In olden days large quantities of snuff . . . were sold [by Dubois] and the community was 'up to snuff' . . . suffered but little with colds in the head," "In olden days the Dubois drugstore supplied the veterinary doctors with tincture aconite for fever, laudanum for colic, horse balls as a physic, tartar emetic against worms . . ."; "The old family doctor used to come to the drugstore to have his saddlebag filled with the different remedies."

The letterhead of his stone reads: "Wm L. Dubois Druggist, Wholesale and Retail Dealer in Drugs and Medicines; Acids, Dye Stuffs, Paints, Oils; Perfumery, Toilet Articles, Etc. Sole Agent for Huyler's Candies." Said one mourner: "How . . . unassuming! He simply styles himself 'druggist' though he was a 'pharmacist' with two state licenses."

His son, James Mortimer, became owner of both the house and the business. In the mid-1970s a young optometrist, Damon Pouyat, purchased the practice of "Chip" Hallenbeck and opened state-of-the-art offices on Main Street. He and his wife purchased the house, then known as the Fray home. They brought up their sons, Scott, now an optometrist in Illinois, and Christopher, now a realtor in the South. For 33 years the integrity and beauty of this historic landmark has been maintained.

CALEB ATWATER DAY HOUSE

The land on which this house is located was originally part of the Lindsay Patent acquired by George Charles, the lieutenant governor of the Province of New York in 1741, 1766, and 1773. This piece of land was sold to J. Day in 1811; he built a simple two-room structure with side roof gables on a stone foundation with no basement. Mr. Day was attorney for and secretary of the Catskill Mountain House Association.

Up to the turn of the 20th century, several additions and a basement resulted in front rooms, front gables, and a central hall to produce today's beautiful, simple house. The Victorian porch was added before 1925.

The three interior chimneys, the stone fireplace mantels, and the original floorboards remain, as does the bluestone basement. Of special note is the antique original three-seated privy. In fact, this is one of only two Catskill Village houses with a surviving privy, the other being the Thomas Cole Cedar Grove Historic Site.

The Caleb Atwater Day House also boasts the original carriage house and grain bins. A chain-link fence surrounds the property, as does a bluestone patio.

Below: The original three-seated privy.

Gloria Dei Episcopal Church

According to records kept by Dr. Charles H. Chubb, monthly worship services were held in Palenville homes from 1853 to 1878. Then, in 1878, the decision was made to raise money for building a sanctuary. Ground was cleared of underbrush in 1879. Loose stones, mostly cobblestones, were dug up to be used with cut native quarry stones for the walls. Pointed arches above the windows and doors are of these quarry stones. A New York City architect, William H. Day, was responsible for the lovely quaint church.

During construction of this Gothic-style structure, services were held in a temporary wooden building about which is recorded, "Delightful was the task of hiding its roughness with hemlock and laurel, and decorating this chancel with flowers, mosses and ferns."

From 1880 to 1885 the chimney and the arches of the sanctuary window took form. Cut stones to make the jambs of the large west window were donated by a resident of Malden, "the more appreciated because he was a methodist." Rafters were set, and a "good friend offered the funds necessary to put on the slate roof." Behind the altar, a hand carving by Rufus Smith, a local artisan at the time the church was built, beautified the space. Open beams at the roof line and four small dormer windows allowed for a more spacious feeling in the diminutive structure.

In the winter of 1880 an organ was presented by the Trinity Church of Saugerties. Piece by piece the precious furniture was acquired. Rustic benches and other fixtures were transferred from the temporary church, and on special Sundays the tradition of decorating with flowers was continued. The bell was mounted. A solid oak door made by a communicant of the church was installed. An altar cloth and the lectern hanging were sewed, the handiwork of a lady who said she "loved every stone in the church." Dedicated on September 20, 1885, the church recorded the total cost at about $5,000. Today, serving the spiritual needs of the community, this beautiful stone building still stands in its quiet setting of tall evergreen trees at the foot of the Catskill Mountains.

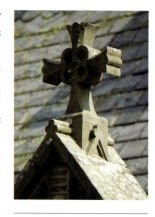

Detail of stone cross over the front entrance.

Christ Presbyterian Church

The historical Presbyterian church, dissolved in November 1997 by the Albany Presbytery, has been a landmark in the Village of Catskill since 1808 when construction was begun. Having served the religious life of thousands of Catskill residents, this church still has a lingering impact on the community. Its Greek Revival style was skillfully blended with the Federal. Six 30-foot-high fluted classical Corinthian columns, created at the same time and by the same factory that manufactured those of the Catskill Mountain House, dominate the front façade. Charles Beach, one major owner of the famous hostelry and a member of the Presbyterian church, donated the columns.

On February 7, 1803, an organizational meeting was held with the association to be known as Christ's Church of Catskill. This group met at the Academy, a building where court was held west of the present jail site. Trustees were elected to bear the expense of support, their fees based on the preceding year's assessment. For the first five years this Presbyterian Society, as they were commonly called, continued meeting at the Academy Courthouse.

The first construction, started in 1808, served as the central part of the church for more than 190 years. Modeled in the style of that time, the square auditorium held boxed family pews with galleries along the side. The narrow elevated pulpit allowed for a clear and uninterrupted view of the speaker. Thirty-nine years later, the interior of the church underwent some modifications, but the exterior remained unchanged until 1853, when the original clapboard structure was significantly enlarged and remodeled. Included was a steeple crowning the structure, which one year later succumbed to heavy fire caused by a lightening strike.

Ground was donated by Thomas Thomson, as was the alley leading from Main Street up to the church. When the church was built, Franklin Street, on which it is located, did not yet exist. So the grass-lined alley, now called Howard Street, was the easiest access to the church. Built above the noise, clutter, and commercialism of Main Street, the church could maintain its seclusion.

The 1826 addition, attached to the church by a passageway, was used for meetings, for Sunday school, for church suppers, for winter services, and for other religious activities. Purchased for use as a private home in 2005, the addition was detached from the original church. Installed in the church in 1897 was a prestigious pipe organ given by Helen Mackey to honor her parents, Ebenezer and Ann Mackey.

With changing times and decreasing attendance, the necessary dissolution was carried out in November 1997. Documents and church papers are held for posterity in the archives of the Albany Presbytery. Major restorations have been undertaken by three owners since that time; the most extensive, beginning in 2006, has been undertaken by its present owners: the buildings, now separated, are two unique houses, and the tower that replaced the steeple has been strengthened structurally under the supervision of Dimensions North's owner, Richard Rappleyea, a professional in historic restorations.

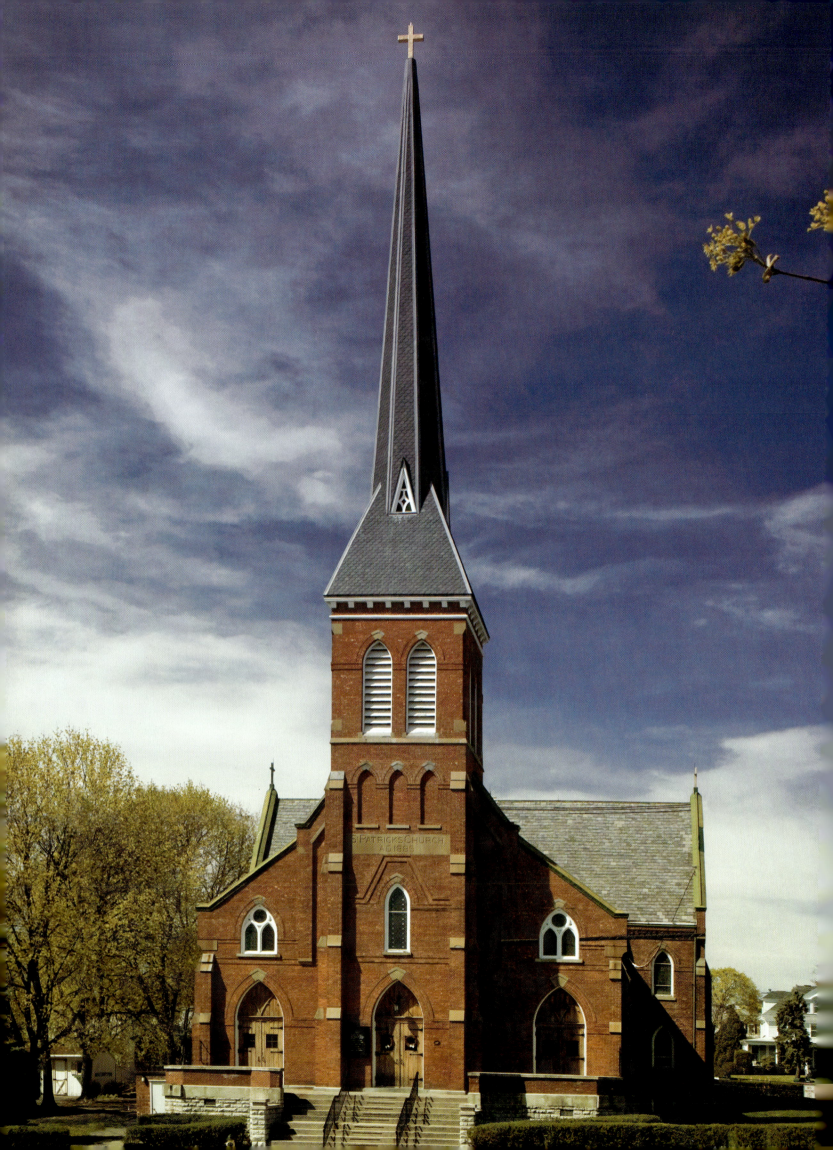

St. Patrick's Church

During the summer of 1853, the Catholic church was established at Catskill. This came about through the efforts of Hudson's Reverend Father Howard. He and his successor, Father Sullivan, would make the weekly journey to Catskill to celebrate Mass. At that time the congregation would gather for Mass in a building on William Street.

Father Myers was the first pastor to reside at Catskill. Father Gratten succeeded him, serving from 1859 to 1869, when Father O'Driscoll—who was instrumental in the construction of the original St. Bridget's Church in nearby Leeds—became pastor. Upon his death in 1884, Father William J. Finneran was appointed to succeed him.

This restrained high-Victorian Gothic-style stately church, with its more than 130-foot-long steeple, was erected in 1885 under the supervision of Father Finneran. The cornerstone for St. Patrick's was laid on August 23, 1885, and the first Sunday Mass was celebrated on April 25, 1886. At that time the location was isolated: horse-drawn carts stood in the field where the rectory is now located. Barely four years after the erection of the church building, Father Finneran embarked upon the creation of a parish school, St. Patrick's Academy, which survived in different forms at different locations until it was closed by the Albany Diocese at the end of the 2006–2007 school year.

While Father Finneran could be eminently proud of the achievements during his pastorate, he was "frail in body" and was "soon called to lay down the work," passing away in April 1900, according to Greene County historian Jessie Van Vechten Vedder in her 1928 work *Historic Catskill*. His successor was Father William Fitzgerald, who supervised the construction of the rectory, which sits next to the church at the corner of Spring and Bridge streets.

Father Fitzgerald served until 1918, replaced by Father James C. Carey (1918–1921). He was succeeded in turn by Father Cox (1921–1925). The next pastor was Father John Smith, who brought the parish school through its first two crises. He served from 1925 until his death in 1946. The list of pastors goes on, each shepherding both the parish church and the parish school through expansion and change, a total of six—including two monsignors—between 1946 and 1971.

The next pastor of St. Patrick's was Father John Murphy, who served from 1971 until his retirement in 2005. During his tenure Father John saw the parish through many struggles, but even more accomplishments. He oversaw restoration and rededication of the elegant church building, and expansion of the parish school, adding a full-day kindergarten, a move to the former parish high school building, and the addition of grades seven and eight in the expanded space. He was also there to calm the parishioners and oversee repairs after a lightning strike threatened to destroy the church building itself.

The steeple of St. Patrick's Church contains a large projecting square central lancet tower, with a pair of lancet-louvered openings under the denticulate cornice of the tall spire, and is topped by a huge metal cross. That cross was struck by lightning on May 6, 1995. A construction detail that seemed unusual before the lightning strike, a full barrier of brick between the side of the steeple and the main structure of the church building proper, is what saved St. Patrick's itself from destruction that day, confining the ensuing fire to the steeple structure itself.

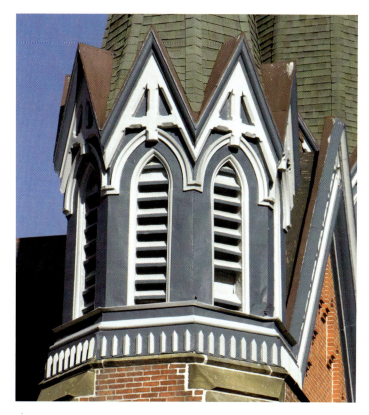

Careful planning and construction work by communicants, friends, and the parish's popular long-term priest and pastor, Father John Murphy, replaced the steeple, maintaining its former grace and elegance. During the period of reconstruction, all religious services were transferred to the parish's "summer tourist church" in nearby Leeds, St. Bridget's, now closed after a minor electrical fire in that building.

The wood entrances and the beautiful Gothic stained-glass windows of St. Patrick's foretell the elegant interior renovation, which is continually maintained.

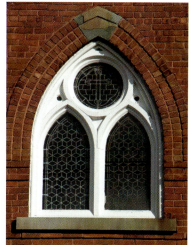

Above: Detail of lancet-louvered opening under the denticulate cornice.

Right: View of the Gothic stained-glass window.

ST. LUKE'S EPISCOPAL CHURCH

St. Luke's Church, constructed between 1893 and 1899, houses the oldest church organization in Catskill, started in 1801. Before they had their own church building, the congregation held services in a schoolhouse located on Thompson Street. In 1803, construction of the first church in the Village of Catskill provided the fledgling flock with their first true house of worship. This new building, constructed of brick, was located near the Catskill Creek, on a dirt road that would soon be formally named Church Street. It was in this first church that artist Thomas Cole and his wife, Maria, were communicants.

Unfortunately, on September 11, 1839, that building was destroyed by fire. The plans for the replacement building were drawn up quickly by artist Cole (in addition to being a parishioner he was also on the building committee). The replacement church, built on the original site, was consecrated on June 10, 1841. Fourteen years later, in 1855, that building, too, was damaged by fire. In the rebuilding of the structure, the artistic details that Cole had lent to the building were lost. In June 1877, fire destroyed much of the church.

Construction of the present church was mentioned in minutes of the vestry on November 9, 1891. During the early 1890s, when the congregation decided to build anew, this time on William Street, the Cole children made a special donation: the stained-glass window that sits above the altar, a memorial to their parents. The other stained-glass windows were memorials as well: J. Atwater Cooke donated the rose window in the front of the church, in memory of his parents. The side windows were memorials to Mrs. E. D. Boyd and C. C. W. Cleveland.

Henry Congdon, a well-known architect of the era, was hired to design the new church building, to be constructed of limestone. This new St. Luke's would become the only Richardsonian-style church in Greene County. The huge limestone blocks, mined in builder George Holdridge's quarry just outside of Catskill, required 50 horses to back down the William Street hill, their load behind them. This feat brought out Catskill crowds to cheer at the unusual parade. The construction of St. Luke's cost $35,000. Holdridge bought the old St. Luke's for $2,700.

The beautiful stained-glass windows, the oak and brass chancel rail, and the Tennessee marble altar provide an aura of solemnity and splendor. With the first service held on June 6, 1899, the dedication ceremonies of the new church spanned the first week of June.

The massive church maintains its original dimensions of 225 by 50 feet. The outside height of the nave is 48 feet, but its overall height to the peak of the spire is 107½ feet. Attached is a two-story parish house of 70 feet by 46½ feet. The original was torn down in the late 1920s and a new one (the present one) was built in 1930.

Many community groups have used the facilities of St. Luke's, including "Big Book," New Leaf Beginner, and Al-Anon.

Opposite: View of the memorial window dedicated to Thomas and Maria Cole.

THE LEEDS REFORMED CHURCH

This early-19th-century stone Reformed church in Leeds reflects its memorable past. The first Reformed church of Old Katskill was erected in 1732 on a hill west of Leeds, perhaps a half mile from the present church. The Reverend Michael Weiss served both Leeds and "Kocksackey" (Coxsackie) for 30 "Sabbaths" a year, preaching in Dutch at Katskill. Similarly, 22 Dutch sermons were expected in Kocksackey. According to Ruth Vedder Schmidt's history of the church, Weiss was to receive each year £50, a residence, a garden, firewood, a horse, a saddle, and a bridle. There was only one extra perk given: if the horse died, he was loaned another. Understandably, the good reverend resigned after four winters. No one filled his position for 17 years, until Johannes Schuneman preached his first sermon. The Reverend Schuneman remained for 40 years.

The descendant of this first church was erected by 1818. The replacement was constructed on a rock at its present location in Leeds. The land was donated by the son of Johannes Schuneman. Stone, quarried on the Rouse farm near Green Lake, was hauled by farmer and oxen to the building site. Foundation stones were laid just before "the year without a summer" arrived, when ice and snow made their presence felt in every single month! Perseverance and determination, however, were victorious. On July 4, 1818, patriotic services rang out in the yet-unfinished church.

The church had yet to boast its graceful spire, a later addition. Ms. Schmidt relates that the "floor was uncarpeted, the seats without cushions, the pews of which formed a box stall with small door openings into aisles on each side of the church. The pulpit resembled a huge barrel with spiderlike legs, was reached by a short and narrow stairway, and above the pulpit was a sounding board."

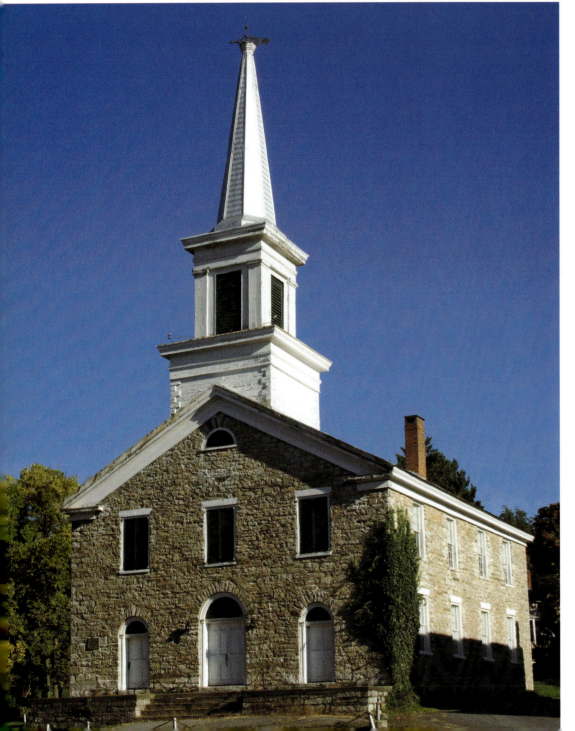

Originally the gallery, still in use today, was entered by means of crooked stairways at both ends. There, the tiers of pews were first reserved for slaves. Later, the last two rows in the body of the church served that purpose. Four windows in the north end of the church have been closed up, but the building has maintained much of its original integrity.

The present lighting replaces the candles and candlesticks of an earlier era. Heating the edifice evolved through many steps. Originally, foot stoves were filled with hot coals. These were replaced by a single box stove on long iron legs, which was in turn replaced by two large box stoves with pipe running the entire length of the church. Next, globe stoves and coal stoves made their appearances in the back corners. Today, propane gas has finally brought the system into modern times.

Originally, stone steps ran the full length of the church beneath the three entrance doors. When autos came into vogue, flagstone was placed on these so that the cars could approach from either end and families could discharge easily. Finally, despite several strong objections, a more formal raised platform with center steps was built. Rocks encase its sides.

When the church was constructed two pews faced each other. The space between, closed by a small door, helped to maintain a semblance of warmth. Each family paid for its own "set" of pews. Even after the pews were rearranged, all to face in the same direction, the practice of payment —now for two pews—continued for years. Objections soon became hotter than any heat put out by those antique foot stoves! The objectors left, forming the beginning of the Leeds Methodist Church. The practice of pew payment no longer exists, though research has not revealed when the custom ended.

Sunday school classes were held in the pews. Festivals, much like today's church suppers, and other special religious activities were crowded. When the Madison area of Leeds became a manufacturing center, mills churned out products sought by thousands. Church pews filled with worshippers not only from Leeds but also from towns throughout Greene County. With the closing of the mills, however, gone were those days and those extra worshippers.

On the front grounds of the church, an old mill stone has been incorporated into a memorial to the men and women of Leeds who served in World War II. Mindful of a past era, the faithful, hardworking members have helped the church survive and prosper in this historic Greene County village.

BEACHVIEW

An excellent example of the high Victorian style, Beachview is one of the last remaining houses belonging to the well-known Beach family that has not been converted into apartments. It is one of several stately brick structures on Liberty Street in Catskill's East Side National Historic District. The house, now in well-preserved condition, contributes to the visual appeal of the wide tree-lined street among other regularly spaced 19th-century Victorian houses uniformly set back along the long expanse of landscape.

The Italianate asymmetrical gable and the cross-gabled roof with a bull's-eye window reflect the 1872 construction date. Similarly, the wide-bracketed eaves and the iron-hooded segmental window crowns demonstrate its original popular style. Step through the paired front door to be awed by 11-foot ceilings, original ornamental plaster crown moldings, medallions, white marble Italianate fireplaces, and oak and cherry patterned floors.

According to 1873 tax rolls, the first occupants of the house were Edgar and Lydia Russel, who sold it to the Beach family in 1874.

J. C. Tallmade, a surrogate judge of Greene County, handcrafted and installed the original woodwork himself. He was the father-in-law of Louis T. Beach, the part-owner of the Catskill Mountain House and brother of one of the major owners, Charles T. Beach. In 1874 Louis T. passed the house and an insurance business, which evolved through the generations, to TB Beach and Sons Insurance. Continuing the business, descendants and generations of the Beach family resided here from 1906 to 1995.

The porch and shutters were removed in the 1950s, as was a front bull's-eye window frame. The latter was filled with cement. The present owners, even realizing the many necessary repairs, purchased the house and have been reviving it ever since.

Sylvester Sage House

The unusual offset gable roof and the dormers on this lovely circa 1890 home give it an air of unique elegance. Two-story bays, one with a tent roof, the pediment dormer, the box-sloped cornice soffit, the decorated frieze, and the open porch with its railing provide additional charm to the home.

The interior boasts the original oak woodwork throughout, as well as brass doorknobs and pocket doors. Transoms sit above every room on the second floor. A tall oak fireplace façade holds an inlaid mirror, its hearth surrounded by imported tiles as well as tile flooring. During the 1950s the kitchen and bathroom were updated.

A skilled architect and builder, Charles Beardsley, constructed this house on Liberty Street in the Village of Catskill. He and his family were the first occupants. Charles Beardsley learned his craft from L. S. and William Smith, who built a considerable part of Catskill. For over 40 years Charles was the head architect for Edwin Lampman, who also had trained with the Smiths. The Beardsley family sold the house in 1895.

Clarence B. Sage, son of Sylvester B. Sage, who was Greene County's representative to the New York State Assembly in 1897 and 1898, purchased this house in 1901. It is plausible that he and his wife, Augusta V. V. Abreet, of Catskill, were renting before the purchase.

After arriving in Catskill, where Clarence was born in 1876, the Sage family first owned a grocery, then later a carriage business. Clarence joined his father in Sage's Carriage Repository, a retail and wholesale business reported to be the largest of this kind between Albany and New York City. In addition to carriages, all types of accessories of the trade were also sold. The firm manufactured some of the accessories in Catskill, keeping several workers employed year-round. After his father's death Clarence carried on the family business, and was also involved with his uncle, a coal dealer in Catskill.

During February 1926, Clarence died at the early age of 50, leaving his wife and two daughters. The popular Catskill man's funeral was held at home. Sadness arrived here again, when during April 1927 29-year-old daughter Virginia passed away.

Two months later a joyous event took place in this house. Daughter Mary Alice was married to George Madison Reaves of Louisiana. The bride wore white satin, and a veil covered with orange blossoms. Piano and violin music filled the rooms.

Widow Augusta continued to live in this house, and after her death, other family members did as well. Shelby Sage Reaves, administrator of Mary Alice's estate, sold the Clarence Sage house in 1985, ending 84 years of Sage family ownership.

Above: Sage's Carriage Repository on Main Street.

WALTON VAN LOAN HOUSE

Sited on a street of high-style 19th-century homes, the Walton Van Loan House boasts a spectacular view of the Hudson River, with the castlelike Olana soaring atop the hills beyond the water. Built in 1863–1864 by Walton Van Loan on a ridge of the Hudson River's west bank, this two-story stucco house has a shallow hipped roof and a three-bay wide rectangular main block. The front of the building has a door set to the right of double windows. This area contains a side entrance hall, a parlor, a sitting room, and a diminutive library.

A smaller recessed block, encompassing an attractively shaped dining room in front of a well-designed kitchen, completes the south end. In the 1990s owners James Ryan, the executive director of Olana State Historic Site, and his partner, David Seamon, a professor of architecture, restored the interior to its original Victorian splendor. In addition to making cosmetic improvements, they searched for and found a Victorian fireplace and mantel to replace the modern mirrored wall and fireplace that earlier habitants had preferred.

The enormously popular bracketed style was used in construction, the brackets sitting under the projecting eaves. This modification of the classical rectangular shape made for a highly picturesque building. Originally sheathed in either board and batten or flat horizontal board, it was covered with stucco around 1914. The side porch was added to the house in 1998. One of the owners at that time wrote: "The column and half columns of this porch were rescued from an 1870s Gothic Revival house in Hudson, NY." Richard Rappleyea of Dimensions North ensured that the columns, brackets, and roof pitch echoed similar features of the early entry porch and front bay.

Van Loan was born in New York City on January 8, 1834, to Matthew Dies Van Loan and Julia Thompson, both originally from Catskill. Matthew Van Loan was a pioneer in photography. When the family lived in Washington, D.C., he improved on the daguerreotype process and was famous for his daguerreotypes of Henry Clay and the aged Dolly Madison. Walton, at the same time, was a page boy in Congress from 1846 to 1850. By the 1850s Matthew had moved to California. The family followed but in 1856, Walton returned with his mother and brother to Catskill. There he purchased part ownership of Van Gorden's News Shop and Bookstore on Main Street and for the next 22 years was involved in that business.

In 1874 he married Lucy Beach, a native of Michigan. The wedding took place at the Catskill Mountain House. In attendance were Mr. and Mrs. C. L. Beach, the Reverend and Mrs. Horton, and many other socialites. In 1879 Van Loan published the first of his *Van Loan's Catskill Mountain Guide* booklets with "Bird's-Eye View" maps of the Catskill region surveyed and drawn by him. Perhaps he transferred his experiences from his earlier transient existence to his books: during the last quarter of the 19th century he published some 39,000 guidebooks and 50,000 maps of the Catskills. When he died in 1921 at the ripe old age of 87, his obituary proudly stated, "He has been to every peak in the entire range."

CHARLES AND EMILY TROWBRIDGE HOUSE

On February 5, 1998, in his column "Greene County Gleanings," Raymond Beecher recounted the story of the 19th-century firm of Trowbridge and Company, whose founder, Charles Trowbridge, envisioned the potential for a lucrative soap and candle business. At the age of 21 Charles left his birthplace, New Haven, Connecticut, and as part of the "Yankee Invasion" settled in Catskill. Some family history suggests that he moved to Catskill to join his "uncle or brother" in a soap business. In 1829 he wed Emily Scott, who also had been born in Connecticut.

An enterprising young businessman, Charles Trowbridge respected the value of advertising and used it effectively to build a prosperous soap and candle "manufactory." First housed on Main Street, the business was shortly thereafter moved to Broad Street, at what is believed to be the site of the Christian Scientist Church Building. Charles' brother, James, was involved in the business, as were, in later years, his sons. In one ad that announced the move it was declared that the business was "manufacturing mould and dipped candles of all sorts and sizes to suit purchasers. The patronage of the village and its vicinity thus far has been gratefully received—a continuance of the same custom is respectively solicited. Merchants in the country, who have heretofore brought supplies from New York, will be furnished on the most favorable terms."

Toward the end of the 19th century, as gas and electric lighting progressed and the competition from large metropolitan firms increased, the Trowbridges closed down their soap and candle factory. Charles Trowbridge had spent 54 years working effectively in his mercantile career.

Unlike many of his business colleagues, Charles never constructed an elaborate businessman's home, remaining in this simple but lovely house for over 50 years. The Charles and Emily Trowbridge House provides a unique journey into the past. Charles built the house in 1829 for his bride. There they resided, and there they celebrated their 50th wedding anniversary.

The house was inherited by Charles Jr., a Civil War veteran and one of the six Trowbridge children, all of whom, most likely, had been born in the house. It then passed on through the family until early 1995. For over 166 years this same family owned the house and, for most of those years, lived there.

Originally, the front room had a fireplace on the same wall as in the next room. The fireplace extended upstairs to the front bedroom. During the 20th century many improvements were made. In 1931 the metal roof was put on. The electricity and plumbing were updated several years later. Cracks in the living room ceiling, thought to have been caused by blasting at the Thruway construction site, were repaired.

On the exterior the wooden clapboards, the pediment with square windows, the pilasters surrounding the front door, and the stepping stone where family and guests discharged from horse and carriage help complete the story of this historic home.

Left: Advertisement for the Trowbridge & Co. Soap and Candle Manufactory, circa 1871.

JACOB VAN LOAN/WALTER PAGLIANI HOUSE

The original sections of this interesting house date to approximately 1805 and 1815. In 1853 the title of the house went to a Jacob Van Loan. Twenty-five years later, in 1878, the O'Grady family gained title. Generations of the O'Grady family lived there for a full century, until 1978.

Additions were made to the house in 1878, including the front porch. Other Victorian details were carefully added as well. At that time the soffit was extended with spandrel work. Some renovations were undertaken in 1975 and 1993. While these were under way, workers uncovered many antiquated shards of redware, Albany slip, blue-edged creamware, and transfer-type pottery pieces buried 100 feet from the house; about eight to ten inches below ground level.

During the 1993 construction, the 1878 metal roof was restored. Wooden shingles were found under the original metal roof, and the clapboard siding was refurbished. Original-period glass replaced the newer windows. Prerevolutionary brick from a demolished historic house in the Esperance, New York, area was used to rebuild the chimneys in their original style.

Amazingly, despite the fact that they had been removed during the 1878 face-lift, the original doors, trim, stairs, and floors still exist. The transom, once used on the front of the house but eliminated in 1878, was returned to its true location over the original door. Both of these items were found in the basement when a new kitchen extension was constructed.

HOLCOMB/BROOKS HOMESTEAD

Much of the history of this wood-framed house appears nonexistent, but local lore suggests that it is one of the oldest houses in town. Through the decades it has served as a general store, a hospital, and as doctors' offices before becoming a residence. The barn was the first firehouse in town.

According to the owners, their documents state that the property is marked by an iron pipe set in the ground in the northwest corner of and proceeding southeast on Malden Turnpike to the easterly side of a maple tree. It then proceeds southwest along Woodstock Avenue to an iron pipe before going west.

This wood-frame house as it stands now was probably erected by Chauncey and Emma Goodwin, who received the property in June 1863. Details of any earlier structure built here are not available, although it is believed there was one. This house now includes 15 rooms, two baths, and two fireplaces. An engraved stone on the side of the house was used to climb on one's horse. In the early 1990s restorations were made as electricity was upgraded and a roof replaced.

The next family featured as owners are the Holcombs, represented by Sherwood A. Holcomb, who passed away in 1929, leaving his estate to Frederick W. Holcomb and John Hobart Holcomb. From that time to the present it has been considered the homestead of the Holcombs and their extended families. Descendants often visit this century-old property from their urban areas to relax in the quiet and beauty of the country.

Day & Holt Company

One of the oldest business establishments in Catskill, the Day and Holt Company, had its origins in 1810 when Thomas Burrage Cooke and his brother, Apollos Cooke, started a business just off Catskill's Main Street, near the Catskill Creek. For almost 200 years the history of this business has been convoluted but interesting.

In addition to hardware, the Cooke brothers sold groceries, drugs, and dry goods, making the ancestor of today's Day and Holt Hardware a village general store. Then, just prior to 1817, the Cookes dissolved their commercial partnership and moved their enterprise to the current two-sectioned brick structure—which they built on Main Street in 1817. Apollos acquired the north half of the new building for his general store, and Thomas acquired the south half for a "good line" of hardware. Business was brisk—the recently incorporated village was alive with construction. Thomas provided the ladders, nails, screws, hammers, saws, and other building materials to the continuing influx of carpenters and builders.

From that time forward the hardware firm was in the hands of Thomas and his successors. Thomas worked alone at times, and with a series of four partners at others. He hired John T. Mann as a clerk, but by 1838 the two men had entered the partnership of Mann & Cooke. For a short period Thomas appears to have maintained his place in the business, which he moved to the north side of the building. Mann left in 1843 but repurchased the business in 1855. Just before and during Mann's separation, the enterprise was taken over by two new workers, the Atwater brothers—who promptly decided to compete with each other in different stores on Main Street! A series of other merchants, often splitting and establishing rival businesses, continued this "hardware feud" in Catskill until 1883. Returning to the business after a 12-year hiatus, Mann changed its name to "the Sign of the Key," symbolized by the large wooden key which had hung over a rival business on the opposite side of Main, but that he then hung over his newly acquired door. (The key later hung over the cash register.) During the Civil War

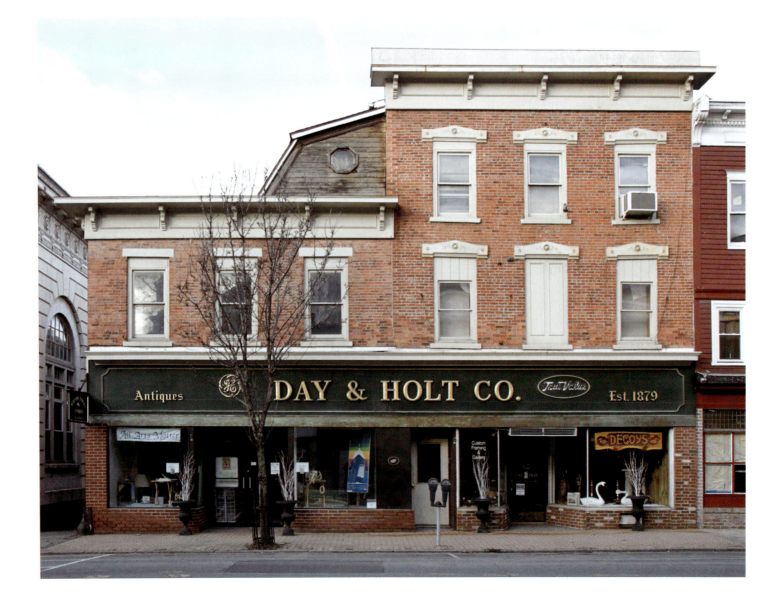

the vast increase in business afforded Mann a wealthy existence in a beautiful entrepreneur's home just north of Catskill.

In 1883, Mann sold the business to two men: Samuel E. Holt and Jeremiah Day. Day was president of the Catskill Savings Bank. Holt, on the other hand, had started in the business in 1874, as a youth. The new owners changed the name to Day and Holt, creating an important identity in Catskill's history for over 130 years. Incorporated in 1904, Day and Holt, one of the earliest surviving corporations in New York state, established itself as the premier hardware store in Catskill. One advertisement announced simply, "We have it, will get it, or it isn't made."

In 1911 Mr. Holt sold his controlling shares to D. Dewitt Hitchcock and Philip L. Walsh, an 11-year employee who, according to his grandson Patrick Walsh, "probably knew the ropes as well—or perhaps better than—anybody." After Philip died in 1926, his widow, Katherine, and son Philip T. Walsh ran the business. They purchased the north half of the double store in 1930 from the estate of Mann's daughter. Widow Katherine separated the two sections of the store, leasing the southern half to the Endicott Johnson Shoe Company, which carried on a business far removed from hardware until 1987, when, once again, Day and Holt occupied both store areas. After Katherine's death, Philip T. operated Day and Holt with his sister, Betty Clark, a kindergarten teacher for the Catskill School District.

The business continued until 2006 under the ownership of Philip T. Walsh's son Patrick, and Patrick's wife, Stephanie. The south section was devoted to Swamp Angel Antiques, while the north housed the hardware business. Then, in September 2006, a surprising story appeared in the *Catskill Daily Mail*. After over 123 years, Day and Holt, the hardware business that had become almost an institution, was closing its doors. Well, "not exactly," some would correct: Swamp River Antiques would move to the north section of the store and the south section would most likely become a rental, as it had been for 50-some years during Katherine Walsh's tenure.

The front of the building has been sandblasted to reveal the original brick and stonework above and below each window. The tragic 1981 fire that destroyed a story and a half of the south end's original three and a half stories may have dimmed in people's memories, but the loss of historical documents is still strongly felt. The Day and Holt Hardware business may be lost, but the historic brick building continues as a landmark on Main Street.

STEVEN DAY HOUSE

If walls could talk, the tales from this home would be awesome! Built in 1791, it is considered to be the oldest house on the east side of Main Street in the Village of Catskill. The solid brick structure, hand-hewn black walnut roof beams, and pegged mortise-and-tenon construction attest to this fact.

Originally, the house had a balcony and a second-floor porch that stretched the length of the structure. In the 1930s, however, the town fathers, fearing danger to passersby—since the porch overhung the sidewalk—ordered that it be torn down.

The first residents, the Steven Day family, ran a private bank in the home prior to 1831—the vault, in fact, is still in place. That bank became the forerunner of the Tanners National Bank, which was organized in May 1831. Other Day families continued in residence, and the local Elks Lodge chapter used the building for a short time as well.

Sadly, the family of George Day suffered two family tragedies while living there. One son, walking the verandah rail one day, fell to his death. Two of his brothers, sailing with their father on the Catskill Creek, had their boat overturn; both were drowned.

Happier days arrived when the families of two physicians purchased the home. In 1932, Dr. M. K. G. Colle and his family lived here. Then, in 1962, Dr. John Myers and his wife, Janet (Deedee), began raising their young family in this historic home, until Dr. Myers passed away in the 1990s. Both doctors held their office hours in the building.

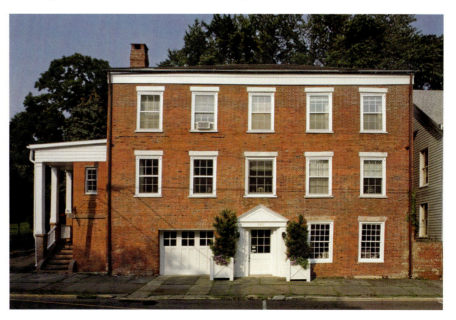

Thorpe-O'Grady Residence

Surrounded by beautiful landscaping, this stately, deep red brick Italianate house boasts two ornate bay windows in each of its two stories. Ornamental stone window heads, similar to one other 19th-century brick house in Catskill, express the builder's ingenuity. Indoor shutters grace these bays. Beamed ceilings and three marble-mantled fireplaces of Italian stone add to the beauty of the interior. The 19th-century basement has been restored to pristine perfection.

The first residents of this home were Douglas and Catherine H. Thorpe, who purchased the property from James and Rachael Stead on April 13, 1892, for the princely sum of $1.00. The Victorian house, sited on the property, was built for Douglas Thorpe in 1891 by George W. Holdridge, an esteemed local contractor and grandfather of George F. Holdridge, secretary of the Catskill Savings Bank. For many years the attractive yellow front door was this house's landmark.

Douglas Thorpe was born in Conesville in 1832. He worked a bit with his smithy father, traveled to Pennsylvania to assist in the construction of a tannery, and then returned to Conesville. He finally relocated to Catskill with his wife and 12-year-old son, William. After William's graduation from Catskill Academy, he became heavily involved with Malcolm and Company, a pioneer manufacturing mill producing fleece-lined products. Beginning office work at $6 a week, William rose to the highly respected wage of $24 per week, much to the pride of his parents, who at that point were aging and in questionable health.

An active Republican, William was elected a trustee of the Village of Catskill in 1898 and, after one year, president of the Village. In addition to being a civic-minded citizen, joining many secular and religious organizations, he was also deemed a "singer of unusual merit," singing at numerous public events.

William attained his greatest success when chosen Greene County judge and surrogate. Presiding over cases for years, he occupied the family home until his death in his mid-80s. His influence on the house is still evident. Originally the house had two small parlors and a center entrance hall, with the staircase rising directly from that hall. He changed this and added a large sleeping porch as well. The judge's sister, Jessie, spent winters with the family while teaching at the Catskill Free Academy.

Judge Thorpe played an important role in community activities. He was especially remembered for his master-of-ceremonies presentation when the Court House Monument to the World War Veterans was erected in 1925. His Memorial Day testimonial to those who served in the Civil, Spanish-American, and First World wars was heralded throughout the County.

During the era of Prohibition, it was alleged that the respected judge issued gun permits to "Legs" Diamond and other notorious gangsters who often used different locales in Greene County as their hideouts. Perhaps they supplied him with the bootleg liquor later found in the wine cellar, a converted cistern.

Including the judge's first sale of the property in 1945, three families have preceded the present owners. On June 7, 1948, Ray Harring, an insurance agent, and his wife, Ethel, bought the property, later conveying it to the popular Main Street department store merchant Jack Lemelman and his wife, Rebecca. They, in turn, sold to Livingston and Virginia Cody in 1955. On October 22, 1969, a Catskill pharmacist and his wife, Julia, purchased the residence, raising their family in this handsome home.

GIORDANO HOUSE

Thought to be the oldest house in the area, this Federal Greek Revival structure has been beautifully restored by the present owners, who prize an antique handwritten deed to the property. The brick-lined house covered in clapboards is situated on the Susquehanna Turnpike of colonial days, now route 23B in Jefferson Heights. It was built circa 1805; an addition was constructed in 1835.

A keeping-room's Rumford fireplace, boasting an original crane, in what is now the dining room, a Count Rumford fireplace in the living room, and wide-board floors grace the interior. A Dutch oven also exists. An enclosed staircase leads from the living room up to a bedroom. In 1946 a kitchen, a patio, and a garage were added to expand the living space. At some point in time a fireplace in the master bedroom was removed to provide space for a closet.

The first occupant was probably a Mr. Benjamin, who placed the original hardware on the doors. He later sold the house to Peter Platt and family of New York City. On March 26, 1835, however, the Platts sold the house to Abner Austin of the Town of Catskill. Abner owned huge tracts of land in the area and his descendants continued to live in the house until 1944, when a tax sale turned it over to Lillian C. DeNyse and Bruce Crane. Within a month of the tax sale the house was purchased by newlyweds Harvey and Muriel Young, who furnished the front hall with antiques, including a 1730s church bench from a New Hampshire family church. Muriel was a music teacher and Harvey an insurance agent. They raised their only son, David, here. David became an educator in New England, where his ancestors had dwelled.

Muriel and Harvey owned the house for a total of 53 years. Then, on July 1, 1988, they sold the property to the present owners. It might be said that these owners stumbled upon the property. New Yorkers who enjoyed their urban life, "Pete" and Betty Giordano decided it would be pleasant to own a weekend vacation home in the country. Reading the *New York Times* one Sunday, they came upon an ad extolling the joys of country living in a house in Cairo, Greene County. Next came the ride upstate, driving around in completely unfamiliar territory. Returning from Cairo to wherever the roads took them, they encountered the "for sale" sign in front of Harvey and Muriel Young's house. The Youngs had recently moved, and had cleared out everything except for a World War II crutch in the attic and dozens of canning jars in the basement.

Stopping, the Giordanos peeked in the windows of the completely bare residence and knew they had found what they were looking for. Meanwhile, neighbors had called the Realtor to alert him to the intruders. Thus they met and the Giordanos decided to telephone with a decision. Back in the city, they made the call to close the deal. Pete's final words to the Realtor were: "By the way, what is the name of that town?"

The year was 1988. Pete was still with the Federal Reserve Bank in New York City. He had been occupied in international banking all his life and would continue a few years more. Betty was a broker with Thomson McKinnon Securities (now Wachovia) and would also continue. So it wasn't until 1992 that they were able to move into their chosen house, refurbishing its antiquity and charisma.

Today the beautiful keystone fan in the front gable foreshadows the elegant antique interior. Since 1978 the house has been on several home tours in the area.

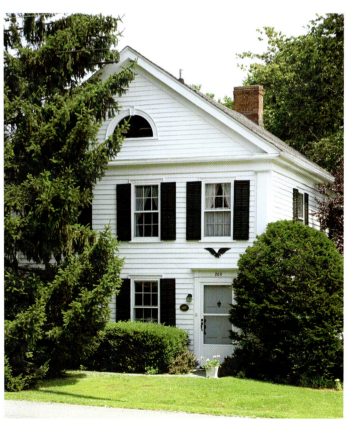

MULBURY HOUSE

In 1846 the Foote and Grant families purchased this property from Eliza Winans. They, in turn, sold it to the Lowe family in 1862. The Lowes are the most likely candidates for those who built the house. Charles H. Lowe and his wife, Esther, paid $400 for the site.

The house remained in the Lowe family for 41 years. On 1903, six Lowe descendants from Mount Vernon, in New York's Westchester County, sold the property to Vernon E. Ford for $1,300. In 1910, Franklin Mulbury, maintenance head at the Catskill Savings Bank, purchased the badly deteriorated house for $1,305 from Vernon Ford's widow, Cornelia. He began restoration of the interior and finished both interior and exterior work in 1912. During some of the restoration period the family used the concrete basement as their living quarters. He and his wife raised two children here, Helen, who became a nurse, and George, who in 1950 opened and operated a retail business in Athens. His son and his daughter-in-law inherited the property in the late 1940s. When George died in 1982, his wife, Ruth, dwelled there, maintaining the architectural integrity of the solid brick house, gardens, and grounds until her passing in the late 1990s.

Out-buildings had been added before 1920 and in that year a garage housed an early automobile. The "L-shaped" wraparound porch covered with old-fashioned flowering vines remained a highlight of the building for many years.

THE McHALE FARMHOUSE

Much of the early history of this residence has been lost over the years. Oral history, however, has it that this was the first farmhouse in the area—and that its first owner was a Dutchman. While it is most likely that the house was built in the later 1700s, the first recorded sale was not until March 17, 1860, when Simon B. Champion sold it to a Mr. Stevens. Stevens, in turn, sold it to the Hodskins family on October 4, 1906. They lived in the house for 40 years. In the 1940s the Post family moved into the farmhouse. Finally, represented by the estate of Etula M. Post, the family sold it to Michael and Katherine McHale on December 30, 1982.

The surrounding farm pastures have long ago given way to the pressures of village expansion. Houses and commercial buildings mask the early agricultural life of the structure, but the original stone foundation still supports the building. Dormers were added in the early 1900s. At that time, also, a metal roof was applied, interior metal ceilings were constructed, and an open front porch was added. Some interior exposed beams and wide-plank wood floors, reminiscent of its Dutch origins, remain as well. The owners continue to undertake interior renovations.

CATSKILL

THE VAN COTT HOUSE

Located on historic Liberty Street in Catskill's East Side National Historic District, this unadorned Victorian house suggests a Greek Revival influence common among many of its neighbors. Constructed of clapboards with entrance to the south of the one bay, the house is conspicuous for its Victorian contemporary dark shade and a delicate porch. Differing from the neighboring mid-19th-century houses, it has two western sleeping porches on the back, one atop the other. Maggie Van Cott had the house built in the 1860s and from it she went forth to energize revival meetings throughout the country. She also used the house as headquarters for her medical endeavors, hoping to heal both the body as well as the spirit.

"She hath done what she could, reads the simple inscription on the Cairo Cemetery monument that marks the resting place of a woman who for 40 years beat the revival circuit, making the name of Maggie Newton Van Cott a household word in the mid-19th century." So wrote Diane Galusha, journalist, in the *Daily Mail* in the November 8, 1976, edition.

Known only as "Mother Maggie" to many of her converts, Van Cott's evangelistic work was done mainly in Greene County, although she traveled throughout the country. Newspapers recorded her revivals in Jefferson (1900), Lebanon Springs (1900), and Ashland (1903). As Maggie aged, it appeared that she became even more dedicated and ventured farther. At the age of 74 she ran a two-week revival in Windham (1904), one in Jefferson, Iowa (1905), at Pittsfield, Massachusetts, and Baltimore, Maryland (1906), and finally at age 89 she held a successful revival in Claverack (1909). The *Windham Journal* described her oratorical style as "more declaratory than argumentative—appealing to passion rather than reason." Bishop Gilhaven noted that "she has done for Christ what has so long been done for antichrist—made women his public helper."

She was the first female licensed to preach in the Methodist Episcopal Church, where much of her revival work originated, and she faced many of her controversies over that licensing. One that raged in 1869 was initiated by the Reverend William Phinney, who proclaimed that she "did not receive sanction of the church's New York General Conference of the Methodist Episcopal Church." Since she was never ordained, she could not conduct sacraments, but according to her obituary in the *Catskill Daily Mail*, she "stormed through the one-horse towns and bustling cities of the east and midwest," and her oratorical magic, which captivated audiences, "brought salvation to an estimated 70,000 converts." Finally, she was licensed by a Stone Ridge minister. An 1872 book by the Reverend John O. Foster describes her evangelical services: "She passed down the aisles and brought in the sinners apparently with no effort, having an almost magical influence on the minds of those with whom she came in contact."

In addition to her spiritual side, Mother Maggie must have had a secular side, for she conducted a cold remedy business out of her house, producing not only the cold remedy Enuf, but also her Frog in the Throat cough lozenges. Her business acumen had most likely come from her early acquaintance with merchandising. Married to a dry goods merchant in New York City, she took over his business in 1848 when he became ill. Female entrepreneurs, especially those in their 20s, were unheard of at that time, but it is likely that the experience provided the skills she needed to continue her lifelong involvement with various industries.

In 1896, after selling the home to May Duncan for the grand sum of $500, Van Cott continued to live with the Duncans for several years before moving to Jefferson Heights to live with her daughter, Mrs John Olney. In 1914, tax records assessed the property at $2,500. In 1928 the house was conveyed to Helena Wiltsie, who raised a family of three children and, after 35 years, sold the property to Salvatore Gangi, a music teacher. In 1969, David Rogers purchased the house and placed it on the Greene County Historical Register.

View of Reed Street, looking east toward the Hudson River, 1903.

TOWN OF COXSACKIE

Anyone looking for a definitive "original" spelling for Coxsackie is completely out of luck: there have been 30 or more spellings, many attempting to transcribe the sound of the Indian name, others attempting to translate it to Dutch or English, even from Dutch to English! The 1662 Bronck deed spelled it Koxhackung, while the Coeymans Patent defined its southern border, being "to the north of a place called by the Indians 'Koxhaexy.'" Attempts to spell it phonetically have yielded variations on "Cooxagy."

Dutch pioneers had been in this area as early as 1652, and Town of Coxsackie was incorporated in 1788 as a division of Albany County. In 1800 the town became part of the newly established Greene County. The land area of this Town was greatly reduced by the later creation of the towns of Durham, Cairo, Greenville, New Baltimore, and Athens, each of which took away a chunk of land from the original, large township. The Village of Coxsackie, which is situated on the bank of the Hudson River, was incorporated in 1867, and the hamlets of Earlton—originally spelled Urlton—and Climax are situated to the west.

From its eastern border on the Hudson River the land rises, meeting a flat fertile area that extends to the base of a high ridge; after, numerous hilly ledges extend to the western border of the town. The lands of Coxsackie fall within several patents granted to early European immigrants in the area. Pieter Bronck and his wife, Hillitje, are acknowledged as the first permanent white settlers. Except for the winter months, they lived on a tract of cleared land that was purchased from the Indians in 1662, and for which Pieter was granted a patent in 1667.

The availability of river transportation and the early turnpikes led to the growth of the hotel business in the area. Farming and its commercial crops were important in development of the town, as was milling, sloop building, and stone quarrying. As time passed, the ice industry, the molding sand industry, the brick industry, and metal foundries also became important to its growth.

The Bronck House
The Greene County Historical Society

The Bronck House itself is only one part of the Bronck Museum complex. Located in the town of Coxsackie, the site is owned and operated by the Greene County Historical Society. The house and ten outbuildings are situated on approximately 18 acres of land, all that remains intact of the 252-plus acres that were deeded on January 13, 1662, by the Mohican Indians to Pieter Bronck (sometimes spelled Bronk). At the time, Pieter was running a tavern and brewery in Beverwyck, which is now the City of Albany.

On June 11, 1667, the governor of New York State confirmed the purchase and granted "Bronck's Patent." The area within the patent was actually larger than the stated acreage because the Dutch only counted cleared land fit for cultivation, not woodland and rocky ridges.

Pieter Bronck cleared the land and in 1663 built a single-room rubble-stone house, which is believed to be the oldest house in the Hudson Valley. The steep single-pitch roof, iron-beam anchors, portholes, casement windows, and other features are characteristic of Dutch houses built in this area during the 17th century. A rubble-stone addition was adjoined to the west wall sometime around the turn of the century. Pieter Bronck, of Scandinavian descent, and his Dutch wife, Helletje Jans, occupied this first dwelling on what would become known as the Bronck farm. Pieter died in 1669, but Helletje continued to run and lease out the farm.

Their son, Jan (John) Bronck, inherited the farm after his mother's death in 1685, but had already built a home for his wife, Commertje Leendertse Conyn, and family in Leeds. Ownership passed to their son, Leendert Bronck, who in 1738 built a house just a few feet north of the rubble-stone structure. The three-story timber-frame building is enclosed with ornamented patterned brickwork and has mouse-toothed parapet gables. Like the earlier house, it also has a steep sloping roof. The hooded porch added to the house in 1792 was later reconstructed. The two dwellings were connected by an enclosed brick passageway.

Leendert Bronck's son, Jan (John) Leendertse Bronck, captain of the militia and a second major in the Revolution, took possession. Jan Leendertse Bronck had only one son, Leonard Bronk (1751–1828), who rose to fame as a soldier, politician, and judge. He was appointed first lieutenant by the convention of New York State in 1777 and 1778, received a similar appointment from Governor George Clinton, and was major of the infantry in 1793. He also was a member of the New York State Senate and Assembly. He served as justice of the peace for Albany County and, in 1800, was appointed the first judge of the court of common pleas, a position he held for many years.

The judge's son, Leonard Bronck, Jr., married Maria Ely. Their daughter, Adelaide Bronck (1843–1918), passed her inheritance not to her surviving husband, Lewis Lampman, but to their son, Leonard Bronck Lampman (see Leonard Warren House, formerly Ely Farm, page 118).

During the late 18th century, a kitchen dependency was erected behind the house to the west, and a New World Dutch barn was erected with a broad thrashing floor and massive grain storage space. The storage area held the wheat that was the family's primary cash crop at that time. In the early 1800s, the Bronck farm was the most valuable single property in the county. With an interest in the new "scientific farming" methods, the family had switched to dairy farming, and by the 1830s had constructed an innovative 13-sided barn. Additional structures also were built during the 19th century.

The farm remained in the family through eight generations, covering 276 years. In 1939, Leonard Bronck Lampman, the last family member to own the farm, donated the 11 structures and surrounding acreage to the Greene County Historical Society. The farm serves as the headquarters for the Society, and on scheduled dates, guided tours are available for visitors to the site, designated as a National Historic Landmark.

Inset: Leonard Bronck Lampman.
Below: Thirteen-sided Dutch barn.

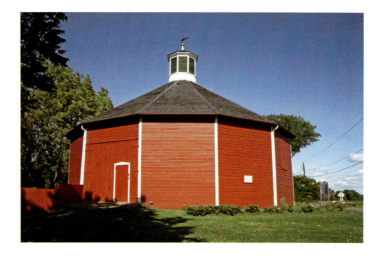

Leonard Bronck Lampman's house, circa 1906.

Raymond Beecher Residence

The Raymond Beecher residence, a wood-framed, Greek Revival–style house, sits atop a rock cliff surrounded by expansive lawns and natural areas that slope down to the west bank of the Hudson River. The two-story, double-chimney home was constructed circa 1899; the barn on the property at a later date. The few houses nearby are situated behind and to the west of the residence.

Scenic Hudson rates the panoramic view that stretches from Four-Mile Point to Little Nutten Hook as one of special merit, with little man-made intrusion. Looking up at the house from the river, the view is impressive as well. It is understandable why Raymond Beecher's parents, Valentine and Maude R. Beecher, chose this as their family residence after a long search for a site along the Hudson River. After the passing of his parents, Raymond Beecher and his late wife, Catharine, took possession and continued to care for the house and property. Maintaining it in excellent condition, Mr. Beecher not long ago had repairs completed on the horse barn that is situated just south of the house.

There have been no additions made to the house since it was constructed by builders Fred Goulde and Charles Duntz. However, the residence was personalized by the Beechers after they purchased the property from the New York Sand and Facing Company in 1939. Valentine Beecher and his son Arthur did most of the work remodeling the house into the Greek Revival style that it displays today. The interior was modified, and the front porch overlooking the river was extended to run the full length of the house. An open staircase and dentil moldings are interior highlights. The plumbing was updated from the cistern system that served the previous tenants, and electricity was installed.

The electricity, however, did not come without cost and tribulation. To reach the property, electric lines had to be strung on poles that were to be placed on a neighbor's property, running along the private right-of-way leading to the house. All seemed well, until the neighbor insisted that before she gave final permission, the Beechers would have to pay for poles and lines to serve her house across the farm fields to the south. An agreement was reached and the electricity installed, and Maude Beecher—who had threatened to leave the primitive living conditions—became more content.

The house was originally built as a caretaker's residence and a boardinghouse for company employees of the New York Sand and Facing Company. At that time, there was a tool house, a dynamite shed, a woodshed, wagon sheds, a three-bay garage, and the horse barn. As superintendent of the company's molding sand bank, George W. Overbaugh and his family were the first to occupy the house. The Overbaughs shared the house with boarders who also were working for the New York Sand and Facing Company.

The present acreage, sold to Annie Bell in 1895, was a section of a large farm owned by Joseph Stephens. Annie Bell and her husband, Thomas, a Scottish immigrant who came to America in 1850, had several enterprises, including the molding sand and ice.

In 1903, the Bells incorporated their various economic enterprises, eventually using the corporate name of the New York Sand and Facing Company.

At one point—the specific date is uncertain—the company constructed a long, high pier on what is now the Beecher property, extending the dock from the Hudson shoreline into deep water. High-quality molding sand was hauled in from surrounding farms using two-wheeled, horse-drawn carts, taken to an overhang platform, and dumped into barges for shipment to customers. It is possible that some of the sand went to the Imperial Facing Mills on Water Street in the Village of Catskill, which Mr. Bell had established in 1880.

In 1897, construction of the Bell icehouse began on the riverbank just north of where the Beecher residence stands today. Ten Broeck Van Orden of Catskill was in charge of the drilling and blasting of the rock cliff that was used as fill for the site. Before the era of modern refrigeration, the need for block ice was constantly increasing; the demand in New York City and other areas led the Bells to almost double the size of their icehouse during the year 1900. The outline of the icehouse foundation can still be seen during dry weather on the western bank of the Hudson River, and the ruins of the brick power engine house remain on the Beecher property. This must have been a bustling spot around the turn of the century, with construction of the house and the businesses running full throttle!

While the Overbaughs were the first to occupy the present house, they were not the first to occupy the present acreage, as there is evidence of an earlier house at the site. There is also evidence that the sloping hillside was inhabited by Native Americans, as a summer fishing camp: tools, flint chips, a few projectile points, and fishing net spools have been found on the property. Many of the articles were made from Flint Mine rock that was "mined" by the Native Americans farther inland in Coxsackie. Mr. Beecher tells of finding various artifacts as a young man when his parents first owned the property.

Above: Valentine and Maude R. Beecher, with children Gladys and Raymond, circa 1918.

COXSACKIE

Leonard Warren House
formerly Ely Farm or Elm Crest Farm

Surrounded by approximately 30 acres of landscaped grounds, the Leonard Warren House sits majestically high on a hill overlooking the Hudson River to the east, and the Catskill Mountains to the west. Prior to 1939, the house was occupied for generations by the prominent Ely, Bronck, and Lampman families. The center section, now the grand entrance with pillars supporting a curved portico topped with a French balcony, is believed to have been built during the 1850s. The south wing was constructed circa 1900–1905. A small farmhouse, believed to have been constructed circa 1805–1812, is incorporated within the north wing.

Dr. John Ely lived and practiced medicine in the town of Greenville from approximately 1797 until serving as surgeon in the War of 1812. Dr. Ely and his family came to Coxsackie after his service in the war; here he continued his medical practice and continued to serve as a New York State assemblyman. The family residence was on Ely Street in the southern end of the village, and it is believed that Dr. Ely never actually lived in the small farmhouse he had constructed on his property. It was possibly used as a farm tenant house. Additional acreage surrounding the farm house was added to the family holdings during the 19th century, increasing the size of what was then known as Ely Farm.

The property was transferred by Dr. Ely to his daughter, Maria, the wife of Leonard Bronck. Remaining in the family, the house and land passed from Maria and Leonard to their daughter, Adelaide, wife of Reverend Lewis Lampman. From 1871 until the early 1900s Adelaide and Lewis resided on Long Island and in New Jersey, where Lewis ministered to his congregations, but they spent summers at the house on the hill. When Adelaide died in 1904 she left the house to their son, Leonard, not to Lewis. The story has been told that Lewis was so angry, he left Ely Farm and stayed at the Bronck house. Reverend Lewis Lampman died in 1918.

Little is known about the operation of Ely Farm itself. It has been said that Leonard Lampman advertised the farm for sale during the 1920s. If this was the case, apparently no deal was completed, because Leonard remained on Ely Farm until his death in 1939. At that time an auction sale was held, and the house and 91 acres were transferred to John O. Yeomans and his wife, Bertha, who called it Elm Crest Farm. Following various sales of acreage by the Yeomans Family, the house and remaining grounds were again auctioned in 1968. At that time it was purchased by the Warren family, who completed extensive restorations during the 1970s.

Inset: Dr. John Ely.

KLINKENBERG

Klinkenberg is situated on approximately three acres of land in the Town of Coxsackie, on the west bank of the Hudson River. The property is surrounded by scattered residences and open land, retaining a rural character. The oldest section of the house dates back to the 1670s and was constructed with stone masonry load-bearing walls. The two-story brick-and-stone section, also with load-bearing walls, was constructed in 1804, followed in 1862 by the clapboard wood-framed section. The builders are unknown. Iron tie-rods characterize the 1804 structure, which boasts four exterior stone chimneys and early 12-over-12 paned sash windows. The interior contains a variety of early woodwork and four authentic Federal-style fireplaces. A three-bay carriage house also occupies the acreage.

Nearby, a former Coast Guard light, some 15 feet tall, sat about 30 feet above the riverbank. The property was purchased by the U.S. government from then-owner George Houghtaling in 1883. Now that land is once again a part of the private property on which Klinkenberg is situated.

When it was established, this Dutch-English farm, known as a bowery in Dutch, consisted of numerous acres that were originally included in the Loonenbergh Patent. The first use of the name Klinkenbergh, which translates as Echo Hill, has been found recorded in a lease dated April 11, 1673, from Mydert Frederickse to Jan Helmsen "of his farm called 'Clinkenbergh.'"

The original stone house was the home for several generations of the Hallenbeck family. Jacob Hallenbeck, baptized in 1684, was the last family member to be in residence. The Hallenbecks welcomed many guests at Klinkenberg, including fellow Tories. The family burying ground is located on a small hill a short distance west of the house. In the 1880s it was reported that the few crude stones were without inscriptions, but church records confirmed that Anna Hallenbeck was buried there in 1711. After the Hallenbecks, the farmstead came into the possession of the Hotaling/Houghtaling family.

Matthias Houghtaling, born circa 1644, was once granted a patent for a large piece of land in the Town of Coxsackie. Six generations later one of his descendants, George Houghtaling, would occupy Klinkenberg, possibly once part of that original land patent. George, born in the early 1800s, must have become a prosperous man, because a lithograph of his residence features his elegant house, a large four- to five-story barn, and numerous outbuildings. The horse and buggy shown sitting on the edge of the river and various water craft indicate the value of river travel to the farmers of that time. Perhaps it was George who built the 1862 wood-framed addition onto the north side of the house.

During 1962, on the 100th anniversary of the clapboard section, Drs. Harold and Isabelle Oaklander took possession and began a long period of restoration to the historic home. These restorations were made with as much authenticity as possible, with advice from Dr. John Mesick, the distinguished restoration architect best known for his extensive work on Thomas Jefferson's main home, Monticello. Today, Klinkenberg's interior still boasts a variety of early woodwork attributable to the three distinctive periods of construction.

Eastern façade with view of the original stone house at right.

COXSACKIE

FOUR MILE POINT
LIGHTHOUSE KEEPER'S COTTAGE

The Keeper's Cottage located on the west bank of the Hudson River sits high on a rock cliff on what is called Paddock's Island, 75 feet above the Hudson River. The name is derived from Laban Paddock, a city of Hudson merchant who had Archibald Doan survey his property in 1821. The following year Paddock and his wife, Elizabeth, sold Four Mile Point Farm, which consisted of 160 acres, two roods, and four perches, to Frederick Barnard of Poughkeepsie.

1824 land records confirm that Barnard held a mortgage for William Jearoms and wife Alida against this large section of land. During February 1831, the Jearoms requested Barnard to release from the mortgaged premises a small section of two acres, two roods, and 25 perches. Later that year the Jearoms sold this small section to the U.S. government for $150.

Due to the treacherous mud flats on the east side of the river, the government had decided to build a lighthouse as a warning beacon to ships traveling between the mud flats and the face of the rock cliff. Congress approved $4,000 toward the land purchase and the erection of a lighthouse and a light keeper residence. One source reports that the government bought an old house and improved it for a "keeper" and family; however, there is government documentation that a contract was signed with master builder Ruel Clapp to construct a dwelling and a stone tower for the light.

The fieldstone house has five rooms. A stone foundation descending the west side of the rock cliff forms a basement under the four northern rooms. A staircase in the center hall gives access to the two upper rooms. A cistern constructed under the southern room can still be accessed through a trapdoor in the current kitchen. A frame addition was attached to the south end, probably in the

1860s. The porch across the front was covered and a small greenhouse room on the southern end was built in more recent years.

The fireplace in the original kitchen was used for cooking meals; in other rooms they were used for heating. The fireplaces have interesting iron mantels that the first private owner believed came from the Netherlands. The keepers who lived here had no central heating, electricity, or plumbing; these conveniences were installed in later years.

The stone lighthouse situated north of the Keeper's Cottage was replaced by an iron tower in 1880. With modernization and automation of lights, there no longer was a need for a light tender at this site. Michael Burke, the last keeper, moved out of the "cottage"

Above: Lighthouse Keeper's cottage, circa early 1930s. (From right) Donald Greene, Debora Greene, and (seated) Harry Reiper.

Opposite: View of the iron lighthouse tower, circa 1930s.

in 1921. Seven years later, the iron tower was torn down and a steel structure placed at water level. In 1931 the house, which was home to various keepers for close to 100 years, was auctioned off via sealed bid.

The winning bid of $1,100 was submitted by Debora (Mrs. Donald) Greene, and in August, the property was transferred to her from the U.S. government. As private owners, Debora and her husband, Donald took on the task of refurbishing the very primitive structure. Using her professional interior decorator skills, Debora designed a new kitchen in the southern room of the stone cottage; the original kitchen became their dining room.

After Donald's and Debora's deaths the Keeper's Cottage came into the possession of their son, Thom Greene, and it is still owned by the Greene family. Unlike the old lighthouse, the Keeper's Cottage remains sturdy and continues its vigil over the Hudson River.

PETER HUBBELL HOUSE

This Greek Revival house was constructed for the Peter Hubbell family by architect and builder Tunis Cochran during 1832 and 1833. The section with the Victorian front bay was constructed in the 1890s while under the ownership of William A. Edwards; the rear upper porches in the 1910s, when Charlotte Fitch was the owner. Three chimneys serve a total of five fireplaces, including the fireplace in the original basement kitchen. The front door opens into a long hall where a staircase leads to the upper level and doors provide entry to the front and back parlors with elaborately carved woodwork. The original flooring of ten-inch-wide white pine contains a rich patina.

Mr. Hubbell was a prosperous businessman in Coxsackie before relocating to Charlestown, Massachusetts. His property ran from this house down to the Hudson River where he operated a brickyard. Unfortunately, he was hurt financially by the panic of 1837, and in 1845 this house was sold to Martin Truesdell in settlement of claims against Hubble. Hubble's wharf, later known as the "stone dock," was sold at about the same time.

In 1848, Judge Anthony Van Bergen, a direct descendant of Martin G. Van Bergen, purchased this house. The Judge and his wife, Clarine, sold their farm in New Baltimore (see Van Bergen-Warren House, page 202), and moved here with their unmarried daughter Maria. The Judge was important in early colonial affairs, and a close friend to President Martin Van Buren. The family settled into the social life of the area and took membership in the Second Reformed Church, then located on the same street. When the Judge died in 1859, he left all of his property to his wife for the remainder of her life; then descending to Maria. Clarine died in 1872, and Maria took her own life a few years later. Maria's brothers sold the property in 1887.

The house passed through several owners until, in 1948, it was purchased by the Whitbeck and Adams families who occupied it for nearly fifty years. In 1997, David Lawler purchased the house situated on a small portion of the original Hubbell property and returned it to a one-family dwelling.

NIGHTINGALE INN

This two-story, wood-framed structure in the hamlet of Earlton sits on two of the original 125 acres of land sold in 1907 to Joseph Karnik, a Czechoslovakian immigrant, and his wife, Anna. The original Nightingale House on this site was destroyed by fire in 1911. The following year the Karniks built a near-duplicate on the same spot. The new boardinghouse, named Nightingale Hall, was completed just as the *Titanic* went down.

Joseph Karnik's granddaughter Julie Karnik Fincke was born in the boardinghouse in 1918 and has told of wonderful times that her family had in the old house, and the many interesting people they encountered. Among these was President Woodrow Wilson, who wired the family in 1917, extending congratulations on the birth of Julie's triplet siblings.

The boardinghouse became a haven for infamous gangsters Al Capone and Jack "Legs" Diamond. It has been reported that Capone's wife and daughters were brought to stay at the Nightingale on many occasions to hide them from rival gangsters. Across the road stood the Nightingale Tavern, also owned by the Karnik family. The tavern was a "hot spot" during Prohibition, with Diamond providing the liquor.

On Sunday afternoons during the summer of 1932, the semifinals of the Best "Voice" of the Catskill Mountains competition were held here. Harry Reiners, a relative of the family and a theater manager for RKO Studios, often brought stage and screen notables such as Lew Ayres, Eddie Cantor, Jimmy Durante, Dorothy Lamour, and Pat O'Brien to stay at the Nightingale and dance in the tavern.

During the 1950s, Nightingale Hall was deeded to Stev-Mar, Inc., and given the name Stev-Mar Lodge. Flyers advertised cool and spacious rooms, and boasted of mountain streams, shady glens, bathing, and pine groves within walking distance. The five-acre lake dug in the 1920s just north of the Nightingale was named Dot's Lake in memory of Joseph Karnik's deceased granddaughter. It was stocked with fish and was available for fishing and boating. The lodge featured square dancing, round dancing, and amateur night. The owners welcomed families with children, advertising that their bar and casino (Nightingale Tavern) were located away from the main house. Perhaps it was during this period that the shutters and the decorative scrollwork on the porch were removed. The interior still retains its original wood moldings and doors, including the pocket doors that lead into the two 17-by-24-foot downstairs rooms.

After Stev-Mar, Inc., sold the property, the house deteriorated as it passed through several different ownerships, until it was purchased in 1999 by Scott McNulty and Neal Fox. The men put much effort into refurbishing the house and rebuilding its reputation. They chose to commemorate part of its original name by christening their incarnation the Nightingale Inn.

HOPEWELL MANOR

This high-quality Victorian house is located within the National Historic District in the Village of Coxsackie, on the west side of Ely Street. The home sits in a dense residential area, with a small front yard bordered by slate flagstone sidewalks. The driveway along the side of the lot extends back to a carriage house/garage. The external highlights of the house include a fan window in the attic area, scrollwork and fluting, the carved design around the windows, and doors resembling gingerbread. Masonry load-bearing walls support the original brick section of the building, and a second-floor wooden bay window projects from the front façade.

While the wood-framed addition at the rear was constructed in the early 1900s, the two-story brick section was built in 1840 by Eli Hunt. It has been said that he was the first occupant, but the property quickly came into the possession of Obadiah Lampman, and it is possible that Hunt built the house for the new Lampman family. On June 5, 1839, Obadiah Lampman, age 22, married Elizabeth Vandenberg. The couple had eight children, the first born in March of 1840. For many years during the latter half of the 19th century, Obadiah was the proprietor of a store at Coxsackie Landing, dealing in staples and fancy dry goods, and advertising everything from groceries to snuffers.

Obadiah's second son, Lewis, served as a Presbyterian minister in parishes on Long Island, in New York and Newark, New Jersey. There, he and his wife, Adelaide Bronck Lampman, raised their family. It is unclear how and why the Coxsackie house passed to Lewis and his wife years before Obadiah's death. We do know that Elizabeth had died in 1889; perhaps Obadiah was infirm, or just did not care to keep the place. At any rate, in 1891 Lewis and Adelaide sold the Coxsackie property to George and Addie Summers.

Less than a year passed before the property changed hands again, this time being transferred to Mark and Miriam Sax. The house remained in the Sax family until 1947. This is the family that added the rear wood-framed section during the early 1900s.

After the Sax family sold the property in 1947, the house passed through four more ownerships, even serving as a nursing home for many years before it was purchased in a deteriorated condition by the Warren family in 1982. Repairs by the Warrens were ongoing for many years. The brick on the oldest section was sandblasted and repointed, and the wood trim repaired and painted. The interior woodwork and the floors were refinished and painted. In 1984, the back woodshed was added. During the late 1990s, a bedroom was converted into a bathroom, an original fireplace was uncovered, the back and front porches were restored, and the garage/carriage house was constructed.

COXSACKIE

HIGH HILL UNITED METHODIST CHURCH

On March 17, 1852, a meeting of the male members of the Congregation of the Methodist Episcopal Church was held at a district schoolhouse in the town of Coxsackie, to elect five trustees. Two days later a meeting was held for the purpose of circulating a petition to solicit funds for building "a house both in size and form that shall be no disgrace to our town." There were 100 subscribers who pledged $697.75. The parcel of land upon which the church still stands was purchased that same year from Moses Weeks and his wife, Jane, for the grand sum of $12.50.

By July 1853 it became necessary for the trustees of High Hill to send a letter to Hiram Brownell (presiding official, along with Moses Mead, at the schoolhouse meeting and one of the first five elected church trustees) requesting that he pay the remainder of his pledge. Perhaps the other trustees were concerned with paying building debts or securing a preacher, since they wrote that the building had been completed for several months.

The plain rectangular church was self-designed and self-built. Although situated in the town of Coxsackie, the surrounding small community straddles the Coxsackie and Athens boundary.

There was extraordinary growth from 1883 through 1885 under Rev. W. W. Shaw. People attended not only from the local community but also from Athens, Leeds, Catskill, Cairo, Sandy Plains, and Earlton. Often, many could not fit into the church.

During 1885 the entrance hall and steeple, which has never had a bell, were added to the building "to appear more like a church." A large chandelier, originally designed as a cluster-type oil fixture, was rewired in 1954 for electricity. That same year, along with electricity, an oil furnace was secured to replace the prior woodstoves and furnace. The simple old stained-glass windows were repaired in 1998.

Older church records were destroyed in a fire but it is well-known that this church was associated with Catskill, and was later on a circuit with Leeds and South Cairo. It has also been connected with St. Paul's Methodist Church and the Federated Church of Athens. In 1968, the Methodist Church and the United Brethren Church combined to form what is now the High Hill United Methodist Church. The High Hill Methodist Church became an independent church in 1993.

VAN DYKE HOUSE

This residence, located in the Village of Coxsackie, has been the home of the Dorpfeld/Kunchala family since 1977. It is believed that the lot on which the residence and barn are situated was once part of the Bronck family's extensive land holdings. The stone east wing of the house is the earliest section, its 18th-century Dutch influence featuring a steep pitched roof and box gutters. It is believed that the addition on the west side was constructed sometime before 1831, and there is evidence that this section also once had a peaked roof. Its current mansard roof was probably added in the late 19th century.

The large Federal-style, two-story brick structure with masonry load-bearing walls was built onto the north side of the existing structure in 1831. Mr. Smith Delamater was the skilled carpenter hired. This addition has a large living room and side hall. The handrail and balusters of the staircase winding to the second story are carved from mahogany. The woodwork in this section is hand-carved, bearing the oak leaf and acorn motif. The side hall extends into the older back section of the house, which contains a stairway, remodeled kitchen, and dining room. The east section has one large room with a fireplace and a low, open-beamed ceiling. Previous owners David and Wanda Dorpfeld believe that the beams in the east wing were probably exposed during the 1920s or 1930s, perhaps as a restoration to its original character.

The earliest known inhabitants, the Van Dyke family, resided here until 1885. Abraham Van Dyck (1778–1835) was the descendant of Hendrich Van Dyck, a Dutchman who came from Holland in 1645 to become one of the leaders of New Amsterdam. Abraham, a prominent attorney, came from the Kinderhook area of Columbia County. Considered an independent thinker for that more conservative era, he supported efforts for church unification and equal education of both sexes. Proof of Abraham's professional success is substantiated by his ability to pay $1,531 for the construction of the large Federal addition. The contract included not only the construction details but also items such as carpeting and furniture. Abraham's wife, Catherine Bronck (1784–1834), also was prominent in the community, as she was the daughter of Judge Leonard Bronck (see The Bronck House, page 114). Abraham and Catherine had a total of 11 children, though only six would reach adulthood and attain a higher education.

Previous owners have said that they once met Abraham and Catherine's grandson William, who told them that his grandparents adorned the front walkway with tomato plants! He was instructed not to eat the tantalizing red fruit, however, as they were considered poisonous. William also said that Abraham's law practice was located on the property itself, and that his grandparents once owned the entire block between Van Dyck and Mansion streets.

The Hoag family, known locally for their plant nursery, owned the property between 1905 and 1927. The family often ate their meals in the cellar kitchen of the oldest section, which contained a Dutch oven. One time the Hoag boys had to climb out on a roof to smother flaming debris originating from a fire at the American Valve Plant. The boys were involved in fire of a different nature when they set the drapes aflame with an oil lamp. This prompted their grandfather to modernize by installing electricity, and their upstairs bathroom was said to be the first in the village to have electricity.

BRONK/SILVESTER HOUSE

Located on Mansion Street in the Village of Coxsackie, the Bronk-Silvester House remains on its original site, near the junction of two streets coming up the hill from the town's two historic shipping areas on the Hudson River. This Federal-style brick building, with its original slate roof and stone foundation, has served as a private residence since it was constructed in 1811.

The large central entry hall contains an impressive circular staircase that winds its way along a rounded wall to the second-floor landing. The hall is flanked on both sides by matching parlors, and there are two corresponding rooms in the rear. This four-room floor plan is repeated on the second floor. Much of the original plaster wall and cornice moldings are still intact, as well as wood moldings, mantelpieces, doors, and period hardware. A rear wing, constructed using brick over a wood frame, is believed to have been built during the late 19th or early 20th century. Most likely used as a service wing and/or law office when first built, it has been transformed into a modern kitchen.

The house was built for John L. Bronk, Esq., who was a direct descendant of one of the earliest and wealthiest prominent pioneers in the area (see The Bronck House, page 114). Following in the footsteps of his ancestors, John was an outstanding citizen. At age 24 when the house was constructed, John had already served as supervisor for the Town of Coxsackie, graduated from Columbia College, and married the daughter of Philip Conine, Jr., another early prominent pioneer.

John L. Bronk and Alida Conine were married on December 22, 1808. The couple had at least five children, but sadly only two daughters reached adulthood. On May 21, 1835, John died at the young age of 48, from injuries sustained in a steamboat accident.

After John's death his daughter, Catherine Susan, and her husband, Peter Henry Silvester, who was one of John's law partners, took possession of this house. Peter had a Greek Revival–style law office built to the east of this house, and at the same time the had a complementing Greek Revival front porch added to this house. Peter grew in prominence; he was elected to the U.S. House of Representatives in 1847 and continually served in Congress until 1851.

After Catherine Susan died, Peter remarried and brought his new bride and stepson to live at this house. In 1864 the property was transferred to John L. B. Silvester, one of the only two surviving children of Catherine Susan and Peter. After the death of John L. B. Silvester, the approximate 30 acres of land was subdivided, and this house and the law office were sold to Rulandus B. Smith and his wife, Bertha, on September 2, 1920. The Smiths moved into the house with their young children. By December Rulandus was operating a meat market in the former law office that had been vacant for a number of years.

After the Smith family sold the house in the 1970s, it was owned by the Gjerfji and Gjonaj families and for at least part of that time was leased as rental property. In 2003 the house was purchased by James W. Dustin and is used as a residence and artist studio. The walls of the large entry hall now serve as a gallery for his creations.

A. M. Hallenbeck Homestead / Sutton Farm

The Hallenbeck homestead is a remaining example of the Dutch influence once so prevalent in the areas of Greene County surrounding the Hudson River. The classic, understated style of the main structure, built circa 1832, is typified by its sound post-and-beam construction, utilizing hand-hewn wood from local trees, mainly eastern white pine. The original farmhouse has eyebrow windows, a front columned porch, and original plank wood flooring.

The homestead's main house is believed to have been built by Abram M. Hallenbeck, on land deeded from his father, Martin C. Hallenbeck, who was a direct descendant of the early settler Jan Casperse Halenbeck (d. 1703). The farmland and homestead, owned and operated by Abram and his wife, is nestled on the eastern slope of Flint Mine Hill—the "rocky ridge" formerly known as Mineburgh (Myneburg) Hill. The northwestern portion of the property is part of the Great Algonquin Flint Mines, a portion of the vast region now recognized as the Flint Mine Hill Archeological District.

The earliest of the barn structures was built circa 1872 on the east side of the Mineburgh dirt road, now Flint Mine Road. A second barn was added to the south side as late as 1890. The signatures of the original builders are visible on several of the interior barn boards, as are Hallenbeck's initials, "A.M.H."

After the death of Abram Hallenbeck in 1897, the homestead passed to his nephew William H. Hallenbeck and his wife, Hattie, who owned the property until 1907. It passed through several hands until 1925, when the homestead and farm became the property of World War I veteran and Durham resident Russell C. Sutton. Russell and his wife, Irene, would, over the course of 40 years, raise nine children while farming and managing the property as the Sutton Dairy Farm.

Throughout the Sutton ownership, the family maintained a prize herd of over 30 purebred Guernsey cows and grew oats, corn, and other grains, as well as apples, pears, cherries, and plums, on the farm. The Sutton farm sold their milk to the Normanskill Dairy, and each day the Suttons would drive their wagon filled with eggs, grain, poultry, and produce down Farm-to-Market Road —now Route 57—to the villagers of Coxsackie.

After Russell Sutton's death in 1966, the farm was partitioned, the livestock and poultry auctioned, and the land parceled. The remaining 43 acres—with the original homestead, barn and surviving structures—were sold in 1970 to the Newcombes. As with many other homes in the area, Barbara Newcombe (Weber) modernized the structure, updating plumbing, electric, and heating. A second-floor master bedroom was added, one of the covered porches was extended, and a cast-iron greenhouse from a Catskill home (circa 1922) was installed to the south exterior of the house.

Today, the homestead consists of the main house, a carriage house (formerly a corn crib), a free-standing milk house and the barn structures with silos. Since acquiring the homestead in 2004, the current owners, Robert Bedford and Linda Pierro, have strived to preserve and restore the home and adjoining structures to their original condition, with further restoration of the barn and buildings to continue over the years to come.

COXSACKIE

OLD STONE HOUSE

Still surrounded by open fields, the Old Stone House is located on Martin Road just outside the Village of Coxsackie. The one-and-a-half-story house has fieldstone load-bearing walls that are more than two feet thick! Built into a bank, the ground entry on the east side goes directly into the basement area. A wood-framed wing projects at ground level on the west side. The original house and the clapboard-covered west wing are sheltered by wood-shingle roofs.

The interior doorway of the attached wing is one of the original front entrances. Its two-section Dutch door is a replacement but may have come from another part of the house. The house has three working fireplaces, exposed beams, and some of the original flooring. An original fireplace and evidence of what was possibly a smoker are still incorporated within the stone foundation in the original walk-in basement kitchen. The farm buildings, which were located west of the house, are gone now and the foundations are the only visible proof of their existence.

Local tradition holds that the original house was built during the 1750s by Peter Vandenberg and that it was the same place sold by Thomas Hotaling to Hendrick Vandenberg. Also, William Vandenberg sold acreage, possibly including this house, to Reverend Henry Ostrander, pastor (1801–1810) of the Dutch Reform church in Coxsackie. Toward the end of the 19th century it was reported that the house was the property of Winslow Case, the tenant being Charles Martin.

In November 1898, James Hayes, who had purchased the house from Winslow Case, agreed that he would deliver a deed to Charles Martin if certain conditions and payments were met. On June 1, 1910, the heirs of James Hayes completed the agreement and issued a deed to the now-married Charles Martin and his wife, Bridget.

This first-generation, Irish-American couple worked their 33-acre general farm and raised their children in this old stone house. After Charles' death in 1948, Bridget continued to live in the house and celebrated her 97th birthday here on August 9, 1963. The house and two acres of land were sold in 1967 to Ronald Mercier and his wife, Mary Martina. Mary Martina "Tina" Mercier (now Gallagher) is to be credited with saving the house. She lived with her family here until major renovations forced them to relocate.

Interior and exterior renovations began in 1988, supervised by John Johnson of Claverack, Columbia County. The mud-and-horsehair mortar between the fieldstones had deteriorated so badly that it was necessary to take down three walls and have them rebuilt. The dirt floor of the basement had to be covered with a layer of concrete, as a support base for temporary columns to support the crossbeams.

The house and two acres were sold in 1994 to Wanda McCoy, MD, from Westchester County, and then became mostly a summer and weekend residence. So complete were the previous renovations that only minor changes were made before its sale in 2001, to Theron and Lisa Gunderman. Since their purchase, the Gundermans have added copper gutters, constructed a garage and a shed in keeping with the period look, and placed the hand pump on the backyard well. Coming full circle, Lisa is the great-granddaughter of Charles and Bridget Martin; once again the Old Stone House is in the possession of the Martin family.

Town Board of Durham, 1910–1911. November 9, 1911.

TOWN OF DURHAM

The settlement of the Town of Durham began during the late 18th century, many of its earliest families arriving from Connecticut. In fact, Durham itself takes its name from the town of Durham, Connecticut, located about 30 miles east of Danbury, from which many of those early settlers had emigrated. Why did Greene County, and Durham in particular, become a mecca for settlers from Connecticut? The answer is the Susquehanna Turnpike, a toll road that started in Connecticut, crossing the Hudson near Catskill and running through the Town of Durham on its way to Unadilla (Wattles Ferry), on the banks of the Susquehanna River.

The villages and hamlets of Greene County's Durham include Cornwallville, Durham Village, East Durham, East Windham, Hervey Street, Oak Hill, South Durham, Sunside, and West Durham. The first settlement in the area was at Oak Hill, formerly called Dewittsburgh. A great deal of the area within these villages, as well as the countryside that surrounds them, remains rural, and scenic. The geography varies widely, from the Durham Valley with its low elevation, which is little more than 500 feet above sea level at East Durham, to the mountain peaks along Durham's southwestern and western boundary; the latter range from a bit over 2,300 feet to more than 2,800 feet above sea level!

East Durham, earlier called Winansville, was originally settled in the 1780s, but by the early 1800s it became a haven for a new group of settlers: Irish immigrants. Their influence can still be felt today, for East Durham is known as the "Emerald Isle of the Catskills." East Durham is also home to the Michael J. Quill Irish Cultural & Sports Center.

It should be noted that the hamlet of Cornwallville was the former home of the church relocated to the Farmers' Museum in Cooperstown, New York. The character and architecture of that house of worship is typical of the early churches built in New York state.

REDBRICK

Redbrick, the William Baldwin House, has been identified by the New York State Office of Parks and Historic Preservation as "eligible for listing on the Federal and NYS Registers of Historic Places," noting that it is "architecturally significant as an outstanding example of 19th-century Federal style architecture in the region. The two-story, five-bay-by-two-bay, center-entry brick residence features numerous elements associated with the style, including as follows: symmetrical fenestration, molded frieze, six-over-six, double-hung sash windows, inset gable-end chimneys, and elaborate arched door surrounds. It remains virtually intact from its period of construction, retaining an outstanding integrity of setting, location, design, materials, and craftsmanship."

The exterior is masonry with load-bearing walls of the original redbrick construction and an impressive fanlight. Phillip Hooker of Albany inspired the architect, and the list of occupants begins with the Shue family, followed by the Baldwins in 1859, Agnes Inglis O'Neill in 1923, and the Garfinkel family since 1964.

The interior is notable for the original wide-board floors, fireplaces in the rooms, doorframes, and attendant architectural details. A pastoral setting graces this clearly outstanding home and barns, evoking a glimpse of the 19th century and the pride of those who built and lived here.

The current owners, the Garfinkel family, have been and still are very active in helping to preserve the integrity not only of their home but of the town of Durham. Mr. Garfinkel was the legal advisor to Citizens to Preserve Durham in the 1970s. He and his law firm successfully represented Durham residents against the Power Authority of the State of New York in their plans to place power transmission lines from Blenheim throughout this scenic area. Years later he was successful again, on that occasion keeping a major dump site from being established in the Durham area.

Left: Center entranceway of the brick Federal-style residence.

TRIPP STORE AND HOMESTEAD

This property was originally a part of the Maitland Patent granted by the British king, George II, to Richard Maitland on June 23, 1767. The Tripp Store was typical of the "general stores" that could be found throughout Greene County in the past. Such stores were notable for their inventory of the vast range of supplies that local residents needed in their daily lives. The store was also an important communication and information center.

In 1888, the "old store was moved back from its original site, turned sideways, and connected to the new store," which had been built that year. In this manner, the "old store" became the warehouse for the "new store."

Today the combined buildings serve as an antique shop for Nick and Mary Lou Nahas, the current owners. The store is painted in its original Victorian style. The Nahases have shown remarkable diligence in their research efforts, and great attention to detail in restoring both the store and the home. Walking into these buildings is truly like stepping into the 19th century.

The house is brick masonry, with load-bearing walls 13 inches thick! The site's Historical Register application reads, in part, "The architecture is late Federal period, Adams style, with elements of Greek Revival in the woodwork. The house, once painted red with black accents on the mortar joints was more recently painted yellow ochre, similar to the siding of the new store (1888). Most of the paint has weathered off, revealing the original red brick. The old store, the main part of the barn, and the outhouse are typical, early Classical Greek Revival. Most of the original interior hardware, e.g., Norfolk latches, is typical of the 1830s."

The interior of the house has grain-painted woodwork and ten-foot ceilings. The parlor and the sitting rooms contain plaster cornices. A large brick fireplace with a bake oven sits in the kitchen. The windows and moldings are all original.

The stores, barns, and other wooden structures use post-and-beam wood-frame construction, with interlocking joints; the "new store" is wood-frame construction with light members. The "cottage" on the property was probably used for other purposes in the past, such as preparing flax.

Opposite top: Front façade of Federal-style brick-mason residence.

Opposite bottom: Interior view of the central sitting room or parlor.

CUTTING BAGLEY HOUSE

John Bagley, a Revolutionary War veteran and captain of the local militia, originally settled this area of East Durham. John also built the first gristmill in this part of town on Thorp Creek. Edward Griswold deeded this property to Cutting Bagley, John's brother, in 1793 and 1796. Cutting Bagley built this house, circa 1802, adjacent to and to the west of his brother's place. The Bagley families moved here from Amesbury, Massachusetts, according to Keith Bagley, great-great-great-grandson of Cutting Bagley, and were among the first to build homes in "New Durham," as it was then called. The Bagley family continued to own this home through at least seven generations, until 1947.

Orlando Bagley, the ancestor of the family, was born in England about 1624, and settled in Boston about 1658, according to the family genealogy. The genealogy traces the family through five generations in New England, including Cutting's arrival at "New Durham" about 1784. Exactly where he lived at that time is not readily apparent, and he may have returned to New England during the winters until eventually establishing a more permanent residence here in the 1790s. Thomas Bagley, Cutting's son, was the next to have the home and property, and is reported to have received a pension for his service in the War of 1812.

As with so many homes of the period, the structure is wood-frame with post-and-beam construction, using interlocking joints. The exterior has the original doors and entrance. On the interior are pine floors with hand-cut nails, original old-glass windows, and hand-hewn and hand-sawn beams in the cellar, indicating both the age of the house and the necessary maintenance and changes over the years. It is likely that much of the wood used in the construction of this house was cut nearby and made ready for use on-site, as was so often done at the time. Sometimes, though, buildings were disassembled and hauled by oxen or horses long distances and then reassembled in the new location, but this was not a frequent practice where timber and labor was readily available.

In 1920, a porch was added, and in 1956, a den was completed to accommodate the needs of later generations and new owners. As we know, these can be agonizing decisions for purists who wish to maintain the character of a 19th-century home and at the same time provide utility for the present day.

New York State has designated the road where this home is located as a scenic highway.

CHITTENDEN/ATKINSON/SWANSON HOUSE

This is a beautiful old farmhouse dating back to 1794–95 for some of its structure. Oriana Atkinson wrote a history of the house in her book, Not Only Ours, *which includes informative sketches of the families who lived here over the years. There are humorous anecdotes about their restoration, which she and Brooks Atkinson, her husband and noted drama critic and war correspondent, carried out during their occupancy from 1928–1982. Oriana was an author, photographer, and correspondent of note in her own right.*

Her book, *Not Only Ours,* should be a joy to read for anyone interested in old homes and local history. She eloquently muses about her home beside the Susquehanna Turnpike, "Sometimes on summer evenings when the stars are low over [Mount] Pisgah we stand in the doorway of our old house which has seen the great days of the Great Road and we fancy we can hear the creaking of the covered wagons, the long-gone shouts, the hoof beats, the lowing of the herds. We can almost see the campfires spangling the darkling fields. And we enjoy the peace and quiet and hope it never changes."

The home, originally built for Leverett and Ruth Chittenden, is a wood-framed structure with interlocking joints. The Chittendens were among the early settlers of Durham and had come here from Connecticut during the latter years of the 18th century. This is a beautiful home with a southern exposure and sweeping panoramic view overlooking the Durham valley and the northern Catskills. Tall, graceful old locusts, privet hedges, lilacs, and period flowers provide attractive landscaping on the lawns around the home.

The windows in the old part of the house are twelve-over-eight; in some panes, "bull's-eye" glass is still in place. The 1830 addition is a Federal-style farmhouse with Greek Revival features, typical to the area. Exposed beams in the kitchen area, original windows, six-over-six, wide-board pine floors, and a fireplace with a Dutch oven remind us of another era. The current owners are Michael and Diana Swanson.

DURHAM

DEERWATCH INN

This home is original to this site, part of the Maitland Patent, and is currently an attractive bed-and-breakfast that maintains all of its 19th-century farmhouse characteristics, including the barn. The building is a two-story post-and-beam structure with wood framing and interlocking joints, and has wood clapboard siding and shutters. The flower gardens are typically resplendent with authentic flowers of the period. The house has been in the family of the current owners since 1944, and has been restored and beautifully maintained.

The original owner appears to have been Deacon John Cleveland, who died in 1823. An 1853 map in the collections of the Durham Museum shows the building. Later owners, circa 1854, added the main section of the house as it now appears from the road. Durham Museum curator Douglas Thomsen provided the current owners with a copy of an outstanding photograph of the house as it appeared in the latter part of the 19th century, showing many people who were guests or visitors to the place. The name "The Carrington Place" is visible, written on the roof in the photo, although there is a possibility that it may also have been known as the Palmer House. The house as it stands in that photograph clearly resembles the house as it appears today, a credit to the restoration work by the current owners.

Restoration was begun in 1975, with some alterations, in keeping with its original style, added in 1997 and 2003–04. The interior has the original wide-board floors and wainscoting. Transoms over the bedroom doors on the second floor indicate its probable use in the latter 1800s and early 1900s as a boardinghouse for summer guests from the environs of New York City, a fairly common practice in this area.

Jack and Joanne Rascoe are the current owners. They have landscaped the property with successive colorful plantings that span the seasons. Pastoral views of meadows, the northern Catskills, and this impressive old farmhouse make this an enticing picture that blends the past with the present.

DURHAM

GROVE COTTAGE

Grove Cottage is a classic Greek Revival with wooden grills in the eyebrow windows and simulated columns at the doors, including Greek pediment, making the home an excellent example of this style. The earliest date of construction was probably late 18th century, with the main house addition dating to 1830.

The list of owners includes Louis Baldwin, Orwell Moss, Edward Slater, Judson Moss, Agnes Inglis, and "Tex" and Elizabeth Wickenden/Goldschmidt. The current owner, Catherine Kayser, has done much to maintain and preserve this beautiful home.

The Goldschmidts and the other recent owners have been meticulous in maintaining this home in excellent condition, and have kept the house as it was intended, with minimal changes.

The original wide-board floors, the drawing room with the original carved mantel, and the window frames and fireplace exhibit the craftsmanship and attention to detail of the artisans who constructed them, and commendable maintenance over the years.

The Goldschmidts, who owned the house from 1946 into the 1990s, were an interesting couple and are still remembered by friends and neighbors. "Tex" was a New Dealer who went to D.C. under FDR and later served under LBJ, working in various capacities, such as on the Economic and Social Council to the United Nations. Elizabeth, "Wickie" as she was known to friends and family, taught at Hunter College. Both were extremely fond of their country place, and friends and family were frequent welcome visitors.

ST. PAUL'S LUTHERAN CHURCH

Records indicate that the organization of St. Paul's Protestant Episcopal Church was established October 16, 1809, at the home of Adijah Dewey. The first minister was the Reverend Samuel Fuller. The church was dedicated on November 21, 1834. The Reverend James Thompson was another early clergyman and served a lengthy pastorate. He died on August 19, 1844, at age 77 and is buried in the churchyard cemetery.

On April 10, 1865, Henry Howard Bates, then the pastor, tolled the church bell for a full half hour to "bring the joyous news to the people of the village" that the Civil War had ended. Bates had served as a chaplain in the 22nd New York State Volunteers from 1861 to 1863. He died on January 14, 1868, and a monument to his memory built by the Masonic Lodge marks his final resting place in the cemetery behind the church. This information and an excellent article by Doug Thomsen, local and Civil War historian, appeared as a "Weekender" edition guest column in the *Catskill Daily Mail*.

Thomsen also writes about the history of the church bell: "It was made by Lewis Aspinwall in 1835 at his Albany, N.Y. foundry." It appears to have been installed in the church that same year. The bell is currently housed in front of the building, since the old belfry had to be removed some years ago. There is a fund that is raising money to replace the belfry at a future date.

Architecturally, of particular interest is the very steep roof on the back section of the building, as well as a cast-iron fence from the Oak Hill Iron Foundry, circa 1840. The stained-glass windows also deserve mention. The Gothic Revival windows are of old glass and add picturesque charm and light to this building. The moldings and trim are Greek Revival style. Originally established as a Protestant Episcopal church, this church has more recently become an Evangelical Lutheran church.

The cemetery in back of the church contains the remains of several early villagers, including those of Levi and Mindwell Tremain, who were the parents of Lyman Tremain, the lawyer and political leader of note: "Lyman Tremain served in various capacities during his career. He was Town Supervisor, District Attorney, Surrogate and County Judge of Greene County, New York State Attorney General, State Assemblyman, and U.S. Congressman." As a favorite son of Oak Hill, the Masonic temple and opera house were, of course, named for him. "His most famous achievement was the 1873 conviction of William Marcy Tweed, the notorious New York City politician. Tremain commissioned his prosecution team to impanel jurors who could not be bribed. Following a lengthy and intense trial, 'Boss Tweed' was convicted and died in prison five years later."

Above: View of the bell at the front entrance.

MT. ZOAR VILLA

The Mt. Zoar Villa boardinghouse dates back to the 1860s. Mary Butts Lamoreau and Isaac Butts were sister and brother. Their father, Barney Butts, had this house built and called it the Summit House. The Butts family was well-known and influential in the area, and Barney Butts was noted as a "skilled landlord" and famous bear hunter and outdoorsman. He reportedly hiked to the top of High Peak in his 80th year. The family was noted for longevity, and Barney's parents were both said to have lived to 100 years of age. Barney apparently captured bears and used them as an attraction at the Summit House. In 1896 Isaac C. Butts purchased it for $100, and it was rechristened the "Butts House Café."

The establishment continued to serve as a boardinghouse or hotel into the 1940s, drawing guests from the New York metropolitan area for its magnificent views. In fact, this is just one of several nearby hotels that drew tourists to this popular location from the 1860s on. This building is one of the few to have survived, and certainly has a colorful and unusual history.

In the 1970s the house was home to Tom and Gladys MacDonald and their family. They renovated the building, replacing the roof and putting in new windows in keeping with the original design.

John and Dawn Giordano now own this elegant 18-room Victorian structure. Having purchased the property in 2001, they are still in the process of restoration. The exterior restoration is nearly complete, having been recently repainted in historic colors. The paint scheme is remarkably faithful to an old photo, which appears to be from an early 1900s postcard.

The interior features hardwood maple floors and Victorian archways in the walls. There are eight rooms and two and a half baths. A second-story observation room, above the five-bay-wide porch, provides a view of five states: New York, New Hampshire, Massachusetts, Vermont, and Connecticut.

DURHAM

Osborn House

This house, which is on both the National Register of Historic Places and the New York State Register, was built about 1850. The building served as a manufacturing site and as a residence. "As such it is a unique architectural hybrid in the community," states the National Register report.

The Osborn House reflects the combination of commercial and residential qualities that gives the hamlet of Oak Hill much of its 19th-century charm. Also called the Mill House, it almost certainly housed a milling operation powered by the adjacent Squirmer Valley Creek—or "Kelsey Creek," as it was called in Beers' 1867 *Atlas of Greene County*. The National Register finds the Osborn House to be "the last intact industrial building and a rare link to the hamlet's industrial development period."

In the latter years of the 18th century, the hamlet was a commercial center, but during the 19th century it was growing into a burgeoning industrial village. After Oak Hill had served as an area milling center in the late 1700s, the local economy began to change during the 1820s and 1830s. The old sawmills and gristmills were converted to iron foundries and woolen mills. The Kimball Foundry was established in 1833, and the Smith Iron Works followed shortly thereafter. In 1844 a local plow manufacturer became the Cherritree and Pierce Iron Foundry. Other supporting crafts and manufactures included a weight-and-scale factory, blacksmiths, and a tin works, to name only a few. By 1857 the village had 57 homes, a school, two churches, two hotels, and five stores.

The Osborn House, along with the nearby buildings of the industries mentioned above and the Paddock store, which later became the Cascade Lodge, formed the industrial heart of the village. Today, only the Osborn House now remains of this group. It is not known what was produced in the Osborn House, but an 1867 list of products made in Oak Hill included "latches, lock hasps, whiffletree hooks, toy horses, match safes, boot jacks, foot scrapers, and many other utilitarian items."

The house is a five- by three-bay timber-framed building, sheathed with clapboards and covered by a hipped roof. The windows are six-over-six sashes, and provide a pleasing balance and symmetrical spacing. The interior of the house uses a center hall plan. Greek Revival influences survive with a high degree of integrity. The front, which faces the road, has a double porch that provides ample outdoor space, and looks out over the creek.

The property contains both the house and a timber-frame barn used for storage. Both buildings "retain a high degree of architectural integrity and stand as an important reminder of the commercial/industrial history of this community," according to the National Register report.

LYMAN TREMAIN OPERA HOUSE

The Lyman Tremain Opera House was constructed circa 1895 and has led a varied but useful existence in the hamlet of Oak Hill and surrounding area. The Opera House raised money by selling shares of capital stock, and apparently this continued for some years. In June of 1901, James Utter purchased ten shares of the Lyman Tremain Opera Company; the sale became finalized on November 13, 1903. About this time the building came to be used as the Lyman Tremain Lodge #265, I.O.O.F.

In addition to being named after one of the village's most famous sons, Lyman Tremain, a renowned lawyer and politician who worked with the prosecution team in the Boss Tweed trial, the building has been used as a theater, a Masonic temple, a dance hall, a grange—and, more recently, a restaurant.

It is clear that Oak Hill took great pride in Lyman Tremain's accomplishments by the place he held in local history. Born in 1819, he died in 1878. But in that brief span of time, he had a very successful career. Admitted to the bar in 1840, he began to practice law in the town of Durham and was elected supervisor there in 1842. He was appointed district attorney for Greene County in 1844. In 1846 he was elected surrogate and county judge. After moving to Albany in 1853, still continuing to practice law, he was elected on the Democrat line to be the attorney general of New York in 1858. By 1862 he had switched to the Republican side, perhaps reflecting concerns over slavery and the Civil War. Tremain served in the state assembly from 1866 to 1868, serving as speaker in 1867. He was elected to the House of Representatives, 43rd Congress, and served there from 1873 to 1875; deciding not to run for another term, he returned to his Albany law practice. Poor health and family considerations may have been contributing factors, but that is a subject for another day.

The construction of this building is of "wood frame with light members." It is among the largest public places in the hamlet, if not the largest. The exterior has an ornate front gable and window cupola of the Victorian period, the time in which it was constructed.

Alterations to the interior have been done tastefully and have been in keeping with the style of the building. The wainscoted walls and lamps and globes that hang from the ceilings add ambience to the rather large dining area on the first floor. Above the wainscot are a stenciled border and a cap rail. The ornamental tin walls and ceiling are attractively painted and further indicate the style of the era in which the structure was built. Period curtains at the windows bring charm and provide a cozier atmosphere. What was once the stage of the Opera House is now partitioned off and serves as the kitchen.

To comply with state law and codes, restrooms and a front entry were added, as well as a fire escape from the second floor, all in 1949. Additional changes were made when it became Sam's Oak Hill Kitchen, and Karl Dratz, the next proprietor made further changes. In 1990, second-floor supports were added, as well as a basement entrance, and the front sill was repaired. The current owners, the Twelve Tribes, have worked to maintain the building and operate it as the Oak Hill Kitchen, continuing to use the name and recent purpose it has served. The interior has had some changes, and many framed photos on the walls recall Oak Hill's past. The restaurant continues to be a popular establishment.

Inset: Lyman Tremain, lawyer, district attorney, congressman.

DURHAM

MAKELY FARM

James Utter, a Revolutionary War veteran, and his family first settled this farm. The earliest construction on this site began in the 1780s. Over time, additions and out-buildings have been added, as with many farms in our area: barns, sheds, tenant house, shop, and garden. The structure is wood-framed, post-and-beam construction, with interlocking joints.

Most additions to the house took place between 1810 and 1840. In the largest part of the house the sills have been restored and the current owners have exhibited a great deal of interest in its history, investing energy and effort to restore the interior, an endeavor that has proved to be an ongoing process.

The interior features large rooms, heavy ornate woodwork, large windows, and two floors with a front stairwell. The attic contains stained-glass octagonal windows, an indication of the "pride of place" taken by owners and craftsmen in the construction process.

Sitting on a plateau high above the village of Oak Hill and surrounded by open fields, the site presents a pastoral scene with an "incredible view of the northern Catskills." From the house a large bay window affords occupants this truly beautiful panorama. The house has a generous porch on two sides that provides similar views.

The late Helen Hilzinger, a schoolteacher and avidly enthusiastic student of local history—and a descendant of James Utter himself—wrote, "The Utters were the first family to settle outside the Village of Oak Hill. They arrived from Saybrooke, Connecticut and staked a claim from the Stewart Patent. James Utter built a log cabin in 1780, planted grain, and then returned to Connecticut to get his wife, returning in 1782. In 1785, he went back to Connecticut to get their children and [they] lived the rest of their lives on the farm."

Panoramic view of the northern Catskill Mountains from the front porch.

COWLES/HULL HOUSE

Records indicate that this Italianate home was built by Cornelius Cowles, the son of David Cowles, one of the earliest settlers of New Durham. Cornelius was by trade a cabinetmaker, and no doubt was responsible for the ornate wood moldings on the eaves and front and sides of the exterior of the home.

The house was built circa 1867–1870. The structure is wood-framed, with light members. The property includes outbuildings, including a privy and carriage house. The carriage house has older windows—pre-1830—which may have been salvaged from another building.

The interior of the house has curved walls on both floors. There are handmade corner cupboards in the dining room. Grained doors and moldings exist throughout the house, with acid-etched glass on the double doors in the main foyer. A handmade fireplace mantel in the front parlor also has faux wood graining.

Mr. And Mrs. Addison O. Hull purchased the home from the Cowles in August of 1887. Addison Hull was a prominent merchant in Durham. The John Hull family, from whom he was descended, was also among the earliest settlers, and came from Connecticut during the latter part of the 18th century. Both David Cowles and John Hull were in Durham about 1784, but may have returned to Connecticut during the winter months for a few years until their New Durham homesteads were ready for their families. Besides being linked in the settlement of New Durham, the two families were united when Anson Hull married Irene Amelia Cowles, daughter of David Cowles, Jr., on September 21, 1848.

Detail view from the west of the Italianate-style cupola.

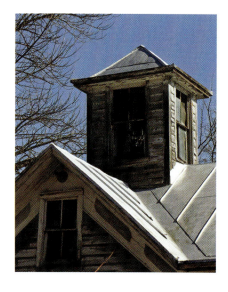

DURHAM

Parks House

This house, currently owned by the James Garfinkel family, is one of the oldest and most beautiful homes in Cornwallville. It is located at the west end of the historic hamlet. The Austins were the first to live here.

Moses Austin was born in Wallingford, Connecticut, in about 1768 and came to Durham at about age 20, according to J. G. Borthwick in 1887, quoted by Greene County historian Jessie Van Vechten Vedder: "He was a wealthy businessman—owned a woolen factory in Cairo, was engaged in various business enterprises, and became very wealthy. He was at one time Judge of the Court of Common Pleas, and in 1819–1822 was a member of the New York State Senate. Mr. Austin spent the evening of his life in Cairo and one of his sons stayed on the Cornwallville farm and became Supervisor of the town."

Austin purchased the farm and built what is now the oldest part of the house, facing the road, in 1806. Over the years the house was extended, maintaining the architectural integrity of the main house, to fit the needs of growing farm families.

After the Austins, the Wetmore, Smith, and Parks families occupied this home for most of its existence. It remained in the Parks family until 1964. All three families were prominent in the church and the community, and were related by marriage. The church is now located at the Farmers' Museum in Cooperstown, having been skillfully disassembled piece by piece, transported, and reassembled there in 1963.

According to the Borthwick papers contained in the collections of the Greene County Historical Society's Vedder Research Library, Dr. Alexander Hunter Parks, a veterinary surgeon and farmer, "built a large pond in 1905. This was the site of the first and successive Cornwallville Church Sunday School picnics." The pond was built by digging out a huge basin and constructing a dam at the lower end, allowing natural springs and small streams to fill the pond. William S. Borthwick, teacher, historian, and chronicler of Cornwallville in his column for a local paper once wryly observed, "Cornwallville was not worth a dam [sic] until Dr. Parks built one."

The outstanding features of this house are the balance and symmetry that typify its Federal style. The fanlight, front entry, and Palladian window above add elegance and charm, and indicate the welcome into the center hall interior, with large rooms opening off the hall. The house contains the original fireplaces and has been well preserved under the ownership of Mrs. Thomforde, 1964–1987, and the Garfinkel family since then.

With its generous proportions, surrounding fields, and agrarian setting at the edge of the village, the Parks House provides an exquisite glimpse into another era. The New York State Office of Parks, Recreation and Historic Preservation has designated the house to be eligible for listing on the State and National Registers of Historic Places. And reportedly, those fields behind the house have their own claim to fame: having been used as drilling grounds for the local militia during the Civil War.

DURHAM

United Methodist Church of Oak Hill

This house of worship is a simple Greek Revival building with an unusual steeple of classical columns, and stone steps and walks. It is typical of the many fine old churches that are found throughout the region. Set back from the road, with old maples in front and with ample space between the church building and the beautiful 19th-century homes adjacent to it, this church has a picturesque beauty that is truly unique and inspiring.

The Methodist people of Oak Hill were organized into a church during the pastorate of A. F. Selleck of the Durham charge, and he became their first pastor. Under his leadership they elected as trustees William Paddock, Charles W. Pierce, Israel P. Utter, and James H. Welch. A building committee was also selected at this time. The builders were Jerome B. Gifford and Stephen B. Osterhout. The contract for the building, which was 40 by 50 feet and also included the belfry, was set at a cost of $1,500.

Construction began sometime in 1859; the building was dedicated on November 2, that same year. The bell was purchased from the West Troy Bell Foundry on June 8, 1863.

The most notable feature of this church building is the previously mentioned "unusual steeple of classical columns, as it juts out from the front facade," according to church trustee O. Winnie in the building's Historical Register application. Working from church documents, Trustee Winnie explains that constructing the unique steeple was not an easy task: "The two front beams over 75 feet tall were hauled into place using oxen and got stuck halfway up. They were only freed by a man climbing up the slanted beams and getting through iron chains with an axe!" However, the documents don't tell us how they finally solved the problem. Now, there is a challenge for a future researcher!

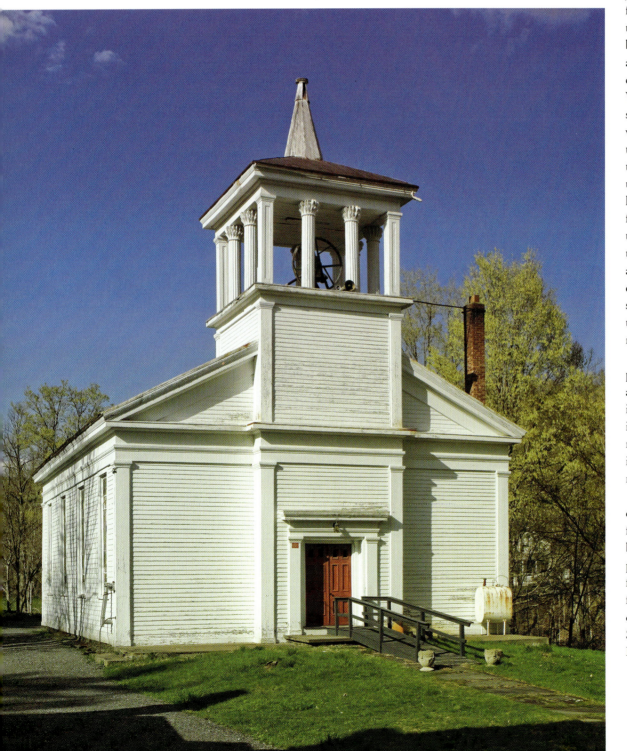

Currently, this church is part of a larger charge: services are still held in Oak Hill during the summer months, while in winter the congregation meets in the Durham building, which is newer and has a more modern heating system.

The Oak Hill Church is currently being repaired, and fund-raising has enabled the bell tower to be repaired and painted, with many other facets of the restoration to follow in the near future. The church has been added to the State and National Historic Registers.

DURHAM

THE PARSONAGE —
OAK HILL UNITED METHODIST CHURCH

This house is a typical village home: wood frame and interlocking joints. Its earliest construction appears to be 1814 or so. Further investigation reveals that the house was built by Lyman Morss, a tanner from Windham who for a period of 12 years worked a tannery built by his father, Foster Morss. Lyman later lost his life in a tanning accident in Carbondale, Pennsylvania.

In the 1830s and 1840s the Egbertson family occupied the home. Mr. Egbertson started the original mill on the Catskill Creek, which later became Dean's Mill. In 1856 the house was listed on *Samuel Geil's Map of Greene County, NY,* which indicated the owners to be Barker and Van Dyck.

Walter Cheritree occupied the home between 1864 and 1868. The Cheritree foundry was reportedly the first industrial complex to make practical use of the malleable iron process. The June 27, 1865, New York State census identifies Walter, then 28, living in the frame house with his 23-year-old wife, Legwina, and their daughter, Ella, who was two years old.

The home is in Beers' 1867 *Atlas of Greene County,* and also appears in one of P. T. Hoagland's 19th-century color postcards of Oak Hill. An 1880 photo shows a white picket fence in front, a graceful reminder of an earlier time. The front porch, added at a later date, uses Victorian trim with bows and is a fine example of Oak Hill's decorated porches. Between 1889 and 1973 the house served as the parsonage for the ministers of the Methodist church. Francis S. Norris, pastor in the 1950s, indicated that the westerly of the two parlors, separated by the original pocket doors, served as a small chapel where wedding ceremonies were performed. A standard glass window is a unique feature in the kitchen, which was originally used as the dining room.

Chestnut woodwork graces the interior. There are steep, narrow stairs, three-quarter-length windows in many rooms; hand-hewn, exposed chestnut beams, original wide-board floors, and a double parlor with sliding doors between the rooms. During a restoration project in the summer of 1995, the signature of an Oak Hill Civil War veteran, Nathan Augustus, who was wounded at the Battle of Gettysburg, was discovered on a wall in the upstairs northeast bedroom.

The original barn on the property, which was restored in 1994, completes this typical 19th-century village home. In 1991 and again in 2001, the Parsonage was included in the Greene County Historical Society's Annual Homes Tour and in 1992 it was added to the Greene County Historical Register.

Above: View of interior parlor.

WHITTLESEY HOUSE

This is a typical center-hall colonial of Georgian style, and has been well maintained. The construction is wood frame with interlocking joints. The date of construction is circa 1820, although a part of the house may date as early as the late 1790s. The property was part of the Stewart's Patent. In the backyard is an ancient camperdown elm, beyond which the beautiful and well-maintained period barns and outbuildings are located. The property includes a carriage house for the storage of wagons and stabling of horses, a necessity in the 19th century.

The current kitchen and woodshed were used as a hatter's shop during bygone days. The interior doors and moldings appear to be of 1830s vintage and are beautifully crafted. In one of the bedrooms is a Federal or early Greek Revival mantel that is noteworthy. The interior still has the original wide-board floors and trim.

The first occupant was Hezekiah Whittlesey. His ancestor, John Whittlesey, was the first of this family to come to America, in 1650. The family was among the early settlers of New Durham and came from Connecticut. The property remained in the Whittlesey family for some years. Zina Whittlesey, who was justice of the peace in 1845, resided there. Dr. Elias Whittlesey was next, and it was later the residence of Dr. George Conklin, Elias' partner in medical practice. More recently, Mae Higgins and Mr. and Mrs. George Bullivant owned the home. Clayton and Shirley Reynolds applied to the Greene County Historic Register in 1992, during their tenure, and the house was approved soon after. The current owner, Alison Slon, is an enthusiastic admirer and preserver of the home.

Rear view of the carriage house and well.

Phineas Tyler House

Phineas Tyler arrived in East Durham with his wife, Sarah, in the late 1780s or early 1790s. Phineas lived in this home until his death on October 4, 1839. According to the Beers' 1884 *History of Greene County*, Phineas Tyler had previously succeeded John Bagley as captain of the Durham militia, and "the first training day ever held in East Durham was held on his farm." Bagley and Tyler were neighbors, and according to a Bagley deed, at one point, they jointly owned about 1,500 acres.

At the time of his death, Phineas retained about 90 acres on his farm, and this he left to his son, Jehiel Tyler. Tragically, on March 4, 1840, at the young age of 39, Jehiel was killed in the wreck of the Canajoharie & Catskill Railroad at High Rock when the bridge gave way and the train plunged to the Catskill Creek below. Jehiel was the sole fatality in the mishap; however, as a result of the accident the Canajoharie & Catskill Railroad succumbed as well. Jehiel and Phineas, as well as other Tyler family members, are buried at Stone Bridge Cemetery in East Durham.

In 1841 Caroline, Jehiel's widow, was forced to sell off much of the farmland to cover expenses. The Tylers continued to live in the house until 1883, when their daughter, Julia Tyler Earl, died. The home then went to Harry Bagley upon mortgage foreclosure. The listing for the Tyler House varies among the different editions of Beers' *Atlas of Greene County*. In the 1856 edition, the owner is listed as Mrs. C. Tyler, but the 1867 edition lists R. R. Earl—who was probably the husband of Julia A. Tyler—as the owner.

The house, with its surrounding 30 acres, still sits on its original site with beautiful views of Windham High Peak and the East Windham Mountain Ridge. The road leading to and from the house is still lined with old sugar maples and has been given DEC scenic road designation. The home has been designated as a historic site by the Durham Historic Preservation Commission.

Carmen and Fred Militello currently own the home and were responsible for applying to have this home placed on the Register. They have been restoring the home since 1988 and hope to repurchase the land sold off by Caroline in 1840—which, amazingly enough, is still vacant farmland—and return the property to its original status as a family-run farm.

Guests relaxing on the porch of the Freehold House, circa 1905.

TOWN OF GREENVILLE

The area we know today as the Town of Greenville was originally a part of Coxsackie, and was separated from it in 1790. The area was organized as a town in 1803—the Town of Greenfield. Five years later it became known as Freehold. It wasn't until 1809 that the name was officially changed to Greenville.

The earliest settlers came from Coxsackie between 1750 and 1772. They were the Brandow, Lampman, and Bogardus families, and they lived on isolated homesteads. After the American Revolution the first settlements began to appear. The people came from New England, in general, with many emigrating from Connecticut. Among the earliest of these settlers were the Spees, Knowles, and Lake families.

Greenville's hamlets, or villages, are East Greenville, Freehold, Gayhead, Greenville Center, Greenville, and Norton Hill. The township lies within portions of the Coeymans, Hallenbeck, and Van Bergen patents, as well as the grant to Augustine Prevost. The town is bounded on the west by Durham, Cairo to the south, Coxsackie and New Baltimore to the east, and the Albany County towns of Coeymans and Westerlo to the north.

Greenville Academy was chartered by the Board of Regents in 1816. It has long been a source of local pride because it was "one of the earlier institutions of higher learning in the state" and a remarkable achievement "for such a small community," as Greene County historian Raymond Beecher observed in *Out to Greenville and Beyond*. This academy served not only nearby locals, but students from distances who would board in the town. One such student in 1822 was John Van Buren, the son of Martin Van Buren. (Martin, of course, was to become our eighth president, serving from 1837 to 1841, and his son, John, would go on to become attorney general of the State of New York.)

The hamlets of the town reflect the crossroads and villages of yesteryear, and the area of public buildings in the village of Greenville is reminiscent of a New England commons. Time has made changes, but much of the charm and history of the town survives for those willing to look for it and those who wish to preserve it.

Prevost Manor
"Hush Hush" Manor House

The Prevost family originally hailed from Poitou, France. They apparently fled to Geneva, Switzerland, after the St. Bartholomew's Day Massacre of the Huguenots, and were granted citizenship there in 1572. The family later migrated to England, becoming prominent members of the British military at a time when many Swiss soldiers became mercenaries, since they were from a neutral country, yet possessed notable military skills.

Major General Augustine Prevost, father of Major Augustine Prevost, was the commander of British troops in Florida, Georgia, and South Carolina against American and French forces. Born in 1723, he died at his estate in Hertfordshire, England, in 1786.

Major Augustine, the son, and the builder of Prevost Manor, married Susannah Croghan in 1765. Her father, George, was Sir William Johnson's agent, and had in his own right huge landholdings of fine land in several states; so it was considered a propitious union for Augustine and Susannah both. Major Prevost tried to save his father-in-law's vast lands, but Croghan was financially overextended and the major likely had to sell his estate in Pennsylvania in an attempt to assist Croghan. This would explain how the major and his family came to live in Greenville, where he also had claims to thousands of acres.

Susannah bore Augustine 14 children. Sadly, many of these children died young, and their mother died in 1790 at about age 40. With his six surviving children in need of a mother, Major Augustine married Ann Bogardus in 1792. She proved to be a very good choice: in addition to being a good stepmother, she would become mother to ten more Prevosts, who survived into adulthood, many into old age. Her father had served in the Revolution on the American side. This would help Augustine's image with the local population, as did his contributions of land to the east of his home that became sites for churches, the academy, and much of what makes up the public common of Greenville today.

The Manor House was built in 1793 by Major Augustine. His original patent from the British king totaled approximately 7,000 acres. Despite the fact that he leaned toward the Tory position on the matter of American independence, it is nonetheless true that after the Revolution he was able to maintain ownership of his land. While there is no doubt that Augustine Prevost's business acumen was helpful, his ability to retain ownership certainly owed a great deal to his personal relationship with men such as Alexander Hamilton and, more significant, Aaron Burr. Burr's influence in the New York State legislature was considerable in recognizing Prevost's claims to this grant.

The family connection between the Burr and the Prevost family was Burr's wife, Theodosia, an attractive, intelligent, and highly regarded woman to whom historians and her contemporaries have paid homage. Theodosia was a widow when she married Burr—specifically, the widow of Augustine's uncle, Marc Prevost, aka "Jacques Marc," who died of wounds in 1779 in Jamaica during the American Revolution while serving as a lieutenant colonel in the British service. He was highly regarded "as a diligent and efficient officer" in British major Patrick Murray's eulogy, but to the American patriots whose towns he burned, he was viewed "not so kindly."

In the final years of the 1700s, according to Beers' 1884 *History of Greene County*, after building a gristmill and a sawmill, he "opened an office for the sale of his lands, which were offered on the most liberal terms, and held out various inducements to all who were disposed to settle on any portion of them. He sold his land in sections to suit purchasers, built roads for the accommodation of the settlers, and donated largely for religious and school purposes." He built a schoolhouse near his residence and hired the teacher, and although both were for the benefit of his own children, he nonetheless admitted, free of charge, the children of all those who had settled near him.

Despite local sources that describe the original house as constructed of "rubblestone," in his article "The Prevosts of the Royal Americans" author Edward G. Williams states that the manor house, built in 1794, was of frame construction. It is possible that there was an earlier stone structure where Prevost and his family lived while the manor house was being constructed.

Describing the manor itself, Williams tells us, "The house was not pretentious, but is a sturdy example of a mid-18th-century English country gentleman's estate house. The ample main room with a large walk-in fireplace served as kitchen and family room together. The visitor is received before a pungent woodsy

redolence as it dispels the chill of an early autumn morning. More recently, a newer kitchen was added. One senses a certain feeling that pervades 18th-century houses—that a lot of living has taken place here. One is conscious of adventurous spirits that emanated from here to foreign shores and battlefields and noted visitors who came to this quiet spot. To the right of the central stair and hall is a spacious drawing room and parlor with fine antique English and early American furniture."

The Prevost manor is known as the "Hush Hush" house because of the serenity and quiet that prevails on the property. Prevost descendants would continue to till the land well into the 20th century. Like the other local farm families, a hilly section was set aside for a family burial site.

Through marriage, the property was handed down to Vanderbilt descendants. Mr. and Mrs. George Vanderbilt did much in the mid-20th century to preserve this house. Mrs. Vanderbilt was proud of her home and allowed Greenville students and their teacher to photograph the home, inside and out, in the 1970s. She was happy to point out a beautiful Chippendale slant-top desk that had "ingeniously designed interior pigeonholes and secret interior compartments" where she claimed Aaron Burr would write during his visits to Hush Hush. The house next passed to the Vanderbilts' daughter, Susan.

The current owners are the Rowans, who beautifully maintain this truly special place. They have owned the home for some time now. Reportedly, Mrs. Rowan has taken great interest in the gardens as well as the home, and they provide a lovely setting that is what Hush Hush is meant to be to all generations.

Opposite left: Prevost Manor, circa 1894.
Opposite right: Detail of one of the original window frames.

PRESBYTERIAN CHURCH

The original church building, erected in 1793, was a hip-roofed structure that was later moved across the street; it became a dwelling. The second church was built by Elon Norton, but that building was destroyed by a fire in 1859. In 1860 the present church was built as its replacement.

D. and E. Griffin constructed the current building. The architect is not known; however, it is noted as "a New England style Meeting House and a fine example of a Christopher Wren Church." The steeple is tall, towering over nearby buildings, with a golden dome. There are fluted Ionic columns with ram's-horn capitals on either side of the recessed front entry door. The stained-glass windows each stands 8 by 16 by 4 feet.

There is a plaque on the church in memory of Beriah Hotchkin, "the first American Missionary West of the Hudson River." He is prominently mentioned in many early sources and had a significant impact on the early religious developments in this region. Hotchkin, a private who served in the Revolutionary War, was ordained in Connecticut in 1785 and preached his first sermon in Benjamin Spees' barn in Greenville on April 5, 1789. He returned home to Connecticut for a brief time, but in the spring of the same year returned to the East Durham area to preach, and by 1793 was called by old friends in that area to come to Greenville, where he could perform all ministerial services in the towns of Greenville, Cairo, Durham, Windham, and Rensselaerville, until his retirement in 1824.

The Presbyterian Church was built on land given for educational and religious purposes by Augustine Prevost, whose original grant, surveyed in 1767, was called the Prevost Patent. The church was organized in 1790 and was the first American church in the Catskill Mountain region. Organized initially as a Congregational church, it became Presbyterian in about 1814. Until recent years, services had been continuous on this site from the time it was organized, except for such periods when the building was being renovated or reconstructed after the 1859 fire. The building today is owned by the Town of Greenville and is used as a performing arts center.

The present church building was placed on the National Register of Historic Places on March 28, 1985, and the inventory notes that the 1860 Presbyterian Church is a "two-acre complex" that includes the Presbyterian Chapel, built in 1885, to the immediate north of the church, and the Greenville Academy building, built in 1906, now the town library to the south of the church. It provided a town-square setting similar to those that many of the early New England settlers to the village were accustomed to. The pond and stately maples make a pleasant scene with the attractive old buildings.

The church steeple was restored and painted in August and September of 1990. In 2008 the exterior of the entire church was thoroughly sanded and painted, a project which was initiated by the local Girl Scout troop for which financial assistance was received. Paint and materials were donated by various companies and individuals, and labor was completed by youths from the Coxsackie Correctional Facility, under the direction of the State of New York.

Left: 1880 program for the first annual meeting of the Sunday School Association at the Presbyterian Church.

Top: Detail view of the cupola with golden dome.

Above: Plaque honoring Beriah Hotchkin, first American missionary of the Hudson River.

GREENVILLE MEMORIAL LIBRARY

The Greenville Memorial Library stands today on the site of the Greenville Free Academy, which was founded in 1816; it was the first free academy in all of Greene County. The original deed states that the land was given in 1800 for religious and educational purposes, a covenant that has been continuously upheld right up to the present day. The building in use today dates from 1906, when it replaced the original structure. The adjacent village green and pond are part of this historic property.

The Free Academy became part of the Greenville Central School in 1930, part of New York State's push for centralization. In 1957 the building was sold to become the Greenville Memorial Library Building and was completely renovated the following year. An extension that had been added to the 1906 building was sold off separately; the new owner moved it just a few miles down Route 81 to Norton Hill, where it was put to use for many years as a barroom.

The library building itself is topped by a pyramidal roof with a large central chimney. On the front, Doric columns support the slightly pitched porch roof topped by an iron railing. In 1975, the front porch was rebuilt to replicate the original entrance of the 1816 Free Academy. The library was listed on the National Register in 1985 as part of the "Greenville Presbyterian Church complex," stating that "the Academy building is a typical example of early 20th-century-school architecture exhibiting such characteristic features as square massing, a two-room central entrance plan, and group windows."

Presently the building serves the community as a public library in various ways. The library mission statement is "to provide information, materials, services, technology and programs to all community residents to meet their personal, educational, cultural and professional needs." It offers numerous programs for children, teens, and folks of all ages. Many civic meetings are held in the building as well, and in this way, it maintains its importance to the village and its surrounding area. Once surrounded by 18th-century New England–style homes, this historic site now stands as a picturesque island amid other buildings, old and new.

Philip and Barbara Flach House

Built in the 1850s by Nathan Swarthout, this is a fine example of a Greek Revival house created in what is called the National style. The original barns were destroyed in a fire and replaced in 1982. Nathan Swarthout, the builder, apparently was skillful and much in demand in the neighborhood, called Newry, where Greene and Albany counties meet. The 1855 New York State census identifies Swarthout as having been born in Albany County, though he had been living in Greenville for one year. His age is listed as 70, his occupation carpenter. His wife, Dorcas, is listed as age 50. He appears in the west district of Greenville in the 1860 federal census.

Within a very short distance of the Flach house, there are as many as four Swarthout-built houses based on the same plan. One such home was built for George W. Conkling; the agreement between Conkling and Swarthout was clearly written by the builder to the owner's specifications. Down the road from the Flach house is another home that is very similar and in the past belonged to Alonzo Holmes. Another nearby home is of the same plan, but has been modernized. That has changed both its appearance and its character.

In its 150 or more years of history, the Flach house has been home to many families, but for most of its existence it has belonged to only two. The early years of the home proved difficult to research because property transfers involving family members appear to have been informal in some instances, and deeds may not have been recorded. The Beers' 1867 *Atlas of Greene County* does show the occupants of the house as the Wallace Dyer family. This same family was listed in Albany County in the federal census of 1860, but the 1870 census confirms the Dyer family to be in Greenville, Greene County, at the home that the *Atlas* indicates. Significantly, Frank Dyer, the 15-year-old son of Wallace and Mary Dyer, and other children appear as part of the family in the 1870 census. In 1879, Frank Dyer married a Miss Emma Palmer. These Dyers went to California, and the Brate family appears to have been the next owners. We suspect Hannah Brate may have been a Palmer before her marriage, although supporting documentation has not yet surfaced. Hannah and her husband, Sylvester Brate, of Rush, Monroe County, New York, deeded the Greenville farm to Emory R. Palmer on March 26, 1894; the document was recorded on July 23, 1894. From this point on the deed sequence is recorded for all owners to the present time. Emory Palmer transferred property by recorded deed to Phoebe Jane Palmer in 1943; she deeded it to the Knudsen family in the same year; and they deeded it to the Flach family in 1947.

During the residency of Emory R. Palmer, the farm was a milk-shipping center for the surrounding Newry area. Farmers brought their labeled milk cans here to a cooling building to be picked up by truck and hauled to Albany and the Normanskill Dairy. This continued for about 50 years.

Joseph and Elizabeth Flach bought the place in 1947 and it was deeded to their son, Philip, and his wife, Barbara, in 1996. The family has beautifully cared for and maintained this classic Greek Revival home and property.

GREENVILLE

FREEHOLD COUNTRY INN

This historic inn has undergone many transformations since it was built in the latter part of the 18th century (circa 1795). The inn began its life as a refuge for travelers and Teamsters passing through the village on the Schoharie Turnpike. The Schoharie Turnpike began at the shore of the Hudson River in Athens, 15 miles away. They could reach the inn at the village crossroads by horse or carriage, or even on foot, by nightfall of the same day.

Through the many decades of the inn's life, the structural façade has been altered and its name changed to reflect each of its owners. These changes are evident in the many photographs now on display at the inn. The original structure was smaller in size than the present-day inn and included an area slightly larger than today's main dining room, with a second floor containing rooms. A copy of the earliest known photograph of the inn hangs over the fireplace in the main dining room. During the 1800s, large, two-story additions were built onto the original structure. Recent renovations have uncovered hand-hewn beams from the original 1795 structure. These have been left exposed.

The Hunt and Parks families gave the inn new identities as the Freehold House, and later as the Freehold Hotel. In 1883, Dr. John Alden Parks built the two-story carriage house that stands east of the inn. In the late 1960s a major restoration was done by the Parks family and it was rechristened again, that time renamed the Old County Inn. Other owners in the 1970s utilized the inn as a tavern and apartments.

Local business owner Ben Buel purchased the property in 1998 and completely renovated the interior. In March 1999 the Buels and their chef, and co-owner, Max Suhner, opened the inn as a fine dining restaurant. In September of the same year they renovated the carriage house and began using it as a banquet facility.

The restaurant is now under new management by Michal Johnson. It is now called Freehold House, as it was known at an earlier time. The specialties of the house are international cuisine with a French influence, creating a new nuance while carrying on an old tradition.

HICKOK HOMESTEAD

This home was built in 1790; it is unusual in that the Hickoks and their descendants, the Wakeleys, owned it until the 1960s, when the Pratt family bought it. The Carlsens, the current owners, purchased the property from the Pratts in 1992. The homestead originally comprised more than 4,000 acres. The house itself was built by Francis Hickok, who operated a sawmill on the nearby Basic Creek with his two brothers. One of the barns on the property was constructed with timbers hauled by oxen from Connecticut when Hickok came to Greenville from his previous home.

It is said that the home was the site of the first town meeting in Greenville, in 1803, and that Hickok was elected assessor at that meeting. He also served as town clerk for the years 1806 through 1809, and in 1816 was elected the second town supervisor.

The house is a Georgian-style farmhouse of the Federal period, with a center hall entry. The woodwork and wideboard floors are original to the structure. There are six original fireplaces, four of them on the first floor. The symmetrical floor plan includes four rooms divided by the center hall. On each side of the hall, one chimney serves a pair of back-to-back fireplaces, one in each room. Each chimney also serves one of the two fireplaces on the second floor. The fireplace in the "keeping room" has a Dutch oven. In 1854 a bay window nook was added to the first floor—but the matching trim, windows, and woodwork give an appearance that it has always been there.

As antique collectors and dealers, the Carlsens describe the house as "an antique they can live in." In fact, it is remarkable that very few changes have been made to the building in more than two centuries, though it has been beautifully renovated and maintained. The major concessions to modern times are an "updated kitchen" and the usual indoor plumbing and bath facilities.

The Carlsens have repainted the interior of the home in colors fitting to the period when the house was built. It has been their good fortune to have old photos, wills, and even the original deed, all of which have been extremely important to the renovation of this fine historic home.

GREENVILLE ARMS

Today the Greenville Arms is a classic country inn that contains 18 guest rooms, each of them unique. This fascinating building is a Queen Anne Revival–style house with a tower and large porch. It had a carriage house to the west, over the creek, which contained a caretaker's apartment. The buildings were constructed for William S. and Mary Reed Chapman Vanderbilt in 1889.

William S. Vanderbilt was a leading citizen of Greenville who also maintained a residence in New York City while serving as treasurer of the Knickerbocker Trust Company. In Greenville, both the large, important Sherrill farm on North Street and Augustine Prevost's 1792 "Hush Hush" manor came into his possession. He was the benefactor behind construction of the Vanderbilt Opera House in Greenville Village and one of the incorporators of the Free Academy (1899), as well as a founding member of the Knights of Pythias Lodge.

For many years during the mid-1900s, the Greenville Arms was owned by Pierce and Ruth Stevens. A daughter of Ferris and Anita Thompson of the Thompson House in Windham, Mrs. Stevens was well versed in the resort business. Collectively, this family and their children have been responsible for four popular Greene County resorts; three in Windham and this one in Greenville. Two are still owned and operated by members of the family: the Thompson House, and Christman's Windham House, which includes a restaurant and golf course. Both are also on the Greene County Historical Register.

Today the owners maintain the unique character and country charm of the Greenville Arms. When the Greene County Historical Society's Tour of Homes focuses on Greenville, the Greenville Arms always a very popular stop on the tour.

Spring Brook Farm

Spring Brook Farm is located on Route 26 in Greenville. The far right wing of the farmhouse is the original section and is believed to have been built in the mid-1800s. At least in later years this section contained a kitchen and woodshed. After their purchase, the Capone family constructed a kitchen with dining area and a family room on the old foundation. The beautifully restored buildings and the surrounding acres of rolling open land retain the appearance of a well-kept 19th-century farmstead.

Mrs. Capone was raised in Brooklyn, New York, but spent summers on a farm that her father had purchased in the Town of New Baltimore. Fifty-some years ago while visiting that farm with her husband, who had returned from the war, the couple took a ride to Greenville and observed the "For Sale" sign on Spring Brook Farm. They had been looking for a place in the country to raise their children, and they spent all summer considering purchasing the property. That fall, the young couple took ownership of the farm from the Abrams family, whose members had worked the farm for over 100 years.

Property records state that this parcel of land was part of Lot No. 1 of the seventh allotment of the Coeymans Patent, and ownership has been traced back to 1851, when one-half interest in a 147-acre parcel of land was conveyed to Daniel Abrams from Lewis and Esther Sherrill. A dozen years later, in 1863, the Sherills conveyed their remaining equal undivided half interest to Daniel. It is unclear how Daniel and the Sherrills shared the farm and/or any profits, but it was Daniel and his family who were working the farm in 1855. The New York State census for 1855 states that Daniel Abrams and his family owned a frame house with a value of $100. This may have been the original section of the farmhouse. The Agricultural & Domestic Manufacturing Schedule in that census states Daniel worked a farm with a cash value of $5,145 that contained 100 acres of improved land plus 47 acres of unimproved land.

Daniel was a general farmer, raising sheep, swine, and poultry, and producing eggs, butter, and apples, along with various grains. His 54 sheep provided 88 pounds of wool in 1855, and he harvested 20 bushels of apples from his 50-acre apple orchard. Some of the products were probably sold locally, the rest shipped down the Hudson River to New York City. Testament to Daniel's business sense can be found across the road from the farmhouse, where a barn and an apple house still stand. Inside the apple house, one can still see the date 1876 written on one of the exposed beams. It would appear that Daniel's produce sold well.

It has been said that Edwin Drake (1819–1890), who is famous for drilling the first oil well, lived in this farmhouse. It is possible that he may have lived with the Abrams for a time, because the Drake and the Abramses families are entwined through marriage and friendship. However, Edwin's father owned a different farm in Greenville, and according to various accountings of Edwin's life he left Greenville with his family at the age of six or eight, living in several places but never returning to Greenville to live. It seems more likely that Edwin was a visitor here.

Christ Episcopal Church

According to the church history, "Christ Church, was organized as a parish, incorporated and recorded in the County Clerk's office, September 7th, 1825, under the auspices and direction of a much beloved and highly respected clergyman, the Reverend Dr. Samuel Fuller, founder of both Presbyterian and Episcopal churches in nearby communities, Durham, Rensselaerville and Windham. The Wardens were Reuben Rundle and Shubal Newman; Vestrymen were Reuben Rundle Jr., Lewis King, Hardy Rundle, John Boyd, Israel Palmer, Aaron Hall and Robert Palmer."

The present church building was first proposed in the minutes of the vestry, January 2, 1852. Architect Richard Upjohn designed this building, which was completed and its first services held in 1857. It is interesting to note that a statement by the clerk at the time indicated that the expense for the stonework for the horse and wagon sheds and for the fence in front of the church was borne by Reuben Rundle, truly a strong financial supporter of the construction. The total cost of the building was $3,325—a large share of which he supplied through labor and money. The total cost was borne by subscriptions from members.

The beauty of this reddish stone church with its Tudor style is that it so quaintly resembles other churches in England, Ireland, and here in this country. The building's reddish stone comes from the Truman Sanford farm. According to the church history, the farm of Truman Sanford was the land in more recent years owned by George Turon, along Route 26, just east of the village.

This construction replaced the original wood-frame church, which had been built in 1827 by Ephraim Russ of Rensselaerville, a famed builder. William Holdridge had been the carpenter in charge. The bell for the older structure cost $800, and the clock, $381. The Reverend John Henry Hobart, Bishop of the State of New York, dedicated the church on September 6, 1827. When the stone church was built, that original building was moved and served for a time as an opera house sponsored by William S. Vanderbilt, a town leader.

The anniversary of the current church was celebrated in 1957. A sesquicentennial event followed in 1975. Over the years, many renovations were necessary to preserve and maintain the building. At one point the struggles to keep up became so worrisome that one vestryman, Orson Hallenbeck, wryly observed that the Rectory should be called "the Wrecktory." Misses Emily and Elizabeth Prevost supplied generous gifts, and further improvements were forthcoming. Significantly, their forebear, Augustine Prevost, had donated the land for the church.

Right: Detail of the vestry door on the eastern side.

Old Methodist Church of Greenville and Norton Hill

The beginning of a Methodist Society was organized February 8, 1825, in West Greenville with 15 members. The church was built on the northwest corner of Ingalside Road and Route 81. Prior to this, the meetings had been held in members' homes. This church moved to Greenville in 1857 and burned in 1873; that same year the congregation divided, one building a church in Greenville and the other building in Norton Hill.

This house of worship was built in 1873. Within its cornerstone lies a box of lead which contains a Bible and a hymn book, church periodicals, and the names of the pastor and members of the congregation at that time. The beautiful stained-glass windows were installed in 1929.

The Greenville church built in 1873 still remains and has recently been painted, but it is no longer in use as a church: in 1947, Norton Hill once again combined with Greenville's Methodist Church. A year later, in 1948, a Wurlitzer organ was purchased for the church. Since 1947, the reunited congregations have been using the Norton Hill building for their services. The bell from the Greenville Methodist Church stands in front of the education wing. It was presented to the combined congregation by the Ladies' Aid Society.

In 1982, the Church Mouse Nursery School opened in the nearby schoolhouse, which had been built in 1871 at a cost of $1,050. The schoolhouse had been purchased by the church in 1940 and had been used for Sunday school and other church activities.

The Greenville–Norton Hill church has had a very active building program in recent years, connecting the church and the old schoolhouse by adding an education building in between in 1982. In 1986 renovations were made to the interior of the church. The balcony and bell were restored, and window trim was painted to enhance the beautiful stained glass. In addition, a large multipurpose and recreation building has been more recently constructed to the rear. To the west, Elliott House, which was bequeathed to the church, serves the church for various other purposes and completes the complex. The 1873 church building, however, rightly dominates the scene. Newly painted in 2006, it is a testament to good stewardship and historic preservation, and is where weekly services are held. It is clearly the heart of this congregation.

Edgett Farm Cemetery
at Sunny Hill Farm on the Sunny Hill Golf Course

The Edgett Family Cemetery is a small family plot located on a hill near the intersection of Sunny Hill Road and Plattekill Road. The property on which it rests can be traced back beyond the Edgett family to an 1816 Blaisdell land grant when the area was still a part of Albany County. There are six graves marked by fieldstones that have no discernible engravings. Thirteen inscribed headstones also stand in the cemetery, the earliest being that of Rufus Edgett, who died January 11, 1826.

Reynolds Edgett, born in 1793 to Henry and Hannah, left the family farm on which this family cemetery sits and moved to Herkimer County, but during the early 1820s he returned home to Greenville. After his parents' death, Reynolds and his family continued to occupy the old homestead.

At the present time the cemetery is well tended and surrounded by a white picket fence, but it was Reynolds's wife, Hannah Baldwin, who determined first to enclose the plot: in her 1877 will Hannah directed that $125 should be spent "in fencing the grounds where I shall be on the farm on which I now reside."

The family farm remained in the family for at least four generations. Henry's niece, Sarah Simpkins-Plank, finally sold the property in 1916.

Freehold Congregational Christian Church

The Freehold Congregational Christian Church is located off Route 32, barely a tenth of a mile east of the Four Corners in the hamlet of Freehold. The organization of this church actually began in Coeymans, Albany County, when Elder Jasper Hazen was called to come to Freehold, where he would serve as its first pastor from 1812–1816. The church was organized with seven members. In 1816, John Spoor took over and named the church: he chose the Freehold Academy.

Freehold would become a "mother church" for the surrounding territory, with separate services being held in Berne, Freehold, Medusa, South Westerlo, Medway, and Stephensville. The congregational church is a descendant of the early puritan church; as such, it attests to the early settlers here being of New England origin. The Constitution of the Freehold congregation states "that each member shall have the undisturbed right to follow the word of God according to the dictates of his own conscience under the enlightenment of the Holy Spirit."

The present sanctuary was raised in September 1854. It was constructed under the general supervisor James H. Hood, assisted by Edgar Jennings and Hiland Lusk. The church bell was purchased that same year from Jones & Hitchcock of Troy. The bell cost $236.35 and weighed in at a hefty 625 pounds.

The interior of the church sanctuary is wainscoting with plaster walls above. A spindle railing encircles the altar that holds

the pulpit and a set of three chairs that are Renaissance Revival rosewood. The wood trim throughout is black walnut. The original stained-glass windows came from Italy in 1902.

There is a historic oak tree behind the church, said to be the second-oldest tree in Freehold. Its huge size indicates that it predates the building by many years. A large, well-kept cemetery stands to the east of the church, and is the final resting place of many generations of families who have lived in this village and its environs. This church has been a unifying force in the community. An ample and neat stone wall separates the church from the cemetery, and an impressive wrought-iron fence extends all along the front of the cemetery, bordering Route 67.

John Spoor is notable among the pastors of this church, serving here for 40 years. A stone monument in the vestry commemorates his contributions. At least two other clergymen served at least two pastorates in the charge, each at different times. One was the Reverend A.C. Youmans in the early 1900s, and the other was the Reverend Sion M. Lynam, whom many will still recall. Reverend Lynam served a 21-year stint from about 1930 to 1951, and returned to pastor the church on March 2, 1967, for about ten more years. After his retirement, he was honored as reverend emeritus in 1977, and still continued to preach when needed. He lived well into his 90s in Freehold. A plaque in the vestry commemorates his service.

The members of this church have carefully documented and preserved the records of the congregation. It is a credit to the continuity of their existence, and provides a wealth of information for future researchers. Like the ancient oak tree at the rear of the edifice, this church is a reminder of the connectedness between the past and the present.

TALMADGE/IRVING HOUSE

The original section of the Talmadge/Irving House is a two-story, five-bay gable-end English colonial structure with a central chimney, a steeply pitched wood-shingle roof, and clapboard siding. Hand-hewn beams supporting the first and second floors are exposed on the basement and first-floor ceilings.

The house is believed to have been built in the 1700s and moved in 1790 to its present location from across the road. As such, it may be the oldest remaining house in Greenville. A gable-end extension and full-length front porch appear to be additions from the late 1800s.

The house has been in the Irving family for more than 100 years. Prior to the Irving ownership, the deed history is traceable to the 1845 sale to Mary Ann Talmadge by Lewis Sherrill for $425, a price that indicates the house was already on the current property at that time. It is likely that Sherrill, who owned many nearby properties at the time, subdivided it from a larger parcel. Unfortunately, the property descriptions prior to this date are based on references such as fences, trees, and adjoining properties, which cannot now be clearly identified.

Postcard view of Lake Wawaka and "Halcottville-in-the-Catskills" as seen from the railroad station, circa 1910.

TOWN OF HALCOTT

The first settlers arrived in Halcott in 1813, when two Van Valkenburgh brothers and their mother took over an area that had been cleared by a wood chopper. A log school was constructed in 1816, and three framed schoolhouses were added between 1834 and 1836. Although the Town of Halcott was set off from Lexington in 1851, it remained in Greene County. This gave it the distinction of being the last Greene County town to be set off. The name honors George W. Halcott, an early settler. Prior to 1838 mail was delivered once a week from Prattsville, where two roads had been constructed over the mountains.

The area was part of the Hardenburgh patent, and the farms were rented. The years 1839 through 1845, during the Catskill rent wars, saw much activity from the "Calico Indians" of Halcott. They even burned a summons a sheriff had tried to serve!

The civil history of the town began at the organizational meeting, held on April 6, 1852. Conger Avery was elected the first supervisor; others were designated as town clerk, tax collector, and justice of the peace.

Beers' 1884 *History of Greene County* details some of the community's early economic life: the tavern of Mr. Applebee, the sawmills of a Mr. Banker and Mr. Brooks, and the blacksmith shop of Mr. Morris. Electricity finally arrived in 1927, providing much-needed living benefits. Today, Halcott is a picturesque rural valley much desired by residents from New York City looking for a second home or to retire.

Okon House

This one-and-three-quarter-story house was built using a combination of stone load-bearing walls and wood-framed construction. It sits on the same site where the original stone section, containing four rooms, was constructed in 1824. The date stone, measuring approximately 12 by 24 inches, is embedded in the façade at eye level, and has been protected for many years by the front porch addition. Though the wood-framed extension has not revealed its construction date, based on the interlocking wood members and the lath-and-plaster inner walls, it likely dates back to the second half of the 19th century.

Although the owners own less than one acre of land, the farmhouse is still surrounded by woods and acres of open land. The immediate area retains its rural character, in part, due to the large dairy barn erected on the farmstead, which still stands behind the house. The large old maple tree in the front yard and a lilac bush add to this image. The property on which the house is situated can be traced back to the Hardenburgh Patent: Lot No. 2, subdivision 34 of Great Lot 20.

In 1855 Conger Avery (1803–1883) owned the stone house, which was valued at $500. He and his sons, Daniel, Isaac, and Harvey, farmed the land around it. It appears likely that the Avery family were the original occupants because Conger and his wife, Hannah, were new settlers in this location 30 years earlier, when the house was built. Here they raised at least eight children.

Over 20 years earlier their neighbor Benjamin Crosby, his wife, Huldah, and their children had arrived in Halcott from a neighboring town in Delaware County. Benjamin Crosby (1797–1893) owned a frame house and was farming with his sons Eli and David. Benjamin's son Edward Crosby was a successful merchant in Kingston.

Edward Crosby purchased the vast land holdings of Conger Avery in 1864 for the sum of $8,000. By June of 1865 his father, Benjamin, Benjamin's second wife, Elizabeth, and at least three of Benjamin's ten children, including his son David and daughter-in-law Bethiah, were living in this stone house. The house, valued at $600, was surrounded by hundreds of acres of farmland. Five years later, in 1870, Benjamin purchased the house and acreage from Edward and Edward's wife, Caroline.

In all, four overlapping generations of the Crosby family lived in this house. Following Benjamin's death in 1893 at the ripe old age of 96, his heirs transferred their share in the house and property to David Crosby (1828–1907). Benjamin and David had been running a farm together since David's youth; both families had been sharing the house for most, if not all of the years since moving there. It seems likely that the wooden extension and the upper floor with its six roof dormers were built to accommodate the extended family, as well as for housing the hired workers who shared the family home.

In addition to the normal farm laborers, the family was joined in 1870 by five Swedish immigrants who served as laborers and house workers. Two other women living in the house during 1870 reported on the federal census that they worked in a dairy. Because of the amount of milk and butter produced on the Crosby farm, and because it was not until 1889 that the first creamery was established in Halcott, one can guess that the "dairy ladies" may have been churning in this house, or at least in one of the farm buildings nearby.

David's son, Wallace Crosby (1878–1956), was the third generation to carry on the family tradition. He farmed with his father and brought his wife, Abbie, to the family homestead where they raised their children. After his father's death, Wallace's mother continued to live in the house with them. In 1911 she and Wallace's two sisters transferred the farm, including the house, to him. By that time farming was apparently less productive, because the house sheltered no hired hands. By the 1930s Abbie was supplementing the family income by running a boardinghouse. Each of the nine bedrooms in the house contained a sink, probably installed to accommodate the quests who used this place as a summer retreat, and who were served meals in the dining room.

Wallace and Abbie's children were the fourth and last Crosby generation to be raised in this house. At the time of Abbie's death in 1956, she was living alone in the house. The couple's surviving sons, Louis E. and George, were married and living in their own homes nearby. There is speculation that Abbie may have been living in a small extension that had been built onto the rear of the stone house.

The stone house, which had been the heart of the family homestead, was also often the hub of local political affairs. In addition to farming, these early settlers fulfilled their civic duties—as did their descendants.

Conger Avery was postmaster at West Lexington and served as supervisor in Lexington prior to the formation of Halcott. He also served as supervisor in Halcott. On April 6, 1852, Conger Avery and Benjamin Crosby presided over the first Halcott town meeting. At that meeting, Benjamin was elected justice. David Crosby built a school for the district in 1871 and he also donated land for the town's first creamery. In the early 20th century, Wallace Crosby served as supervisor of Halcott.

Around the time of his mother's death, Louis E. Crosby, the last to run the family farm, discontinued operation. The stone house, which for over 150 years had sheltered the Avery and Crosby families, became rental property.

During the 1970s Michael and Carol Okon noticed that the house was empty, and they contacted the Crosby family in hopes of arranging a purchase. The December 1977 transfer to the Okons for the first time separated the house from the Crosby family cemetery and farm. The Crosby family did retain a right of way for access to the remaining farm outbuildings and property. Happily, this change in ownership returned the house to a well-maintained, owner-occupied family residence.

Haines Corners Station, offering "Connections by Boat or Rail for All Points North and South," circa 1900.

TOWN OF HUNTER

The Town of Hunter, located high in the northern Catskill Mountains, was first established under the name Greenville on January 27, 1813. The town adopted the name Hunter the following year. The land, taken from the Town of Windham, is a portion of the 1,708-acre land grant given by Queen Anne to Johannes Hardenburgh and six other individuals. Today the Town of Hunter consists of two incorporated villages, Hunter and Tannersville, and three hamlets: Haines Falls, Elka Park, and Lanesville. There are also five private communities that originated as summer camps: Elka, Onteora, Santa Cruz, Sunset, and Twilight Parks.

By the 1890s, hundreds of large wood-frame hotels and boardinghouses accommodated visitors who sought the fresh mountain air for health and diversion. The proliferation of the automobile, the Depression, and then World War II affected tourism in Hunter, and many of the large hotels closed down. After the war Hunter remained in the tourist business, catering to hikers, campers, and other outdoor enthusiasts, although at a slower pace than before.

During the 1960s, skiing on the great mountain refocused the town's commercial base, emphasizing winter sports. This, along with the spin-off of service industries and the conversion of the summer cottages to year-round homes, spurred the local economy. Outdoor activities still thrive, and artistic and cultural events fulfill the needs of the year-round residents, the weekenders, and the tourists who share their town.

Ulster & Delaware Railroad Station
Haines Falls Railroad Station

Owned by the Mountain Top Historical Society, this one-story, wood-framed former train station sits on a low concrete foundation at its original site on the north side of Route 23 in the hamlet of Haines Falls. It is an important regional example of a railroad station serving the many people who once traveled to and from the tourist areas of the Catskill Mountains before the popularity of the personal automobile.

The hipped roof on the station is supported by prominent open brackets and drop pendants. Unfortunately, the old slate shingles were replaced with modern asphalt shingles. At both ends of the station the roof extends several feet beyond the building and is supported by large square columns. The overhang on the west end supplied a large sheltered area for the passengers waiting to board, and for those debarking from the train. The overhang on the east end protected freight and baggage. The main entrance and an entry door into the baggage area are on the south side of the station. On the north, the track side, an entrance led to the stationmaster's office.

The interior of the station was divided into three areas. Directly through the main door was an entrance hall and the ticket/stationmaster's office. On the west side, there was a passenger waiting room with a large stone fireplace on one wall. East of the central office there was a large baggage/freight room, bathroom, and utility area.

Passing through Haines Falls, this route of the Ulster & Delaware Railroad (1870–1979) started in the city of Kingston in Ulster County, made its way to headquarters in Rondout, and then journeyed through the Catskill Mountains to its terminus at Oneonta. In the Catskills, the Ulster & Delaware had two branches, one going to Kaaterskill and the other to Hunter. On its route, the train carried travelers to the many tourist areas with numerous hotels and boardinghouses.

In the early 1910s, New York State determined that the original Haines Falls station was too small for the local and large tourist population, and convinced the Ulster and Delaware Railroad to replace it. In 1913 the old station was torn down, and this station was erected only a few hundred feet away.

This station served as a full-season passenger station until the New York Central Railroad purchased the Ulster & Delaware Railroad in 1932. At that time it continued only as a regular stop during summer months, when tourists were plentiful. During the rest of the year it was necessary to flag down the train as it passed through. Business was handled at a station in the Village of Tannersville. In 1940 the Haines Falls station was closed completely and the tracks removed by the railroad. The railroad bed is still visible north of the station.

The station and property were purchased by Henry Meyer, son-in-law of Christopher A. Martin, who had previously owned the property and the Loxhurst Hotel that sat next to the first station. The Martin family converted the station into a summer residence, and it remained in the Meyer family until December 1995, when it was sold to the Mountain Top Historical Society.

Luckily, the building was not greatly compromised while serving as a residence, retaining much of its original fabric and architectural integrity. Yet it took a great deal of work to restore the station to its original condition. The roof was reconstructed and the room partitions and Sheetrock covering the original wainscoting were removed. The original wainscoting was cleaned and any missing pieces were duplicated. The windows that had been lowered were returned to their original positions, and period lighting was installed.

Returned to its prior prominence, the station is once again a welcome site after you've driven up through the gorge of the Catskill Mountains to Haines Falls.

Western façade of the restored station.

HUNTER

MEMORIAL CHURCH OF ALL ANGELS

Memorial Church of All Angels is a central feature in Twilight Park, the park being one of the private summer communities established in the town of Hunter more than 100 years ago. Owned and occupied by the same Episcopalian congregation since its establishment, the church serves as a summer community house of worship, welcoming many who are not of the Episcopalian faith. The church was founded in 1895 and was originally named the "Mission Church of All Angels."

The building was planned by architect Alexander Mackintosh and constructed by a Mr. Payne, who was supervised by Samuel Rusk of Haines Falls. Funding for the construction came from $1,419.70 in subscriptions and a $2,000 mortgage. The cornerstone was laid on November 9, 1895, and the earliest construction of this lovely small church began in 1896. The main body of the structure is of dry "laid-up" stone with masonry embellishments measuring 43 feet square, including the chancel. Following the local Catskill Mountain tradition, the interior is covered in varnished wood, with laminated "ribs" supporting a vaulted ceiling.

The pulpit was first occupied by Reverend Henry Yates Satterlee, rector of the Calvary Church in New York City, who would go on to become the first bishop of Washington, D.C., at the National Cathedral. The reverend's introduction to Twilight Park was his summer vacation at the cottage of his cousin, the artist Walter Satterlee. Reacting to the need for Episcopal services, the Reverend Satterlee preached at various inns within the private parks until a piece of land was obtained on which to establish this house of worship. He conducted a morning prayer service in the incomplete church on July 19, 1896. Unfortunately, due to his new full-time position as bishop of Washington, D.C., he was unable to conduct the first service of Holy Communion. That honor instead went to Reverend Dr. George Williamson Smith, president of Trinity College, who officiated at the service on August 2, 1896, with 77 people in attendance.

Perhaps the congregation sat on folding chairs during that first summer, because the oak pews were not placed in the church

until the summer of 1897. At that time, the pews joined the oak pulpit and other items donated by various individuals. During the early years of the church, services were conducted on Wednesdays, Fridays, and Sundays, with up to three services on some Sundays. It has been reported that the 5:00 p.m. Sunday service was the most popular.

During his absences, due to his responsibility as bishop, Reverend Satterlee's colleagues and family members assumed his duties here. When Reverend Satterlee passed away in 1908, a committee was formed to change the name of the church to "Memorial Church of All Angels." In tribute to their founder, funds were raised to complete the building.

The stone masonry façade, the porch, and the steps were completed at a cost of $1,947.43, during the winter of 1908–1909. However, due to trouble with the land title, consecration was delayed until July 13, 1913. The church was dedicated in memory of Bishop Satterlee, and the property formally deeded to the Diocese of Albany. After the demise of its founder, the Reverend Canton W. Austin from Washington, D.C., took charge and remained for the next ten years. In 1915, during Reverend Austin's pastorate, the bell tower, designed by the original architect, was completed. The tower along with its bell was a $2,660 gift to the church.

Throughout World War II, much of the congregation consisted of wives and children whose husbands and fathers were fighting in the war. The Reverend Bradford Burnham arrived in 1944, and when peace was declared on August 14, 1945, he gathered with many people at the church to ring the bell and pray. Reverend Burnham continued to serve until his son Frederick succeeded him in 1978. During Frederick's tenure, it was decided to take the step toward full adherence of the canons of the Episcopal Church and also to create a resting place for cremated remains adjacent to the church. On July 10, 1983, a memorial garden was consecrated, which is now graced by stone benches where the living can pause, reflect, and pray overlooking the mountain clove.

While still adhering to the Book of Common Prayer of the Episcopal Church, the Memorial Church of All Angels is still very much a community chapel. Fifty to 100 community members of the Protestant, Catholic, and Jewish faiths worship here during the ten-week summer period when various visiting clergy preside over the single Sunday service. Sometimes as many as 250 community members attend memorial services or weddings conducted by visiting clergy, including Frederick Burnham. Not to be overlooked are the exquisite stained-glass windows, including examples of Connick and Tiffany, which allow a cascade of colored sunlight to enhance these occasions.

OLD PLATT CLOVE POST OFFICE

Old Platt Clove Post Office, now a private residence, is located on the south side of Platt Clove Road in the town of Hunter. It is situated in a small community: approximately eight houses surrounded by woodland. Built in the 1880s, the former Platt Clove Post Office displays some interesting architectural elements. One of the most significant elements is a spiral staircase, hidden behind a door, within a rounded, tower-like enclosure. The door and walls are beautifully stained and covered with "matchstick" board. The house has hardwood floors, including some wide-plank areas.

The majority of the interior walls are covered with the original stained, triple-beaded boardwork in geometric chevron designs. The building's exterior is covered with the original clapboards and shingles. Using fish-scale, cap-tooth, and square shingles, they incorporate the outline of two trees, possibly hemlocks to represent the local tanning industry, so important in this area during the 19th century.

The two-story wood-framed house has circular sawn members that are joined with wire nails, and is constructed on a sloping grade that goes down toward the Plattekill Creek. The foundation, exposed in the rear, is constructed of irregularly laid dry, flat fieldstones, and was reinforced with concealed concrete piers during 2003–2004. The front of the building faces north, with the center projecting forward to create a bay where the main entrance is located. A second entrance is protected by a small porch located in the corner where the west wall of the bay connects to the north wall of the main house.

The main entrance in the bay leads into a small vestibule, where the spiral stair to the five rooms on the second floor is located. A separate doorway in the vestibule allows entry into a first-floor living area, leading directly into the east room which functioned as a parlor for the family. The post office was located in a similar-sized room on the west side, and was accessed from the second exterior door. Significant as a local example of mixed-use late Victorian architecture, the post office room served the community at a time when the area had numerous hotels and boardinghouses that were popular tourist destinations.

The house was used as both a residence and post office by Charles Edgar Cole when he served as the fourth U.S. postmaster of Platt Clove. The former Ulster County quarryman was appointed postmaster of Platt Clove on May 15, 1888. The appointment is believed to be based on his Civil War service. Cole would sort and distribute the mail in the west room until his retirement on November 26, 1911. During 1890, the postmaster's wife, Louisa, purchased the property from the owner, Sarah A. Young. Although prior ownership has not been documented, the account handed down through the Cole family is that the house was first owned and occupied by William Hommel, whose daughter Sarah married Amos D. Young. Land records confirm that William

Hommel purchased 107 acres of land in the area during 1845; it is probable that this property is a small portion of that larger tract of land.

In 1880 the future postmaster and his family were living in Hunter, probably in this same house, with widow Susan Young and her single son, George. George would later marry Ida Cole, one of the postmaster's daughters. It seems plausible that when George and Ida married they remained in the house, because in the 1892 census Ida and George with their two children are listed as residing with the Cole family. Perhaps the front vestibule served as an entry point for two related yet separate families, one using the staircase to the second floor and the other using the door into the first-floor parlor. It has been proposed that the largest of the five rooms on the second floor was used as the master bedchamber, but it's possible that it could have been used as a sitting-room for one family, with the second staircase in the rear providing access to the kitchen area.

Louisa Cole died in 1900, and the postmaster followed in 1926. Their daughter Eva, who was partially blind, continued to reside in the house and sold postcards, candy, and souvenirs to area visitors.

It is possible that this structure housed the United States Post Office even before Mr. Cole's appointment, and perhaps continued as such for a short time after his retirement.

On January 5, 1885, Edward F. Brice was appointed as the third U.S. postmaster of Platt Clove. A topographer's office request for information, signed by Brice, describes the location as being 75 yards on the north side of Plattekill Creek. The description sounds much like the site of this building, unlike former site descriptions when the post office was housed in the Hotel Plattekill. Since there is no new site request on file by Postmaster Cole, it seems likely that Edward Brice was the first to use the period shelving that still remains in the west room.

Following Postmaster Cole's retirement, Theodore Kessel was appointed postmaster on January 26, 1911, with Elizabeth C. Fuller following on August 13, 1915. No new site location request is on file with the postal system until a request in 1917 by Postmaster Fuller.

Postmaster Cole's great-grandson John Dwyer, a resident of nearby Elka Park, can remember as a child purchasing candy from Eva. When Eva died in 1942, the heirs of Louisa sold the house and property to Frank Scialo. Passing through three generations of that family, the house is now owned by Gerard J. Muro, who traces his ancestry back to the Cole family.

A small addition was added on the rear before Mr. Scialo purchased the property, and a bathroom and some other alterations were completed during the 1940s; otherwise, the structure remains unaltered. Mr. Muro takes great pride in his restoration of the building, working with contractor Waldemar Stanick of Greenville and using volunteer help from the Bruderhof community. The improvements completed in 2003–2004 did not compromise the structure's historic integrity.

Washington Irving Inn

Washington Irving Inn is situated on a mostly wooded parcel located on the historic Rip Van Winkle Trail (Route 23A) between the villages of Hunter and Tannersville. Owned and operated by the Jozic family, the inn was chosen in 2006 as one of three finalists in the Bed & Breakfast of Distinction category of the New York State Hospitality & Tourism Association's Stars of the Industry Program. Although now an upscale bed-and-breakfast, the structure began life as a private residence.

The Frederick W. Lilienthal family purchased a 14½-acre parcel of land in 1939 on which to build a summer residence. Frederick was a prominent and prosperous physician, and a pioneer of the Socialist Party in New York City. His wife, Augusta, was editor of the women's section of the New York Volk's Sterns Sunday Magazine. Since the family did not hire an architect, they traveled frequently to the site to consult with the local building crew, and to keep watch on the construction. The following year they settled into Villa Meta, a late Victorian, shingle-style house with a three-story octagonal turret. The house was named to honor their only child, Meta.

Ten years later Meta took possession of the house, which continued to serve as the family's summer residence into the early 20th century. Meta Lilienthal-Stern sold the property in 1928, and following the sale the structure fell on hard times. The Great Depression, World War II, and the family auto that drew tourism away from the Catskill Mountains—all of these had their effect. Through several ownerships the decorative shingles covering the roofs and the exterior walls disappeared. The stylish trim also vanished, including the balustrade atop the turret, and the upper railing that surrounded the wraparound portico. For at least part of this period the structure was used as a boardinghouse, renting rooms to families who shared a common kitchen and two or three existing bathrooms.

The Chebolian family purchased the property in 1941, and for at least part of their 45-year ownership ran the establishment as the Washington Irving Inn. It was most likely during their tenure

that the wings were constructed, additional rooms created, and the portico rebuilt. The story is told that Marderos Chebolian was a great chef and loved to fill the dining room with guests. To accommodate his passion, it is believed that he was instrumental in converting the stable behind the inn into a large kitchen, and changing the porch between the kitchen and dining room into a connecting room. As Marderos grew older he gave up the business, but retained a small portion of the original acreage on which to retire. He lived in a cottage there until he passed away, at about 90 years of age.

The inn and the remaining property were purchased by a hotel corporation, who owned it for about 15 years. For some of this period an Armenian couple, Fred and Victoria Avedis, were the proprietors. The corporation sold off additional acreage to various individuals before the inn and the remaining 6.7 acres were sold to the current owners in 1986.

Mirko and Stefania Jozic were New York City residents looking for a place to start a business, and their love of the mountains lured the couple to the Catskills. When they came upon the hotel named Washington Irving Inn, an immediate bond was forged: they knew about the famous American author when they were still in their native Yugoslavia. They saw the inn's potential and began planning for its renaissance, turning it from an aging hotel into a modern bed-and-breakfast.

Four years into the renovation process, Mirko lost his life in a car accident. Fortunately, the entire family had been included on the improvement plans, so Stefania and their sons, Nash and Danny, persevered. They oversaw all of the construction details, including reinforcement of the foundation and creation of a private bath for each of the rooms. The guest rooms were outfitted with modern amenities, and the lobby, dining room, library, and living room were all refurbished.

The original summer residence is now the core of today's larger structure, and luckily, through the years of decline, the interior Victorian period décor, including the stained hardwood wainscoting and trim, was retained. In the parlor, Stefania provides an elegant afternoon tea using Serbian recipes from her native Yugoslavia, serving desserts and tea sandwiches on her one-of-a-kind antique dish collection. In contrast, the Jozic family's transformation of the exterior of the inn was completed in a modernist design, but following in the Catskill Mountain tradition, they used wood as decorative detail. The dissimilarity between the original structure and the newer additions is erased by the stained-cedar clapboards arranged in ornamental patterns.

Congregation Kol Anshe Yisroyal
Hunter Synagogue

Kol Anshe Yisroyal in Hunter, also known as Hunter Synagogue, is a fine example of an Eastern Orthodox synagogue. The Queen Anne-style structure is located on Main Street in the Village of Hunter. It sits on the original site where construction began in 1913, and where the Jewish community has been welcomed through its doors since 1914.

The building is constructed of wood members; following the Catskill Mountain tradition, decorative woodwork was used on both the interior and exterior of the Synagogue. The original foundation was recently reinforced, retaining the opening where the Schoharie Creek ran through before being diverted by a construction project along Main Street. There have been changes to some of the windows, and the outside walls of the synagogue are now covered with more modern material, but otherwise it remains remarkably intact.

The entrance to the synagogue on its north end is enhanced by decorative corner pilasters, the pediment above the entrance is in-filled with patterned wood shingles, and the gable contains a large oculus with a stained-glass panel depicting the Star of David. The exterior doors open into a deep vestibule that crosses the width of the building. In past years, Sabbath classes were held in this space during the winter.

Oak doors in the vestibule lead into the main sanctuary, where the walls and vaulted ceiling are covered in matchstick wainscoting. Three rows of simple wood pews face the far wall, where, atop a raised platform, an intricately-carved cabinet (Ark) houses the Torah. Two windows with stained-glass panels are situated on each side of the Ark area. Prior to the 1990s these two windows contained opaque glass, as many of the windows still do.

Midway up the sanctuary is a reading table on a bimah, a raised platform, encircled by a balustrade. This is where, when removed from the Ark, the Torah is laid out and read. A stairway in the vestibule leads to the women's gallery, which is situated in the northwest corner. The gallery contains two rows of three pews and is spanned by a balustrade. Light enters through second-story windows.

To complete the history of this synagogue it is necessary to look back to 1905, when the first synagogue in the village of Hunter was constructed. Referred to as the Fischel Synagogue after its founder, Harry Fischel, it was constructed on property adjacent to the west side of the current elementary school. That synagogue accommodated 250 people. The June 26, 1906, edition of the *Hebrew Standard* newspaper contained an article announcing that not only was the edifice a house of worship, but it was also holding Hebrew and religious classes. Not many years after its construction, there was division in the congregation, and many of its working-class members opted to build a second synagogue.

In 1909 a foundation was started on the outskirts of the village, but construction stopped, and the property on which Kol Anshe Yisroyal, Hunter, stands today, was obtained. It was only a short distance from the first synagogue, and construction was completed in 1914. It is not apparent how long the first synagogue continued to operate, but by the 1930s—possibly even earlier—Mr. Fischel and others were attending services at the new synagogue built by the working class. It is interesting to note that Mr. Fischel's home was across the street from the news synagogue. In 1939 the Fischel Synagogue became part of the current site,

Left: The first synagogue structure, circa 1900.
Above: View of the bimah with Ark and parokhet (curtains).

with the understanding that the structure would be carefully disassembled and the materials used to build an addition to serve as a gathering place for the congregation. A plaque in the west wing honors Jane Fischel, who donated funds for this work.

Kol Anshe Yisroyal, Hunter, as the "new" synagogue is known today, is the only all-year Jewish house of worship in Greene County. Many leading rabbis and cantors have been visitors, and a number of resident rabbis have been welcomed in, each bringing a personal style to the services.

The congregation experienced decline in past years, but it is building again. The Sunday Torah school is active, and three worship services a week are conducted in the synagogue. A rabbi is engaged for High Holy Days and special events, and members of the congregation volunteer their services as readers when the rabbi is not present. In addition, on the first Friday of the month the service is followed by a community dinner hosted by members of the congregation.

*Miles Bridge over the East Kill, Jewett, circa 1908.
The Miles Brothers' house on the left was the local post office.*

TOWN OF JEWETT

Set among picturesque hills and sloping mountain peaks, the Town of Jewett is geographically long and narrow, and is shaped a bit like the letter "L" fallen forward. It is in Jewett where one finds the headwaters of the East Kill Creek, which flows into the Schoharie Creek and eventually into the Schoharie Reservoir, which supplies water to the City of New York. Jewett contains some of the tallest peaks in the Catskill Mountains, including Thomas Cole, Blackhead, and Black Dome to the north.

Back in 1783 William Cass and his family, the first settlers to the area, arrived at what is now Jewett Center. Other immigrants followed, settling at Jewett Heights, Mill Hollow, Goshen Street, Beaches Corners, and East Jewett. Most had emigrated from Connecticut; once here they made their living by farming, tanning, and operating small mills.

Some of the settlers brought something else with them from Connecticut: stocks and a whipping post. These were erected in Jewett Heights, near the Presbyterian church. According to the Reverend H. H. Prout, the apparatus was "erected on mere neighborhood views and administered only on local authority." The reverend adds that the stocks were used only once: "A man known as Brom Pete swore terribly on regimental training day. The poor fellow was taken in hand, brought before Justice Ichabod Andrews, and condemned to the stocks for two hours." The demise of the apparatus came not long after that event, as "one night six or eight spirited young fellows demolished the stocks, and carried most of the timbers to Abel Holcomb's swamp."

Formed in mid-November 1849 from lands taken from the Towns of Hunter and Lexington, Jewett has distinction of being named after Freeborn G. Jewett, chief judge of the New York State Court of Appeals. Jewett's first town meeting was held in April 1850, at which time Fisk Beach was elected supervisor and Henry R. Hosford was elected town clerk. Also elected at that time were three assessors, three justices, four highway commissioners, a poor master, a tax collector, a school superintendent, four constables, three election inspectors, and a sealer. The latter inspected and verified weights and measures.

In its heyday, the town had four churches and a dozen school districts, each with its own one- or two-room schoolhouse. Today the schools are gone, as is one of the churches, but the town can boast two post offices.

MILES BRIDGE—ACROSS THE EAST KILL

This iron span across the East Kill just south of Beaches Corners was constructed circa 1897. The Owego Bridge Company of Owego, New York, constructed and supplied the iron framework, but the stone foundation and wood decking were probably constructed from local materials and assembled with local labor. Due to safety concerns, Miles Bridge was closed to vehicle traffic in 1988.

It appears that bonds were issued to cover the cost of Miles Bridge. According to Greene County supervisor reports for 1897, the town account for Jewett lists "Note Owego Bridge Co; $500 plus $13.06 interest claimed and allowed. The following year: Note and interest $625. Amounts in 1901 and 1902 on notes and interest total $1,031. All of these costs may not be for this bridge alone, but the total seems comparable with the price of other iron bridges in Greene County around that time.

The Owego Bridge Company was founded in 1892. Just two years after organizing, the company had completed what was then the longest single-span highway truss bridge in New York state. Perhaps because of this feat, officials put their trust in a relatively new company.

Almost certainly, Miles Bridge got its name from the family whose residence is located at the southern end of the bridge. Members of the Miles family have been farmers and property owners in the town of Jewett since the early 1800s. The U.S. post office was in the Miles house and there was a store nearby.

In 1997, after the collapse of the NYS Thruway bridge, a broad inspection of bridges occurred. The following year Miles Bridge was closed. There was some attempt to rescue the bridge for use as a walking path, but unfortunately it remains barricaded even to pedestrian traffic.

Blue Willow

The house known as the Blue Willow is of classic Victorian design: large rooms, high ceilings, wide-board floors, and exceptional wood trim throughout. The wainscoting in the kitchen includes the ceiling. Sometime after its circa 1898 construction, a dining room and master bedroom were added to the original house.

The Goslee family dates back to late 1700s in this area and the acreage on which Blue Willow sits was subdivided from the Goslee family farm. In 1899 an acre of land opposite the wagon house of Fred M. Goslee (no longer standing) was sold to a piano teacher from Brooklyn, New York. "Professor" August Arnold had boarded at an inn across the street before constructing his family's summer home.

In his land transaction, Professor Arnold was prudent to arrange for a water supply to his property. Secured in his deed is the privilege of transporting spring water from the neighboring property through a one-inch pipe, at a cost of five dollars annually.

Blue Willow was purchased by Frederick J. Seeback of Jersey City, and during the 1920s and 1930s was used as a tea house. Tea and ice cream were served to locals and to boarders from nearby hotels and farms. It was during this time that it quickly earned the name Blue Willow, because all the refreshments were served on the owner's wedding china with the blue willow pattern.

Ethel Peck became its third title-holder in 1943 and owned it for the next 20 years. Blue Willow was transformed into an antique shop that operated until the 1960s. It was then purchased by Kenneth R. Finn of Jamaica, Long Island. When it was purchased by David and Arthur Larsen in 1969, it was restored to a private residence. Presently, the owners rent the house seasonally to families that have been coming to the area for many years, some for generations.

Goslee Cottage Farmhouse

Here is a home with a history in five different towns! While the building has never been moved, the political boundaries around it have—frequently! Over the years, it has been part of Woodstock, Windham, New Goshen, Lexington Heights, and now Jewett.

Actually, such frequent changes are quite apropos for this particular house, which has undergone a number of major changes itself through the years. Today the house is a two-storied, five-vaulted, symmetrical side-gabled Federal and Greek Revival Inn and farmhouse. The one-story entry porch is surrounded by Doric columns constructed with native woods. The original front door—probably stored in the barn—has been replaced with one from the 1890–1910 era, although the original tracery and side lights are intact. Triangular mounts sit above the front windows. The building's original 12 windows were diligently stored in the barn during the renovation.

This current form is quite different from the original. The earliest construction dates to 1797, and the building's original use was as an inn. Local rumor has it that Aaron Burr addressed the population of Jewett Heights from the front parlor on the first floor.

The first owner of record appears to be Dr. Abram Camp, who emigrated from Connecticut. He was the area physician for many years. It may have been during his ownership that the first modifications were made to the building. In 1830, its use and form were shifted to that of a farmhouse, most likely in the Federal style. The next owners were members of the Goslee family. The property remained with this family from 1860 to 1986. The Goslees gave the house a "country" Greek revival renovation in 1888 or so. In 1913, the carriage house, the icehouse, and the creamery were added, as well as a big hearth.

Inspecting the roofing from inside, one can see that the common rafters are pegged together, and that roofing supports still contain vintage board. Although the banister and stairway and an upstairs bedroom still feature wide-board floors, there are drawings that indicate the house has undergone substantial interior changes since the mid-1800s.

In the basement, one can see that foundation stones are uncut and in irregular courses. The basement also reveals the fact that the house once had two other chimneys. But the final surprise is the fact that a gravity-fed spring is still flowing in the "spring room."

Jewett Presbyterian Society
Jewett Presbyterian Church

The earliest records of the Jewett Presbyterian Society date back to July 7, 1797, as "a book of records for the Society Town of Windham." The original meetinghouse was erected by "an association of men of different religious denominations for their mutual accommodation" while the country was yet comparatively new and no one denomination felt able to build for itself. In 1813 the association separated from Windham and became the Lexington Congregational Society. Then, on May 4, 1827, the church changed to a Presbyterian form of government and was received into the Columbia Presbytery, which later became part of the Albany Presbytery, to which the church still belongs.

The current church building was planned and built in 1848; it was 38 feet by 60 feet, and the specifications called for it to be "laid with good hemlock boards." The total cost was not to exceed $2,500, including the old church. "Bees" were held to take down the old church and to erect the new one. J. B. Hinman and William Goslee were contracted to build the new church. Pledges were solicited for money, material, and manpower. The old building was torn down and the timbers used for the new church; the men of the community worked in their spare time to complete the task.

In 1867, Jewett Heights, formerly called Lexington Heights, and formerly a part of Lexington, now became the Town of Jewett. The church was renamed the Jewett Presbyterian Society, a name that survives to this day. The church has a rich history of ongoing renovations: the steeple, which was severely damaged by a 1913 storm, was replaced by George Radcliffe of Kingston; in 1916, a 40-inch bell was purchased from Montgomery Ward for $67.50 to replace an earlier bell that had cracked; in 1923, new pews replaced the original pews and seats, which were once sold as a way to pay preachers; in the 1930s, stained-glass windows were donated by the Kirkman (Soap) family. In more recent years, a new foundation and a full basement were constructed under the church. Grants from the O'Connor Foundation, fund-raising efforts, and gifts have provided for the upkeep and maintenance—the latter two accounting for the greater part.

In 1848, the same year that construction began, a plot of land was deeded to the Methodist Society for five dollars, and the two churches were built on adjoining land. When Methodist attendance declined, the Presbyterian Society purchased the Methodist building and plot for $200 in 1903. Today it is the Presbyterian Church Hall and is listed as part of the church complex on the New York State and National Register.

The church was built in the Greek Revival style, with two doors at the gable end of the exterior. The interior retains the original round, vaulted ceiling, though now it is hidden under a dropped ceiling. The bluestone slabs in front of the church entranceway are enormous and unusual.

It is worthy to note the changes in Society practices, in that women have become Elders of this church since 1980, where previously leadership had been dominated by men. At the church's bicentennial celebrations, in 1999, it was noted that "the spirit of fellowship and worship can always be found in the beautiful old church that stands on a knoll on the heights of Jewett."

Jewett Presbyterian Church, prior to 1901.

The Lexington Catholic church in the Catskill Mountains, circa 1900.

TOWN OF LEXINGTON

Albany and Ulster counties were realigned in 1788, placing the mountaintop in the Town of Woodstock. In 1798 Windham was divided from Woodstock, and by 1800 Greene County was formed. At this point Windham was subdivided, forming the new town of New Goshen, now Lexington, and including Barbertown, now Lexington Heights. Finally, in 1851, Halcott, the last of the Greene County towns to be created, was set off from Lexington.

The Town of Lexington sits surrounded by some of the grandest scenery to be had in the Catskills. Many of the early settlers who migrated here came from the Connecticut town of Goshen—hence the original name, New Goshen. These settlers saw the potential to harness the waterpower of the rushing streams and creeks. They also saw the abundance of timber and fur available in the area. Timber—more specifically, tree bark—played an important role in the emergence of tanning as a major Greene County industry. By 1830, several tanneries were located in the town, though the industry died out locally as it consumed the needed ingredients that had earlier been readily available.

After the Civil War, there was a great boardinghouse business boom, and many boardinghouses sprang up in Lexington. Many farmers got into the act, augmenting their income by expanding their houses to rent a room or two to help accommodate the influx of summer boarders heading to the mountains to escape the heat of the city. But those businesses built specifically for use as boardinghouses and hotels were all the rage, as Beers' 1884 *History of Greene County* comments: "Of the hundreds of summer boarding houses and hotels located in and about the county, very few can compare with Lexington's O'Hara House . . . all in all, the spot is indeed charming . . . a most desirable stopping place." There was also Lexington House, circa 1883, one of the last surviving examples of late-19th-century resort architecture in the Catskills.

The Lexington Creamery, launched in 1899, was a successful local business for 60 years, providing an income for many in the community, including the dairy farms. They produced butter at a rate of eight tons per 24-hour cycle with a crew of 14 men per shift. During the years of butter production, Land O'Lakes was their biggest client. In the mid-1950s, Reddi-wip production replaced butter production, but Reddi-wip moved out in 1959 and the creamery closed its doors. Two years later, the facility burned to the ground.

A progressive town, Lexington at one time boasted 15 schoolhouses; 13 of those sites are still known. Lexington also had three Methodist churches, two Baptist churches, one Baptist church school, and one Catholic church—although the latter was primarily for the city visitors. Today, tourism still plays an important role in the local economy, with major portions of the land now the property of New York State or the City of New York.

COLE HOUSE/TRAILSIDE COTTAGE

This historic structure was constructed early in the 19th century. Later, a rear wing was added. The building uses post-and-beam construction, the timbers probably hewn from local hardwood. As was common on the Mountain Top, the original exterior shingles were of local hemlock. Construction took place during the transition from cooking in fireplaces to using woodstoves. As a result, fireplaces were constructed at both ends of the house. The year 1822 is chiseled on both chimneys. It is believed that this house served as the principal residence on a large farm until the 1860s, when another farmhouse was built farther up the hill.

Mostly surrounded by woodland, this house faces the north bank of the West Kill stream about a mile distant from the village of West Kill. As it is set near the entrance to the scenic Spruceton Valley and along part of the original road to Kingston, prior to the establishment of the so-called Notch Road—now Route 42—the building earned the nickname of Trailside Cottage.

On July 3, 1922, the property was conveyed to Bertram Carter by a Mr. & Mrs. Trede. The property was further conveyed to Lillie M. Cole on May 12, 1928. In all, the house was in the possession of the Carter/Cole families for at least 75 years. Through those years the owners tried to update and repair where needed without drastically changing the house. Some of the moldings on the front of the house are original, as are the window-lights in the front door. To make it more livable, during the 1950s George Cartwright, a local carpenter, was hired to combine three rooms to create a large country kitchen with a fireplace. A rear porch was added in 1982. The Carter/Cole ownership ended in 1997.

Outbuildings on the property include barns and an artist studio. The studio is a reproduction of the small, unheated one used by local artist Hazel Cole Carter, who resided here at the time of her death in 1974. Donald C. Christ is credited for the replication of Hazel's studio. After purchasing the property in 1997 he made a renovation attempt, but her original studio was beyond repair due to termite damage.

Hazel Cole Carter painted in the American primitive style of Grandma Moses, depicting scenes of West Kill, the Catskills, and the Hudson Valley. Local residents report that Hazel's work was displayed at the Whitney Museum of American Art in New York City, and her descendants report that some of her paintings were reproduced on Hallmark greeting cards. One card illustration is a Christmas tree in the bay window of this house. Hazel's descendants dispersed and sold her paintings, but two pieces of her artwork have never left this house. The floor in one room remains just as she painted it, and although somewhat "washed away," remnants of her mermaid linger in the porcelain bathtub. The building was renamed in her honor and is now known as Cole House.

LEXINGTON

LEXINGTON STONE HOUSE

Taking advantage of native stone, this building was constructed circa 1783 by the Crispell family. The house had never been altered by addition or incorporation into another structure until 1973 when a large frame barn was joined to one end. The house contains two large stone cooking fireplaces and what is believed to be original floors and beams.

Local stories that have been passed down declare English people began building the house, went back to England, returned with other family-members and lived in a log cabin on the hillside during the construction of the stone house. Although no date stone has been found, an Ulster County deed for the property confirms that in 1782 Benjamin Crispell (of English descent) purchased 150 acres from Barent Deklyn, a merchant in Trenton, New Jersey. Benjamin is believed to have been born circa 1756 in Hurley, Ulster County, New York.

In both the 1790 and 1800 census, the family was recorded as having one slave. According to local lore, the slave, Black Tom, who was a huge man, came with the original owners and helped to build the stone house—and lived out his life here and asked to be buried on the bank of the Schoharie Creek. No evidence of a grave has been found to document this account.

After the Crispell family, this house passed through several owners. Then it was purchased in 1937 by Howard and Helen Matthews, who possessed it for 35 years. In 1943 Helen wrote of finding the unkempt but sturdy stone house on its own dusty road among the sheltering mountains. Helen must have found the house neither cold nor damp, as previous owners had. Her writings are filled with fondness and attachment to "Benjamin Crispell's Acres," such as when she penned, "Of the quiet of evenings before the great fireplace, came the voice of Stone House's own spirit."

In 1973, owner Natalia Pohrebynska had a large old barn attached to one end for use as "Stone House Gallery" and "Pohrebynska Antiques." During the stone house's bicentennial year, on August 13, 1983, individuals were invited to a tour, an art exhibit, and an outdoor concert to benefit the newly formed Music and Art Center of Greene County, Inc. In 1992 Natalia was one of the hosts on the Greene County Historical Society's 16th Annual Tour of Homes.

LEXINGTON METHODIST CHURCH

Founded in 1845, the First Methodist Episcopal Church of Lexington was the first of the three Methodist churches in the town of Lexington. One hundred years later the Lexington Methodist Church was incorporated. By the turn of the 20th century, the hamlet had four churches, but only the Methodists remain active today. For more than 160 years this church has served the community and, along with its neighbors in this section of the hamlet, has survived several floods.

When the Methodist Episcopal Society was first organized in Lexington, they had no formal place of worship and traveling circuit riders were the only clergy. As their membership grew to 50, an appropriate place of worship seemed necessary.

On March 21, 1845, Bruce C. Smith and his wife, Deborah, deeded 52 rods (a bit more than a quarter acre) of their farm to John Chase, Minor Sanford, Chauncey Williams, Ashael Reynolds, and West Chase, trustees of the First Methodist Episcopal Church of Lexington. The parcel of land was sold for $130.

Included in the deed was a provision of encumbrance on a schoolhouse straddling the division line between Smith and his neighbor Chauncey Williams, a provision Smith had been subject to. Although the property deed does not specify what the encumbrance on the schoolhouse was, perhaps this is the one-room schoolhouse attached to the church known as Lexington Church Hall.

The church was dedicated during Reverend Smith Hubbard's sermon on October 14, 1845. During the early years it was heated by two potbellied stoves, and it is thought there was a balcony in the rear that was later enclosed. The 125th anniversary program for Lexington Methodist Church states that as time passed, additional space was desired for church-related activities, and the trustees purchased a vacant one-room schoolhouse, which was moved to the site.

In 1936, without being dismantled, the schoolhouse was moved behind the church. Fourteen years later, a room was constructed between the two buildings to house a new furnace.

Over time, the church interior has been spruced up with paint and carpet. The exterior has been sheathed in vinyl siding and aluminum, but it still maintains the Greek Revival appearance of the structure as it was originally designed and built.

TOWN OF LEXINGTON HISTORICAL SOCIETY
St. Frances De Sales Church

The land for this Lexington Catholic church was purchased in March 1896, and construction began immediately. Today, the church building remains essentially as it was when it was first constructed. The front porch was enclosed at some point in time, but has since been changed back to the original open-porch design.

St. Frances De Sales Church is representative of late Gothic Revival ecclesiastic architecture in the community of Lexington. The church building, with its soaring scissor-truss system, features Gothic characteristics and elements inspired by the theories associated with the ecclesiology movement.

The architectural significance of St. Frances De Sales Church is enhanced by the survival of many of its interior features. The church is characterized by a large auditorium, with strong visual emphasis placed on the altar and chancel. Such linear orientation is typical for Roman Catholic church design. A varnished wood interior and the absence of standard bench pews—a deliberate choice, and part of the original design—all contribute to the building's significance as an outstanding local example of a tourist-economy church design in the northern Catskill Mountain region.

The church building was inactive for about ten years, until the newly formed Lexington Historical Society was able to purchase the property on June 3, 1999.

Packing apples at the Stanton Hill Farm, for shipment to New York City, circa 1914.

TOWN OF NEW BALTIMORE

Tucked away in the northeast corner of Greene County, New Baltimore extends westward from the Hudson River, a hilly, rocky, rural area. The Town of New Baltimore was established as a separate town in 1811, from lands formerly part of Town of Coxsackie. In 1823 New Baltimore annexed three islands located in the Hudson River from Columbia County's Town of Kinderhook.

Due to the availability of river transportation and the area's proximity to Albany, the settlement of this area by the Europeans began early in the 18th century. Much of the land within the town had been part of the land patent granted to the Barent Pietersen Coeyman, a Dutch immigrant, and confirmed by a new patent to his son Andries in 1714. The remaining lands had either been part of the Thomas Houghtaling Grant, or the Coxsackie Patent. The Bronck, Vander Zee, and Van Slyke families were among the early settlers along the river. The earliest settler in the center section of the town was Jonathan Miller, who came in 1791.

Milling, stone quarrying, ship building, and ice harvesting were all important industries here. General farming, with its crops of vegetables, grains, and fruits—especially apples—added to the town's prosperity.

While there are no incorporated cities or villages within the town, the hamlet in the northeast corner, situated on the steep west bank of the Hudson, is often spoken of as the "village of New Baltimore." Other hamlets within the town include Grapeville, Hannacroix, Medway, Stanton Hill, and Sylvandale.

New Baltimore retains its small-town character even today. Many of the homes built by the prosperous businessmen and farmers during the 19th and early 20th centuries survive; many are now the homes of those employed in surrounding areas, some as far away as New York City.

The Town of New Baltimore was honored in 1995, when the core of the hamlet (95 contributing buildings on approximately 113 acres) was listed on the National Register of Historic Places. Designated as "New Baltimore Hamlet Historic District," it stands out as one of only five remaining Hudson River communities to survive with an intact collection of architecture spanning the full range of its history.

VAN BERGEN/WARREN HOUSE
"OLD STONE HOUSE"

This two-story Georgian-style, square-fieldstone house sits atop a small hill on approximately six acres of land at the southern end of the town of New Baltimore. Construction of the original stone house took place during the first years of the 18th century. The interior contains a full-length center hallway with two rooms on both sides. The original Federal-style, covered formal entrance faces east, where extensive lawns extend down to New York State Route 9W. A one-story porch, added in the early 20th century, is attached to the south side.

Near the residence is a stone smokehouse that was reconstructed using the original materials following its demolition by a falling tree branch. The remodeled wooden carriage house, once part of the original tract, sits on an adjoining parcel. Woodland on the west end of the property helps to screen a more modern garage.

The house and 150 acres of land comprised the dowry that Hester Houghtaling brought to her marriage with Peter A. Van Bergen in February 1786. The bride and groom both came from families with money and political prestige. Peter's father was a military leader in the Revolution, as well as a direct descendant of one of those who came to the colony under the patronage of Killian Van Rensselaer. Hester was the only daughter of Captain Thomas Houghtaling, also an active participant in the rebellion. Additionally, the captain held various town political positions and was a wealthy landowner.

Peter developed the farm and also became a prominent politician, holding offices such as tax collector and senator. In 1807, Peter and Hester transferred ownership of the farm to their only surviving child, Judge Anthony A. Van Bergen.

At age 21 and recently married, the young Anthony and his wife, Clarine, took things into hand, running the farm and starting a family. Their growing family expanded to ten children, so additional space became necessary. Thus, in the early 1820s, Anthony and Clarine doubled the size of the original stone house, adding to the rear of the structure an exact match of the existing house. Over the years, they also expanded their farm acreage, increasing it to approximately 700 acres. A supporter of what was then known as "scientific farming," Anthony was instrumental in forming farmer organizations and agricultural schools. He promoted new farming methods such as plowing the subsoil, spreading limestone on fields, constructing underground drains, and using compost. Specializing in livestock and hay, Anthony was a leader in the use of the hay press for compressing large amounts of hay into tight bales. He contracted the cutting of his own hay to local men and bought hay from other local farmers as well, shipping it down the Hudson River to the New York City market.

Unfortunately, their sons apparently had no interest in taking over the family farm, and in 1848 it was sold to someone outside the family. Over the course of the next 114 years, most of the farm acreage was sold off, and the frequent change of ownership led to neglect and deterioration of the house. When the Warren family purchased the house in 1962, they also purchased an adjoining three acres on which the carriage house is situated, as well as a portion of the original acreage across Route 9W. They spent two years renovating the stone house, restoring all the woodwork. As much as possible, period construction materials were used in the rehabilitation. A corner fireplace uncovered during the renovation was incorporated into the contemporary kitchen. On the west side of the house, they removed a deteriorated wooden kitchen wing that was believed to have been added in 1899. For the rear entrance, a Federal-period doorway was taken from a soon-to-be-razed hotel.

Today the old stone house continues to be used as a private residence. Although the farm buildings no longer grace the site and the land holdings are diminished, the stone house still remains, sitting grandly atop its hill, fitting comfortably into what is now a suburban setting.

Left: Smokehouse, circa 1970.
Above: South view of the "Old Stone House," circa 1970.

NEW BALTIMORE

ALBERT T. HOTALING FARMSTEAD

This two-story, wood-framed Greek Revival house, circa 1850, along with its outbuildings, is located in the southern end of the town of New Baltimore on approximately eighteen acres of rural land. The land on which it sits was owned by one family for more than 300 years. The Albert T. Hotaling farmstead, part of the family's larger parcel, was worked and called home by the same family until its sale in 1974. In 1986, the current owner, Anita Hermesdorf, purchased the farm and put great effort into restoring the house and the exterior of the fruit barn that sits west of the house. The house remains a private residence, but regrettably it is no longer a working farm.

The main section of the original house is oriented north/south, with an east wing, and is situated on a knoll atop a T-intersection of roads. From the house one can look, either through the original floor-to-ceiling windows or from the full-length front porch on the south face, down a spacious lawn and across the road to the main complex of barns.

The land on which the farm sits is a minuscule portion of the 5,400 acres obtained by the Dutch settler Matthias (Mathias) Hoogteeling (Houghtaling/Hotaling). The Houghtaling Patent was granted to Mathias Houghtaling on July 8, 1697, by Governor Benjamin Fletcher, who represented the English crown. When Mathias died, much of the lands of the Houghtaling Patent passed to a son and daughter; in later years, the land was acquired by Mathias' great-grandson Thomas Hotaling. Thomas gave a small portion of this land to his son Peter, who, in 1850, sold approximately 68 acres to his grandson, Albert T. Hotaling. It was Albert T. Hotaling and his wife, Caroline Lisk, who built the 1850 house and established the 19th-century farmstead that would be farmed by the family for 174 years. In 1864, Albert T. and Caroline constructed the two-story, wood-framed animal barn that still stands today.

Albert T. Hotaling died in 1903. At that time the property was in possession of his brother, Richard Andrew Hotaling, and his family. Richard died one year later and the property was sold to his son, Albert R. Hotaling, and his wife, Caroline. It was Albert and his wife who established the farmstead as a fruit farm, tending the orchards and building a double-wall fruit storage barn in 1910.

Apparently, Albert R. and Caroline were sharing the house with other family members, because around 1933–1934 their son, Alburtus Hotaling, and his wife added a kitchen wing. Alburtus also built the one-story shed that they came to use for canning, for storage, and as a washroom. In 1955, three additional parcels were added to the farmstead and Alburtus and his brother, Irving E. Hotaling, were added as owners.

Alburtus died in 1974, leaving as heirs his wife, Laura, and son Richard. At that time, there had been several additions and other outbuildings erected to accommodate the expanding Hotaling family, but no major modifications had been made. The farm contained at least 100 acres.

Apparently, no family member was inclined to purchase the property, because that same year Richard and his mother sold the farmstead to a non–family member for farming purposes. For a dozen years following the sale, four different owners took possession of the property. During that period, major modifications were made, with little attention to the historic character of the house, partly because it was used as a two-family home for at least part of that period.

Examples of modifications in conflict with the Greek Revival style of the historic structure included poured-concrete front-porch floors; a small bath, den, and bedroom on the first floor in the northwest corner that were converted to a large bath, closet, and hall; the conversion of the original kitchen/mudroom and adjoining porch into one large room; the removal and replacement of original doors on the east and west sides with windows; and a closet constructed on the second floor which concealed a south window from the stair hall. Along with the house, the outbuildings also deteriorated.

After purchasing the farm in 1986, the current owner began restoration reusing original materials when possible. The work proceeded according to the U.S. secretary of interior's standards for historic restoration. Along with extensive interior restorations, the

exterior also received attention, including the re-creation of any missing exterior wooden details, and the restoration of the copper-lined, wooden rain gutters. Eloise Marinos, an architect from Connecticut, oversaw the project. Local craftsmen Wayne Myhre and David Ameer were hired to repair and re-create the wooden details, including the sophisticated front entry door with transom and sidelights. In 1993, Anita Hermesdorf was the winner of the Third Annual Residential Design Awards Program, co-sponsored by the Westchester/Mid-Hudson and Eastern New York Chapter of the American Institute of Architects. The house and fruit storage barn were featured in *Hudson Valley* magazine.

Top: Panoramic view of the Hotaling Farmstead, circa 1993.

Bottom: Blueprint of main house.

ALLEN DEANE PLACE

This farmstead, which still contains 80 of its original 100 acres, is located on Gedney Hill Road in a hilly section of northern New Baltimore. The name was chosen to honor Allen L. Deane, who owned and, with his family, operated the farmstead for 80 years, from 1875 to 1956. An 1856 area map and property records verify that the farmstead dates back to at least 1851–1861, when Stephenson Thorn Salter farmed the land. The current owner states that this farm should not be confused with the A. Dean Place that is no longer in existence. The two did, however, coexist in the same area of the town.

Based on the upright-and-wing style and construction techniques, the one-and-a-half-story farmhouse is believed to have been built circa 1830–1840. The builder and the first occupants are unknown. An old photograph of the house, with its attached alleged smokehouse, is thought to have been taken around the end of the 19th century, based on garments worn by the ladies standing in front. The photograph shows a porch with Victorian scrollwork trim and columns.

In more recent years, the roofline on the back of the wing section was changed to supply more headroom on the second floor, and the porch was altered. Otherwise, the outside appears much the same as in that early photograph. In that same photograph, there are flower gardens on each side of the front walkway leading to the road. At that time the road ran between the house and the two-and-a-half-story English-style barn built into the bank.

The road was rerouted in the 1970s, bypassing the farmhouse and a small stone quarry, but the flower gardens remain in the same position leading toward the barn. The main section of the barn, almost beyond repair, was stabilized and trussed between posts with wire. The shed roof addition on the north side, which housed the horses, was torn down, and the wooden stanchions that secured the milk cows were removed to create storage space.

Based on the dated signature of Isaac Deane, son of Allen L. Deane, the barn is believed to have been built circa 1899. It was Isaac whose name was found on remaining apple barrels that had, in earlier years, been filled and shipped by train from New Baltimore Station. In fact, a few of his apple trees continued to live in the old orchard for many years. Jonathan Donald tried to save them by propping up their branches, but, alas, the single remaining tree succumbed in 2002.

The farm's carriage house may have been built in 1876, since that date is written on the original stairs. Modernization of its interior relegated the old stairs and the cutter sled to storage in the barn. However, aside from the addition of a cupola, the outside of the carriage house appears unchanged, since its doors close to hide the modern windows.

The hog barn, and a wagon shed full of tires, pulleys, and pieces of machinery, were beyond repair; they were torn down. A small milk shed remains, although the cool stream water that once filled its pits now bypasses it, running through a "blind ditch" to the old 12-foot hand-dug well beneath the farmhouse porch. The inside of the farmhouse was completely refurbished, and a new water supply and updated plumbing replaced the privy (which was also torn down).

The farmstead and orchard ceased to be productive during the first half of the 20th century. Three children of Allen L. Deane who were remaining on the farm grew aged and frail, and moved to a nursing home. As they were unable to keep up the farmstead, it deteriorated and then passed through four different owners before the Donalds purchased it in 1967. Their massive restoration was completed over a 30-year period, principally in 1968, 1991, and 1998. Along with refurbishing the buildings, they trucked away years worth of accumulated material, including items from the dump behind the farmhouse. Although it is no longer a working farm, the fields are kept open, and the old fence lines are still evident, preserving the character of this 19th-century farmstead.

Front view of the farmhouse, with attached smokehouse and porch with Victorian-style trim and columns, circa late 1890s.

Orchard Farm
Miller-Woodhull Homestead

The Miller-Woodhull Homestead, known as Orchard Farm, is an active farm, currently containing approximately 115 acres in the rural Medway area of the Town of New Baltimore. The two-story wood-frame house, with its mid-Victorian porch, was rebuilt in 1859 by one of Jonathan Miller's grandsons, incorporating materials from the family's first frame house (built in 1798). The house contains the traditional plain woodwork and floorboards from the older structure.

The original 67¾-acre farm was part of the lands in the Coeymans Patent and was settled by Jonathan Miller and his wife, Lydia, in 1791, and later purchased from Isaac D. Verplanck in 1797. Over time, Mr. Miller gradually cleared several hundred acres of land. It is believed that the first commercial apple orchard in the area was set out on this farm circa 1852.

Jonathan and his family first lived in a log cabin on the south side of the road, across from the site of the present house. History has it that Lydia blew on a conch shell to warn the men clearing the fields when wolves were near the cabin, also blowing on it to call them to meals. Lydia had married Jonathan when she was very young, against her parents' wishes. On her leaving her childhood home, Lydia's father gave her permission to take along one cow. Lydia must have been quite a savvy young woman, because the story goes that she went to her father's barn and chose his best animal. Sadly, after that visit to the farm, she never saw her parents again.

The Miller family was instrumental in the creation of the First Church Christian Society of the Town of New Baltimore, now incorporated as the Medway Congregational Christian Church. As early as 1832, the Millers transferred farmland to the church trustees on which to build a house of worship. For several years before that gift, the congregation had been meeting in Jonathan's house and barns.

In 1861, Jonathan's great-granddaughter Annie married into the Woodhull family, whose descendants still own and reside on the farm, and still hold membership in the church.

Medway Congregational Christian Church

This two-story New England–style wood-framed church with its square belfry sits on two acres in the town of New Baltimore. The church and the 326-plot cemetery adjoining to the north and west of the building are located in the rural Medway/Four Corners area of the town, surrounded by farms and single-family homes. In front of the church an aged lone pine tree grows, and beside it a stone horse block rests, both reminders of earlier times.

Dating back to 1807, the Christian Church of New Baltimore is distinguished as the first church of the Christian denomination to be organized in the state of New York. The members first worshipped in the house and barns of Jonathan Miller (now Orchard Farm/Miller-Woodhull Homestead). Deciding to build a formal house of worship, the congregation chose a spot on the Miller farm, which by then belonged to his son Jonathan Jr. Construction of the earliest building on the site dates back to 1832, with a land transfer from Jonathan Miller, Jr. and his wife, Margaret, to the trustees of the First Christian Society of the Town of New Baltimore. In 1856 additional property was transferred to the trustees of the society from other family members.

In 1861 a new and larger wood-framed church was built on the site of the 1832 building. Tin walls and ceiling with fleur-de-lis accents adorn the sanctuary of the 1861 white clapboard church. In 1895 the church bell was hung in the belfry. The congregation continued to grow and resources increased, which led to later additions and renovations.

Changes in the 1920s included new frescoes, seats, and carpeting, as well as hardwood stairways and polished oak floors. The entrance was changed and new doors installed. The dark basement walls were brightened with paint and the floor covered with linoleum. In 1928 the pipe organ was installed. Further renovations followed in the 1930s. In 1936, after the church had been wired for electricity, fixtures and an electric stove were installed. Two years later a kitchen wing was completed on the north end.

Now incorporated as the Medway Congregational Christian Church, this congregation is still active in the community.

Above: Medway Congregational Christian Church and congregation, circa 1906.

New Baltimore

Prospect Place

Although over the years the property size has been reduced, Prospect Place remains on its original site, located within a village setting. The house and garage sit high on a hill overlooking the Hudson River to the east. Extensive grounds enclosed by stone retaining walls still roll down toward Main Street in the hamlet of New Baltimore.

The picturesque-style, two-story brick residence was built circa 1850 by Captain Edward Ely Sherman (1817–1898), and the house is said to be one of the hamlet's most important architectural features. The house is one of only two structures in the Hamlet that contain elements of the Gothic Cottage movement. Although it has fewer ornamental details than some, this gives it a more stately appearance. Its intersecting medium-low pitched jerkinhead roof is an element to be found on only one other structure in the hamlet.

Edward, his wife, Anna Hotaling Sherman, and their three children were the first occupants of Prospect Place. The captain was descended from a prominent family dating back to when his grandfather Paul (1763–1820) came to the town in 1791 and built a house on a riverside lot in the hamlet. Paul began building sloops along the waterfront as early as 1815, and engaged in profitable trade in New York City and in the West Indies. It is said that after two or three trips to the latter location, the sloops were sold and new ones built. Son Joseph (1786–1876) did not build ships, but carried on the commerce between New York City and New Baltimore. Joseph built his house on or near where his father's house had stood.

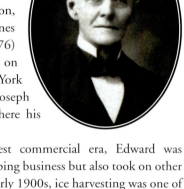

During the town's richest commercial era, Edward was associated with his father's shipping business but also took on other endeavors. From 1854 to the early 1900s, ice harvesting was one of the principal industries, and in 1881 Edward went into partnership with two other residents, erecting and running a 12,000-ton-capacity icehouse, which was located on Hotaling Island, opposite the hamlet.

Inset: Edward Ely Sherman

Fairview

This house—which was built before the formation of Greene County—and its adjoining structures sit on their original site in the eastern section of the town of New Baltimore. The main house, carriage house, and privy, once part of a 276-acre tract, sit on 14 acres surrounded by open and wooded lands overlooking the Berkshire Mountains, the Taghkanic Hills, and the New York State Thruway.

The wood-framed one-and-three-quarter-story residence was built circa 1793 using a framing plan similar to that used for houses in the Connecticut River valley. It boasts brick-lined exterior walls, and a central chimney with four fireplaces. The original owners are unknown, but it is believed that the Hawley family took possession in 1815 or so. Later owners included the Shears and the Broncks, both well-established families associated with early New Baltimore.

A summer-kitchen addition was constructed circa 1850. In 1885 a library, a second stairway, and three bedrooms were added. Upgrades in the 20th century included the addition of a south porch in 1932 and a garage in 1967. Extensive restorations between 1975 and 1982, based on on-site artifacts and family papers, included restoring the paneling, the fireplaces, and the early kitchen.

Interesting features on the property include a carriage house, and a privy with its original stenciling by an itinerant artist.

It is believed that Fairview is what was once known as "Friendship's Asylum," a name given to this house by Honoré Chaurand in the 1790s. Chaurand was one of three French refugees who at that time purchased farmland in the area from pre-Revolutionary families.

Lisk/Hallock Homestead and Farm

The approximately 80-acre Lisk-Hallock Homestead and Farm was purchased by Charles Lisk from Daniel Gregory and his wife, Zadey, in 1824. The current house, farm buildings, and family cemetery are surrounded by open fields and woodland, situated in a still-rural area of the town of New Baltimore.

Charles Lisk willed the farm to his youngest son, Benjamin C. Lisk. Benjamin, a fruit farmer and Mason, built the current house. Evidence for this includes the cornerstone, which reads B. C. Lisk 1868. This house sits on the site of an earlier house that was torn down. Many beams in the basement still retain some bark, and crafted holes are visible. These things indicate that the beams were part of earlier construction that used the mortise-and-tenon technique for joints.

Some notable features of the interior are the four marble fireplaces, a butler's pantry, and plaster cornice-work in the formal living room. Circular walls, starting at the cellar level, continue up to the first and second floors, and are most prominent in the oval-shaped dining room. The exterior of the two-story wood-frame house displays bracketed cornices and pedimented crowns over the windows.

The site contains 11 other structures, the oldest one built in 1846. Nine of these retain slate roofs, and many have simple pedimented crowns over the windows and doors. The largest barn was built in 1853 with hand-hewn beams up to 13½ inches square and 45 feet in length, using mortise-and-tenon joints. It has a rock-bottom, air-cooled fruit storage area under one end, a hayloft, and 12 cow stanchions. The wing of this barn once contained a hay press. Later, it housed equipment for sorting, grading, and packing fruit. It was built by Benjamin C. Lisk, and the painted Masonic emblem still remains over the large barn doors along with his initials and the date. Charles J. Lisk inherited the farm and orchards after his father Benjamin's death. It is reported that Charles was an amateur artist, and that he studied under Frederic Church.

Other structures on the site include a carriage house; a pig barn; a chicken house with an angled southern wall to admit maximum sunlight; a corn crib; a smokehouse; a five-seat, wallpapered privy; a small shed; a garage; and two smaller barns. The family cemetery, surrounded by a superbly crafted stone wall, sits atop a knoll in a field a short distance away. Photos taken between 1913 and the late 1960s by Charles J. Lisk's only child, Abby Lisk-Hallock, document that the buildings have existed in their current configuration for at least 78 years. One structure now missing is the icehouse, which was removed in the early 1900s.

Another small barn that sits across the road, on an adjoining property-owner's land, was once part of the farm complex. It housed the farm's apple press and was later equipped as a farm shop. In addition to the cider-making equipment, the building contained two cellars for storage. The Lisk family's "champagne cider" was enjoyed as far away as New York City, shipped in wooden barrels by boat down the Hudson River.

Four generations of the Lisk family occupied the farm until 1964, when it was sold to a new owner. The property changed owners again in 1983. The present owners, the Hilscher family, have had possession since 1990, and have put considerable time, money, and effort into restoration of the buildings. Although the property is no longer a working farm, the Hilschers appreciate its history and enjoy hosting "barn-bees" for special occasions.

Inset top: Charles and Jennie Lisk.
Inset bottom: Abby Lisk-Hallock.
Left: Apple spraying on the farm, circa 1914.

Below: Panoramic view of the Lisk barn and farm buildings.

213

NEW BALTIMORE

LISK HOMESTEAD

For more than 100 years, two houses stood on this site, separated only by the driveway. The house on the south side was razed in 1952. This surviving two-story, side-hall Greek Revival–style house with its one-and-a-half-story wing probably dates back to the early 19th century. A large two-story addition was attached to the rear of the wing in 1830. Decorative scrollwork panels decorate the front porch, and the front door is framed with squared columns topped with a frieze and cornice.

The interior of the house has been wonderfully preserved. The kitchen contains a fireplace with a "beehive" baking oven that sports a door from the O. G. De Groff foundry. The dining room has exposed wooden beams, some retaining their original tree bark, and the original gaslight fixture in the ceiling. Modern heating and plumbing have been installed, yet the acetylene generator still remains in the basement.

The Lisk Homestead dates back to the late 18th century, located in an area of New Baltimore known as Stanton Hill. The family home and other remaining structures, including a barn, carriage house, apple-sorting shed, and chicken coop, are still surrounded by approximately 80 acres of fence-lined, open land.

Benjamin and his wife, Elizabeth, are buried east of the barn, in the family cemetery. Elizabeth died four years after Benjamin and left all her property to their unmarried daughter, Deborah. It is unclear why the other children were excluded, but perhaps they had received dowries from their father when starting their own farms and families. Deborah lived on the farmstead, along with her married sister Patty.

Patty and Samuel T. Powell's son, Benjamin L. Powell, and daughter-in-law Jerusha welcomed their first child in 1830. Probably one of the houses on the homestead was built to accommodate Benjamin's new family.

The farm passed to Benjamin, and by 1865 he owned 150 acres with 200 apple trees. The barn, carriage house, and apple-sorting shed that remain on the property today were probably built during his ownership. Construction details point to 1880 and 1890. Benjamin lived on the farm until his death in 1901.

Charles Friend purchased the farm, established a boardinghouse and renamed the Lisk Homestead Locust Grove, most likely after the black locust trees that then lined the driveway. Square dances were held in the lower house, there was ice skating on the swamp, and comforters were created in the dining room. Charles' wife, Hattie, pitched hay, patched the roof, and drove their wagon and team. The story goes that when the Friends purchased the farm, the kitchen was in such bad condition that Hattie sat down and cried. Considering her toughness, the kitchen must have

Above: The apple-sorting shed.

been archaic! One can easily surmise that it was Hattie who had the removable numbered shelving installed in the walk-in kitchen pantry. That shelving is still in use by the present owners.

After its life as a boardinghouse, the homestead was used only as a summer home by various owners. Since 1971, Edward and Priscilla Coates have enjoyed living and raising their family on the Lisk Homestead, and truly appreciate the homestead's heritage. Unable to save an old, falling-down barn as a structure, they gifted its various parts to numerous friends who have integrated these parts into their own homes.

MAPLE GROVE FARM

Maple Grove Farm retains approximately half of the original 118 acres owned by the Powell family in the 1700s. The house, barn, privy, shop, and garage sit in a country setting surrounded by open land, woodland, and a few newer homes. Donald Berkhofer, the current owner, says that one locust tree on the property is almost as old as the house. It is believed that the house sits about 50 feet southwest of a former log cabin built on the site, possibly the homestead of the Dutchman David Verplank, who transferred the property to the Powell family.

The two-family, Federal- and country-style house with its center hall was built circa 1785, as was the middle section of the barn. The original one-and-a-half-story, 30-by-50-foot wood-framed house was built by an early settler named Thomas Powell. A west wing was added by his son in 1815, and at that time the barn was enlarged as well. A small shed-type addition was attached to the east side of the house in 1820.

After being occupied by three generations of Powells, in 1830 the farm was sold for $800. During the early 1900s, the owner at that time, George Robbins, increased its value by raising the roof to create a full two-story house.

The next owner was Martha Hoube. The Berkhofer family purchased the farm from Martha in 1965. Restorations by Donald Berkhofer were ongoing between 1965 and 1980. The original doors, retaining much of their hardware, the floors, and the moldings in the house are still intact, as well as two fireplaces.

Hillcrest Road, which runs in front of Maple Grove Farm, was once known as the Coxsackie-Westerlo Turnpike. A legend passed down through generations of owners is that Ethan Allen stopped at the farm for a drink of water before finishing the last two-and-a-half miles of his walk from the Hudson River to the settlement of Newry, where he was to visit his friend Charles Wooster.

Maple Grove Farm, circa 1897.

New Baltimore Reformed Church

The New Baltimore Reformed Church is a one-and-a-half-story red brick Gothic Revival–inspired house of worship that was built during 1833–1834. Constructed using wood timbers joined in the mortise-and-tenon method, it sits high on a hill above the Hudson River, its majestic 100-foot white steeple still stretching skyward. An active church for more than 175 years, it was incorporated in 1861 as the Protestant Dutch Reformed Church of New Baltimore, New York. It still sits on the original site in the hamlet of New Baltimore.

In the early 1830s a group of New Baltimore's residents met to discuss erecting a church building in the hamlet. A parcel of land was deeded, and a building committee suggested a brick building measuring 36 feet by 46 feet, arched with an end "galary" in front of the pulpit, posts of 20 feet, and a belfry. Lewis Crandell was hired as the master mason for the foundation, and the cornerstone service was held on July 4, 1833. Architect Thomas Gibbons finished the building in 1834.

There was one entrance, on the south end, with a low square belfry above it. A stepping stone used at the front entrance was obtained from the 1793 Reformed Church of Coeymans Square, which was being razed at the time of the New Baltimore construction; the stone was transported to New Baltimore by Mr. James Hotaling. The windows were of plain glass, demurely covered with curtains. Some of the pews were square, while others had doors at their entrance. The gallery extended across the south end, opposite the pulpit.

The first consistory was appointed May 3, 1834, and the first members were received on July 19 of that same year. While a sexton was hired for more rigorous work, the church women took on the task of general cleaning. A Sabbath school was started in 1843 and grew to accommodate 160 students. Classes were held in the sanctuary's gallery, meeting only during the summer months.

By 1854, the congregation had outgrown the building's seating capacity, and a 12-foot extension was added on the north end to accommodate 16 new pews. Lewis Crandell once again used his expertise, taking charge of the project to repair and extend the foundation. It was around this time that stoves and elegant kerosene lamps and chandeliers were installed.

The original cupola on top of the church was removed in 1870. (It is interesting to note that one of the church members, William H. Baldwin, Sr., loved woodworking and used the wood from the old cupola to create novelties inside bottles, which he sold at church events.) Then, during 1872 and 1873, new and more extensive alterations were completed. The gallery was removed from the sanctuary and the south end of the church was extended by the addition of a bell tower and steeple, a small pinnacle, two vestibules, and a choir alcove. A new front was completed, buttresses added to the sides, and the single entrance was replaced by a double entrance. A furnace room was excavated for the installation of a wood/coal furnace. The front walk was paved with flagstone.

The west wing that still stands today was added in 1885, after the Young Peoples Association had been given permission to raise money to build a chapel that could be used for meetings, suppers, and social events.

Electric lights replaced the kerosene lamps in 1909. The following year, the first of several stained-glass windows was installed to replace the plain-glass windows in the sanctuary. During late 1929 or the early 1930s, the roof was reshingled and copper gutters were installed. New wiring and electric lights were installed in the chapel as well. In 1930, the wagon sheds east of the church knoll were removed. An Orgatron and chimes replaced the old-fashioned hand-pumped organ.

In 1945 and 1946 the church was completely redecorated and dedicated to those serving in the military. A divided chancel replaced the central pulpit, and a lectern matching the pulpit and an altar were built and placed on an enlarged platform. Unique cast-brass chandeliers and wall sconces—salvaged from the United States Hotel in Saratoga Springs, which was being razed—still decorate the sanctuary. More than 300 pieces in each chandelier were replated before reassembly and installation.

Over the years, leakage in the bell tower had caused structural damage in the southeast corner of the church. So when a new chimney was added, the supporting roof rafters, and the tenons in the floor joists connecting them to the foundation plate, were fixed and reglued. The windows in the bell tower received copper flashing, and new lights were installed in the sashes. At the same time, all of the walls and ceilings in the bell tower, the choir-loft and the church were replaced or patched where necessary.

On July 18, 1954, the cornerstone was laid for a new addition at the north end of the chapel, to house a large kitchen, lavatories, and a basement room. The plans were drawn and the carpentry performed by Burton Albright. The gallery was also enlarged. The final modification was made in 1970, when the large folding glass partition doors between the chapel and church were replaced by a solid partition and a single door.

In the 1990s the congregation, facing formidable costs, reached out to the surrounding community for support of the historic structure. The community responded with donations to help cover the cost of cleaning the red bricks and repointing the mortar. The original founders would be proud to know that some of their descendants still welcome the community through the building's beautifully restored arched wooden doors, which lead them into the sanctuary for worship, and into the chapel for community events.

THE PARSONS HOMESTEAD

This pre-Revolutionary, one-and-a-half-story rubblestone house is the oldest home in the hamlet of New Baltimore. The exact date that Stephen Parsons built the house is unknown, but it is believed that it was constructed during the 1770s. The house has since been enlarged by a two-story framed addition on the north side.

Once dominating the hill rising from the west bank of the Hudson River, the Parsons' home was surrounded by barns, other outbuildings, and open farmland. Today the house, a privy, and a shed are surrounded by well-kept gardens on a quarter-acre lot in a village setting.

Stephen Parsons was born in 1754 and moved to New Baltimore from East Hampton, Long Island. It was in East Hampton where his Puritan great-grandfather, Samuel Parsons, settled in the 1600s, and where many family members remained. The record of the first land transaction cannot be found, so the original acreage is unknown. However, it is known that more than 181 additional acres of land were purchased in 1804; and by the time the town was formed in 1811, the family owned more than 300 acres.

During the 1800s there were many markets for farm produce up and down the Hudson River. Stephen Parsons must have been a good farmer on top of being a prominent businessman and citizen, because in 1827 the family purchased a $1,000 square-stern sloop.

Stephen was also a religious man: his encouragement and gift of $100 in 1833 led to the construction of the New Baltimore Reformed Church building, and he became one of the first elders of the redbrick church that still sits a short distance south of his stone house.

In 1840 Stephen's son, Melvin, added land to the north and east of the farm. Therefore, the size of the farm was reduced. Due to the area's increasing population, building lots were sold off during the 1840s and 1850s. In 1852, 100 acres were transferred to Stephen's grandson. Additional lots were sold during the 1860s.

The core property was passed down through the family, and was still owned by Stephen's great-grandson, Clarence Bronk Parsons, when Stephen died in 1851 at the age of 97. Descendants lived in the rubble-stone house until 1929, and then the house and farm were rented for several years. A cider mill built by Clarence beside the barn buildings burned in 1930. Approximately two years later, Clarence raised a large frame addition at the back of the stone house.

Until the 1940s, the Parsons Homestead remained a prosperous dairy farm. In 1945, the house was sold to George and Isabel Ellrott, who did considerable restoration. Most of the outbuildings were removed after that time.

The Wolf family purchased the property in 1973; they also have carefully restored the house and beautified its grounds. A wood-framed kitchen addition was erected on the north side of the house in 1995, which blends well with the house and surrounding gardens.

New Baltimore Reformed Church Parsonage

The parsonage of the New Baltimore Reformed Church is situated on a hill above the Hudson River, across the street and to the west of the church, in the hamlet of New Baltimore. Built in 1861 using an interlocking wood frame, the two-story house contains a central hallway and flanking parlors. The front porch extends across the entire length of the house; at some point, the north end was enclosed. In 1992–1993, the wooden clapboards were covered with more modern materials. Despite this, with its white color and green shutters, the house retains much of its New England colonial character.

For many years, the New Baltimore congregation had shared a pastor with the Reformed church at Coeymans. This was not an uncommon practice for smaller churches of that era. As the congregation grew in New Baltimore and additional funds became available, the co-pastorate was discontinued. It all must have seemed quite impressive for Reverend Robert G. Strong, arriving with his new wife in 1861 to take charge as the first full-time pastor, and moving into the newly built parsonage that had cost $1,900 to construct.

Since its construction, the parsonage has received various improvements and repairs. Records indicate that a new furnace was installed in 1884. Until a new chapel was constructed in 1885, which added a west wing to the church building across the street, the double parlors in the parsonage were used by the Young People's Association and other groups as a place for meetings and other events. Even today, one of the twin parlors is occasionally used as a meeting place.

When the parsonage was painted in 1910, the cost was $94.58. The following year, the consistory agreed to have the building wired for electricity and to have a bathroom and hot-water heater installed. In 1926, another replacement furnace was installed. That same year, the parsonage, the chapel, and the church were painted by Charles W. Mead & Son, a local contractor, for $840.

Reverend Henry Wells Brink accepted the pastorate in 1929 and enjoyed working at the rural church. Popular with the youth, he was always ready to transport them and other parishioners of the church in his automobile to meetings and rallies. The congregation must have greatly appreciated this generosity, because during his very first year of service, a garage to house his car was constructed north of the parsonage. In 1936, the parsonage roof was reshingled and fitted with copper gutters; this work was performed by Ralph A. Hotaling and Arthur L. Kniffen at a cost of $300. The cement-block garage, enlarged in 1940, was razed at a later, unspecified date.

Presently, a small paved area in front and to the side of the parsonage serves as church parking. Since its erection, the parsonage structure has continuously served as a home for numerous pastors and their families. The congregation continues to maintain the house: in 2005, while conducting a search for a new resident pastor, the New Baltimore Reformed Church congregation used the interval to make repairs and give the parsonage interior a face-lift.

NEW BALTIMORE

ROCKY STORE SCHOOL
NEW BALTIMORE TOWN HALL

Located west of the hamlet of New Baltimore, the Rocky Store School—now the New Baltimore Town Hall - and the double outhouse marked for boys and girls remain in a rural setting surrounded mostly by woodland, with a few homes here and there. What are believed to be the original double-hung windows remain in place, and the square bell tower still contains the working school bell.

Changes were made over time. The clapboards, reported to have been painted in various colors through the years, have now been covered in more modern material. The cloakrooms have been removed and alterations made to the original entranceway and foundation. Plumbing and central heating have been added. Although the hardwood floors were recently refinished, they still show evidence of the placement of the screwed-down student desks and the position of the wood stove that once kept them warm.

The Rocky Store School was built in 1892 as a replacement to the district's previous stone schoolhouse. Rocky Store remained an active one-room schoolhouse for grades one through eight until the 1960s. A shrinking student population, combined with the popularity of centralized school districts, led to the closing of the school. In the mid-1960s, the school district transferred the building to the town government of New Baltimore. The first town meeting was held in the building on May 25, 1965. From then until the mid-1990s, all town government offices and public meeting spaces, with the exception of the highway garage, were contained in this one-room school building.

To bring town government into the 21st century, a wing for office space was constructed to the rear of the original building, effectively doubling the size. Connected to the addition by a common door, the original one-room school continues to be the meeting hall for town government. Some restoration of the schoolhouse has been completed to reflect its original interior, and more is planned for the future.

Until a couple of years ago, a withering old maple tree stood in front of the building, reminding former students of its use as a base during their many ball games. Numerous town residents have fond memories or enjoy tales of community events that took place at the one-room school, including church services and sing-alongs.

VOSBURGH RESIDENCE

The Vosburgh residence is situated on a small parcel of land in the hamlet of New Baltimore on the Hudson River's west bank. It's likely that Gildersleve Bedell constructed the house. From construction details and design, it is believed that this two story residence was built circa 1845; this was one of several buildings constructed in the hamlet during that time, which imitated the Greek Revival style, but on a smaller scale.

Although the exact year when Bedell took ownership of the property has not been determined, when he sold it in 1847 the sale included a dock and steamboat office. Since the house is built into a bank, the basement can be entered at ground level on the river side. Perhaps this is the area where the steamboat office was located. In 1852 the owner was granted a letter of patent from New York State officials for land extending from the east lot line 200 feet into the Hudson River, which was intended for docking facilities.

The next owner held title for only two years before selling it in 1857 to William L. Davis, who was in the shipbuilding business. The property remained in the Davis family for 25 years. They had the Corinthian façade redone during 1875 using the Ionic style, which at that time was considered a "modern" improvement. For the next 34 years it was owned by the William Fuller family, who sold it to John H. Wagoner, a Hudson River pilot. In 1941 it was purchased by Fred and Virginia Bagley, who lived here until 1984, owning it longer than any other family. During their tenure a hand pump on a dug well in the front yard provided drinking water; for water for other purposes, they depended on a tidal well pumped into a basement cistern.

After the Vosburgh family purchased the property, they upgraded the water system with a drilled well and restored the old bulkhead. In 2001 architect Chris Hoppe drew up plans for alterations to the house, including a two-story addition in keeping with the main house design. The new addition built by Tim Meier and Matthew Pacuk replaced an existing small one-story kitchen wing. Asbestos shingles, perhaps added in the early 1940s, were replaced with traditional cedar siding. The conversion of two rooms on the first floor of the main house into one large room was done tastefully, retaining the original varied-width wood floorboards, and the existing windows, door moldings, and exterior doors.

Above: Probably an old ship building, now razed, stood between the house and the river.

NEW BALTIMORE

SUNSET HILL FARM
OSSIE SMITH FARM

Currently the barns stand empty of livestock, but this 125-acre farm is still active in conjunction with its neighbor, Valley View Farm. The Smith homestead is located in the hilly western section of the town of New Baltimore. Over time, there have been numerous alterations, additions, and restorations, making it difficult to know the exact date of the original construction. However, some evidence suggests that the earliest section of the one-and-a-half-story wooden post-and-beam family home dates back to the 1790s.

Although now sided with new materials, the house retains its farmhouse appearance, surrounded by open fields, woodlands, and scattered outbuildings including a barn, a garage, and sheds.

Family history recounts that the original house, built by John Smith circa 1790, was later incorporated into a small barn that still exists on the property. During the Depression years, many farm families earned income by renting out rooms, and Ossie and Cora Smith did this on their farm.

They also hosted dances as entertainment for their boarders. The lack of resources during World War II kept most families close to home, and word spread locally about the Saturday night dances at the farm's "dance hall," with many friends and neighbors joining in the camaraderie. There is no record of a charge, but there may have been a small cash donation requested. The participants were responsible for their own refreshments, and perhaps they brought along a little extra that ended up in the boardinghouse larder.

The dances in the small barn were illuminated by lantern light, and a local black family occupied the bandstand, daughter on the piano and father on the fiddle. After Ossie and Cora Smith's deaths, a neighbor ran the dances, adding a guitarist and another fiddler.

Since 1792, when the land was purchased by John Smith from the Ten Eyck family, excepting a brief period during the 1930s, several generations of the Smith family have resided on and worked this farm, as well as the adjoining Valley View Farm located just down the hill. During the 1970s, Irving Smith continued to work both farms as one. He improved the buildings on Valley View Farm, where his parents resided, to accommodate the family's growing herd of registered Guernsey milk cows. In the later part of the 20th century, when small dairy farming was no longer profitable, the family sold their dairy herd and switched to raising beef cattle.

It was recorded in the *Heritage of New Baltimore*, published in 1976, that the road past the farm had been changed to accommodate the automobile. The road no longer went straight down the hill past the farm toward Valley View Farm on Staco Road; instead it followed the driveway of Sunset Hill Farm between the house and barns. Or, as current owner Irving Smith related, the rerouting was the result of so many visitors! At the present time, however, Sunset Hill Road once again bypasses the "dance hall" and the farm driveway.

The barns at Sunset Hill Farm.

NEW BALTIMORE

VALLEY VIEW FARM
FLOYD SMITH FARM

Located on Staco Road in the western section of the town of New Baltimore, Valley View Farm is an active cattle farm containing 210 acres. The wooden post-and-beam structure dates back to the 1800s. This beautifully restored upright-and-wing-style house owned by I. Todd Smith and family is believed to have been built in 1838 by an ancestor named Samuel Y. Smith. The home is complemented by well-kept lawns, a garden, and a pond. The numerous outbuildings, including a barn, sheds, and garage, are surrounded by open fields, wood lots, and a stone quarrying area. Beautiful mountain views serve as a backdrop for the nostalgic agrarian setting.

Since the late 1700s, several generations of Smiths have resided and farmed the land in this area, which became part of the Town of New Baltimore when the town was established in 1811. Valley View Farm's owner continues to operate this farm in connection with his parents' adjoining property, which is known as Sunset Hill Farm. Working both farms as one, Smith and his father, Irving, continue the tradition of a one-family operation, just as generations of Smiths have done in the past. I. Todd and family reside in the home where his grandparents once lived.

The animals used by their ancestors to help till the land and harvest the crops were replaced by the farm tractor in the early 20th century, and other mechanization followed as well. During the 1970s, Irving Smith built an addition on the Valley View Farm barn and erected a new silo to accommodate the family's growing herd of registered Guernsey milk cows. Due to the increasing costs for hired farm laborers, Irving installed many labor-saving devices to permit him to operate the dairy farm with mostly family labor. Eventually, however, high land taxes and low milk prices, among other things, caused small dairy farming to become unprofitable, and the family sold their dairy herd. In place of the dairy herd, the family farm began raising beef cattle. Some of the herd are sent away to be slaughtered, while others end up as another farm's stock. The black cattle can be seen grazing on the farm hills, and the Smiths' hay crop helps to feed the cattle when the grazing fields are covered with snow.

View of Pratt's farm buildings in Prattsville, circa early 1900s.

TOWN OF PRATTSVILLE

Referring to Prattsville, in 1907 Harold Bell Wright, the author of The Shepherd of the Hills, *wrote, "Tain't no wonder at all God rested when he made these here hills, he just naturally had to quit, for he done his best, and was plumb tuckered out." Residents and travelers before and after often agree, intrigued by the beauty of this mountain town lying in a sheltered valley of the Catskills. Known first as Schoharie Kill, "Schoharie" meaning "floating driftwood" in the local Native American language, this "gem of the Catskills" did not exist as a town until March 6, 1833, when it was named in honor of Colonel Zadock Pratt.*

Prattsville was formed from the Town of Windham. A large group of Schoharie settlers made camp in this section of the famous colonial Hardenburgh Patent prior to the Revolution. During the war they were attacked by Indians and Tories incited by British leadership. The Schoharie camp won, with some of the victors remaining in the area to form the nucleus of a new town.

Zadock Pratt moved to Greene County when he was 12 years old and, through his later renowned tanning exploits, was responsible for developing one of the first planned communities in New York state. In 1824 his tanning business was the world's largest, but this was not his sole achievement. Serving in the House of Representatives, he was appalled by the condition of the White House and worked to allocate funds to purchase new curtains for the presidential residence. He backed a number of bills, one to reduce postage costs, another to require the use of durable materials in the construction of government buildings, and yet another for construction of a cross-continental railroad. He was also instrumental in passing legislation to formally accept the gift of James Smithson, a British chemist and philanthropist who had died in 1829 and had bequeathed to the United States the tidy sum of £100,000 in gold bullion, which had remained under lock and key since its arrival. Thanks to Pratt's efforts, this "national inheritance" was used to establish a national museum: the Smithsonian Institution.

Prattsville is a long, one-highway town. Along its eastern end a park, donated by Pratt and bearing his name, is fenced by stone walls. There, a winding path climbs to 500 feet above the Schoharie Creek and showcases a breathtaking view of these wide vistas, valleys, and mountain peaks. Nearby are two monuments, the first in memory of Pratt's horses and dogs. The other is dedicated to the boys of the World War. Pratt's mansion, now home to the Zadock Pratt Museum, attests to his influence—both as a member of the House of Representatives, and as a local philanthropist who disbursed wealth and care to make Prattsville attractive and inviting.

PRATTSVILLE

ZADOCK PRATT MUSEUM

Zadock Pratt was born in 1790 in Rensselaer County. In 1802 his family moved to Jewett, Greene County, where his father established a tannery business. At the age of 34, Zadock left the family business and purchased the land where Prattsville now stands, erecting a tannery that grew to become one of the largest tanning operations in the nation. Pratt was known as a tanner, farmer, builder, banker, churchman, and philanthropist. His generosity and his acumen were instrumental in the building of Prattsville. His political accomplishments were many; Windham justice of the peace, New York State senator, presidential elector, member of the U.S. House of Representatives; chairman of public buildings and grounds in Washington, D.C.

His most famous motto was to not to live off the people but among them. He died in 1871, ten years after his only son was killed in battle during the Civil War. According to local mountain lore, Zadock Pratt's greatest achievement was his succession of wives, five in all: two sets of sisters, and finally a young lady of 28 from New York City. (And yes, she did outlive him!)

Pratt's homestead is a two-storied structure of sawn hemlock using post-and-beam framing, with clapboard siding and a gable roof over projecting eaves with 1850 brackets. The building features split Shaker shingles, double-hung windows, louvered shutters, and cross-and-bible doors.

Incorporated within the current museum is the original house built in 1828 as a two-story Federal-style structure. Over the years the homestead was enlarged and greatly modified. Circa 1856, the original center hall façade and gable roof were greatly altered with the addition of wings and extensions.

The west wing of the main house started life as the Prattsville Bank building. The small Greek Revival–style building was moved circa 1856 from its position on Main Street and attached to the house. Also at that time, Pratt had his carriage house attached to the rear of the homestead by means of a two-story hyphen. With the addition of numerous architectural details, the homestead shed its Greek Revival design to conform to the Victorian style. The orientation of the side and rear wings creates a multi-gable roof, enhancing the picturesque design.

The early-19th-century stone-lined well, approximately 20 feet deep, is located in the hyphen behind the main block of buildings, sheltered under a recessed porch. The landscaping remains mostly as it was in the 1850s, except for an old-fashioned herb

garden added in 1981, and the stone flower garden and wooden trellis, both added in 2003.

Descendants of Pratt's daughter Julie acquired the homestead in 1959. The structure was being used as an apartment building and needed extensive restoration to return it to its former beauty. During the 1970s it was refurbished to its current mid-19th-century appearance, and now serves as a house museum and collection repository. A carriage house was added to the property in 1975 for office, meeting, and storage space. Its replicated 19th-century design features complement the homestead.

The significance of the homestead/museum goes beyond its 19th-century architecture and its association with Zadock Pratt, and Prattsville as the center of the Catskill Mountain tanning industry. It represents the history and growth of a town and its people, beginning with the early German settlers, who during the 18th century built their homes and farmed the fertile soils of the Schoharie Valley; it also represents the establishment of small tanneries, gristmills, and sawmills on the banks of the Schoharie Kill, and the desire of the people in Prattsville to preserve the history of their mountain town.

Opposite inset: The Honorable Zadock Pratt.

Above: Etching of Zadock Pratt's residence, circa 1848.

Right: Main parlor in the restored Pratt homestead/museum.

Pratt Rock/Pratt Rock Park

While the sandstone itself is several hundred thousand years old, the carvings known as Pratt Rock began in 1841 and were the work of four different stonecutters: John Fair, Charles Kissock, E. Brenefind, and H. Vermilya. A set of exact dates for each carving is not known, however, because a carving was begun only when Colonel Zadock Pratt thought of some specific design or scene and decided that he wanted it chiseled into the cliffs. The cutters continued working on the carvings until the colonel's death in 1871.

The carvings, all symbolic of pieces of his life, are sometimes of himself. One intricate carving shows the face of his son, George Watson Pratt, himself a colonel in the Union army. George died from wounds he sustained during the Second Battle of Manassas during the Civil War. Each of the faces is approximately five or six feet high, and the various symbols are about two feet high. They are all cut into the gray sandstone.

Pratt loved to entertain both friends and dignitaries at the rocks. With this in mind, in addition to the designs, he had caves, tables, and benches carved as well. The caves always remained quite cool, and he stored his champagne in them, waiting until just the right moment to spring that little surprise on them!

Pratt ultimately turned the 20 acres of land occupied by the rocks over to the Town of Prattsville, which has been caring for the area ever since. In 1980, the Prattsville Recreational Committee sponsored "Save the Rocks," raising enough money to completely restore the designs. Because of this, they are still available for all to see, and are well worth a jaunt up to the caves.

On July 3, 1985, the nationally syndicated *Ripley's Believe it or Not!* cartoon featured Zadock Pratt's rock project. The text proclaimed that "Pratt's Rocks [sic] are often referred to as New York's Mount Rushmore and the only one like them in the country."

Pratt Rock earned a spot on both the New York State Historic Register and the National Register of Historic Places in 1986.

Views of Pratt Rock, circa 1922.

PRATTSVILLE COMMERCIAL BUILDING
DRESSER HOUSE

Built into the east bank of the Schoharie Creek, this is one of the earliest of more than 100 houses and commercial buildings that Zadock Pratt had constructed in the village of Prattsville. It is one of only a few surviving commercial structures representative of early American industry. Constructed circa 1824 with massive hemlock beams, this building originally served as the felt mill office/sleeping quarters of Zadock Pratt when he owned and operated the largest tannery in the world. Pratt hired and fired many men of all ages to run a competitive tannery business.

Representative commercial uses of this small three-room building include use as a blacksmith shop, paint shop, lathe shop, art-glass shop, and storage. The exterior, painted red and with a rear shed addition, is illustrated on the map of Prattsville, dated 1833 by A. H. Jackson.

This building was given to the Pratt Museum in 1955 by a former member of the board of trustees, Andrew Dresser, who had inherited it from his grandparents. While under Dresser ownership, the building served as a residence. There is an adjoining building labeled as a workshop that is shown on other early maps. It is believed the workshop was moved to the building's north end to be used as the kitchen wing in the 1920s. During the 1970s there was a relocation of the entrance, and a brick chimney and fireplace were installed.

Matching grants from the Catskill Watershed Corporation and the O'Connor Foundation have helped fund the many improvements undertaken in the last few years, including a new foundation in 1996, replacement of the roof and windows, and altering the landscaping to replicate the original tree and flowering bushes. The museum's plans for the Commercial Building include using it as an informational office that they've christened "Gateway to the West."

PRATTSVILLE

THE REFORMED DUTCH CHURCH OF PRATTSVILLE

Fronting on the main street, this is the oldest church in the town of Prattsville. The Dutch Reformed congregation was established here in 1802 by Reverend Lopaugh. Their first church was erected on this site in 1804. After being damaged by fire in 1833, the church was soon rebuilt. Above the entrance is a plaque that reads "Reformed Dutch Church Built 1804 Rebuilt 1835." One-third of the rebuilding costs for the church were generated through the generosity of Zadock Pratt, founder and benefactor of the hamlet of Prattsville.

The interior of this church has been described as "superior," retaining its original plan of an entry vestibule and hall. It is the only church on the mountaintop that contains original pew doors. Deteriorated box pews were replaced with replicas during a 1971 and 1972 restoration, funded by a grant from the O'Connor Foundation. The original chancel survives, with a raised platform surrounded on three sides by a low raised paneled enclosure. On the wall behind the chancel, the altar is set within a Gothic arched niche that was added as part of an 1881 renovation.

The small land parcel on which the church was erected meets the steep east embankment of the Schoharie Creek. Although a deed to the church has not been found, it is believed that the parcel was given by the Laraway brothers, as they were benefactors of a parcel deeded to the elders and deacons for use as a cemetery. John Laraway and his sons John, Jonas, Derrick, and Martinus were pioneers in Schoharie Kill before Zadock Pratt enlarged it and it was renamed Prattsville.

The two-story church is constructed with heavy timbers on a rubble-stone foundation designed in a New England country style, with a Greek Revival influence. Before the single-story church hall and office was erected in the 1950s, a driveway went around the building, passing in the rear the spot where carriage sheds stood. The church is noteworthy for its detailed façade and bell tower, markedly similar to that of the Centre Presbyterian Church of Windham. The multi-tiered tower was originally topped with a fourth tier and a domed roof.

The original 12-over-12 windows are intact, some with original panes. The window moldings, door, and columns remain untouched, despite the fire that required a great deal of rebuilding. Over the main entrance and the dedication plaque is a large Federal-style oval window. Originally, two doors flanked the double-door entrance but were removed as part of a late-19th-century restoration. Although the exterior is sheathed in synthetic clapboards and has modern replacement shutters, the building still maintains its original character.

OLD EPISCOPAL MANSE
SAYERS LUTZ HOUSE
REFORMED DUTCH CHURCH PARSONAGE

Constructed circa 1845 on a rubble-stone foundation in the shape of a cross, the Manse, also known as the Sayers Lutz House, is located on the west side of Route 23 in the village of Prattsville. It was built by the Protestant Episcopal congregation as a home for their pastor, and was probably constructed by the same carpenter, Nelson Finch, who constructed their church. The first occupant was probably the Reverend Thomas S. Judd, first pastor of the newly formed Episcopal congregation.

The exterior features are done in a Gothic Revival style: pointed windows and a steeply pitched gable. The casement windows have been described as exceptional. A simple gingerbreading accentuates the trim on the house. Interior features include a spiral staircase with two right angles built into it, as well as two doors leading to two parlors with back-to-back fireplaces, their wooden mantels carved in Greek Revival style.

The Episcopal church flourished for about ten years, but during the mid-1800s, when the tanneries in Prattsville started closing, membership declined. By 1884 services were held only during a few of the summer months, leaving little need for a pastor's residence.

Many have lived in and owned this house. The owner in 1867 was a local miller named William A. Richtmyer. As part of his estate, it was sold in 1872 at public auction, which was held at the hotel of Isaiah Houghtaling in Prattsville. Beginning in 1883, three generations of the Lutz family owned the property. In 2000 it was purchased by the Reformed Dutch church from the Sayer Lutz estate, to be used as a parsonage.

Despite minor alterations and additions, including the one-story addition on the rear that housed an apartment during the 1950s, the house still retains its original integrity. A carriage barn on the property built in a similar style during the latter half of the 19th century complements the character of the site.

Vetter House— Original Methodist Parsonage

This beautiful and well-kept single-family home in the village of Prattsville was built in the early 1800s, and for many years served as the district office for the local United Methodist Conference. With wings added in 1847 and 1880, the house now contains 14 rooms, including a summer kitchen.

In 1907 Mary Mix sold this house, which she had taken ownership of in 1897. Elmer Krieger, the new owner, assumed two mortgages against the property. It is interesting to note that at an earlier date Mary had given a right-of-way across her property for a railroad trolley line from Oneonta to Cairo. Apparently, it was one of the several proposed trolley lines that were never constructed.

Edwin L. Moore and Blanche Turk were married in 1908. The couple moved to Prattsville four years later, and Edwin became manager of the Prattsville Dairy Company. In 1919, while working at the dairy, Edwin purchased this house in partnership with Frank Rosecrans, from the estate of Elmer Krieger.

After ten years Edwin left his position at the dairy and started a feed and hardware business, which he remained active in until it was sold in 1928. Frank Rosecrans was also in the hardware business, apparently either working for or in partnership with Edwin. In the U.S. census Frank reports his occupation as retailer in hardware, while Edwin reports himself as a merchant in hardware.

After the sale of his business, Edwin ran and was elected to the office of Prattsville town supervisor, a position he held for 14 years. Edwin also served as the director of the Stamford National Bank for 30 years. Frank become clerk on the Prattsville board of supervisors.

Both men shared ownership of the house and resided in it with their families for numerous years. In 1943, by then a widower, Frank sold his undivided one-half interest to Edwin. Edwin passed away at home on a Sunday morning in 1952.

During the 1900s the house was known as Moore's Tourist Home, a hospitable place accommodating business travelers and tourists. Blanche and Frank's wife, Susan, probably ran the boardinghouse. In 1972 Blanche deeded the property to Lawrence Gardiner and his wife, Gertrude. From that year until 1975 the house served as the editorial office for the regional quarterly magazine, *The Catskills,* published by Mr. Gardiner.

Frayer Barn

The interior of this barn was constructed using parts of older buildings, as the large support beams and the long and short boards show evidence of prior use. One of the two rooms was designed to store a carriage, the other is a small room with horse stalls. There is also a "let-down" or "moving ladder" to the hayloft. One other barn on Washington Avenue also has this feature.

In April 1883, Medad Frayer and his neighbor Thomas Fitch legally declared that they, and their heirs, would maintain the well and water pump between their houses on Washington Avenue, provide a wide gate for teams of horses and vehicles, and provide a narrow gate for people to pass through the property. The dirt road, used as a shortcut up to Huntersfield, where it is said cattle passed down from one mountain meadow and up to the next, left the main road and crossed the property.

The agreement arose after Frayer's purchase on March 27, 1883, and perhaps from his intention to construct this 1884 barn on the back of his lot. An older house and this barn passed through several owners, until 1944 when the house was moved to Slater Road. A new house replaced the former in more recent years, but the old barn remains as a reminder of earlier times.

This barn is identified as a stable on the 1887 fire insurance map created by Sanborn Map and Publishing Company, Limited. The amount the Frayer family paid for insurance is unknown, but they were protected by a volunteer fire company with 500 feet of hose, and the reservoir (Schoharie Creek) only a short distance from the corner of Washington and Main streets.

In 1980, steps were taken to stabilize the building, which was bowed due to age. Some of the deteriorated, older wide clapboards in the rear exterior were replaced with particleboard. Then, in 1996, the barn received a new roof. The late Muriel Pons, former Prattsville town historian and past owner of this property, reported in 2003 that the two front windows are completely original, right down to the hinges.

SCHOHARIE CREEK HOMESTEAD

Encompassing more than 100 acres of farmland, this was a dairy farm owned by three generations of the Conine family. The barn is a significant structure, three stories high. The farmhouse has a summer kitchen complete with the original chimney. Various changes and additions over the years have altered the design. During the 1940s a two-room addition was constructed to accommodate boarders. The original log and timber section of the house may possibly date back to the 18th century and may be a surviving structure from the settlement historically called both Federal City and Red Falls.

The earliest history of this house is elusive. Possibly it was the family homestead of the Soule family, who sold the 66-acre parcel to the Conines, or a tenant house for tannery or mill workers. Just upstream from this house was a tannery, which was built at the waterfall circa 1829 by Foster Morss. After it was closed in 1849, Foster's son Burton utilized the water power of Red Falls to run a foundry that manufactured cotton mill machinery. At a later date, Burton owned a cotton mill and several tenant houses in this area. The mill was in operation until 1880, just one year before David H. Conine and Dwight Conine purchased this property from Ebenezer and Rachel Soule.

The Conine family and their farm complex were an essential part of the economic, political, and social forces that shaped Prattsville. Four members of the Conine family from Prattsville served in the 120th Regiment of New York State Volunteers during the Civil War: Dwight, Ezra, Solomon, and Eli. In 1896, members of the Conine family were farming more than 1,000 acres in the town of Prattsville.

In the 1940s this homestead became, in the words of its ads and brochures, an "upstate Catskill Mt. Boarding House—with lots of good 'home cookin'.'" One member of the Conine family still remembers serving food to the guests in the boardinghouse when it was owned by Chester and Myra Conine.

Since 1966, the farmstead and surrounding acreage has been owned by the Owad family. In more recent years, Christine Owad had a small chapel constructed on the property in memory of her parents.

O'Hara/Fowler/Laraway House

This building is an early stagecoach inn and tavern. The building was originally designed in the Federal style; the Greek Revival façade with its two-story porch and four fluted pillars date to about 1840. Martinus Laraway established this first inn—the building was also used as his home—shortly after the Revolution.

This tavern first appears on Jackson's map of 1833. On Samuel Geil's 1856 *Map of Greene County,* it is identified as C. Smith's Hotel. This name predates Colonel Pratt's purchase, and served through the 19th century. The building has the architectural integrity of the typical tavern style, including many early features such as two exterior doors, one with a fanlight, and an early-style banister and rail. It also contains an early cranberry kerosene pull-chain fixture in the hall.

The first Prattsville town board meeting was held in this building—then the home of Colonel Henry Laraway. The names Decker, Munson, and Dickerman are listed as being in attendance. In business conducted at that meeting, Zadock Pratt was given the title of "Overseer of the Poor."

During the 19th century, four sisters owned competing inns in Prattsville. The sisters took the competition so seriously that they would not even speak to one another! During that time, this was the inn of one of those sisters. In 1882, the inn was purchased by Charles Fowler, a Lexington native. After refurbishment, it opened as the Fowler House with accommodations for 50 guests. Today the building is a residence, commonly known as Fowler House, or the O'Hara Homestead.

Hotel Fowler stationery, circa 1917.

LUTZ/MAFFAT HOUSE
MCGINNIS-LUTZ HOUSE

It is believed the first occupants of this house were settlers in the 1770s. They lived in the oldest section, a simple northern colonial–style structure that was moved during the 1820s from along the Schoharie Creek to its present location on Main Street. The Greek Revival section was built around the same time. The house is constructed of exposed hand-hewn hemlock post-and-beam, with batten doors and blacksmith-forged door latches. It rests on a dry, laid-up stone foundation. The front porch added in the 1840s is Gothic Revival style with gingerbread brackets.

The Greek Revival section was built by Zadock Pratt, who constructed more than 100 houses in the village to shelter his tannery workers. The repositioning and construction of the house came about due to his realignment of the settlement's main road, which originally ran along the bank of Schoharie Creek. It is thought that this was once the office for the Gilbert Foundry and Mill.

In 1968 the roof was raised on the back section to accommodate a bedroom and bath. The interior of the front section originally had the typical four-over-four rooms. There are no hallways, making it necessary on the upper floor to walk through one bedroom in order to enter the others. The ladderlike stairway that once went almost straight up has been replaced. At some point, the four downstairs rooms were converted into two long parlors. This change had already taken place when the house was purchased by Claude and Frances Lutz in 1951. One room still had the old 12-over-8 bubbled window panes in sashes without any hardware.

Since that time the property has remained under the ownership of the Lutz family, an old and well-known family in Prattsville. Claude served in the U.S. Navy during World War II and in 1989 was buried in Fairlawn Cemetery. He joined other relatives in the cemetery, including children with the Lutz name, interred as early as 1886. When the village was incorporated in 1883, Andrew Lutz, who emigrated from Germany to the United States in 1845, was one of the three appointed trustees. Andrew, his wife, and at least some of their children are also interred in Fairlawn.

PRATTSVILLE

ELM TREE FILLING STATION
O'HARA'S TRADING POST

To date, this business has been owned and operated by five generations of the O'Hara family; the sixth generation is there now. Thomas J. O'Hara, Sr., the builder and original owner, passed this business on to his son Albert; he, in turn, passed it on to his son Thomas. Tom passed it to his son Michael, who plans to pass it on to his two sons, Kipp and Kory, who currently display merchandise from their business located elsewhere in Prattsville.

Between 1948 and 1998, Tom and his wife added snow plowing, travel trailers, and a towing service, hunting and fishing supplies, a gift shop, and even a Radio Shack outlet. The building itself has survived 15 floods since 1948, as well as a fire, and has always been repaired and even improved to fit the times.

"'Tis said" that this is probably the oldest gas station in the entire state of New York, but that is not its only claim to fame: it is also known for having the largest roadside "elm tree standing." And in 1861, that tree is said to have had an army tent stationed under its weighty branches. The tent acted as a reception office for local recruits into the Union army, to fight in the Civil War. The commander of that specific regiment was Colonel George Watson Pratt, the son of Zadock Pratt. Unfortunately, that tree no longer stands: New York State took it down in the 1950s because it was diseased, a victim of the elm tree beetle, as were many other trees in Prattsville at that time. After it was pulled down, its annual growth rings were counted, and it was determined that the tree was 325 years old.

During 2008 the O'Hara family closed the service station, due to increasingly stringent New York City regulations and environmental rules governing the so-called watershed communities along the creeks and streams that feed the city's vast upstate reservoirs. Only time will tell whether this building and business of 80-plus years will continue or become a legend of the past.

Elm Tree Filling Station, circa 1930.

Country Hutt Antique Center

The earliest construction at this site, located on Main Street a short distance from Zadock Pratt's home, is documented on Lot No. 16 on A. H. Jackson's 1835 survey map, which was drafted June 5, 1833. This building originally had a roof overhang, which was later incorporated into a balcony porch. The building uses peg/post construction, with wide-plank boards. Among other features, the interior contains French doors.

At one point, this building may have been used as living quarters for Colonel Pratt's tannery workers, and from available resources it appears to have later served as a commercial building.

According to an 1838 deed, Albert B. Austin and his wife, Jane Elizabeth, who were living in the city of Hudson, sold Lot No. 16, two adjoining parcels, and one parcel across the Schoharie Turnpike to Consider King of Prattsville. The price tag was $1,300. It seems possible that Dr. King may have had his medical practice in this structure next to the "PrattsVille House."

Consider King was practicing in Milford, New Jersey, during 1821. By 1830, at age 33, he and his brother Levi King, also a doctor, who would later set up practice in Cairo, New York, became members of the newly formed Greene County Medical Society. In 1831 Consider King and his wife, Lucina, joined the Windham Congregational Church, and in 1834 began buying property in the town of Prattsville. By 1850 Dr. King and his family had left Prattsville, but he did not sell Lot No. 16 until 1854.

The new owner was James B. Gregory and his wife, Cyntha Elizabeth Myers. James served as Prattsville clerk from 1852–1853 and was a member of the Oasis Lodge No. 119, F. & A.M. Unfortunately, we do not know for what purpose he used the building, but he owned it for more than ten years. In April 1865, while living in Sing Sing, New York, the Gregorys sold Lot No. 16 to Sarah Laraway.

The next owner was George Hoagland, although it is unclear how the building came into his possession. George was Prattsville town clerk in 1865, and he also served as justice of the peace. In the May 9, 1864, *Mountain Sentinel* it was reported that George ran a credible drugstore. Perhaps he had his drugstore in this building prior to his purchase, or moved in afterwards. He sold it to Edward Walters in March of 1866.

The Beers' 1867 *Atlas of Greene County* shows that John N. Bullis and Robert Hoffman had a store in this building situated between the "Hotel G. W. Martin" and C. Platner's saloon. Apparently they did not own the property, since an 1875 deed documents its sale to Edwin Bouton, Lewis Palmer's executor. Palmer had purchased it from Edward and Lydia Walters.

After additions to the original structure, and passing through many owners, in recent years the building became an antique center owned by Christl and Valentine Riedman. They made a number of repairs to the structure in 2003. Country Hutt Antiques featured all types of interesting artifacts in the sales booths rented out to antique buffs. The antique center recently relocated, and this building on Main Street is waiting for a new occupant.

Waterfall House and Clark Falls

The Waterfall House is an old building even by Greene County standards: the original construction may predate the creation of the county itself! While the exact date is not known, the second story was added sometime during the early 1800s.

From 1854 to 1869, owner Isaac Searles ran a carpentry shop out of the building. He specialized in cabinetry and furniture, especially chairs. Unfortunately, 1869 turned out to be a very bad year for Searles: during a flood, the Huntersfield Stream swept through the building, putting Searles out of business. He did rebuild, only to have an even greater tragedy strike five years later: in 1874, his 18-year-old daughter, Abby Searles, drowned during another flood.

Oddly enough, 1874 also marked the opening of a funeral parlor that would be operated out of this home for more than 100 years, under a number of different owners, the first being Ed Brown. Business must have been good, because the building was rebuilt during 1885 and 1886. Ceiling beams were exposed in the middle room and living room; the deck and porches were added later.

In 1905 the beautiful, gorgeous, wonderful Clark Falls was becoming very popular. Huntersfield Stream, Huntersfield Creek, and Huntersfield Falls all flow into Clark Falls, over many tiers of stone and rock.

An old iron bridge was moved from Prattsville's Main Street to this Washington Street property in 1945. From the house, this bridge crosses the stream and then crosses the creek to the outer banks, where the owner put in a lovely flower garden.

The funeral parlor's 111-year run came to an end in 1985. After Ed Brown's time, the next owner/operator was Al Shaver, and finally the Fred Deckers—first senior, and then junior. After their tenure, in 1985 the property was purchased by Tom and Barbara Cemikvasky, who live part-time in Guatemala. In 1987 the Cemikvaskys graciously opened their lovely and interesting home to visitors, participating in the 11th Annual Old Homes Tour sponsored by the Greene County Historical Society.

Prattsville's Old Town Hall

While this 1-story building, constructed circa 1900, is a basic structure, it nonetheless displays a few Victorian touches. The gable has four rows of fish-scale shingles, a central medallion, and an oval double fan. The building was probably constructed by a local carpenter, and the shingles may have been made by Mr. Deyoe, who owned a gristmill at the swinging bridge. His mill used water power and was later run by steam.

In preparation for "Historic Prattsville Pathways to the Past," the Zadock Pratt Museum provided information on the historic inventory of Prattsville. They concluded that the Old Town Hall was built circa 1900; this was based in part on the building's placement in the area across the turnpike road (Main Street) from Zadock Pratt's home, where his showy ponds and gardens stood.

Main Street in Prattsville has suffered flood damage several times because it is so near the Schoharie Creek. At least two catastrophic events devastated the area where Prattsville's Old Town Hall sits. A local newspaper reporting on an 1869 flood stated the water was five feet deep and its power had washed the cabinet shop away, which had lodged near the Episcopal church. The James Frayer house was washed away, as was the bridge, hat shop, gristmill, and several barns and sheds. In fact, all of the buildings on the creek side of Main Street were damaged to some degree.

The *Prattsville News* reported in 1874 that nearly every house on Main Street from just above the bridge by the Episcopal church, down to the Reformed church was three to five feet deep in water filled with logs and debris. If this small building had been standing at either time, it seems unlikely it would have survived such catastrophic events.

Oral history relates that the first occupant was the Grace Episcopal Church, whose congregation used it as a chapel. Grace Episcopal Church was constructed in 1845, and around the same time a manse for their minister was also built. The church flourished for only about ten years, then during the mid-1800s, when the tanneries started closing, membership declined. By 1884 services were held only during a few of the summer months. Perhaps the dwindling congregation downsized to this building.

Regardless of its age, this building has played many different roles in the development of Prattsville. History reveals that it served as a school before its use as a town hall and polling place. In later years, the town's old records were stored here, as well as firefighting equipment and items relating to the town's water district. The rescue squad has also used the building, and at one time it was even used as a recreation hall for young people. At present it houses the sheriff's cars.

Silas Lewis Munson and wife Phoebe Fuller Munson, circa 1905.

TOWN OF WINDHAM

Windham was originally a part of Woodstock, Ulster County. In March 1798, two years before the creation of Greene County, Windham was set off as a separate town. In 1800, after Greene County had been created and the young Windham town placed within it, the Town grew: a portion of what was then known as Freehold, today known as Durham, was annexed to the Town of Windham.

Unfortunately for Windham, the town's land mass would soon be placed on a diet of sorts, as Greene County's other mountaintop towns were created by paring away pieces of the Town of Windham. Ashland, Halcott, Hunter (Greenland), Jewett, Lexington (New Goshen), and Prattsville (Schoharie Kill) were created in this manner between 1813 and 1851.

The hamlet of Windham was originally called Osbornville when a post office was established there on February 22, 1831, and Bennett Osborn was appointed the first postmaster. "In 1836, when Zadock Pratt became a candidate for Congress, Bennett Osborn campaigned for his [Pratt's] opponent, so during his first term, Pratt saw to it that Osbornville was changed to Windham Centre, and William Robinson replaced Bennett Osborn as postmaster. The name of the hamlet was shortened to Windham on June 24, 1873."

From the outset, Windham was a farming area. By the mid-1800s, to supplement their income, families with a spare room or two began taking in summer boarders. As tourism became the major source of income in the area, some private homes expanded into full-time boardinghouses and hotels. In fact, there is an area in Windham known as Brooklyn, even boasting its own local "Brooklyn Bridge." Located close to where Route 296 and Route 23 meet, the area most likely got its name from the large number of Brooklynites who spent their summers in the area.

Windham today enjoys its nicknames, "Land in the Sky" and "Gem of the Catskills." The present Town of Windham includes the hamlets of Hensonville (formerly called Bailey's Four Corners), Maplecrest (originally Big Hollow), and Windham; areas that today are called Brooklyn; Brooksburg (the Union Society named it thus because a meetinghouse there was open to all denominations); Mitchell Hollow, aka Mitchell's Hollow (named after an early settler); Nauvoo (named for the Illinois Mormon settlement, because of some of the Windham settlers who had lived here went west with the Mormon migration); North Settlement; and a part of East Windham.

By most accounts, the early settlers of Windham were mainly of English stock, from elsewhere in the British Isles, and from Connecticut, but some were of Dutch or Palatine German ancestry. Today, families have migrated to other areas and new folks have moved into Windham. It is significant, however, that there are still a large number of descendants of the early settlers who continue to live here, and their newer neighbors, too, are justly proud of their scenic community and interested in its heritage. Its mountains are filled with hiking trails, two 18-hole golf courses, a ski slope, rich opportunities for hunting and fishing, and fine restaurants.

Munson/Durnan House

This is a wood-framed, Queen Anne–style Victorian house constructed in 1887. The exterior is finished in clapboard using a fish-scale design. The exterior also has filigree and gingerbread trim, front and second-floor porches, and a third floor cupola or "widow's watch" peak.

The architect who designed this house, George F. Barber, was incredibly prolific. He is responsible for literally thousands of houses built across the country, and for popularizing the elaborate exterior shape and gingerbread we associate with Victorian styling. He accomplished this by thinking "outside the box"—in his case, outside the floor plan—running a mail-order business selling house plans. The design of this residence was straight out of his catalogue: home design #61, new model dwelling.

Construction of this particular "new model dwelling" began in 1884 and was completed in 1887. A small photo studio was added in 1923 by Donald Munson. The house was a Munson family home for eight decades. At one point in its life, it was known as Elmhurst Inn.

This home was built for Silas Lewis Munson and Phoebe Fuller Munson. Silas was a farmer and a carpenter by trade and it is believed that the house was largely built by him or under his direction. In the Elmhurst Inn period it was a vacation place for visitors to the mountaintop area. The Munson family is among the oldest families in Windham, having arrived here from Wallingford, Connecticut, about 1800, although research indicates that some Munson relatives may have been here during the 1790s.

The Munsons had originally emigrated from England, and by 1637 Thomas Munson was in Hartford colony and a veteran of the Pequot War. *The Munson Family History*, by Emma L. Patterson—a direct descendant of Silas Lewis Munson, and former librarian at Peekskill High School—contains a great deal of interesting historical background on the family odyssey and lineage. She obtained much of the early history of the family from the Munson record that is housed in the New York Public Library.

Left: View of "widow's watch" cupola.

CENTRE PRESBYTERIAN CHURCH
WINDHAM LIBRARY AND CIVIC CENTER

Occupied by the Centre Presbyterian Church, this site was originally donated by Merritt Osborn early in 1834 for use as a cemetery. In fact, several interments were made here, but water from the creek poured into newly dug graves and the ground was soon abandoned for burial purposes.

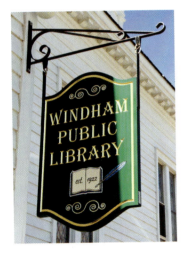

Because of this, later that same year the Presbyterian Society purchased one acre of land for $30 from Colonel George Robertson. This acre was located just east of Windham Village, and the remains of those originally buried in the Merritt Osborn Cemetery were reinterred. That acre is now considered the old part of the Windham Village Cemetery.

The Osborn plot was then used for this church building erected in 1834 and dedicated to the worship of God on January 1, 1835; the sermon was given by the Reverend David Porter. The pastor chosen by the congregation was the Reverend Leonard Van Dyke, who served in that post from 1835 to 1860, when his failing voice made it necessary for him to resign.

This is a one-and-a-half-story, Greek Revival–style building. It is very similar to a church in Rensselaerville, New York, that is believed to have been a sister building in the early days. This building has original clapboard siding and fenestration, and a one-story rear addition that used to be the Sunday school and kitchen, but now houses the public library.

The main part of the church is three bays wide and four bays deep, using a wood frame and post-and-beam construction. It has a medium-pitch gable roof with full pediments on the façade. Tall, rectangular stained-glass windows adorn the east and west sides of the sanctuary. The original cornice moldings and frieze, the corner pilasters with molded capitals and bases, and the belfry and steeple are impressive. The entry has double-paneled wood doors, and the doors are flanked by double Greek Doric columns or pilasters.

The iron fence that still surrounds the churchyard was purchased through the efforts of S. Henry Atwater and erected in July 1880. T. G. Sellers furnished the pews bought in 1905 during the redecoration of the church. The church was not redecorated again until 1922, which was the same year that the church was wired for electricity. The electric service replaced an acetylene gas machine that had been in use since 1910.

The church organ, holding between 2,500 and 3,000 pipes, had tones exceptionally mellow and sweet. It weighed more than 10 tons and cost the congregation nearly $8,000. The organ's wonderful sound was especially joyous during the Christmas holidays, when one of the talented town youths played Christmas hymns that would be heard up and down Main Street.

The Centre Presbyterian Church congregation merged with the Windham United Methodist Church in 1972. This building stood empty for a few years and was scheduled for demolition, but through the efforts of Larry Tompkins, a Centre Church committee was formed in 1978 to raise money for restoration. It was placed on the National Register of Historic Places in 1979.

Now that the town has taken over the building, it has been overseeing the renovations necessary to preserve the building, such as new floor timbers, and interior work to meet the needs of the town library and the civic center. All work has been done while preserving the character of the building. The church has twice been painted, the second time in May–June 2006, and the beauty of the building has been greatly enhanced. The next project is reported to be the refurbishing of the wrought-iron fence that has surrounded the churchyard since 1880.

The civic center is frequently used for various concert series that are well attended and feature gifted artists. The library serves the community actively, offering a wide variety of media, including computer access to people of all ages. In this way, the old church has taken on a new life and continues to serve the community in meaningful ways.

Left: Windham Public Library sign.

Below: Site of the original church organ, which once contained nearly 3,000 pipes.

WINDHAM

OLD PUBLIC LIBRARY

Constructed in 1899 for Prentice Mack, this structure was built by local carpenter Pratt Brewer, who had served the Union in the Civil War as a member of Company E, 15th New York Engineers. The front portion of the building served as a jewelry store, and the addition in back was a shop for gun and bicycle repair. In 1922 it became the Windham Public Library, and served as such until 1988, at which point the library moved on to larger quarters.

This one-and-a-half-story Queen Anne-style structure is largely intact and is totally unique in the village. It is constructed of wood frame with narrow clapboard and decorative wooden shingles. The front entrance is recessed, with a single door and stained-glass transom lights above. The entry porch extends out from the building at a 45-degree angle. It has a molded cornice, bracketed eaves, and paneled and spindle friezes with segmented arches and turned posts and balusters.

On the siding are scalloped, diamond, and hexagonal shapes. The building has an irregular plan and massing, which is typical of the Queen Anne style. Looking up, one will notice the complex roofline, the two gabled-roof dormers, and a polygon-shaped corner turret, plus the use of stained glass in the panes of the windows. As noted in a publication by Christine Owad, an architectural historian, "the use of decorative wooden shingles creates a rich textural quality." This is particularly noticeable on the turret and other decorative rooflines. There is a Greek Revival element in the front gable that is also very appealing to the eye.

Though there are many homes in Windham and throughout the greater area with decorative shingles, few can match this building, although the Munson/Durnan House on the Greene County Historical Register would be one.

This unique building caught the attention of artist Harry Devlin, who painted it in 1989. The painting was then reproduced as a poster in March 1991 for a retrospective at the Morris Museum in Morristown, New Jersey.

MITCHELL HOLLOW UNION SOCIETY CHAPEL

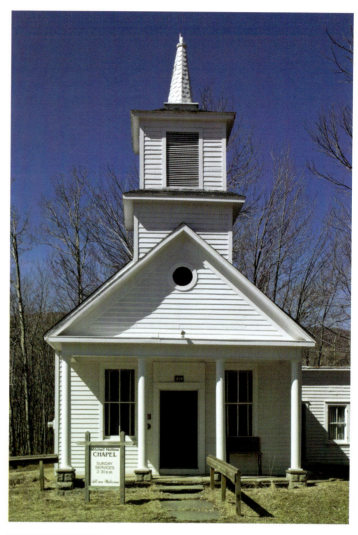

The Mitchell Hollow Chapel was originally housed in an old schoolhouse across the road from the present structure. In that old schoolhouse they taught spelling, had a debating society and a dramatic association, and held religious services. In the 1800s it was customary for people, after working all day, to arrive in horse and buggy for an evening Mass. Each family had its own area. Amazingly, the same well-worn old hymnals are still in use today.

In 1898 the congregation decided that the old schoolhouse would no longer be used for religious purposes and that a new building would be needed. Land and lumber were donated. Parishioners, including the pastor, all worked on the project, and soon the building was in place. It took only a year to both construct the new church and pay for it.

This small, quaint, and charming chapel is all original, including the wainscoting used throughout the chapel. The finial used on the steeple is handstretched up toward heaven. Use of this finial is exceedingly rare: apparently there are only four or five steeples in the country that have integrated such a design element. But here, in a setting at a fork in the road, with the mountain ridge framing the background, the design is especially captivating.

The official name of the Mitchell Hollow Chapel is the Mitchell Hollow Methodist Episcopalian Presbyterian Union Society Chapel. The significance of this long official name is that the church is open to all faiths.

Inset: Detail of the rare finial "hand."
Below: View of chapel interior with the original wainscoting.

Cobb/Brockett/Blakeslee House

The original section of this residence, the "western" half, is a five-bay Greek Revival–style structure. It was built in 1856 for Alphonso Cobb. The builder was N. P. Cowles. This part of the house has a medium-low pitch hip roof with molded cornices and a wide molded frieze with Greek Revival–style frieze windows, and extends out on the north façade over a three-bay portico. The portico itself features tall, fluted Ionic columns. Corner pilasters with molded capitals hover in the corners of this section.

The main entrance is located in the central bay, and features flanking pilasters with molded capitals and wide crowning entablature. Fenestration in this section of the house consists of double-hung windows with pediment-shaped lintels and lowered shutters.

The eastern side was built in 1912 using frame construction. The gambrel roof has wide projecting eaves with cornices and a triple-window dormer on the north. A second-story balcony is located on the north façade, in the corner formed by the intersection of the old and new wings. It has a knobbed roof with a molded cornice, and decorative wooden shingled siding, as well as a spindled frieze, turned post, and turned balustrade.

A one-story porch wraps around the north and east sides of the addition and is partially recessed on the north side under the gambrel roof. The porch features turned posts and turned balustrades. Fenestration consists of one-over-one double-hung windows with molded lintel heads and at least one small multipanel easement window. The house contains an interior brick chimney.

Alphonso's daughter Lucia Cobb Brockett and her husband, Irving, added the Queen Anne edition. Deeds indicate the land and property were granted to them on April 4, 1898. Irving Brockett—he had been Alphonso's choice for Lucia's hand—served as town justice from 1866–1869, and as supervisor from 1869 to 1870. Other deeds and land records record Irving Brockett's death; the parcel of land with the building was granted to Lucia Cobb Brockett on April 4, 1898.

In 1947 the young Dr. Robert Blakeslee was discharged from the army. He had just completed his internship at Cook County Hospital in Chicago. He returned home with the idea of practicing medicine in his hometown of Windham, New York. In 1950 he bought the property, then the Haines House, practicing medicine in the 1856 Greek Revival section of the house. His family used the 1912 Queen Anne side of the house as their home.

In those days it was common for a physician to practice medicine in his home, assuming immediate availability. Old and young alike were treated. Mothers unexpectedly delivered their babies in the office. Bones were set; lacerations were sewn together. The doctor's practice grew quickly, and he often found himself working until ten o'clock at night; each morning the doctor drove to the hospital in Catskill and tended to his patients there.

Sometimes payments came in the form of fruits and vegetables, craft items, pies and other baked goods, or, in the fall, deer meat.

Behind the parking area in the garage, there is a room known as the dog room: before the family doctor had purchased the property, a veterinarian had owned the house. The dog room had been the vet's animal operating theater. One of the vet's children owned a horse, so the property also has a horse barn.

A consultation room for the doctor and a family room were added on the south side in 1958, enlarging the house.

Presbyterian Manse/Dr. Hubbard House
The Parsonage

This two-and-a-half-story vernacular Victorian-style residence was built using post-and-beam construction. It is a wood-framed structure, five bays wide, with clapboard siding and a laid-up stone foundation. The roof has a medium-steep pitch, intersecting gable roof with projecting eaves, and ornamental large-board trim. The main gable is sheathed with decorative wooden shingle siding and has a single window with decorative wooden surrounds and a pedimented lintel.

One of the distinguishing features of the house is the magnificently detailed third-floor window. A decorative molded and ornamental frieze continues around the house above the second-story level. Fenestration consists of two-over-two double-hung windows with ornamental lintel beads. The main bay features molds, surrounds, and a decorative pediment lintel bead. The single-bay entrance porch is highly decorative, with a low-pitched hip roof, a molded cornice, a molded and spindled frieze, large as well as small jigsawn brackets and braces, wooded posts, and turned balustrades.

This historic building is believed to have been built prior to 1840. The building is shown on the maps in Beers' 1867 *Atlas of Greene County*. The building was originally known as Dr. Hubbard's house, but it was purchased by the Centre Presbyterian Society from E. J. Story in 1866, at which time it is believed the Queen Anne addition and renovation were completed.

The Centre Presbyterian Church was consolidated with the Methodist Church of Windham on August 30, 1972. The manse was subsequently sold to Josephine Blakeslee on July 27, 1982. The new owner promptly ordered extensive repairs, including updating the electrical service capacity, and putting in a new heating system, new plumbing, and a new kitchen. The house was also repainted, maintaining its original style.

ALBERGO ALLEGRIA

Here we have two Victorian houses, both built in 1876. They were originally part of the Osborn House boarding complex, which was built in 1876 by Elbert Osborn, who had been a farmer in North Settlement. It was Osborn, in fact, who told his North Settlement neighbor Ira Thompson to give up farming and try the boardinghouse business. The North Settlement neighbors found themselves neighbors again in the Brooklyn area of Windham, halfway between Windham and Hensonville.

Osborn House was a successful complex for more than a century, housing up to 300 summertime guests in several Victorian homes. These "city people" came with their trunks, some to stay the entire summer, others just for a week or two. In those days it was common for working fathers to send their families to breathe the good, healthy mountain air, especially during the polio epidemic of the 1940s.

The Gooss, Rubrecht, and Jacobs families bought the Osborn House in about 1946, operating it for 30 years. John Goettsche and his family lived and worked on the premises. The Thompson House was next door, where Ferris and Anita Thompson had five daughters. One of them was bound to catch John's eye, and on October 17, 1953, he married Mickey Thompson.

Eventually, Osborn House became the Albergo Allegria bed-and-breakfast. In 1983, two of the houses were joined together at the middle foyer. The combined building features gingerbread trim, the original stained glass, a keyhole window, a dining room alcove, and a widow's watch. A side porch has the original banisters and railings intact. These have been beautifully restored and create a prominent display. The current owners are Lenore and Vito Radelich, former owners of La Griglia, long a popular restaurant on the mountaintop. The Radelich family has done a remarkable and noteworthy restoration of Albergo Allegria.

This property also has a Hollywood connection: one of the first Johnny Weismuller Tarzan movies was filmed in the rear of the property, on the Batavia Kill.

Windham Hardware

The Windham Hardware Store has been run as a hardware store since it was built by Samuel Atwater in 1886. Atwater was followed by Brockett and Strong. Mr. and Mrs. James Lawrence, the present owners, have had at least two generations of their family operating the store. In fact, almost all of the owners have run the store for at least two generations.

It is interesting to review the deeds of earlier times, for many contained very specific details. The old deeds for this property, for example, were quite explicit in stating that the east driveway had to remain open at all times, the only exception being when wagons were unloading merchandise.

The store still retains its old wood floors, original shelving, and some original hardware. The front door is original as well, with stained-glass plates. The building has a stone foundation, but the structure's most notable feature sits skyward: the tower atop the building. The tower was removed by one generation, but restored by the generation that immediately followed.

The 2003 restoration of this building by the Lawrences was beautifully accomplished, and makes this building an outstanding example of the period when it was constructed, and the important place it held in the community's enterprises. It represents a time when nearly all needs were purchased in the village. Though times have changed, this hardware store is still a very busy and viable business.

John Howard/Van Valin House

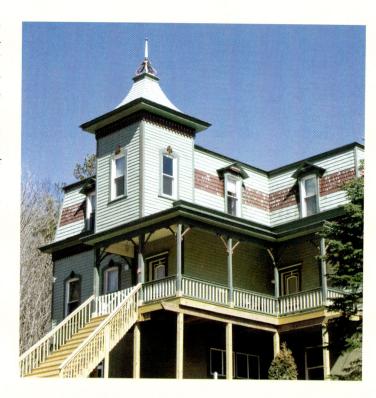

The year of original construction for this house is thought to have been 1851. The kitchen was added in 1920; repairs were made to it in 1950. In 1928, owner John Howard decided that he wanted to add a greenhouse to the property. Built from the ground up in 1908, the greenhouse was equipped with a heating system designed and installed by John Howard.

While away at school during her childhood, John Howard's daughter, Josephine, had met a Pennsylvania man named Ernest Van Valin. Years later, he finally succumbed to his boyhood love of Josephine and journeyed to find a home and to marry her. In 1928, Ernest joined his father-in-law in the family business. In 1970, Van Valin's son, Phil, joined his father in business, operating the greenhouse and related enterprises.

Today, under the ownership of Natasha and Drew Schuster, the greenhouse has been expanded and is in use as the Catskill Mountain Country Store, which operates as a greenhouse, a grocery store, and a breakfast and lunch spot. They sell home-cooked pies, cakes, and rolls, as well as fresh vegetables.

Attractions of this house include its decorative shingling and a tricolor paint scheme. In 2008, the building was moved a short distance back from the highway for business and personal considerations.

DR. FORD HOUSE

In the hamlet of Hensonville, on a hill overlooking much of the village, is an attractive Victorian home in the Queen Anne style. Over the years there have been only a few owners. During most of those years, in fact, the house was home to two families: Ford and Jacob.

Dr. Sidney L. Ford had this home constructed in 1893, and it was owned by his family until 1948. Dr. Ford was highly respected and loved by the people of the mountaintop communities, and served as family physician to many for more than 50 years. According to Gault's *Dear Old Greene County*, Dr. Ford's forebears had come to Jewett in the late 1700s from Connecticut, as did so many early families in this area. Born in Jewett on February 28, 1865, to Horace N. Ford and Matilda Haines Ford, Sidney was the only son among four sisters. While he was still an infant, the family moved to a farm in Big Hollow (Maplecrest). There, he later attended a one-room school, and having shown ability there, he was then sent to a preparatory school in Burlington, Vermont.

Ford's uncle, after whom he was named, was a medical doctor, and in his will had bequeathed his medical books to young Sidney, "if he is a mind to study, and go through with them." Evidently he was, graduating from New York University with a doctor of medicine degree in 1891, at the age of 26. He soon returned to the mountains of his boyhood home to practice his profession among the families he knew so well. A very fine source of information about Dr. Ford is Elwood Hitchcock's book, *Hensonville: A Mountaintop History*. It is especially interesting because he knew Dr. Ford personally, and the good doctor was also his family's physician.

In addition to his medical practice, Dr. Ford served the community in many other ways. He served as county coroner from

1899 to 1905, and again from 1911 to 1914. He was president of the First National Bank of Windham and served as supervisor of the Town of Windham for more than a decade. (He was a Democrat.) In 1910 he became chairman of the Greene County Board of Supervisors and became instrumental in the building of the new county courthouse, presiding over the first meeting of the board of supervisors held there. He was known to be an effective advocate of good roads in Greene County.

Dr. Ford was a member of various medical societies and served on the staffs of the Greene County Memorial Hospital and the Kingston City Hospital. He was also active in the Hensonville Methodist Church, and a member of the local Masonic Lodge.

A remarkable example of a man who served his community with excellence, Dr. Ford died on April 16, 1945. He was 80 years old. He is buried in the family plot in the Windham Cemetery.

The Jacobs family, who next lived in the house, was important in the community also, operating the grocery store just down the road for many years.

In 1997 Mary Lawyer, who had been searching for an ideal place to operate a bed-and-breakfast, purchased the property. She began a fine restoration of the old home with details according to the architecture of the period. It was renamed "Be My Guest." Most notable on the exterior is the multi-colored paint application, the graceful porches, and the octagonal room at the top of the house that once served as a sleeping porch. The interior of the home has Greek Revival columns in the dining room, and what has been described as a "magnificent Victorian staircase" in wood paneling that covers much of the front parlor wall, and provides dramatic access to the second floor. Recently, the Miller brothers purchased the property and continue to operate it as a bed-and-breakfast.

WINDHAM CEMETERY

The current location of the Windham Cemetery is not the site of the original cemetery for the Town of Windham. The original location was at the site of the Centre Presbyterian Church, which now houses the Windham library and civic center. However, the original site was neither sufficient nor suitable for use as a burial ground, due to constant flooding from the nearby creek. Therefore, in 1834, the Presbyterian Society purchased one acre of land from Colonel George Robertson for the princely sum of $30.

The new cemetery site was located just east of Windham Village, and there the remains from the earlier site were reinterred. This acre is now known as the "old part" of the Windham Village Cemetery. Veterans of the Revolutionary War, as well as the Civil War, are also buried here.

CHRISTMAN'S WINDHAM HOUSE

The siting of Windham House was originally determined by its use as a farm. The farm fields spread out directly across the road, and a barn was close to the road as well. The building was constructed in 1805. One of the earliest owners was Perez Steele, who was at one time a member of the New York State legislature. He also served as justice of the peace for many years. The Steele family had arrived from Connecticut in 1795 or so, and included six children. When they first arrived they settled on a farm in North Settlement. They were very homesick and unhappy there, and finally relocated on the Turnpike, which housed a better farm. This is the place we now know as Christman's Windham House.

The design is typical of the early inns of New York state. The farmhouse was ideally suited to become a roadside inn, and the farm buildings were suited to livery functions attached to the Catskill and Delhi stage, which carried the mail. So in the 1840s Windham House was put to use as a stagecoach hotel for commercial travelers.

The dining room had large tables seating twelve. Meals were served family style, nothing fancy, but good food and plenty of it. At every meal on each table was a large pitcher of milk and a smaller one of cream. If you stayed here in 1927, a girl would walk through the halls at 7:00 a.m. ringing the "rising bell." It would be rung again at 8:00 a.m. for breakfast, 1:00 p.m. for dinner, and 6:00 p.m. for supper.

Breakfast consisted of juice, oatmeal, or cold cereal, bacon and eggs, toast or hot muffins, coffee cakes, and a beverage. The offering would occasionally include a small steak and creamed potatoes. For the midday dinner, the hot meal of the day, the main dish was meat with a choice of roasted or broiled potatoes, a salad, vegetable, hot biscuits, homemade desserts, and beverages. However, on Sundays and Thursdays you had no choice: they served chicken, riced potatoes, a vegetable and coleslaw, homemade ice cream, and a choice of beverage. Supper included cold meat, potato or macaroni salad, home-fried potatoes or Spanish rice, hot biscuits, dessert, and a beverage.

The building is a handsome Greek Revival–style inn. The six large Ionic columns were added in 1867; the third floor was added in 1872. Interestingly, the New York State Historical Museum's Bump Tavern in Cooperstown looks a great deal like Windham House—and originally, it was set about a half mile down the road toward Ashland. Therefore, it seems likely that the same builder

constructed both of them. The Bump Tavern builder is thought to be Captain Medad Hunt, who was by profession a carpenter and joiner. The building was erected about 1795 and later became the property of Ephraim Bump, hence the name. (The Bump Tavern lives on as a living history site at the Farmers' Museum in Cooperstown, New York.) The similarities between these two beautiful old inns, built about ten years apart, and once standing so close, are striking. Today, Christman's Windham House is operated as a fine resort and restaurant with a golf course, and remains the oldest continuously operating inn in the Catskill Mountains.

POTTER/TIBBALS/TICHO HOUSE

This one-and-a-half-story Greek Revival residence is presently occupied by William and Nancy Ticho. It is a wood-framed house with clapboard siding except for the front (north) façade, which is sheathed with flush horizontal-board siding. The building, with a central interior brick chimney, is topped by a low-pitched hip roof with slightly projecting eaves and molded cornices. Fenestration consists of six-over-one double-hung windows on the first story that have pediment-shaped molded lintel heads and wooden lowered shutters. The wide-molded frieze contains Greek Revival–style frieze windows of three panels each, again with lowered shutters.

The house was constructed by N. P. Cowles. Cowles was a tailor by trade and had a shop in the village. He was apparently a good businessman, owning several buildings in town. It is also apparent that he was a builder both in demand and of considerable skill, for he is known to have built at least three houses in town, possibly more. The buildings at the Sokoll residence near the western edge of the village have been built by him. Two of his efforts appear in this book: the Cobb/Brockett/Blakeslee House (see page 250) and this house.

Cowles was postmaster at Windham from 1852 to 1861, and supervisor of Windham in 1877–1878. He and his family had moved to Windham from Connecticut when he was a young man. They continued to live here for many years, although in his later years, when his children were grown, he and his wife moved to Catskill and established a tailor business again.

One particularly notable feature of the house is the three bay front portico, recessed on the north façade beneath the frieze window of the upper story, which is supported by fluid Ionic-order columns. The corner pilasters with molded capitals are also worthy of note.

The date of the earliest construction here is 1843: that was the year that the first occupants, George W. Potter and his bride, Antoinette Doty, were married.

Windham Journal / Phantasma Gallery Building

This lovely old building is located on Main Street in the heart of downtown Windham. It was built in 1825 by N. C. Cowles and operated as a mercantile business—he was a tailor by trade, as well as a skilled builder of many homes in the village. It could at one time have been a part of another building. One occupant is believed to have operated a comb factory on the site. The town newspaper, The Windham Journal, took over the building in 1885, using it until 1990. Today it houses the Phantasma Gallery and is also used for art exhibitions.

The Windham Journal was a weekly newspaper begun in 1857. Beers' 1884 *History of Greene County* states that the paper's premiere edition on March 1, 1857, held 20 columns of news, and that by the third issue the paper had 305 subscribers. By July 1859, publisher W. R. Steele boasted that his paper had "subscribers in every state of the Union except Arkansas" and had a circulation 500 copies greater than that of any other paper published in the county.

After Steele, the founder and original editor, the editor for much of *The Windham Journal*'s early period was Edward M. Cole. While he was "wielding the editorial pen," as it was described, the paper was significantly different than the other local papers of its day: national and state news was reported and discussed in the editorial columns and in the letters to the editor. Cole had a keen interest in politics and was active in the Democratic Party— so much so, in fact, that even while he sat on the county's board of supervisors in 1884, he was forced to file a suit for his paper against Greene County, for failing to pay for court-ordered legal notices printed in the paper.

After his term as a Greene County supervisor, Cole held state political office: he was elected to the New York State Assembly in 1892 and served a stint as Windham's postmaster from 1893 to 1897. He also served as a member of the town board and the board of education, and spent many years as Windham's justice of the peace. He was held in high esteem throughout the county, as evidenced by his obituary and the tributes paid him by so many, after his death in 1915. His son, Keeler M. Cole, took over the paper after his father's death.

While the interior walls of the building have been Sheetrocked, the building nonetheless retains a great deal of its history. It still contains the original wood and windows, and pine floors. The building's attic also retains the original glass and frames. The exterior siding is original, except in the areas where it's been patched. The building has a fresh coat of paint, tastefully representative of the period.

Inset: Edward M. Cole, editor of The Windham Journal.

Above: The Windham Journal, boasting the "largest circulation in the county," April 20, 1876.

MANSFIELD/ARTEMISIA HOUSE

This building appears to date back to the early 1800s, and the lights that sit over the front door are reported to be original to the house. The property was called the Hollister Hotel and was for a long time known as the Mansfield place. The Mansfield family came to Windham from Connecticut and several generations continued to live in the area. Clippings from The Windham Journal, dating from 1886, were given to Patricia Morrow, current town historian, by Dorothy Talmadge, her predecessor. Morrow then went through Windham house by house and had written a sketch about each family. In fact, much of what we know of this family and the house comes from Ms. Morrow's excellent research, including census information; deeds; birth, death, and marriage notices; and the information the Journal article provided.

This is a fine-ranked Greek Revival house with a simple façade. In 1871 alterations were made to the windows by Truman Johnson, and an addition was put on. The change in the windows has removed the symmetry of the original home, as before-and-after photographs can attest. Some 12-over-12 windows still remain in the upper part of the house, and the gable ends still retain their typical Greek Revival beauty in the cornice and returns.

One of the most interesting stories about this house is "The Curious Case of the Framingham Frame," by Patricia Morrow, which appeared in *The Hemlock*, a local history paper in the 1990s. The story begins on August 24, 1879, eight years after those changes were made, when the house was professionally photographed. The image was labeled W. H. Mansfield House, Windham, Greene County, NY. Unfortunately, that photograph would disappear at some point. But 111 years later, in an antique shop in Framingham, Massachusetts, near Boston, a gentleman would find an old picture frame and purchase it. "In the frame, behind the glass were dried flowers, according to the Victorian custom. He removed six, small nails from the back that appeared to hold two small pieces of cardboard to the frame. One piece was an old Bull Durham advertisement. On the back of the other was a penciled notation in the upper right hand corner that read W. H. Mansfield House, Windham, Greene Co., N.Y. August 24, 1879; and upon turning it over he found a photograph pasted to the front. Below the photo someone had written Mansfield House in ornate script. To the left was printed Windham, and to the right, Green Co. [*sic*] N.Y." The gentleman was able to contact Ms. Morrow and kindly offered to return the picture to Windham. And so it was that on July 11, 1990, the photo began its journey back to Windham, which led to Patricia's investigation into the history of the house and its occupants.

A group of business associates purchased the property and ran an advertising business called Artemisia out of the house. Windham artist Robert Cepale and his wife, Christine, later purchased the property; and recently, new owners have acquired it. A sign above the front entrance now reads: "The William H. Mansfield House."

A rather humorous note to conclude with is that the house once stood next to Potter & Newell's Furniture Store. The old deed mentioned "the right of allowing the eaves of George Potter's shop to drip on said premises." That was indeed an era when civility was present even in legal matters. The Potter building is better remembered as the Windham Laundromat, which burned down in 1976. Fortunately, the Mansfield House survives, "dripping eaves" no more.

STIMSON/IVES/REYNOLDS HOUSE

George Stimson was one of the very first settlers of the Batavia Valley, and probably the first within the present-day boundaries of the village of Windham. He is said to have come from Framingham, Massachusetts, in 1785. He was the herdsman for Chancellor Livingston, who owned land in the Hardenburgh Patent, and Stimson experimented with the old-world custom of pasturing herds in the high country during the summer.

For shelter, Stimson built a brush shanty by the side of a great rock, a short distance from the current house. He is said to have had no neighbors nearer than either Cairo or Prattsville—either way, a trip of at least 15 miles. The rock is located just outside the west end of town, on the north side of Main Street —Route 23— in Windham. Today, a New York State Historic Marker recognizes the site.

Sometime after constructing his shanty, Stimson built himself a more substantial log cabin, living there for a dozen years. During that tenure, Stimson made a trip to Framingham, bringing his wife and several children back with him to Windham. By 1818, however, the Stimson family had money problems. At one point, Sheriff Jacob Haight was authorized by a writ of *fieri facias,* issued out of the court of common pleas for the County of Greene, to sell off as much of the family's "goods, chattels, lands and tenements" as necessary to settle the family's debt to a John Adams, who was owed $71.31 in costs and damages.

In time, the family began construction of a more substantial home, to which they added over the

The Stimson Rock, site of George L. Stimson's original 1785 log cabin.

ensuing years. The earliest construction was done in the second quarter of the 19th century. Additions were carried out in the later 1800s. The original house, with beams in the cellar, now exists as the center portion of the house.

By the time that William Stimson, George's son, became the owner of the place, it was known as the Stimson Farm. But the Stimson family's ownership would end in the 1860s.

Samuel Ives was the progenitor of his family in this area in 1789. He hailed from Wallingford, Connecticut, where he and three of his brothers had been soldiers in the American Revolution. He settled in Jewett Heights. His descendant Roma Ives—either a son or grandson, as there was a Roma in each generation—was to become the owner of the Stimson Farm by 1865. He kept it for only four short years, however: records show that in 1869 Thomas Branough, whose family had also been residents of the Windham area for some time before this, bought the farm from Roma R. Ives. Unlike their immediate predecessor, the Branough family kept the house in the family into the 20th century.

The Reynolds family, the current owners, have owned, maintained, and preserved the home for many years now.

ROBINSON/DOTY/PATTERSON HOUSE

Construction of this wood-framed, clapboard-sided house took place in 1833. The house was originally designed in the Greek Revival style; additions were completed later, in 1905–1906. The most recent restoration occurred in 1998.

The first occupants were members of the Eli P. Robinson family. This Eli Robinson was a "lineal descendant of the Reverend John Robinson," 1576–1625. The Reverend Robinson had been a well known Pilgrim leader in England whose church was instrumental in the creation of the Plymouth Colony. Eli was also a captain of the militia during the War of 1812. And Eli was also the father of Lucius Robinson, born at Windham on November 4, 1810. Lucius practiced law at Catskill and served as district attorney of Greene County from 1837 to 1840. Moving on to New York City, he practiced law there from 1840 to 1855, organizing the Republican Party the following year. This "native son" of Greene County was elected governor of the State of New York in 1876. He died on March 21, 1891.

At one time Bennett Osborn operated a distillery called "Windham Whiskey" on this property, producing a drink considered better than the "Bluegrass" variety of whiskey.

The name Doty in the historic title of the house comes from the married name of one of Eli Robinson's daughters. In the mid-20th century Emma Patterson, a librarian and Munson family genealogist, resided here.

THOMPSON HOUSE

In the latter part of the 19th century, two farmers were neighbors in North Settlement. They were not particularly happy in their occupation, wondering if there wasn't a better way to make a living. Elbert Osborn, one of the farmers, built a boardinghouse in the Brooklyn area of Windham, midway between Windham and Hensonville. He soon found that he was a lot happier running a boardinghouse than a farm, and mentioned this to Ira Thompson, his old neighbor.

Eventually Thompson was convinced, and in 1886 he purchased the Manor House, also in Windham's Brooklyn area, from Elias J. Reynolds. Ira's wife, Christine, was not totally convinced that this was an easier way of life because she found herself cooking, cleaning, and washing for their 25 guests—and she was doing so with the 19th-century cooking and laundering facilities she had at her disposal. Lanterns had to be brought to the kitchen each day to be cleaned, refilled with oil, and have their chimneys washed. Laundering the bedclothes involved heating water and carrying it outside, rinsing sheets in several wooden tubs, and line-drying.

The well-kept lawns and sweeping front porch of the Manor House provided summer guests with a feeling of tranquillity. The business prospered, and in 1893 a second house, Spruce Cottage, was built. Herbert Thompson, Ira's son, turned all of the fancy woodwork on his lathe and covered the exterior with multicolored patterns of wood shingles.

A third building was added to the Thompson complex in 1950: Tamarack Lodge. This was the first hotel facility in the area to have bedrooms with carpeting and private baths. In 1958 the Thompsons put in a swimming pool. They also bought the Soper Inn across the road, which had originally been a box factory that was then renovated into a boardinghouse.

In 1967 a new main building was built, which included office space, a dining room, and a kitchen. A coffee shop was added in 1968, and a recreation/game room in 1969. Ferris Thompson, Herbert's son and Ira's grandson, died in 1969, but he left behind a unique and substantial way of life for his family. Anita, his widow, continued to be involved for many years and lived well into her 90s, providing a wonderful role model for generations to come. Family ownership continued in the hands of Ferris' daughter and son-in-law, Mr. and Mrs. John Goettsche. Today, the establishment is operated by their son, Eric, and his wife, Debbie. It continues to be very much a family-run business involving several generations.

Over the past 125 years, five generations of the Thompson family have greeted and served summer guests. The Thompson House now accommodates winter guests for skiing in their Evergreens complex, built in 1986.

WINDHAMERE

The Lewis and Munson families, who were united in marriage, constructed the present building in about 1833; several additions were made through the 1920s. Silas Lewis Munson operated it as a farm until 1875, when he diversified into the boardinghouse and resort business. There were several buildings along South Street at the top of Church Street that belonged to various members of the family. The Munson/Durnan House (see page 245) contains more information on the family's background.

Windhamere, as it is known today, was operated as a summer resort for most of its existence. It was called the Munson House at first, and became a popular boardinghouse where city people could enjoy the good mountain air during the summer resort era of the Catskill Mountains. At least four generations of the Munson family ran the boardinghouse for over a century during its heyday.

This is a two-and-a-half-story house with large center gables, front and back, that balance with the end gables for a most appealing architectural style. Victorian touches were added during the latter part of the 19th century and porches were tastefully added to accommodate the summer guests' views of the mountains. In fact, the house has a beautiful setting, facing South Mountain and the ski area. A large lawn with landscaping surrounds the building, and the Windham golf course borders the property to the east.

In 1997 Peter and Mona Kliegman bought the Munson House from Chilton Cammer, the great-grandson of Silas Lewis Munson, as a retreat from the city where they could enjoy the skiing and golfing seasons in the Catskill Mountains. Windhamere remains a private home today.

PHOTOGRAPHY & ILLUSTRATIONS

ORIGINAL PHOTOGRAPHY

Collection of the Greene County Historical Society, Coxsackie: cover, back cover, pp. ii–iii, xii, 6–7, 9, 10, 11, 12, 13, 14, 19, 20, 21 (bottom right), 22 (top), 23, 24–25, 26, 27 (bottom), 29 (top), 30, 31 (bottom), 34, 38, 39 (bottom), 41 (top), 42, 43, 44, 45 (bottom), 48–49 (bottom spread), 50 (bottom), 51, 52, 56, 58, 61, 62 (top & bottom), 63, 64, 65, 66 (top), 67, 69 (top & bottom), 70 (top), 71, 72, 73, 74, 75 (left & right), 77 (top), 78, 79, 80, 81, 82, 83, 86 (bottom), 87, 88, 89, 90, 91, 92, 93 (right), 94 (top & bottom), 95, 96, 97 (top), 98–99, 100, 101, 102, 103, 104 (top), 105 (top & bottom), 107, 108, 109, 110 (bottom), 111, 115 (top), 117, 118–119, 120, 121, 123 (top), 124, 125, 126, 127, 128, 129, 130–131, 134, 135, 136, 137 (top & bottom), 138, 139, 140, 141, 142 (bottom), 143, 144–145, 146 (bottom), 147 (top), 148 (top & bottom), 149, 150, 151 (top & bottom), 152 (top & bottom), 153, 156 (bottom), 157, 158, 159 (top), 160, 161, 162, 163, 164, 165, 166, 167, 168, 170, 171, 175, 178, 179, 180–181, 181 (bottom), 183, 184–185, 187, 190, 191, 192, 196, 197, 198, 199, 203, 204, 207, 208, 209 (bottom), 210 (bottom), 211, 213 (bottom), 214 (top), 215 (top), 218, 219, 223, 226 (bottom), 227 (bottom), 229, 230, 232, 233, 234, 235, 236 (top), 237, 238 (bottom), 239, 240, 241, 244, 245, 247, 248, 249 (top right & bottom), 250, 252, 253 (top), 254, 256, 257, 258 (bottom), 259, 260, 261 (top & bottom), 262, 263.

Thomas J. Satterlee, Catskill: pp. xii, 1, 2 (top & bottom), 27 (top right), 29 (bottom), 36, 40, 59 (bottom), 66 (bottom), 70 (bottom), 77 (bottom), 84, 97 (bottom), 98 (inset), 106, 142 (top), 147 (bottom), 159 (bottom), 186 (bottom), 213 (top), 214 (bottom), 217, 220, 221 (bottom), 222 (top), 231, 246 (top & bottom), 249 (top inset), 251, 253 (bottom).

Timothy Albright, Jr., Athens: pp. 28, 32, 33.

Jean Bush, New Baltimore: pp. 53, 85, 169, 255.

Greene County Tourism, Catskill: p. 114 (bottom).

HISTORIC AND PERIOD IMAGES

Archives of The Greene County Historical Society, Coxsackie: pp. ix, 3, 4, 15 (inset), 18 (top & bottom), 21 (bottom left), 22 (bottom right), 27 (top left), 31 (top), 35, 45 (top), 46, 49 (top inset), 50 (top inset), 54, 57 (top & bottom), 59 (top), 60, 76 (bottom), 93 (left), 102 (top), 104 (bottom), 110 (bottom), 112, 114 (top), 115 (bottom), 116, 118 (inset), 122 (top & bottom), 123 (bottom), 132, 146 (top), 156 (top), 159 (left), 172, 176, 186 (top), 193, 194, 200, 202 (top & bottom), 205 (top & bottom), 209 (top), 210 (top), 212 (all), 213 (top), 221 (top), 224, 225 (inset), 228 (top & bottom), 237 (bottom), 238 (top), 258 (top, bottom inset).

The following were reproduced from Beers' *History of Greene County, New York*. Published by J. B. Beers & Co. New York, 1884: back cover (inset), pp. 19 (inset), 21 (inset), 25 (inset), 37, 39, 41, 86, 101 (top); and Beers' *Atlas of Greene County, New York*. Published by F. W. Beers, A. D. Ellis & C. G. Soule. New York, 1867: p. viii.

The authors and publisher are grateful to the following individuals for permission to reproduce photographs and documents in their possession:

Donald Berkhofer, New Baltimore: p. 215 (bottom).

Roy Davis, Windham: p. 242.

Jonathan Donald, New Baltimore: p. 206.

Pauline Munger Lawrence, Windham: p. 15 (bottom right).

Ken Mabey, Durham: p. 154.

Janet Nichols, Jewett: p. 188.

Linda Pierro, Coxsackie: p. 176.

Kelton and Eilleen Vosburgh, New Baltimore: p. 221.

Retouching and photo restoration by Robert Bedford, Flint Mine Press, Coxsackie.

SOURCES

The Vedder Research Library is a noncirculating research center making available to Greene County Historical Society members and the general public a wide range of primary and secondary resource materials depicting the historical development of Greene County. The majority of sources for this volume are in the library collection.

"A Bit of Local History! The following Is a Brief Sketch of How the Farm Now Occupied by C.A. Platner Derived Its Name of Stanley Hall." *The Prattsville News.* May 15, 1909.

"A Bit of Church History." *The Prattsville News.* July 3, 1909.

"A Look at History" and "Inn Will Stage Mystery." *The Greene County News.* Catskill, NY. October 14, 1999.

"Advertisement for Lampman's store." *The Coxsackie Union.* April 4, 1861.

Alarcon, Alvaro E. "Good Deeds Rewarded." *The Daily Mail.* Catskill, NY. January 24, 2007.

Alarcon, Alvaro E. "Reception Hall Evokes Elegance, Memories." *The Daily Mail.* Catskill, NY. February 6, 2007.

Albany Emmanuel Baptist Church. *Celebration of the One Hundredth Anniversary of Emmanuel Baptist Church of Albany, New York, October 28th to November 4th, 1934.* Circa 1934.

"American Painters." *The Examiner.* Catskill, NY. June 8, 1967.

Anderson, George Baker. *Landmarks of Rensselaer County New York.* Published under the auspices of the Troy Press. Syracuse, NY, 1897.

"Anniversary Celebration Trinity Church, Ashland." *The Windham Journal.* August 24, 1933.

Assessment Records, Cairo Town: 1908 & 1911.

Assessment Records, Catskill Village: 1922 & 1929.

"At Home" Section. *Times Union.* Albany, NY. February 4, 1996: pp. H1, H2.

Athens Sesquicentennial August 19-20-21, 1955. (n.p., brochure).

Athens Trinity Episcopal Church; Records:
    Burials, 1847–1868.
    Church Marriages, 1847–1875.
    Communicants, 1835–1866.
    Funerals, 1815.

Atkinson, Oriana. *Not Only Ours: A Story of Greene County, N.Y.* Reprinted by Hope Farm Press. Cornwallville, NY, 1974.

Bachand, Robert G. *Northeast Lights: Lighthouses and Lightships, Rhode Island to Cape May, New Jersey.* Sea Sports Publications. n.p., 1989.

Bagley Family; Genealogy. File Vedder Research Library.

Barkley, Frank G. "Tribute of a Friend, April 19, 1915." *The Windham Journal.* April 22, 1915.

Basini, Senior Warden Ronald Joseph. "Celebrating 100 Years of Service and Worship." n.p., July 21, 1996.

Beecher, Raymond (editor). *Greene County: A Bicentennial Overview.* Greene County Historical Society. Coxsackie, NY, 2000.

Beecher, Raymond (Greene County Historian). "Greene County Gleanings." *The Daily Mail.* Catskill, NY. December 18, 1993.

———. "Greene County Gleanings." *The Daily Mail.* Catskill, NY. February 5, 1998.

———. "Greene County Gleanings." *The Greene County News.* Catskill, NY. August 15, 2002.

———. *The Houghtalings: A Dutch-American Family.* Published by R. Beecher. n.p., June 1994.

———. "Honorè Chaurand's Friendship Asylum." *Greene County Historical Journal.* Coxsackie, NY. Volume 10, Number 3, Fall 1986.

———. "Mike Dolan's Company Strip Mines Moulding Sand." *Greene County Historical Journal.* Coxsackie, NY. Volume 6, Number 3, Fall 1982.

———. *Out to Greenville and Beyond.* Greene County Historical Society. 1997.

———. "The Thomsons of Catskill Landing: An In-Depth Study." *Greene County Historical Journal.* Coxsackie, NY. Volume 23, Number 2, Summer 1999 (Part I); Volume 23, Number 3, Fall 1999 (Part II).

———. "A Van Bergen Legacy." *Greene County Historical Journal.* Coxsackie, NY. Volume 12, Number 4, Winter 1988.

———. "The Wilcoxsons and Badeaus at Home and Abroad." *Greene County Historical Journal.* Coxsackie, NY. Volume 14, Number 4, Winter 1990.

Beers, F. W. *Atlas of Greene County, New York: From actual Surveys by and under the direction of F. W. Beers, assisted by Geo. E. Warner & others.* F. W. Beers, A. D. Ellis & C. G. Soule. New York, 1867.

Beers, J. B. *History of Greene County, New York: With Biographical Sketches of Its Prominent Men [1788–1884].* J. B. Beers & Co. New York, 1884; reprint edition: Hope Farm Press. Cornwallville, NY, 1969.

Best, Gerald M. *The Ulster and Delaware: Railroad Through the Catskills.* Golden West Books. San Marino, CA, 1972.

Biographical Review: Biographical Sketches of the Leading Citizens of Delaware County, New York. Biographical Review Publishing Company. Boston, 1895: pp. 318–20.

Biographical Review: Containing Life Sketches of Leading Citizens of Greene, Schoharie and Schenectady Counties, Volume XXXIII. Biographical Review Publishing Company. Boston, 1899.

Blumenson, John G. *Identifying American Architecture—A Pictorial Guide to Styles and Terms, 1600–1945.* W. W. Norton & Company. New York, 1981.

Board of Supervisors of Greene County New York. *Journal of Proceedings of the Board of Supervisors of Greene County, NY:* 1928, 1932, 1935, 1937, 1939, 1962, 1964.

"Board of Supervisors Special Meeting Cairo, Tuesday, June 5th 1883." *The Recorder.* Catskill, NY. June 29, 1883.

Bonafide, John. *Walking Tour of the Hamlet of New Baltimore Historic District.* New York, n.d. (pamphlet)

Book of Record for the Society Town of Windham; *Lexington Congregational Society Minutes 1799–1859.*

Borthwick, William S. "Events of Cornwallville Community, 1888 to 1947, Inclusive." *Greene County Examiner-Recorder.* Catskill, NY, circa 1947.

Bronck Museum. *Bronck Museum: The Hudson Valley's Oldest Home* (brochure). Bronck Museum. Coxsackie, NY, n.d.

Buel, Terry. *Welcome to Freehold Country Inn* (brochure). Freehold, NY, n.d.

Burnham, Fred. Correspondence, from February 2006.

Cairo Herald. Cairo, NY. Issues dated April 4, 1935; July 25, 1935; February 13, 1936; February 27, 1936; March 26, 1936; June 4, 1936; September 3, 1936; December 9, 1937.

Cairo pictorial collections. Vedder Research Library of the Greene County Historical Society.

"Calvary Episcopal Church at Cairo Celebrates Its Hundredth Anniversary. Centennial Service Held Saturday and Sunday, With Corporate Communion and Reception—History of the Parish Since Its Organization." n.p., August 18, 1932.

Cameron, Evelyn. "Coxsackie News Corner, Looking Back." *The Greene County News.* Catskill, NY. November 4, 1983.

Catskill Center for Conservation & Development. *Catskills Domestic Architecture. A Series of Driving Tours and a Guide to Architectural Styles.* The Catskill Center. Arkville, NY, n.d. (brochure based on the book "On the Mountain, in the Valley," the Catskill Center, 1977)

"[The Catskill Daily Mail] Recalls Big Flood of the Last Century: Prattsville News Reprints Story of Catastrophe Which Occurred in 1874." *Catskill Daily Mail.* July 2, 1930: pp. 6–7.

Catskill Directory, 1896. n.p.

Catskill Examiner Centennial Edition. August 1930.

"Catskill Public Library: Interim Report Draft." *Preservation Architecture.* May 26, 1998.

Centennial History of the Memorial Church of All Angels 1886–1996, Twilight Park, Haines Falls, New York. Haines Falls, NY, circa 1996.

Chronological Biography of Hon. Zadock Pratt, of Prattsville, NY. William H. Romeyn & Sons, Printers. Journal Office, Kingston, NY, 1866.

Church Directory Year Book: Athens, Leeds and High Hill Parish Methodist Church. 1929.

Church Directory: Federated Church/High Hill United Methodist Church, 1973. n.p. Circa 1973.

Close, Stuart, MD. "Colonel Zadock Pratt." n.p., n.d. Gift to Greene County Historical Society by Elizabeth Stuart Close, June 1952.

Cohen, David Steven. *The Dutch-American Farm.* New York University Press. New York, 1992.

Cohen, Jill. "What Has Happened to the Greene County Farmer? A Look at the Agricultural History of our Area, from Inception, to Boom, to Decline. Part Three." *Ravena News Herald.* October 7, 2004.

Columbia County at the end of the Century, A Historical Record of its Resources, Its Institutions, Its Industries and Its People. Edited and published under the auspices of the Hudson Gazette. Volume II: p. 177.

Congressional Biographical Directory; Letters; and other supporting documents from Keith Bagley to the Livanos. n.p. n.d.

Conkling, George. "Conkling-Swarthout Building Contract." Account book, 1810s–1860s.

"County Almshouse Annex Assured." *The Cairo Herald.* March 26, 1936.

"County Office Building Notes 100th Anniversary." *The Greene County News.* Catskill, NY. November 10, 1983.

D'Agostino, Robert A. "At the Bench: Greene County on Trial – Part Three." *Greene County Historical Journal.* Coxsackie, NY. Volume 19, Number 1, Spring 1995.

———. "Edward M. Cole: More Than Just a Country Editor." *Greene County Historical Journal.* Coxsackie, NY. Volume 19, Number 1, Spring 1995.

———. "Searching for The Windham Journal." *Greene County Historical Journal.* Coxsackie, NY. Volume 19, Number 1, Spring 1995.

———. "Thomas Cole's House Was Never Thomas Cole's House." *Greene County Historical Journal.* Coxsackie, NY. Volume 20, Number 4, Winter 1996.

Davom-Lane, M. A. "Historical Society Buys Old Rail Station." *Daily Mail.* Catskill, NY. December 16, 1995.

deBoer, Louis P. *Jan Van Loon. His Ancestry in Europe and His Descendants in America. A Biographical and Genealogical Sketch.* n.p. New York. 1917.

Delaware County, New York: History of the Century, 1797-1897 Centennial Celebration, June 9 and 10, 1897. Published by W. Clark. 1897.

De Lisser, Richard Lionel. *Picturesque Catskills: Greene County.* Picturesque Publishing Company. Northampton, MA, 1894. Reprint by Hope Farm Press. Saugerties, NY, 1983.

Dietz, Frances. "Elizabeth Miller Hathaway: Further Information Comes to Light." *Greene County Historical Journal.* Coxsackie, NY. Volume 20, Number 2, Summer 1996.

———. "The Life of Elizabeth Miller – Part One: Elizabeth Miller, Diarist." *Greene County Historical Journal.* Coxsackie, NY. Volume 19, Number 4, Winter 1995.

———. "The Life of Elizabeth Miller – Part Two: Elizabeth Miller, Author & Helpmeet." *Greene County Historical Journal.* Coxsackie, NY. Volume 20, Number 1, Spring 1996.

"Dr. F. W. Lilienthal Dead." *The New York Times.* July 29, 1910: p. 9.

Dodd, Rev. Henry Martyn, AM. "1803–1903 Centennial of the Old First Congregational Church, Windham, New York, June 16th 1903. The History of the Old Church with Shorter Histories of the Daughter Churches of Windham, Jewett and Ashland. And Other Historical Matters." *Windham Journal Print.* June 16, 1903.

———. "The First Presbyterian Church Ashland, A Short History." *Windham Journal Print.* June 16, 1903.

Downing, Andrew Jackson. *The Architecture of Country Houses.* New introduction by George B. Tatum. Da Capo Press. New York, 1968.

Dunn, Shirley W. *The Mohicans and Their Land, 1609–1730.* Purple Mountain Press. Fleischmanns, NY, 2000.

Dunn, Shirley W., and Allison P. Bennett. *Dutch Architecture Near Albany: The Polgreen Photographs.* Purple Mountain Press. Fleischmanns, NY, 1996: pp. 67-71.

"Early Settlers of Prattsville, Who They Were and How They Arrived Here." *The Prattsville News.* May 29, 1909.

"Early Settlers of Prattsville, Stirring Times During the Revolutionary War." *The Prattsville News.* June 12, 1909.

"Echos of the Past: 100 Years Ago, July 31, 1880." *The Greene County News.* Catskill, NY. August 2, 1990.

"Echos of the Past: 50 Years Ago, September 19, 1919." *The Greene County News.* Catskill, NY. September 21, 1989.

"Edgett Cemetery/Nicholsen Farm, compiled by Mr. & Mrs. W. A. Carl; Indexed by Peter R. Christoph; Typed by Vicki DiNovo." New York State Library. Albany, NY, August 1971. Copy: Cemetery Records, Vedder Research Library.

"Edward M. Cole." *The Windham Journal.* April 15, 1915.

Edwards, Mary Jane (comp.) *Mark Twain's The Adventures of Tom Sawyer (with illustrations of the Northrup House).* Reprint edition, n.p. 1981.

"1840–1965, The Lexington Methodist Church Lexington, NY 125th Anniversary Service Sunday, October 17, 1965." *History of the Lexington Methodist Church.* n.p. Circa 1965.

"1869 News." *The Prattsville News.* April 23, 1910.

Ellis, Franklin. *History of Columbia County, New York: With Illustrations and Biographical Sketches of Some of Its Prominent Men and Pioneers, 1825–1885.* Higgson Book Co. Salem, MA, circa 1990.

Ensign and Everts Everts. *Combination Atlas Map of Greene County.* Everts, Ensign & Everts. Philadelphia, 1876. Reprint edition by Martin Wehle. Churchville, NY, 1973.

The Examiner. Catskill, NY. January 29, 1925; February 5, 1925; February 12, 1925.

"Fairlawn Cemetery Listing, Transcribed by Sylvia Hasenkopf." *Tracing Your Roots in Greene County, Greene County, New York History & Genealogy.* 2006. (Web design and site coordination by Sylvia Hasenkopf.)

Falk, Peter Hastings (editor). *Who Was Who in American Art: Compiled from the Original Thirty-Four Volumes of American Art Annual—Who's Who in Art, Biographies of American Artists Active from 1898-1947.* Sound View Press. Madison, CT, 1985.

Falk, Peter Hastings (editor–in–chief), Georgia Kuchen, Audrey M. Lewis, and Veronika Roessler. *Who Was Who in American Art, 1564–1975: 400 Years of Artists in America.* Sound View Press. Madison, CT, 1999.

"First American Church in the Catskill Mountain Region, 1790, Presbyterian Church of Greenville, New York—A Heritage." n.p., n.d.

First Congregational Church of Old Windham Centennial: 1803–1903. n.p., n.d. (booklet)

First Reformed Church, Athens, NY. Records: Baptisms, various years.

Fone, Byrne. *Historic Hudson: An Architectural Portrait.* Foreword by John Ashbery; Introduction by Rudy Wurlitzer and Lynn Davis. Black Dome Press. Hensonville, NY. 2005.

"Ford Genealogy." Genealogy file, Vedder Research Library.

"From the Foothills, Cairo in the Spring." *The Greene County News.* Catskill, NY. May 2, 1996.

Gallt, Frank A. *Dear Old Greene County; Embracing Facts and Figures, Portraits and Sketches, of Leading Men Who Will Live in Her History, Those at the Front To-day and Others Who Made Good in the Past.* Catskill Enterprise Printers. Catskill, NY, 1915.

Galusha, Diane. "Greene County Heritage. 'She Did What She Could' to Save Souls in Greene County." *The Daily Mail.* Catskill, NY., November 8, 1976.

Geil, Samuel. *Map of Greene County, New York.* E. A. Blach. Philadelphia, 1856.

Giddings, Edward D. *Coeymans and the Past.* Tri-centennial Committee of the Town of Coeymans. n.p. 1973: p. 53.

Glassie, Henry H. *Pattern in the Material Folk Culture of the Eastern United States.* University of Pennsylvania Press. Philadelphia, 1968.

Glunt, Ruth Reynolds. *Old Lighthouses of the Hudson River.* Moran Printing Company. Rhinebeck, NY, 1969.

Goldstein, Rabbi Herbert S. (editor). *Forty Years of Struggle for a Principle: The Biography of Harry Fischel.* New York Publishing Company, "The Jewish Book Concern." New York, 1928.

Goltz, Susan Brydon, Ph.D. *History of Crescent Lawn, Main Street Ashland, New York.* Unpublished manuscript. n.d.

Greene County Deed Indices. Various.

The Greene County Directory Containing a General Listing of the Citizens, also a Town and County Register and a Business Directory, Besides Much Other Useful Information Regarding Greene County Affairs. No. 2. Compiled to September 1, 1896. Fred E. Craigie, Publisher. Catskill, NY, 1896.

Greene County Historical Society's 11th Annual Tour of Homes. June 6, 1987. (brochure)

Greene County Historical Society's Historical Register application files.

Greene County Mortgage Indices. Various.

Greene County Historical Society's 26th Annual Tour of Homes. June 1, 2002. (brochure)

Greene County Surrogate Court Probate Records. Various.

Griffen, George. *Slater Family.* Genealogy File at Vedder Research Library.

"Haines Falls Station Purchased by Society." *Catskill Mountain News.* January 17, 1996.

Halcott Valley, 1851–1976. Published by the Town of Halcott. 1976. (booklet)

Hallenbeck, Francis Arthur (editor), Robert Henry Van Bergen, and Rev. Delbert W. Clark. *Ye Olden Time, as compiled from The Coxsackie News of 1889. The Coxsackie Union News.* Coxsackie, NY, 1935.

Handbook of the Christian Church of Freehold, New York. n.p. 1903.

Hansen, Harry (text and illustrations). *Historic Resources Reconnaissance Survey. Town of Durham, Greene County, NY.* Prepared for Town of Durham Preservation Commission by Kyserike Restorations, Inc. High Falls, NY, 1997.

Hasenkopf, Sylvia. *Headstones List – Edget Family Cemetery.*

Haskins, Vernon. *The Canajoharie & Catskill Railroad Disaster.* Durham Center Museum. Durham, NY.

"Have You the 'Voice' of the Catskill Mountains?" *Albany Times-Union.* Albany, NY. Circa Summer 1932.

Heins, Frances Ingraham. "The Older the Better to Abby and Russ Carlsen, a 1790 Greenville Homestead is Just an Antique That You Can Live In." *Times-Union.* Albany, NY. June 1, 2003.

Heritage of New Baltimore. Sponsored by the Bicentennial, Town of New Baltimore, NY. Hillcrest Press. Hannacroix, NY, 1976.

Herman, D., and R. Philp. Statement made on June 18, 1993.

Hewitt, Mark Allen. "Winning Home Designs." *Hudson Valley Magazine.* Volume XXII, Number 6. 1993: pp. 52–54.

High Hill Methodist Church 100th Anniversary Brochure. n.p. May 4, 1952.

High Hill Methodist Episcopal Church: Lime Street, New York; 82nd Anniversary Brochure, 1852–1934. n.p. Circa 1934.

High Hill United Methodist Church: 150th Anniversary Brochure, 1852–2002. August 11, 2002.

Hine, Charles Gilbert. *The West Bank of the Hudson River, Albany to Tappan: Notes on Its History and Legends, Its Ghost Stories and Romances. Gathered by a wayfaring man who may now and then have erred therein.* Privately printed by C. G. Hine. n.p., 1906.

"Historical Review." *The Windham Journal.* November 11, 1976.

"Historical Society Buys Old Rail Station." *The Daily Mail.* Catskill, NY. December 16, 1995.

History and Remembrances. Diamond Jubilee, Congregation Anshe Kol Yisroyal, Hunter Synagogue Hunter, NY, Established 1914. Unpublished paper. May 21, 1989.

History of Christ Church Greenville 1825–1975. Greenville, NY, circa 1975.

History of the United Methodist Church of Greenville and Norton Hill on the Centennial of Their Sanctuaries, 1873-1973. Greenville, NY, circa 1973.

Hitchcock, Elwood. *Hensonville: A Mountaintop History, Windham, New York.* Black Dome Press. Hensonville, NY, 1998.

Hollander, P. *The Catskill Public Library, A Brief History with Sources.* n.p. July 4, 1976.

Howat, John K. *Hudson River and Its Painters.* Viking Press. New York, 1972.

Howland Collection; at the Vedder Research Library of the Greene County Historical Society.

Howland Family; Vertical File at the Vedder Research Library of the Greene County Historical Society.

"In the Town Hall on Thursday Feb. 27th." *The Prattsville News.* February 22, 1919.

"Interesting Letter from a Former Prattsville Resident," *The Prattsville News.* August 3, 1910.

Jackson, A. H. (Surveyor and Draughtsman). *Survey Map.* 1835.

Jensis, Annabar. "Old County Poorhouse." *The Daily Mail.* Catskill, NY. November 4, 1983.

Kamenoff, Mary Vedder. "Digressions on the Journal of Lovisa King, 1808–1902." *Greene County Historical Journal.* Coxsackie, NY. Vol. 3, No. 3; Vol. 3, No. 4; Vol. 4, No. 1; Vol. 4, No. 2; Vol. 4, No. 3.

Kelly, Henry Russel. *Imprints on the Sands of Time: Left by Certain Kelly's, Lampman's, Craig's, Ferguson's.* n.p. Towson, MD, 1972: pp. 86-88. Fifth edition, reprinted 1997: pp. 81, 89, 91.

"King's Daughters Visit Almshouse." *The Cairo Herald.* February 27, 1936.

"Landscaping at County Home to Start Soon." *The Recorder.* Catskill, NY. April 2, 1937.

Larson, Betty (Catskill Town Historian), and Robert A. D'Agostino. "Thomas Cole Also Designed for Wood, Mortar, and Brick." *Greene County Historical Journal.* Coxsackie, NY. Volume 20, Number 3, Fall 1996 (Part I); Volume 20, Number 4, Winter 1996 (Part II).

Letter of Patent, bearing date March 19th, 1852, granting "certain lands lying in the said Hudson River adjoining the before named and described lands, for docking purposes." Executed by Washington Hunt, Governor of the State of New York, and Archibald Campbell, Secretary of State. 1852.

"Letter to the Publisher." *The Palenville Zephyr.* August 16, 1899.

"Life: Section C." *Daily Freeman.* Kingston, NY. August 22, 2000.

Lilienthal, Meta. *Dear Remembered World: Childhood Memories of an Old New Yorker.* Richard R. Smith. New York, 1947.

"The Little Church in the Valley: Ashland's St. Joseph's Oldest Catholic Church in Catskills." *The Mountain Eagle.* Hunter, NY. September 4, 1984.

Lorton, John. A series of articles in *The Windham Journal,* 1886. (Lorton went from house to house and obtained family histories of the people living in the town at the time.)

Mather, Frank Jewett Jr. *Charles Herbert Moore Landscape Painter.* Chapter IV, "Marriage, Move to Catskill. His Activities Described for Charles Eliot Norton." Princeton University Press. Princeton, NJ, 1957.

"May Build New Almshouse Annex." *The Cairo Herald.* April 4, 1935.

McKnight, Nellie. *Joseph Prentiss and the Early History of Trinity Church Athens, New York.* n.p. April 9, 1934.

"McNulty Brings Creative Flair and Drama to Nightingale." Business Section of *The Greenville Press.* July 18, 2002.

"Memorial Address on the Life and Character of Dr. Levi King, at the Request of the Members of the Greene County Medical Society, Delivered by Dr. J. B. Cowles, of Durham." Article in unknown newspaper: Vedder Research Library collection, Scrapbook 18, p. 77.

"Memorial Contributions, Memories [on death of the editor]." *The Windham Journal.* April 22, 1915.

Militello, Carmen and Fred. "The Phinias Tyler House Cornwallville Road, Durham Township. A Brief History." Unpublished. Historical Register file. n.d.

"Mr. S. J. Thorne of Grapeville, NY. Graduate of the Albany Business College, now Book-Keeper for Copley & Dolen, New York." Unknown newspaper, Scrapbook 16: p. 30. Vedder Research Library Collections, Greene County Historical Society.

Morrow, Patricia (Windham Town Historian). "The Curious Case of the Framingham Frame." *The Hemlock.* A Mountain Top Historical Society Publication. Haines Falls, NY. n.d.

Moul, Henry S. *Modern Buildings by Henry S. Moul, Architect, 443 Warren St., Hudson, N.Y.* Published by Henry S. Moul. Hudson, NY, circa 1898.

Munson, Donald F. *Methodism in Windham.* n.p. December 6, 1934.

Munson Family Record. Family records at the New York Public Library.

Nahas, N. C. "Why the Tremain House Should be Saved." Unknown newspaper article. April 19, 2004.

"New Baltimore" column. *Coeymans Herald.* June 10, 1875.

"The New County House." *The Recorder.* Catskill, NY. November 23, 1883.

"The New Greene County Home." *The Cairo Herald.* December 9, 1937.

New York State Census: *Greene County—Population and Farm Schedules.* Various years.

New York's State and National Registers of Historic Places:
    Ashland:
        02NR04997 Elias Strong House.
        96NR00979 North Settlement Methodist Church.
        96NR01066 West Settlement Methodist Church.
        96NR01068 Trinity Episcopal Church: Ashland.
    Athens:
        90MRA00030 Historic Resources of the Village of Athens.
        90NR00555 Athens Lower Village Historic District.
        90NR00558 Van Loon, Albertus, House.
        90NR00559 Zion Lutheran Church.
    Catskill:
        02NR01924 Rowena Memorial School.
        90NR00548 East Side Historic District.
        90NR00549 Cole, Thomas, House.
        96NR00930 Leeds Dutch Reformed Church.
    Coxsackie:
        02NR01905 Bronk-Silvester House.
        90NR00537 Bronck Farm 13-Sided Barn.
        90NR00540 Bronck, Pieter, House.
        90NR00553 Reed Street Historic District.

Durham:
　01NR01743 Tripp House and Store Complex.
　01NR01818 Mrs. Osborn House.
　04NR05382 The Parsonage.
　04NR05384 St. Paul's Lutheran Church.
Greenville:
　90NR00541 Greenville Presbyterian Church Complex.
　90NR00542 Prevost Manor House.
Hunter:
　00NR01595 Fischel, Harry, House.
　99NR01559 Hunter Synagogue.
　04NR05325 Old Platte Clove Post Office.
　06NR01036 Twilight Park Historic District Hains Falls.
　96NR01036 Ulster and Delaware Railroad Station.
Jewett:
　01NR01850 Jewett Presbyterian Church Complex.
New Baltimore:
　90NR00544 Houghtaling, Peter, Farm and Lime Kiln.
　90NR03282 Van Bergen House.
　96NR00928 New Baltimore Hamlet Historic District.
Prattsville:
　00NR01695 Old Episcopal Manse.
　90NR00545 Pratt, Zadock, House.
　92NR00413 Pratt Rock Park.
　96NR00936 Prattsville Commercial Building.
　96NR01067 Prattsville Reformed Dutch Church.
Windham:
　90NR00547 Centre Presbyterian Church.

"Nightingale Inn Makes Historical Register." *The Greene County News.* Catskill, NY. July 18, 2002.

"Notice of Sale." *The Catskill Examiner.* December 21, 1872.

"Notice to the Public!" *The Windham Journal.* April 22, 1915.

"Obituary: Abram Bedell." *The Catskill Examiner.* February 15, 1890.

"Obituary: Edwin Moore." *The Prattsville News.* May 1952.

"Obituary: Jacob Decker." *The Catskill Examiner.* May 29, 1897.

"Obituary: Philip Conine." *The Windham Journal.* May 27, 1858.

"Obituary: Sylvester Baldwin Sage." *The Recorder.* Catskill, NY. Friday, June 16, 1905.

"Old House in Athens, Built in 1706, is Saved." *The Recorder.* June 11, 1937.

"Old Lighthouse at Coxsackie sold for $50." *Catskill Daily Mail.* March 27, 1935.

"Old Time Prattsville!" *The Prattsville News.* December 11, 1909.

"Our Coxsackie Homes." *The Greene County News.* Catskill, NY. November 14, 1963; January 30, 1964; March 5, 1964.

"Over the Hill." *The Examiner.* Catskill, NY. February 12, 1925.

"Over the Hill to What? A Plain Talk to the Plain Tax Payers of Greene County." *The Examiner.* Catskill, NY. January 29, 1925.

Owad, Christine. *A Guide to Windham's Architectural History.* n.p., n.d.

Palmer, Horace Wilbur, and Nellie Morse Palmer. *Palmer Families in America: William Palmer of Plymouth and Duxbury, Mass.* Neshanic Printing Company. Neshanic, NJ, 1973.

Patterson, Emma L. *The Munson Family History: For the Descendants of Silas Lewis Munson.* n.p., n.d.

"Perhaps a New Almshouse Annex." *The Cairo Herald.* February 13, 1936.

Personal reflections and conversations in 2004, 2005, 2006, 2007, and 2008 with:
　Badrotti, Norma; Round Top Cemetery Assoc. Secretary
　Beecher, Dr. Raymond; Greene County Historian
　Berkhofer, Donald
　Blakeslee, the late Josephine
　Boice, the late Betsy
　Bouton, Cindy; Halcott Town Historian
　Bush, Clesson; New Baltimore Town Historian
　Cammer, Chilton; Munson descendant
　Carlsens, the
　Crosby, Hazel; widow of George Crosby
　Daley, Natalie
　Davis, Roy; Munson descendant
　Dwyer, John; great-grandson of Charles Edgar Cole
　Feit, Ronna
　Flach, Phillip
　Fox, Neal
　Gallagher, Tina (née Mary Martina Mercer)
　Glynn, Margaret; Munson descendant
　Goldschmidts, the
　Greene, the late Thom
　Gunderman, Theron and Lisa
　Hayes, Michael
　Hommel, Justine; Hunter Town Historian/President, Mountain Top Historical Society
　Hunter, the late Florence
　Jozic, Stefania
　Kayser, Ms.
　Lawrence, Pauline M.
　Mabey, Ken
　Meyer, Bernhard
　Modra, Deborah
　Muro, Gerard
　Myers, Hattie
　Okon, Michael and Carol
　Pearsall, Gwen Munson
　Rascoe, Jack and Joanne
　Tenerowicz, Carol Slutzky
　Van Valin, Wayne
　Whitcomb, Lenore

Peters, Alice A. and George H. Peters (compilers). *Powells of the Hudson Valley, Descendants and Related Families.* Volume 5. Greene County Historical Society. Coxsackie, NY, 1985.

Phillips, Sandra S., Linda Weintraub, Len Jenshel, James Marston Fitch, et al. *Charmed Places: Hudson River Artists and Their Houses, Studios and Vistas.* "Conceived and curated by Sandra S. Phillips, compiled and edited by Sandra S. Phillips and Linda Weintraub, color photographs by Len Jenshel, with essays by James Marston Fitch . . . [et al.]" Edith C. Blum Art Institute, Bard College, and Vassar College Art Gallery, in association with H. N. Abrams. New York, 1988.

Pinkney, James D. *Biographical Sketches.* J. B. Hall, Publisher. 1868: pp. 24–28.

Pons, Muriel. "George Watson Pratt: Part Three." *Greene County Historical Journal.* Coxsackie, NY. Volume 28, Number 2, Summer 2004.

———. "The Mystery of the Pratt Book Collection: Part Two." *Greene County Historical Journal.* Coxsackie, NY. Volume 28, Number 1, Spring 2004.

———. *Old Town Hall.* n.p., n.d. (A brief history based on her research.)

———. "The Vedder Catalogue and the Mystery of the Pratt Collection." *Greene County Historical Journal.* Coxsackie, NY. Volume 27, Number 4, Winter 2003.

Post Office Department. National Archives Microfilm Publication M1131:
　Record of Postmasters 1874–1889. Volume 46, p. 218.
　Record of Postmasters 1889–1900. Volume 63, p. 202.
　Record of Postmasters 1901–1930. Volume 97, p. 228.

Post Office Department: Report of site locations 1837–1950. National Archives Microfilm Publication M1126.

"Prattsville Dairy Company Certificate of Incorporation." Vertical file at Vedder Research Library.

Prattsville Recreational Improvement Committee. *Historic Prattsville: Pathways to the Past.* Pratt Museum. Prattsville, NY, 1995.

Presbyterian Church, Greenville, New York, April 27th and 28th 1913. (pamphlet)

Priest, Josiah. *The Low Dutch Prisoner: Being an account of the capture of Frederick Schermerhorn.* n.p. Albany, 1839.

Prout, Henry Hedges. "Old Times in Windham" - published in The Windham Journal from February 18, 1869 to March 31, 1879. Transcribed by Olive N. Woodworth and reprinted by Hope Farm Press. Cornwallville, NY, 1970.

"Real Estate." *The Catskill Examiner.* March 11, 1871.

"Realty advertisement, Sunday Magazine Section." *The New York Times.* May 23, 1993.

Rededication Service, Methodist Church of Greenville and Norton Hill. April 14, 1957. (pamphlet).

"Reformed Church History. A History of One of the Early Ministers of the Reformed Church in this Village." *The Prattsville News.* May 23, 1909.

Reformed Dutch Church, 1798–1998. Publication made through the A. Lindsay and Olive B. O'Connor Foundation Inc. and Prattsville Reformed Church Women in Mission and Friends. Circa 1998.

"Refuted by the Facts." *The Examiner.* Catskill, NY. February 26, 1925.

"Reminiscences: The Years of '60–'66, A Souvenir of Those Years." *The Mountain Sentinel.* September 14, 1918.

"Resorts of the Catskills." (Exhibit at Columbia-Greene Community College.) *The Daily Mail.* Catskill, NY. November 17, 1980.

Reynold, Helen Wilkinson. *Dutch Houses in the Hudson Valley Before 1776.* Prepared under the auspices of the Holland Society of New York. Dover Publications. New York, 1965: pp. 66–68, 133–134.

Robb, Sarah C. and Harriet C. Crane. *History of the Memorial Church of All Angels 1896–1971, Twilight Park, Haines Falls, New York.* Wayside Press. Palenville, NY, 1971.

"Round Top—Guardian of Catskill." *The Greenville Press.* March 26, 1998.

"Round Top Village Cemetery, compiled by On-Ti-Ora Chapter DAR-1-122, NY Catskill. Copied by Jessie S. Rossi, 1940–1950s rechecked." Veronica S. Chalmers except where otherwise noted. Typed by Hannah W. Whittle, 1986. Indexed by Lawrence V. Rickhard, November 1992. Copy, Cemetery Records, Vedder Research Library.

Ryan, Michael. "Pratt Museum's circa 1824 'Commercial Building' gets $12.5K from CWC." *The Windham Journal / Hudson Valley Newspapers.* June 6, 2002: B7, p. 4.

Sage Family Genealogy File, Vedder Research Library.

St. Patrick's Parish of Catskill: 100 Years of Service in the Community—Celebrating the Centennial of St. Patrick's Church 1885–1985 & Celebrating the Centennial of Our Parish School 1890–1990. E & G Press. Catskill, NY, 1991.

Slater Family Genealogy. File at Vedder Research Library of the Greene County Historical Society.

"Smith Farm, New Baltimore; A Historic Family Farm." *The Greene County News.* Catskill, NY. November 11, 1971.

Stev-Mar Lodge flyer of undetermined date. Copy on file at the Vedder Research Library.

Stilgoe, John R. *Common Landscape of America, 1580 to 1845.* Yale University Press. New Haven, 1982.

"Sylvester House, or Mansion House West Coxsackie." *Coxsackie Union.* December 3, 1920.

Talmadge, Dorothy M. *"West Settlement Methodist Church."* 1976.

"Tannersville: 'Special to The New York Times.'" *The New York Times.* June 19, 1910: p. X2.

Tax Assessment Records, various years: Town of Catskill; Town of Coxsackie; Village of Coxsackie.

Thomas, Sidney P. *Phoenix Family Research (Pensacola Beach, Florida).* Copy on file at the Vedder Research Library of the Greene County Historical Society.

———. "Klinkenberg, an Ancient Dutch Bouwerij: A Record of Early Ownership." *Greene County Historical Journal.* Coxsackie, NY. Volume 4, Number 3, Fall 1980.

Thomsen, Doug. "Bell Rang End of Civil War." *The Catskill Daily Mail.* n.d.

Thomsen, Doug (compiler/curator). *List of Greene County Men in the Civil War by Regiment.* Durham Center Museum. n.d.

"Tintypes of Yesteryear—Neighborhood Anchor." *The Greenville Press.* n.d.

"Tour of Old Houses Highlight of Sesquicentennial." Newspaper clipping. n.p. Circa 1955.

Town of Durham: A Bicentennial Booklet. Big Acorn Press. n.p., 1976.

Trinity Church of Ashland, New York. History. One Hundred Fiftieth Anniversary of the Founding: May 11, 1799 – May 11, 1949. Published by the Ladies' Guild of Trinity Church. Ashland, NY, 1949. (pamphlet)

Trustees High Hill Methodist Episcopal Church. "Letter to Hiram Brownell for payment of the remainder of his subscription." Dated July 1853.

Twain, Mark (pseud). *Tom Sawyer.* Adapted by June Edwards, illustrated by Joel Naprstek. Raintree Publishers. Austin, TX, 1981.

"230 Men Now on Work Projects." *The Recorder.* Catskill, NY. January 29, 1937.

"232 Now Work on WPA Jobs." *The Recorder.* Catskill, NY. February 19, 1937.

Ulster County Deeds. Book 35, p. 163.

United States Census. "New York State Population and Agricultural Schedules." Various years:
    Columbia County: City of Hudson;
    Delaware County: Town of Middletown;
    Greene County:
        Town of Athens
        Town of Cairo
        Town of Catskill
        Town of Coxsackie
        Town of Greenville
        Town of Halcott
        Town of Hunter
        Town of New Baltimore
        Town of Prattsville
    Oneida County: Town of Whitestown
    Otsego County: Town of Springfield
    Ulster County: City of Kingston.

United States Census. "Pennsylvania Population Schedule 1860: Wayne County; Town of Honesdale."

Uzzilia, Robert (Cairo Town Historian). "Little Church on the Hill Has Long History in Faith." *Greenville Press.* June 3, 1999.

——— (compiled by). *One Hundred and Fiftieth Anniversary Book of Calvary Church, Cairo, NY, August 13, 1832 – August 13, 1982.* n.p. Circa 1982.

Van Bergen, Robert Henry. *Ye Olden Times: As compiled from The Coxsackie News, 1889.* Printed by the Coxsackie Union News.

Vedder, J. Van Vechten *Historic Catskill.* J. C. & A. L. Fawcett. Astoria, NY. n.d.

——— (County Historian). *History of Greene County. Volume 1, 1651–1800.* n.p. Catskill, NY, 1927.

The Village of Athens Bicentennial Walking Tour Guide. GreeneTourism.com. Info compiled by Carrie Feder, Sharon Palmateer, and Carol Pfister, 2003. Layout and design by Matthew Palmateer, 2003.

Wade, William. *Panorama of the Hudson River from New York to Albany, drawn and engraved by William Wade.* William Wade, New York; William Croome, Philadelphia, 1845.

Walsh, Patrick. "The Almost Bicentennial Hardware Store on Main Street: Catskill's Day and Holt." *The Daily Mail.* Catskill, NY. September 2006.

Walsh, Patrick. Greene County Historical Register application file.

Webber, Grace Story (Cairo Town Historian). "Cairo Historian Gives Details on Town Newspapers." *The Catskill Daily Mail.* May 21, 1953.

———. "Town Historian Compiles Facts on Cairo Hotels." *The Catskill Daily Mail.* April 6, 1953.

"We Lost So Much in That Fire." *Greene County Historical Journal.* Coxsackie, NY. Volume 16, Number 3, Fall 1992.

Whitcomb, Charlotte. *The Whitcomb Family in America: A biographical genealogy with a chapter on our English forbears "by the name of Whetcombe."* n.p. Minneapolis, MN, circa 1904: pp. 365, 379, 392.

Whitney, W. A., and R. I. Bonner. *History and Biographical Record of Lenawee County, Michigan, containing a History of the Organization and Early Settlement of the County together with a Biographical Record of Many of the Oldest and Most Prominent Settlers and Preset Residents, Obtained from Personal Interviews with Themselves or Their Children: Volume 1.* Adrian W. Stearns & Co., Printers. Hudson, MI, 1879.

Whittlesey Family. Genealogy File, Vedder Research Library of the Greene County Historical Society.

Wilkinson Family photo, in front of High Hill Methodist Church, circa 1920-1930; Pictorial File, Vedder Research Library of the Greene County Historical Society.

Williams, Edward G. "The Prevosts of the Royal Americans." *The Western Pennsylvania Historical Magazine.* Volume 56, Number. 1. January 1973.

"Wiltse Explains WPA Projects." *The Recorder.* Catskill, NY. October 18, 1935.

Winans, George Woodruff. *First Presbyterian Church of Jamaica, New York, 1662–1942: A narrative history of its two hundred and eighty years of continuous service.* Published by The Church. n.p., 1943: pp. 160–167.

Woodworth, Olive Newell (member On-Ti-Ora Chapter, Daughters of the American Revolution), and Hassie Fuller Lane. *East Kill Valley Genealogy. A Record of the Burials in Two Catskill Mountain Graveyards with Genealogical Information from 1620 to 1964.* Greene & Ulster Printing Co., Catskill, NY. 1964.

"Work on Almshouse Annex Starts." *The Cairo Herald.* June 4, 1936.

"Work on Almshouse Annex Progresses." *The Cairo Herald.* September 3, 1936.

"WPA Workers are Laid Off." *The Recorder.* Catskill, NY. January 1, 1937.

Zirkel, Don. *"Deserted Church Made into Shrine: Restoring of Catskills Monument is Aided by Local Catholics."* n.p. August 1950.

Zukowsky, John, and Robbe Pierce Stimson. *Hudson River Villas.* Rizzoli. New York, 1985.

INDEX

A

A. P. Lombard Company, 57
Abeel, Rev. David, 35
Abrams, Daniel, 165
Abreet, Augusta V. V. (later Sage), 102
Adams family, 123
Adams, John, 260
Administrative Center of the Bank of Greene County, 62
Albany Circuit (Methodist), 8
Albergo Allegria, 252
Albert T. Hotaling Farmstead, 204–205
Albertus Van Loon House, 1, 24–25
Albright, Burton, 216
Albright, Elizabeth Conine, 33, 40
Albright, Timothy, 33, 40, 62
Albright, Timothy, Jr., 32
Algonquin Indians, 18, 55
Allen, Ethan, 215
Allen Deane Place, 206–207
A.M. Hallenbeck Homestead/Sutton Farm, 129
Ameer, David, 205
Andrews, Ichabod, 189
Apfel, Richard and Janet, 23
apple industry
    buildings used for, 214
    first commercial orchard, 208
    individuals involved in, 165, 200, 206, 212
    in New Baltimore, 201
    overseas shipping, 88
Applebee, Mr., 173
architectural styles, 1–2, 32
Arnold, August, 190
artisan's houses, 45
Ashland, 2, 4, 5, 8, 10, 12, 13, 111, 243, 257
Ashland Historical Society, 8
Aspinwall, Lewis, 142
Athens, 1, 16, 17, 18, 21, 22, 23, 25, 27, 28, 29, 31, 32, 33, 35, 37, 38, 39, 40, 41, 42, 43, 44, 65, 110, 113, 126, 162
Athens First Episcopal Church, 41
Athens Generating Corporation, 18
Athens National Bank, 42
Atkinson, Brooks, 139
Atkinson, Dr. Mahlon and Lillon, 72
Atkinson, Oriana, 139
Atwater, Henry, 72
Atwater, Joshua, 72
Atwater, S. Henry, 246
Atwater, Samuel, 253
Atwater brothers, 106
Augustus, Nathan, 151
Austin, Abner, 89, 109
Austin, Rev. Canton W., 182
Austin, Moses, 149
Auston, Albert B. and Jane Elizabeth, 239
Avedis, Fred and Victoria, 185
Avery, Conger, 173, 174
Avery, Daniel, 174
Avery, Hannah, 174
Avery, Harvey, 174
Avery, Isaac, 174

B

Badeau, Amelia and Marie, 79
Badeau, Phoebe, 79
Bagley, Cutting, 138
Bagley, Fred and Virginia, 221
Bagley, Harry, 153
Bagley, John, 66, 138, 153
Bagley, Keith, 138
Bagley, Orlando, 138
Bagley, Thomas, 138
Baldwin, Hannah (later Edgett), 169
Baldwin, Louis, 141
Baldwin, William H., Sr., 216
Baldwin family, 135
Bank of Greene County, 2, 62
Banker, Mr., 173
Barber, George F., 245
Barker (Parsonage owner), 151
Barnard, Frederick, 122

Barnes, Bob, 83
Bartow, Maria (later Cole), 76, 77, 99
Bartow family, 76
Batavia Kill, 4
Bates, Henry Howard, 142
Be My Guest B&B (Dr. Ford House), 254–255
Beach, Charles T., 95, 101
Beach, Fisk, 189
Beach, Louis T., 101
Beach, Lucy (later Van Loan), 103
Beach, Mr. and Mrs. C. L., 103
Beach, Sarah (later Slater), 48
Beach family, 87
Beachview, 101
Beardsley, Charles, 102
Beardsley, William A., 57
Becker, Emily F., 84
Beckman, William, 55
Bedell, Abram, 31
Bedell, Bradbury, 31
Bedell, Gildersleve, 221
Bedell, Margaret, 31
Bedell, Minnie (Mary), 31
Bedell/Nichols House, 30–31
Bedford, Robert and Linda Pierro, 129
Beecher, Arthur, 116
Beecher, Catherine, 116
Beecher, Gladys, 116
Beecher, Raymond, 104, 116, 155
Beecher, Valentine and Maude R., 116
Bell, Annie, 116
Bell, Mary, 82
Bell, Thomas, 116
Benham, Dr. Thomas (father), 7
Benham, Thomas (son), 7
Benjamin, Mr., 109
Bennet, Abby, 40
Bennet, Amanda, 40
Bennet, Elsie (née Scot), 40
Bennet, Hobart, 40
Bennet, John and Phebe, 40
Bennet, Mary Elisa, 40
Berkenmeyer, Rev. Wilhelm Christoph, 37
Berkhofer, Donald, 215
Berkhofer family, 215
Betts, Judson A., 57
Bird family, 68
Black, Michael, 32
Black Rock Farm, 22
Black Rock Site, 17, 18, 22
Black Tom (slave), 197
Blaisdell Land Grant, 169
Blakeslee, Josephine, 251
Blakeslee, Dr. Robert, 250
Blue Willow, 190
boardinghouses
    in Cairo, 47
    Deerwatch Inn, 140
    in Hunter, 177
    in Lexington, 195
    Lisk Homestead, 214, 215
    Mt. Zoar Villa, 143
    Nightingale Inn, 124
    Okon House, 174
Thompson House, 262
Washington Irving Inn, 184
Bogaert, Gysbert Cornelise uyt den, 55
Bogardus, Ann (later Prevost), 156
Bogardus family, 155
Borthwick, J. G., 149
Borthwick, William S., 149
Boughton, Howard L., 74
Bourke, Eleanor, 82
Bourke, Oliver, 82
Bouton, Edwin, 239
Boyd, John, 166
Boyd, Mrs. E. D., 98
Bradbury House, 31
Brady, Edith, 39
Brady, William C., 39
Brandow, Ed, 88
Brandow family, 155
Branough, Thomas, 261

Brate, Hannah, 161
Brate, Sylvester, 161
Brenefind, E., 228
Brewer, Pratt, 248
Brice, Edward F., 183
Brink, Catherine Susan (later Silvester), 128
Brink, Rev. Henry Wells, 219
Brockett, Irving, 250
Brockett, Lucia Cobb, 250
Brom Pete, 189
Bronck, Annatje, 68
Bronck, Catherine (later Van Dyck), 127
Bronck, Commertje Leendertse (née Conyn), 114
Bronck, Heletje (Hillitje, née Jans), 113, 114
Bronck, Jan (John), 68, 114
Bronck, Jan (John) Leendertse, 114
Bronck, Leendert, 114
Bronck, Maria (née Ely), 114, 118
Bronck (Bronk), Pieter, 113, 114
Bronck family, 127, 201, 211
Bronck House, 1, 114–115, 118
Bronck's Patent, 114
Bronk, Adelaide (later Lampman), 114, 118, 125
Bronk, Alida (née Conine), 128
Bronk, John L., 128
Bronk, Leonard, 114, 118
Bronk, Leonard, Jr., 114
Bronk family, 118
Bronk/Silvester House, 128
Brooks, Mr., 173
Brown, Ed, 240
Brownell, Hiram, 126
Bryant, William Cullen, 77
Buckel, Howken, 53
Buel, Ben, 162
Bull, William, 83
Bull House (Harmon Pettingill House), 82–83
Bullis, John N., 239
Bullivant, Mr. and Mrs. George, 152
Bump, Ephraim, 257
Bump Tavern, 257
Bunce, Charles and Katherine, 82
Bunce House (Harmon Pettingill House), 82–83
Burke, Michael, 122
Burnham, Dr. Bradford, 182
Burnham, Frederick, 182
Burns, Francis, 8
Burr, Aaron, 156, 157, 191
Burr, Theodosia (earlier Prevost), 156
Burroughs, John, 5
Butts, Barney, 143
Butts, Isaac, 143
Butts, Isaac C., 143
Butts, Mary (later Lamoreau), 143
Butts House Café (Mt. Zoar Villa), 143
Byrnes, James, 25

C

Cairo, 2, 17, 46–47, 48, 49, 50, 51, 53, 68, 109, 111, 113, 126, 148, 155, 159
Caleb Atwater Day House, 93
Calvary Episcopal Church, 51
Cammer, Chilton, 263
Camp, Dr. Abram, 191
Canajoharie & Catskill Railroad, 153
Cannime, Rev. S. J., 10
Cantline, John, 82
Canton. *See Cairo*
Capone, Al, 124
Capone family, 165
Carbine Farm, 52
Carey, Father James C., 97
Carlsen family, 163
Carman, Joseph and Lydia, 52
Carnegie, Andrew, 84, 85
Carnegie Corporaton of New York, 35
Carrington Place (Deerwatch Inn), 140
Carter, Bertram, 196
Carter, Hattie C., 65
Carter, Hazel Cole, 196
Cartwright, George, 196
Casazza, John J., 59
Cascade Lodge, 145

270

Case, John and Mary, 50
Case, Winslow, 131
Case Store and Residence, 50
Cass, William, 189
Catskill, 1, 2, 13, 17, 33,43, 44, 47, 54–55, 59, 60, 62, 63, 65, 66, 67, 70, 72, 73, 74, 75, 76, 78, 79, 80, 81, 82, 83, 84, 85, 86, 87, 88, 89, 90, 91, 92, 95, 97, 98, 101, 102, 103, 104, 106, 107, 108, 109, 111, 116, 126, 129, 176, 253, 256, 257, 261
Catskill Creek, 55, 68, 82, 87, 98, 106, 107, 151, 153
Catskill Daily Mail, 66, 107, 111, 142
Catskill Examiner, 59, 74, 80
Catskill Library Association, 84
Catskill Mountain Country Store, 253
Catskill Mountain House, 2, 55, 75, 87, 93, 95, 101, 103
Catskill Mountain Railway, 55, 87
Catskill Mountains, 10, 47, 48, 53, 55, 59, 76, 94, 118, 124, 147, 159, 177, 178, 181, 184, 186, 189, 194, 227, 256, 263
Catskill Packet, 72
Catskill Park and Forest Preserve, 48
Catskill Patent, 17, 55
Catskill Point, 55, 87
Catskill Public Library, 2, 84–85
Catskill rent wars, 173
Catskill Recorder, 92
Catskill Route (railroad), 177
Catskill Savings Bank, 82, 92, 107, 108, 110,
Catskill Watershed Corporation, 229
The Catskills, 76, 77, 78, 87, 133, 139, 140, 147, 173, 178, 184, 195, 196, 199, 103, 225, 235
The Catskills (magazine), 233
Catwalk, 58–59
Cauterskill, 55
Cedar Grove. *See Thomas Cole's Cedar Grove*
Cementon, 55
Cemikvasky, Tom and Barbara, 240
Centre Presbyterian Church, 246–247, 251, 255
Cepale, Robert and Christine, 259
Champagne Cider, 212
Champion, Simon B., 110
Charles, George, 93
Charles and Emily Trowbridge House, 104
Charles W. Mead & Son, 219
Chase, Albert, 60
Chase, Emory A., 57, 60, 84, 90
Chase, John, 198
Chase, Philander, 15
Chase, West, 198
Chase/Lane/Shanks House, 60–61
Chaurand, Honorè, 211
Chebolian, Marderos, 185
Chebolian family, 184–185
Cheritree, Ella, 151
Cheritree, Legwina, 151
Cheritree, Walter, 151
Cherritree, Olive, 80
Cherritree and Pierce Iron Foundry, 145
Cherritree–River View Cottage, 80
Chittenden, Leverett and Ruth, 139
Chittenden/Atkinson/Swanson House, 139
Christ, Donald C., 196
Christ Episcopal Church, 166–167
Christ Presbyterian Church, 95
Christian Church (New Baltimore), 209
Christman's Windham House, 164, 256–257
Christ's Church of Catskill, 95
Chubb, Dr. Charles H., 94
Church, Frederick, 76
Cimmorelli, Michael, 79
Clapp, Ruel, 122
Clark, Betty, 107
Clark, Franklin B., 27
Clark, George, Esq., 82
Clark, William J., 27
Clark, Winifred, 27
Clark House (Cowles House), 64–65
Clarke, Champlain and Rachel Fiero, 65
Clarke, George (father), 82
Clarke (Clark), George (son), 82
Clarke Scholarship, 65
Clay, Henry, 5, 103
Cleveland, C. C. W., 98
Cleveland, John, 140
Clinton, George, 114
Close, Minetta, 90

Clouw family, 18
Coates, Edward and Priscilla, 215
Cobb, Alphonso, 250
Cobb/Brockett/Blakeslee House, 250, 257
Cochran family members, 53
Cochran, Tunis, 123
Cody, Livingston and Virginia, 109
Coeyman, Andries, 201
Coeyman, Barent Pietersen, 201
Coeymans Patent, 155, 165, 201, 208
Coffin, Lydia, 23
Coffin, Reuben, 23
Coffin, William, 23
Coffin family, 40
Cole, Charles Edgar, 182, 183
Cole, Edward M., 258
Cole, Eva, 183
Cole, Ida (later Young), 183
Cole, Keeler M., 258
Cole, Lillie M., 196
Cole, Louisa, 182, 183
Cole, Maria (née Bartow), 76, 77, 99
Cole, Theodore A., 86
Cole, Thomas, 66, 76–77, 78, 85, 98, 99
Cole, Thomas, Jr., 59, 76
Cole family, 98
Cole House/Trailside Cottage, 196
Colgrave and Purdy (contractors), 81
Colle, Dr. M. K. G., 107
Columbia County Court House, 50
Congdon, Henry, 98
Congdon, Minerva, 92
Congregation Kol Anshe Yisroyal (Hunter Synagogue), 186–187
Conine, Chester and Myra, 235
Conine, David H., 235
Conine, Dwight, 235
Conine, Eli, 235
Conine, Ezra, 235
Conine, Frances Daley, 33
Conine, Philip, Jr., 128
Conine, Phillip, 8
Conine, Solomon, 235
Conine family, 235
Conklin, Arthur and Lola, 60
Conklin, Dr. George, 152
Conkling, George W., 161
Conyn, Commertje Leendertse (later Bronck), 114
Cooke, Apollos, 106
Cooke, Frank, 66
Cooke, J. Atwater, 98
Cooke, Thomas Burrage, 106
Cooke family, 79
Corlaers Kill Patent, 17
Cornelius Van Loan House, 29
Cornell, Joseph and Ellam, 80
Cornell, Samuel, 79
Cornwall, Amos, 52
Country Home, 42
Country Hutt Antique Center, 239
Courthouse (1813), 86–87
Courthouse (1909), 2
Cowles, Charles, 55
Cowles, Cornelius, 148
Cowles, David, 148
Cowles, David, Jr., 148
Cowles, Irene Amelia (later Hull), 148
Cowles, N. P., 258
Cowles, Noble P., 65, 250, 257
Cowles House (Clark House), 64–65
Cowles/Hull House, 148
Cox, Father, 97
Coxsackie, 1, 3, 17, 21, 35, 39, 47, 100, 112–113, 114, 116, 118, 121, 125, 126, 127, 128, 129, 131, 155, 159, 201
Coxsackie Patent, 201
Coxsackie-Westerlo Turnpike, 215
Crandell, Lewis, 216
Crane, Bruce, 109
Crane, Daniel, 89
Crescent Lawn/Jeralds House, 12
Crispell, Benjamin, 197
Crispell family, 197
Croghan, George, 156
Croghan, Susannah (later Prevost), 156
Crosby family members, 174
Croswell, Dr. Thomas O'Hara, 92
Crowell, Rev. Seth, 8
Cummings, John, 72

"Curious Case of the Framingham Frame" (Morrow), 259
Cutting Bagley House, 138

D

D. R. Evarts Library, 38
dairy farming, 129, 161, 222, 223
Daley, Dr. Alton B., 33, 39
Daley, Frances (née Shufelt), 40
Daley, Frank and Natalie, 67
Davidson, John A., 63
Davis, William L., 221
Day, Emily (Emily Seymour), 33
Day, George, 107
Day, J., 93
Day, Jeremiah, 107
Day, William H., 94
Day & Holt Company, 2, 106–107
Day families, 107
Dayton, Warner F. B., 74
De Masi Sand Blasting Company, 53
Deane, Allen L., 206
Deane, Isaac, 206
Decker family, 42
Deckers, Fred, Sr. and Jr., 240
Decklyn, Barent, 197
Deerwatch Inn, 140
Delamater, Smith, 127
Delaware Indians, 18, 22, 68
den Bogaert, Gysbert Cornelise uyt, 55
DeNyse, Lillian C., 109
Dernell-Clark House, 26–27
Dernell, Harman F. (Herman Dernehl), 17, 27, 38, 41
Dernell, Leonora (later Eichorn), 28
Dernell-Lang, Emilie, 35
Devlin, Harry, 248
Dewey, Adijah, 142
Deyoe, Mr., 241
Diamond, John (Jack) "Legs," 2, 109, 124
DiCaprio, Alfred and Marjorie, 80
Dimensions North. *See Rappleyea, Richard*
Dimmick House, 45
Doan, Archibald, 122
Doane, Rt. Rev. William Croswell, 15
Donahue, William, 65
Donald, Jonathan, 206
Doney, Carol, 73
Donnelly family, 79
Dorpfeld, David and Wanda, 127
Dorpfeld/Kunchala family, 127
Dot's Lake, 124
Doty, Antoinette (later Potter), 257
Doty, Lucius R., 74
Downing, Andrew Jackson, 2
Dr. Ford House, 254–255
Drake, Edwin, 165
Dratz, Karl, 146
Dresser, Andrew, 229
Dresser House (Prattsville Commercial Building), 229
Dubois, J. Mortimer, 93
Dubois, William Larremore, 92–93
Dubois/Fray/Pouyat House, 92–93
Duncan, May, 111
Dunn, Carlos, Jr. and Nancy, 90–91
Dunn, Steven, 90
Duntz, Charles, 116
Durand, Asher B., 76, 77
Durham, 8, 47, 113, 129, 132–133, 135, 138, 139, 140, 146, 148, 149, 150, 153, 155, 159, 166, 243, 259
Dustin, James W., 128
Dutch architecture, 1
Dutcher, Elias and Elizabeth, 53
Dwyer, John, 183
Dyer family members, 161

E

Earl, Julia A. (née Tyler), 153
Earl, R. R., 153
Edgett, Hannah (née Baldwin), 169
Edgett, Henry and Hannah, 169
Edgett, Reynolds, 169
Edgett, Rufus, 169
Edgett Farm Cemetery, 169
Edwards, William A., 123
Egbertson family, 151
Eichorn, Charles, 28

Eichorn, Laura, 28
Eichorn, Leonora (née Dernell), 28
Eichorn/Zar/Kurdziel House, 28
1813 Court House, 86–87
Elizabeth House, 68–69
Elliot, Mabel, 90
Ellrott, George and Isabel, 218
Elm Crest Farm (Leonard Warren House), 118–119
Elm Tree Filling Station (O'Hara's Trading Post), 238
Elmhurst Inn (Munson/Durnan House), 244–245
Ely, Dr. John, 118
Ely, Maria (later Bronck), 114, 118
Ely family, 118
Ely Farm (Leonard Warren House), 118–119
Empire Quarry, 63
Endicott Johnson Shoe Company, 107
Englert, Dr. Paul and Marcia, 60
English, Jay, 80
Episcopal Church (Ashland), 2
Episcopal Church (Greenville), 2
Episcopal Parsonage (Ashland), 7
Episcopal Parsonage (Prattsville), 2
Erickson, Jane (née Van Loan), 21, 22
Esperanza, 17
Euiler, Barbara Van Deusen, 31
Evans, Randall ("Randy"), 18, 25, 45
Evarts, Daniel Redfield and Elizabeth, 38
Everitt, Charles, 85
Every, Minnie, 41

F
Fair, John, 228
Fairview, 211
Falckner, Reverend Justice, 37
Feder, Carrie, 25, 45
Fiddler's Green (Grant/Foote House), 88–89
Fiero, Joshua and Mary, 65
Fiero, Peter, 53
Finan, Katherine M., 59
Finch, Nelson, 232
finial hands, 249
Finn, Kenneth R., 190
Finneran, Father William J., 97
First Christian Church Society (New Baltimore), 208, 209
First Congregational Church (Windham), 15
First Presbyterian Church (Ashland), 6
First Reformed Church (Athens), 34–35
First Reformed Church of Catskill, 81
Fischel, Harry, 186
Fischel, Jane, 187
Fischel Synagogue, 186
Fitch, Charlotte, 123
Fitch, Thomas, 234
Fitzgerald, Father William, 97
Flach, Joseph and Elizabeth, 161
Flach, Philip and Barbara, 161
Flach family, 161
Fletcher, Benjamin, 204
Flint, Orin Q., 41
Flint Mine Hill, 129
Floyd Smith Farm (Valley View Farm), 222, 223
folk buildings, 1
Foote, John B., 88
Foote, John C., 88
Foote family, 110
Ford, Cornelia, 110
Ford, Gerald, 60
Ford, Horace N. and Matilda Haines, 254
Ford, Dr. Sidney L., 254–255
Ford, Vernon E., 110
Foster, Rev. John O., 111
Four Mile Point Lighthouse Keeper's Cottage, 122–123
Fowler, Charles, 236
Fowler, Orson, 86
Fox, Ilse, 43
Fox, Neal, 124
Fox, Walter, 43
Frayer, Medad, 234
Frayer Barn, 234
Fredericske, Mydert, 121
Freehold Congregational Christian Church, 170–171
Freehold Country Inn (Freehold House/Hotel), 154, 162
Freightmaster's Building at Historic Catskill Point, 87
Friend, Charles, 214, 215
Friend, Hattie, 214–215
Friendship's Asylum (Fairview), 211

Fruisen, Fred, 73
Fuller, Elizabeth C., 183
Fuller, Phebe (later Munson), 242, 245
Fuller, Rev. Dr. Samuel, 142, 166
Fuller, William, 221
funeral parlors, 240

G
Gabriele family members, 45
Gabriele/Maher House, 45
Gale, Samuel, 92
Gallagher, John M., 50
Gallagher, Mary Martina (earlier Mercier), 131
Gallery 42, 70
Galusha, Diane, 111
Gangi, Salvatore, 111
Gantley, Daniel W., 21, 22
Gardiner, Lawrence and Gertrude, 233
Garfinckel family, 135
Garfinkel, Mr., 135
Garfinkel family, 149
Gateway to the West (museum building), 229
Geritse, Marte (Van Bergen), 47
Gibbons, Thomas, 216
Gibson, Tom and Dianne, 70
Gifford, Jerome B., 150
Gilbride, Rev. Michael, 10
Gilhaven, Bishop, 111
Giordano, John and Dawn, 143
Giordano, Pete and Betty, 109
Giordano House, 109
Gjerfji family, 128
Gjonaj family, 128
Gladfelter, Stanley, 33
Gladfelter, Jennie, 33
Glassie, Henry, 1
Gleason, Daniel S. and Helen, 79
glebes, 37
Gloria Dei Episcopal Church, 94
Goettsche family members, 252, 262
Goldberg, Frank and Sarah, 72
Goldecklag, Eugene and Elizabeth, 65
Goldschmidt, Tex and Elizabeth Wickenden, 141
Goodwin, Chauncey and Emma, 105
Goose Meadow, 32
Gooss family, 252
Goslee, Fred M., 190
Goslee, William, 193
Goslee Cottage Farmhouse, 191
Goslee family, 190, 191
Gould, A., 7
Goulde, Fred, 116
Grace Episcopal Church (Prattsville), 241
Grant, Alexander, 88
Grant family, 110
Grant/Foote House, 88–89
Gratten, Father, 97
Great Algonquin Flint Mines, 129
Greek Revival movement, 1–2
Greene, Debora and Donald, 122, 123
Greene, Frederick Stuart, 18
Greene, Thom, 123
Greene County
    Agricultural Society, 47
    Courthouse, 56–57
    Courthouse (1813), 86–87
    formation of, 195
    Historical Register, purpose, ix
    Historical Society, 114–115
    map, viii
    Planning Board, 50
Greene County Poorhouse/Almshouse/Home (Greene County Office Building), 52–53
Greenville, 2, 15, 113, 118, 154–155, 156, 157, 159, 160, 161, 163, 164, 165, 169, 171, 177, 183
Greenville Arms, 164
Greenville Free Academy, 155, 160, 164
Greenville Memorial Library, 160
Greenville Presbyterian Church, 158–159
Gregory, Cyntha Elizabeth (née Myers), 239
Gregory, Daniel and Zadey, 212
Gregory, James B., 239
Griffin, D. and E., 159
Griswold, Edward, 138
Grossman, Alex, 73
Grossman, Edwin, 88
Grove Cottage, 141
Gunderman, Theron and Lisa, 131

H
H. F. Dernell Ice Tool Company, 27, 38
Haight, Jacob, 260
Haight, Lydia, 21
Haight, General Samuel, 21, 22
Haight, William, 21
Haight/Gantley/Van Loan House, 20–21
Haines Falls Railroad Station, 178–179
Haines House (Cobb/Brockett/Blakeslee House), 250
Halcott, 172–173, 174, 195, 243
Halcott, George C., 85
Halcott, George W., 173
Halcott, John B., 52
Halenbeck, Jan Casperse, 129
Hall, Aaron, 166
Hall, Electa Day (later Johnston), 72
Hall, Lyman, 72
Hall/Ursprung House, 72
Hallenbeck, Abram M., 129
Hallenbeck, Anna, 121
Hallenbeck, Chip, 93
Hallenbeck, Francis and Catherine, 21
Hallenbeck, Jacob, 121
Hallenbeck, Martin C., 129
Hallenbeck, Orson, 166
Hallenbeck, William H. and Hattie, 129
Hallenbeck family, 18, 121
Hallenbeck Patent, 155
Hallock, Abby (née Lisk), 212
Hardenburgh, Johannes, 177
Hardenburgh Patent, 173, 174, 225, 260
Harmon Pettingill House (Bunce House, Bull House), 82–83
Harring, Ray and Ethel, 109
Hartwick, Richard, 55
Haunted House on Chestnut Hill (King House), 91
Hawkins, Ashton, 21
Hawley family, 211
Haxton, Benjamin, 41
Hayes, James, 131
Hazen, Jasper, 170–171
Helmsen, Jan, 121
Herman, David, 65
Hermesdorf, Anita, 204, 205
Hickok, Francis, 163
Hickok Homestead, 163
Higgins, Mae, 152
High Hill Methodist Church, 126
High Hill United Methodist Church, 126
Hight, Samuel, 21
Hildridge, William, 166
Hill family members, 90
Hill/Tannenbaum House, 90–91
Hilltop (Catwalk), 58–59
Hilscher, Ted and Nancy, 86, 87
Hilscher family, 212
Hilzinger, Helen, 147
Hinman, J. B., 193
History of Greene County (Beers)
    on Athens' geography, 17
    on boardinghouses, 78
    on Halcott, economic life in, 173
    on Leeds' Indians, 68
    on Prevost (Augustine), 156
    on slave owners, 78
    on Tyler (Phileas), 153
    on Windham Journal, 258
Hitchcock, D. Dewitt, 107
Hitchcock, Elwood, 254
Hoag family, 127
Hoagland, George, 239
Hoagland, P. T., 151
Hobart, John Henry, 166
Hobbs, Pamela Newcombe, 80
Hodskins family, 110
Hoff, Ben, 28
Hoffman, Robert, 239
Holcomb, Abel, 189
Holcomb, Frederick W., 105
Holcomb, John Hobart, 105
Holcomb, Sherwood A., 105
Holcomb/Brooks Homestead, 105
Holderidge, George, 98
Holdridge, George F., 108
Holdridge, George W., 85, 108
Holdridge, James, 63
Holdridge, William
Hollister Hotel (Mansfield/Artemisia House), 259

Holloway, Charles H., 12
Holridge, George W., 85
Holt, Samuel E., 107
Hommel family members, 182
Hood, James H., 170
Hoogteeling. *See Houghtaling*
Hooker, Phillip, 135
Hopewell Manor, 125
Hoppe, Chris, 221
Horton, Reverend and Mrs., 103
Hosford, Henry R., 189
Hosmer, Maria, 21
Hotaling. *See also Houghtaling*
Hotaling, Albert R. and Caroline, 204
Hotaling, Albert T., 204
Hotaling, Albertus, 204–205
Hotaling, Irving E., 205
Hotaling, James, 216
Hotaling, Laura, 205
Hotaling, Peter, 204
Hotaling, Ralph A., 219
Hotaling, Richard Andrew, 204, 205
Hotaling, Thomas, 131, 204
Hotchkin, Beriah, 159
Hoube, Martha, 215
Houghtaling, George, 121
Houghtaling, Hester (later Van Bergen), 202
Houghtaling, Isaiah, 232
Houghtaling, Matthias (Mathias), 121, 204
Houghtaling, Thomas, 202
Houghtaling family, 121
Houghtaling Patent, 121, 204
Howard, John, 253
Howard, Josephine (later Van Valin), 253
Howard, Reverend Father, 97
Howe, William E., 93
Howland, Benjamin, 59
Howland, Clarence, 59
Howland, Edith, 59
Howland, William Slocum, 59
Howland family, 59
Hubbard, Dr., 251
Hubbard, Jedediah, 6
Hubbard, Rev. Smith, 198
Hubbard, Timothy, 6
Hubbard/Benham/Tompkins House, 6–7
Hubbell family, 123
Hudson, 17
Hudson-Athens Ferry, 41
Hudson Heights (Catwalk), 58–59
Hudson River Day Line, 87
Hull, Dr. A. Cooke, 66, 90
Hull, Anson, 148
Hull, Irene Amelia (née Cowles), 148
Hull, Isaac, 8
Hull, John, 148
Hull, Lydia Cooke, 66
Hull, Mr. and Mrs. Addison O., 148
Hull/Gamble-Roby House, 66
Humphrey, O. T., 74
Hunt, Eli, 125
Hunt, Medad, 257
Hunt, W. I., 154
Hunt family, 162
Hunter, 2, 176–177, 178, 181, 182, 183, 184, 186, 189, 243
Hunter Synagogue (Congregation Kol Anshe Yisroyal), 186–187
Huntersfield, 234, 240
Hush Hush Manor House (Prevost Manor), 156–157, 164
Hutchinson family, 79
Hyer, James, 23

I

ice houses, 116, 210
Ice Tool Company (H. F. Dernell), 27, 38
in-law houses, 28
Indians. *See individual tribes*
Inglis, Agnes, 141
Iroquois Indians, 55
Irving family, 171
Ives family members, 261

J

J. B. Beers and Co. *See History of Greene County*
Jackson (architect), 81
Jacob Van Loan/Walter Pagliani House, 105
Jacobs family, 252, 255

James Frayer house, 241
Jan Van Loon House, 18–19
Jans, Heletje (Hillitje, later Bronck), 113, 114
Jearoms, William and Alida, 122
Jennings, Dean W. and Margaret, 65
Jennings, Edgar, 170
Jennings, W. Irving, 84
Jeralds, Frances (née Tuttle), 12
Jeralds, Thomas W., 12
Jewett, Freeborn G., 189
Jewett, 48, 188–189, 191, 193, 226, 243, 254
Jewett Heights, 189, 191, 193, 261
Jewett Presbyterian Church, 192–193
John Howard/Van Valin House, 253
John L. Thomson Son & Co., 92
Johnson, John, 131
Johnson, L. Scott, 75
Johnson, Michal, 162
Johnson, Truman, 259
Johnson, William, 156
Johnston, Electa Day (née Hall), 72
Johnston, General John C., 72
Jones, Samuel and Eve, 53
Joyce, James, 3
Jozic family, 184, 185
Judd, Gideon, 70–71
Judd, Rev. Thomas S., 232
Judd/Olney House, 70–71
Jurgsatis, George, 83

K

Karnik, Joseph and Anna, 124
Karnik-Fincke, Julie, 124
Kavelle, James, 82
Keefe Architects, 92
Keeper, Robert, 29
Keeper's Cottage, 122–123
Keller and Company, 57
Kennedy, Robert, 57
Kesinger, Philip, 65
Kessel, Theodore, 183
Kevin Berry Builders, 62
Kimball Foundry, 145
King, Dr. Consider, 239
King, Ebenezer, 35
King, Levi, 239
King, Lewis, 166
King, Lucia, 91
King, Lucina, 239
King, Rufus, 91
King House, 91
Kirkman (Soap) family, 193
Kissock, Charles, 228
Kliegman, Peter and Mona, 263
Klinkenberg, 1, 120–121
Knickerbocker Ice Company, 25, 87
Kniffen, Arthur L., 219
Knowles family, 155
Knudsen family, 161
Kol Anshe Yisroyal (Hunter Synagogue), 186–187
Kortz family, 66
Koster, James, 32–33
Kretchmer, Steven and Alma, 63
Krieger, Elmer, 233

L

La Grange family, 18
Lake family, 155
Lamoreau, Mary (née Butts), 143
Lampman, Adelaide (née Bronk), 114, 118, 125
Lampman, Edwin, 102
Lampman, Elizabeth (née Vandenberg), 125
Lampman, Leonard Bronk, 114, 118
Lampman, Rev. Lewis, 114, 118, 125
Lampman, Obadiah, 125
Lampman family, 118, 155
Lanahan, Hope, 42
Lanahan, Thomas, 42
land grants. *See Patents*
Lane, Patricia, 60
Lang, Emilie Dernell, 27
Laraway, Derrick, 231
Laraway, John, 231
Laraway, Jonas, 231
Laraway, Martinus, 231, 236
Laraway, Sarah, 239
Larsen, David and Arthur, 190
Lasry, Eric N. and Margaret, 59
Lasry, Gabriel, 59

Lassen, Eleanor D., 33
Lawler, David, 123
Lawrence, Mr. and Mrs. James, 253
Lawrence, Pauline, 7
Lawrence, Pauline Munger, 15
Lawrence, Rowena Eloise Banning, 63
Lawyer, Mary, 255
Leeds Bridge, 68, 69
Leeds Methodist Church, 101
Leeds Reformed Church, 81, 100–101
Lemelman, Jack, 75
Lemelman, Jack and Rebecca, 109
Leonard, James and Mary, 60
Leonard Warren House, 118–119
Lewis family, 263
Lexington, 173, 174, 189, 191, 193, 194–195, 197, 198, 199, 243
Lexington Catholic Church, 194, 199
Lexington Congregational Society, 193
Lexington Creamery, 195
Lexington Heights, 191, 193
Lexington Historical Society, 199
Lexington House, 195
Lexington Methodist Church, 198
Lexington Stone House, 197
Light, Betty and Ray, 83
lighthouses, 122–123
Lilienthal, Augusta, 184
Lilienthal family members, 184
Lindsay Patent, 93
Lisk, Benjamin C., 212, 214
Lisk, Caroline (later Hotaling), 204
Lisk, Charles and Jennie, 212
Lisk, Charles J., 212
Lisk, Deborah, 214
Lisk, Elizabeth, 214
Lisk-Hallock, Abby, 212
Lisk/Hallock Homestead and Farm, 212–213
Lisk Homestead, 214–215
Little Red Schoolhouse, 89
Livingston, Anthony, 23
Livingston, Anthony A., 25
Livingston, Chancellor, 260
Livingston, Rev. Gilbert R., 35
Livingston, Philip, 23
Livingston/Coffin/Apfel House, 23
Livingston family, 17
Locust Grove (Lisk Homestead), 214–215
Loonenburg (Loonenburgh), 17, 18, 37
Loonenburg (Loonenburgh) Patent, 17, 18, 22, 25, 121
Lopaugh, Rev., 231
Lowe, Charles H. and Esther, 110
Lowe family, 110
Lowell, James, 60
Loxhurst Hotel, 178
Lusk, Hiland, 170
Lutz, Andrew, 237
Lutz, Claude and Frances, 237
Lutz family, 232, 237
Lutz/Maffat House (McGinnis-Lutz House), 237
Lyman Tremain Opera House, 146
Lynam, Rev. Sion M., 171

M

Mac Braswell, J. P. and Frieda, 43
MacDonald, Tom and Gladys, 143
Mack, Prentice, 248
Mackey, Ebenezer and Ann, 95
Mackey, Helen, 95
Mackintosh, Alexander, 181
Madison, Dolly, 103
Magee, Peter, 39, 44
Maher, Kathleen Gabriele, 45
Maher, William J., 45
mail-order homes, 245
Maitland, Richard, 136
Maitland Patent, 136, 140
Makely Farm, 147
Mann, John T., 106–107
Manor House, 262
Mansfield/Artemisia House, 259
Mansfield family, 259
Maple Grove Farm, 215
Marinos, Eloise, 205
Marner, William, 7
Marquis, Arthur, 29
Martin, Charles and Bridget, 131
Martin, Christopher A., 178

Martin, David, 78
Masonic lodges, 86
Mather, Frank Jewett, 59
Matthews, Howard and Helen, 197
Matthias Van Loon/Palmer House, 39
McCarthy, Reverend, 10
McCoy, Wanda, 131
McGinnis-Lutz House (Lutz/Maffat House), 237
McHale, Michael and Katherine, 110
McHale Farmhouse, 110
McNulty, Scott, 124
McRobert, John, 89
McTague (owner of Grant/Foote House), 88
Mead, Moses, 126
Medway Congregational Church, 208, 209
Meier, Tim, 221
Memorial Church of All Angels, 180–182
Mercier, Ronald and Mary Martina, 131
Mesick, Dr. John, 121
Methodist Episcopal Church (Round Top), 53
Meyer, Henry, 178
Michael J. Quill Irish Cultural & Sports Center, 133
Miles Bridge (Jewett), 188, 189
Miles family, 188, 189
Militello, Carmen and Fred, 153
milk farming, 129, 161, 222, 223
Mill House (Osborn House), 144–145
Miller, Annie (later Woodhull), 208
Miller, Catherine (later Titus), 33
Miller, Harry and Betty, 73
Miller, Jonathan, 201, 208, 209
Miller, Jonathan, Jr., 209
Miller, Louis A., 50
Miller, Lydia, 208
Miller, Margaret, 209
Miller brothers, 255
Miller-Woodhull Homestead (Orchard Farm), 208
Mineburgh (Myneburg) Hill, 129
Mission Church of All Angels, 181
Mitchell Hollow Union Society Chapel, 249
Mix, Mary, 233
Mohican Indians, 17, 22, 55, 68, 114
Moon, Roy C., 88
Moore, Blanche (née Turk), 233
Moore, Charles Herbert, 59, 77
Moore, Edwin L., 233
Moore, Johnnie, 21
Moore, Mary Jane (née Tomlinson), 59
Moore's Tourist Home (Vetter House), 233
Morris, Mr., 173
Morrow, Patricia, 259
Morss family members, 6, 151, 235
Morton, Cynthia, 43
Morton, Levi P., 44
Morton, Maria (née Wait), 44
Morton, William H., 44
Morton/Reinsdorf House, 44
Moss, Judson, 141
Moss, Orwell, 141
Mother Maggie (Maggie Newton Van Cott), 111
Moul, Henry S., 50
Mountain Top Historical Society, 178
Mt. Zoar Villa, 143
Mulbury family members, 110
Mulbury House, 110
Munn and Sons (architects), 80
Munson, A. B. (photographer), 4
Munson, Donald, 245
Munson, Donald F., 8
Munson, Silas Lewis, 242, 245, 263
Munson, Thomas, 245
Munson/Durnan House, 244–245, 248
Munson family, 263
Munson House (Windhamere), 263
Muro, Gerard J., 183
Murphy, Father John, 97
Murray, Patrick, 156
Myers, Cyntha Elizabeth (later Gregory), 239
Myers, Father, 97
Myers, Hattie, 75
Myers, Jr. John and Janet (Deedee), 107
Myers Stone House, 75
Myhre, Wayne, 205

N
Nahas, Nick and Mary Lou, 136
Nanticoke Indians, 68
Naprstek, Joel, 43
Native Americans. *See names of individual tribes*

Neal, Glen, 70
New Baltimore, 33, 113, 155, 165, 200–201, 202, 204, 206, 208, 209, 210, 211, 212, 216, 213, 216, 218, 219, 220, 221, 222, 223
New Baltimore Reformed Church, 216–217, 218
New Baltimore Reformed Church Parsonage, 219
New Baltimore Town Hall (Rocky Store School), 220
New Durham, 138, 148, 152,
New York-Catskill-Athens Steamboat Company Limited, 44
New York Central Railroad, 178
New York Ice Company, 25
New York State Pharmaceutical Association, 92, 93
Newcombe, Barbara (née Weber), 66, 70, 80, 129
Newkirk, Jacob, 78
Newman, Shubal, 166
Newry (neighborhood), 161
Nicholas/Daley/Albright Home, 40
Nichols, Annie (later Shufelt), 33
Nichols, General George Sylvester, 31, 35, 38
Nichols, John, 31
Nichols, S. H., 38
Nichols, Sarah, 40
Nichols, Sylvester, 23, 41, 45
Nichols family, 31
Nightingale Inn/Tavern, 124
Norris, Pastor Francis S., 151
North Settlement Methodist Church, 8, 9
Northrup, Isaac, 17, 18, 35, 43, 44
Northrup House, 43
Norton, Elon, 159
Not Only Ours (Atkinson), 139

O
Oak Hill Iron Foundry, 142
Oak Hill Kitchen (Lyman Treamin Opera House), 146
Oak Hill United Methodist Church, 150
Oak Hill United Methodist Church Parsonage, 151
Oaklander, Harold and Isabelle, 121
Ober Back (Overbagh), Johann Peter, 85
O'Connor Foundation, 193, 229, 231
O'Driscoll, Father, 97
Ogden, Sybil Ludington, 72
O'Grady family, 105
O'Hara family members, 238
O'Hara/Fowler/Laraway House, 236
O'Hara House, 195
O'Hara's Trading Post (Elm Tree Filling Station), 238
Okon, Michael and Carol, 174
Okon House, 174–175
Old County Inn (Freehold Country Inn), 162
Old Episcopal Manse, 232
Old Leeds Bridge, 68
Old Meeting House (First Congregational Church, Windham), 15
Old Methodist Church of Greenville and Norton Hill, 168–169
Old Platt Clove Post Office, 182–183
Old Public Library (Windham), 248
Old Stone House (Coxsackie), 130–131
Old Stone House (Van Bergen/Warren House), 202–203
Old Times in Windham (Prout), 6
Old Windham, 5
Olney, Danforth, 70–71
Olney, Mrs. John, 111
Olsen, Early S., 31
O'Neill, Agnes Inglis, 135
Orchard Farm (Miller-Woodhull Homestead), 208
Osborn, Bennett, 243, 261
Osborn, Elbert, 252, 262
Osborn, Merritt, 246
Osborn House, 144–145
Osborn House Boarding complex, 252
Osbornville. *See Windham*
Ossie Smith Farm (Sunset Hill Farm), 222, 223
Osterhout, Stephen B., 150
Ostrander, Rev. Henry, 81, 131
Otis Elevating Railway, 55, 87
Overbagh/Everitt Cemetary, 85
Overbaugh, George W., 116
Owad, Christine, 235, 248
Owad family, 235
Owego Bridge Company, 189

P
Pacuk, Matthew, 221
Paddock, Laban and Elizabeth, 122
Paddock, William, 150
Paddock store (Oak Hill), 145
Paddock's Island, 122, 123
Palen, Jonathon, 55
Palmateer family members, 32, 33
Palmer, Emma (later Dyer), 161
Palmer, Emory R., 161
Palmer, Harry, 39
Palmer, Lewis, 239
Palmer, Phoebe Jane, 161
Palmer, Robert, 166
Palmer family, 59
Palmer Foundation, 59
Palmer House (Deerwatch Inn), 140
Parks, Dr. Alexander Hunter, 149
Parks, Dr. John Alden, 162
Parks family, 149, 162
Parks House, 149
Parsonage (Presbyterian Manse/Dr. Hubbard House), 251
Parsonage, Oak Hill United Methodist Church, 151
Parsons, Clarence Bronk, 218
Parsons, Melvin, 218
Parsons, Samuel, 218
Parsons, Stephen, 218
Parsons Homestead, 218
Patents (land grants)
  Blaisdell Land Grant, 169
  Bronck's Patent, 114
  Catskill Patent, 17
  Coeymans Patent, 155, 165, 201, 208
  Corlaers Kill Patent, 17
  Coxsackie Patent, 201
  Hallenbeck Patent, 155
  Hardenburgh Patent, 173, 174, 225, 260
  Houghtaling Patent, 121, 204
  Lindsay Patent, 17
  Loonenburg (Loonenburgh) Patent, 17, 18, 22, 25, 121
  Maitland Patent, 136, 140
  Prevost Patent, 159
  Roseboom Patent, 17
  Stewart's Patent, 152
  Thomas Houghtaling Grant, 201
  Van Bergen Patent, 155
Patterson, Emma L., 245, 261
Payne, Mr., 181
Peck, Ethel, 190
Peloubet, Harriet Clark, 27
Penacook Indians, 68
Persen, Jan, 78
Peter family, 68
Peter Hubble House, 123
Pettingill, Harmon P. and Mary, 82
Phantasma Gallery, 258
Philip and Barbara Flach House, 161
Philp, Richard, 65, 78
Phineas Tyler House, 153
Phinney, Rev. William, 111
Pierce, Charles W., 150
Pierro, Linda and Robert Bedford, 129
Plamer, Israel, 166
Plank, Lillie, 49
Platt, Peter, 109
Pohrebynska, Natalia, 197
Pons, Muriel, 234
Porter, C., 38
Porter, Rev. David, 246
Porter, Israel, 42
Post family, 110
Potter, Antoinette (née Doty), 257
Potter, George W., 257
Potter & Newell's Furniture Store, 259
Potter/Tibbals/Ticho House, 257
Pouyat family members, 93
Powell family and members, 214, 215
Powers, James, 79
Pratt, Freelove, 41
Pratt, George Watson, 228, 238
Pratt, Julie, 227
Pratt, Zadock
  buildings constructed by, 224, 229, 237
  life of, 225, 226, 236
  Osborn and, 243
  Pratt Rock and, 228
  Reformed Dutch Church, benefactor of, 231

Pratt family, 163
Pratt Rock/Pratt Rock Park, 228
Prattsville, 2, 5, 10, 173, 224–225, 226, 227, 228, 229, 231, 233, 234, 235, 236, 237, 238, 239, 240, 241, 243, 260
Prattsville Bank building, 226
Prattsville Commercial Building (Dresser House), 229
Prattsville Dairy Company, 233
Prattsville News, 241
Prattsville's Old Town Hall, 241
Presbyterian Church (Ashland), 13
Presbyterian Church (Greenville), 158–159
Presbyterian Manse/Dr. Hubbard House, 251
Prevost, Ann (née Bogardus), 156
Prevost, Major General Augustine (father), 156
Prevost, Major Augustine (son), 155, 156, 159, 166
Prevost, Elizabeth, 166
Prevost, Emily, 166
Prevost, Marc (Jacques Marc), 156
Prevost, Susannah (née Croghan), 156
Prevost, Theodosia (later Burr), 156
Prevost family, 156
Prevost Manor, 156–157, 164
Prevost Patent, 159
privy/privies, 21, 32, 73, 77, 93, 148, 206, 211, 212, 215, 218
Prometheus Bound (Cole), 85
Prospect Place, 210
Protestant Dutch Reformed Church (New Baltimore), 216
Prout, Caroline (later Tuttle), 12
Prout, Rev. Henry Hedges, 6, 7, 15, 189
Prout, John, 6
Purdy, Rev. M. Seymour, 38
Purling (Cairo), 47

R
Radcliffe, George, 193
Radelich, Lenore and Vito, 252
Ramsen (Remsen), John, 73
Ramsey (Remsen) Schoolhouse, 73
Rappleyea, Richard, 78, 79, 95, 103
Rappleyea family, 80
Rascoe, Jack and Joanne, 140
Raymond Beecher Residence, 116–117
Reaves, George Madison, 102
Reaves, Shelby Sage, 102
Redbrick (William Baldwin House), 134–135
Reformed Church (Coeymans Square), 216
Reformed Dutch Chuch of Prattsville, 230–231
Reformed Dutch Church Parsonage, 232
Reiners, Harry, 124
Reinsdorf, Walter and Lucille, 44
Rennie, Father, 10
Reynolds, Ashael, 198
Reynolds, Clayton and Shirley, 152
Reynolds, Elias J., 262
Reynolds family, 261
Richtmyer, William A., 232
Riedman, Christl and Valentine, 239
Rip Van Winkle Bridge, 17
Ripley's Believe it or Not, 228
Robbins, George, 215
Robertson, George, 246, 255
Robinson, Rev. Eli P., 261
Robinson, John, 261
Robinson, Lucius, 261
Robinson, William, 243
Robinson/Doty/Patterson House, 261
Rockefeller, Nelson A., 57
Rocky Store School, 220
Rogers, David, 111
Roosevelt, Theodore, 57, 86
Roseboom Patent, 17
Rosecrans family members, 233
Round Top (Cairo), 47
Round Top Cemetery, 53
Rowan family, 157
Rowena Memorial School, 63
Rubrecht family, 252
Ruf, Francis, 86
Rundle family members, 166
Rusk, Samuel, 181
Russ, Ephraim, 15, 166
Russel, Edgar and Lydia, 101
Ryan, James, 103

S
Sage family members, 102
Sage's Carriage Repository, 102
Saint Francis De Sales Church, 199
Saint Joseph's Villa, 70
Salisbury, Sylvester, 47
Salter, Stephenson Thorn, 206
Sam's Oak Hill Kitchen (Lyman Tremain Opera House), 146
Sanderson-Bedell, Sarah W., 31
Sanford, Minor, 198
Sanford, Mitchell, 79
Sanford, Truman, 166
Satterlee, Rev. Henry Yates, 181, 182
Satterlee, Walter, 181
Sax, Mark and Miriam, 125
Sayers Lutz House, 232
Sayre, Daniel, 50
Schaefer, Louis H., 73
Schermerhorn, Frederick, 53
Schlefer, Mack, 89
Schmidt, Ruth Vedder, 100
Schoharie, meaning of term, 225
Schoharie Creek Homestead, 235
Schoharie Turnpike, 162
Schram, Ralph, 75
Schuneman, Rev. Johannes, 100
Schuneman, William, 66
Schuneman House, 66
Schuster, Natasha and Drew, 253
Schwerbel, John A. and Claudette D., 50
Scialo, Frank, 183
Scienceville (later Ashland), 5, 13
Scot, Elsie (later Bogardus), 40
Scott, Emily (later Trowbridge), 104
Seamon, David, 103
Searles family members, 240
Second Reformed Church, 35
Seeback, Frederick J., 190
Selleck, A. F., 150
Sellers, T. G., 246
Seymour, Emily (Emily Day), 33
Shadley, Stephen, 68
Shanks, Richard and Sherry, 60
Shanneger family, 68
Shaver, Al, 240
Shear family, 211
Sherman family members, 210
Sherrill (Sherill, Sherrell), Esther, 165
Sherrill (Sherill, Sherrell), Lewis, 165, 171
Shook, Warner, 75
Shrine Church of St. Joseph, 10–11
Shue family, 135
Shufelt, Annie (née Nichols), 33
Shufelt, Frances (later Daley), 40
Shufelt, Frank R., 40
Sickles, Valorous, 65
Sign of the Key, 106
Silberstein, Edith Cole, 76
Silvester family members, 128
Simpkins-Plank, Sarah, 169
Slater, Edward, 141
Slater, Elihu, 48
Slater, Hugh, 48
Slater, Mary E. (later Whitcomb), 48, 49
Slater, Sarah (née Beach), 48
Slon, Alison, 152
Smallwood, Andrea, 29
Smallwood, Robert, 29
Smith, Austin, 7
Smith, Bruce C. and Deborah, 198
Smith, Rev. Dr. George Williamson, 181
Smith, Grace and Victor, 88–89
Smith, I. Todd, 223
Smith, Irving, 222, 223
Smith, Father John, 97, 222
Smith, L. S., 102
Smith, Lydia, 79
Smith, Ossie and Cora, 222
Smith, Rufus, 55, 94
Smith, Rulandus B. and Bertha, 128
Smith, Samuel Y., 223
Smith, William, 102
Smith family, 149, 222, 223
Smith Iron Works, 145
Smithson, James, 225
smoke houses, 202
Soap (Kirkman) family, 193

Soper Inn, 262
Soule, Ebenezer and Rachel, 235
Spees family, 155
Spencer family members, 41
Spoor, John, 170–171
Spoor, John D., 43
Spring Brook Farm, 165
Spruce Cottage, 262
St. Elizabeth's Academy, 70
St. Joseph's Chapel, 10–11
St. Luke's Episcopal Church, 98–99
St. Patrick's Academy, 97
St. Patrick's Church, 96–97
St. Paul's Lutheran Church, 142
stagecoach hotels, 256
Stalker, Jeffrey and Ann Marie, 41
Stanick, Waldemar, 183
Stanley, Ashbel, 47
Stanton Hill Farm, 200
Staphes, Moses, 72
Stead, James and Rachel, 108
Steele, Harry Addison and Frances Vosburgh, 15
Steele, Perez, 256
Steele, W. R., 258
Steele family, 256
Stephens, Joseph, 116
Stern, Meta (née Lilienthal), 184
Steven Day House, 107
Stevens, Mr., 110
Stevens, Pierce and Ruth, 164
Stewart House, 17
Stewart's Patent, 152
Stilgoe, John, 1
Stillwood, 74–75
Stimson, George, 5, 260, 261
Stimson, William, 261
Stimson/Ives/Reynolds House, 260–261
Stimson Rock, 260, 261
Stoddard, Harvey and Emily Hunt, 53
Stone, Benjamin, 77
Story, E. J., 251
Story, Lester H. and Eva, 50
Story, Virginia, 73
Straley, Rev. Luther, 37
Stratton, Edward, 12
Strong, Elijah, 13
Strong, Elisha, 5, 13
Strong, Jairus, 13
Strong, Rev. Robert G., 219
Strong Farmhouse, 13
Strong homestead, 12
Strope, Johannes, 53
styles, architectural, 1–2
Suhner, Max, 162
Sullivan, Father, 97
Summers, George and Addie, 125
Summers, James and Jean, 75
Summit House (Mt. Zoar Villa), 143
Sunset Hill Farm (Ossie Smith Farm), 222, 223
Susquehanna Turnpike, 133
Sutton, Russell C. and Irene, 3, 129
Sutton Dairy Farm, 129
Swanson, Michael and Diana, 139
Swarthout, Dorcas, 161
Swarthout, Nathan, 161
Sweeney, John, 42
Sweeney family, 42
Swim, Frank, 75
Sylvester Sage House, 102

T
Tallmade, J. C., 101
Talmadge, Dorothy, 8, 259
Talmadge, Mary Ann, 171
Talmadge/Irving House, 171
Tamarack Lodge, 262
Tannenbaum family members, 91
tanneries, 226, 229
Tanners National Bank, 107
tanning industry, 195
Ten Eyck family, 222
Thomas Cole's Cedar Grove, 76–78. *See also* Cole, Thomas
Thomas Houghtaling Grant, 201
Thomforde, Mrs., 149
Thompson, Anita, 262
Thompson, Christine, 262
Thompson, Ferris and Anita, 164, 252, 262
Thompson, Herbert, 262

Thompson, Ira, 252, 262
Thompson, Rev. James, 142
Thompson, Julia (later Van Loan), 103
Thompson, Mickey (later Goettsche), 252, 262
Thompson, Thomas T., 76
Thompson House, 2, 164, 252, 262
Thomsen, Douglas, 140, 142
Thomson, John Alexander, 76
Thomson, Thomas, 95
Thorpe, Douglas and Catherine H., 108
Thorpe, Jessie, 108
Thorpe, William, 108
Thorpe-O'Grady Residence, 108–109
Ticho, William and Nancy, 257
Titus/Connine/Palmateer House, 32–33
Titus family members, 33
Tolley, Fred, 33
Tolley, William, 32–33
Tom Sawyer (Twain), 43
Tom Thumb, General, 86
Tomlinson, Mary Jane (later Moore), 59
Tompkins, Audrey, 7
Tompkins, Frank, 7
Tompkins, Larry, 246
Tompkins, Samuel, 8
Town of Lexington Historical Society Building, 199
Trailside Cottage (Cole House), 196
traveling preachers, 8
Trede, Mr. & Mrs., 196
Tree House (Cimorelli House), 79–80
Tremain, Levi and Mindwell, 142
Tremain, Lyman, 142, 146
Trinity Episcopal Church, 7, 14–15
Tripp Store and Homestead, 136–137
trolley lines, 233
Trowbridge family members, 104
Truesdell, Martin, 123
Turk, Blanche (later Moore), 233
Turon, George, 166
Tuttle, Albert, 12
Tuttle, Aurelia, 12
Tuttle, Caroline (née Prout), 12
Tuttle, Rev. Daniel Sylvester, 15
Tuttle, Ellen, 12
Tuttle, Frances (later Jeralds), 12
Tuttle, John, 15
Tuttle, Sidney, 7
Tweed, William Marcy ("Boss"), 142
Twelve Tribes, 146
Twilight Park, 181
Tyler, Caroline, 153
Tyler, Jehiel, 153
Tyler, Julia A. (later Earl), 153
Tyler, Phineas and Sarah, 153

U

Ulster & Delaware Railroad Station, 178–179
United Methodist Church of Oak Hill, 150
United States Hotel (Saratoga Springs), 216
Upjohn, Richard, 166
Urspring, Jack and Nancy, 72
Utter, Israel P., 150
Utter, James, 146, 147
Uzzilia, Robert, 51

V

Valkenberg, E. P., 62
Valley View Farm (Floyd Smith Farm), 222, 223
Van Bergen, Anthony A. and Clarine, 123, 202
Van Bergen, Garret, 78
Van Bergen, Maria, 123
Van Bergen, Martin G., 123
Van Bergen, Peter A., 202
Van Bergen Patent, 155
Van Bergen/Warren House, 202–203
Van Buren, John, 155
Van Buren, Martin, 86, 155
Van Cleef, Rev. Cornelius, 35
Van Cott, Maggie Newton (Mother Maggie), 111
Van Cott House, 111
Van Deusen, Edna Nichols, 31
Van Dyck, Catherine (née Bronck), 127
Van Dyck, Hendrich, 127
Van Dyck, William, 127
Van Dyke (Parsonage owner), 151
Van Dyke, Abraham, 127
Van Dyke, Rev. Leonard, 246
Van Dyke House, 127
Van Gelder Octagon House, 2

Van Gorden's News Shop and Bookstore, 103
Van Hoesen, Sarah (later Schermerhorn), 53
Van Ilpendam, Maria Jansen (later Van Loon), 18
Van Loan. *See also* Van Loon
Van Loan, Albert (Albertus), 18, 37
Van Loan, Charles, 60
Van Loan, Charles, Jr., 67
Van Loan, Charles, Sr., 67
Van Loan, Cornelius, 29
Van Loan, Eugene, 21, 22
Van Loan, Eugene, Jr., 18, 20
Van Loan, Helene, 21
Van Loan, Henry, 44
Van Loan, Jack and Cindy, 66
Van Loan, Jacob, 37, 105
Van Loan, Jane (later Erickson), 21, 22
Van Loan, Julia (née Thompson), 103
Van Loan, Louise, 67
Van Loan, Lucy (née Beach), 103
Van Loan, Mary Helene, 21
Van Loan, Mathyes, 37
Van Loan, Matthew Dies, 103
Van Loan, Schuyler, 22
Van Loan, Thomas, 21
Van Loan, Walton, 103
Van Loan/Daley House, 67
Van Loan's Catskill Mountain Guides (Van Loan), 103
Van Loon, Albert (Albertus, d. 1838), 25
Van Loon, Albert (Albertus, son of Jan), 18, 25
Van Loon, Cornelia, 25
Van Loon, Ilsje, 18
Van Loon, Jan (father), 17, 22, 25
Van Loon, Jan (son), 18
Van Loon, Jane, 21
Van Loon, John M., 43
Van Loon, Maria, 18
Van Loon, Maria Jansen (née Van Ilpendam), 18
Van Loon, Matthias (Mathias, b. 1822), 39, 44
Van Loon, Matthias (son of Jan the elder), 18
Van Loon, Nicholas, 18
Van Orden, Ten Broeck, 116
Van Rensselaer, Killian, 202
Van Slichtenhorst, Brant Arent, 55
Van Slyke family, 201
Van Valin family members, 253
Van Valkenburgh family, 173
Van Vechtan (Vechten), Peter, 68, 89
Van Vechten, Jan, 89
Van Vechten, John and Anna Marie, 68
Van Vechten, Samuel and Sarah, 68
Van Vecten, Teunis, 89
Van Winkle, Dr. Roger and Patricia, 60
Van Wort, Harmon, 38
Vandenberg, Elizabeth (later Lampman), 125
Vandenberg, Hendrick, 131
Vandenberg, Peter, 131
Vandenberg, William, 131
Vander Zee family, 201
Vanderbilt, Mr. and Mrs. George, 157
Vanderbilt, Susan, 157
Vanderbilt, William S., 166
Vanderbilt Opera House, 164
Vanderbuilt, William S. and Mary Reed Chapman, 164
Vandervoort, M., 53
Vedder, Jessie Van Vechten, 68, 97, 149
Vermilya, H., 228
vernacular (folk) buildings, 1
Verplanck, Isaac D., 208
Verplank, David, 215
Vetter House—Original Methodist Parsonage, 233
Victorian period, 2
Villa Meta, 184
Vincent, Florence, 85
Vosburgh, Cornell, 17
Vosburgh family, 221
Vosburgh Residence, 221

W

Waggoner family and members, 42
Wagoner, John H., 221
Wait, Maria (later Morton), 44
Wakeley family, 163
Walsh, Katherine, 107
Walsh, Patrick, 107
Walsh, Philip L., 107
Walsh, Philip T., 107
Walsh, Stephanie, 66, 107
Walters, Edward and Julia, 239

Walton Van Loan House, 103
Warren family, 118, 125, 202
Washington Irving Inn, 184–185
Waterfall House and Clark Falls, 240
Waterman, Barnabas, 23
Wawaka, Lake, 172–173
Weber, Anne, 70
Weber, Barbara (later Newcombe), 66, 70, 80, 129
Weed, Antoinette, 74
Weeks, Moses, 126
Weismuller, Johnny, 252
Weiss, Rev. Michael, 100
Welch, James H., 150
West Hollow Brook, 13
West Settlement Methodist Church, 8, 9
Wetmore family, 149
Wey, Benjamin, 92
Whelan, Louise Howland Beddow, 59
Whitbeck, John and Catherine, 68
Whitbeck family, 123
Whitcomb, Edward Burdette, 49
Whitcomb, Henry Barber, 48–49
Whitcomb, Mary E. (née Slater), 48, 49
White, Bill and Mary, 75
Whiting, Benjamin C., 39
Whiting, Jeannette, 39
Whittlesey, Dr. Elias, 152
Whittlesey, John, 152
Whittlesey family members, 152
Whittlesey House, 152
Wickenden, Elizabeth (later Goldschmidt), 141
Wilbur, Howard C., 90
Wilcoxson, Martino Niles, 79
William Baldwin House (Redbrick), 134–135
Williams, Chauncey, 198
Williams, Edward G., 156
Wilson, Woodrow, 124
Wiltsie, Helena, 111
Winans, Eliza, 110
Windham, 1, 2, 5, 8, 13, 15, 74, 111, 133, 151, 153, 159, 164, 166, 177, 191, 193, 195, 225, 226, 231, 239, 242–243, 245, 246, 248, 250, 251, 252, 253, 255, 256, 257, 258, 259, 260, 261, 262, 263
Windham Cemetery, 255
Windham Hardware, 253
Windham House, 2
Windham Journal (newspaper), 111, 258
Windham Journal/Phantasma Gallery Building, 258
Windham Laundromat, 259
Windham Library and Civic Center, 246–247
Windham Whiskey (distillery), 261
Windhamere (Munson House), 263
Winnie, O., 150
Winter Clove Inn, 2, 48–49
Witherill/Stalker House, 41
Wolf family, 218
women, in the church, 111, 193
Woodhull family, 208
Woodworth, Sally, 48
Wooster, Charles, 215
workingman's houses, 45
Wright, Harold Bell, 225
Wycoff, Rev. Isaac N., 35
Wyncoop, Reverend, 81

Y

Ye Olde Stone House, 78
Yeomans, John O. and Bertha, 118
Youmans, A. C., Rev., 171
Young, Amos D., 182
Young, David, 109
Young, George, 183
Young, Harvey and Muriel, 109
Young, Sarah (née Hommel), 182
Young, Sarah A., 182
Young, Susan, 183
Young, Ida (née Cole), 183

Z

Zadock Pratt Museum, 225, 226–227, 241
Zimmerman, Frederick L. and Grace, 59
Zion Evangelical Lutheran Church, 36–37, 45